D1491861

K07732

MEDICAL CONFIDENTIALITY AND CRIME

Medical Confidentiality and Crime

SABINE MICHALOWSKI

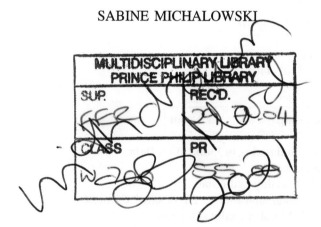
ASHGATE

Published by
Ashgate Publishing Limited
Gower House
Croft Road
Aldershot
Hants GU11 3HR
England

Ashgate Publishing Company
Suite 420
101 Cherry Street
Burlington, VT 05401-4405
USA

Ashgate website: http://www.ashgate.com

British Library Cataloguing in Publication Data
Michalowski, Sabine
   Medical confidentiality and crime
   1.Confidential communications - Physicians 2.Criminal
   investigations - Moral and ethical aspects
   I.Title
   344'.0412

Library of Congress Control Number: 2002117154

ISBN 0 7546 2294 0

Printed and bound in Great Britain by Antony Rowe Ltd
Chippenham Wiltshire

Contents

Acknowledgements

This book is based on my PhD thesis and would not have been possible without the guidance and support of my adviser and former colleague, Di Longley, whom I wish to thank for her support and patience. I also wish to thank my Examiners, Michael Jones and Vivian Harpwood, for their comments on the thesis. I am grateful to Jane Wright, Jim Gobert, Audrey Guinchard, Steve Anderman, Sheldon Leader and Lorna Woods for their constructive comments on various chapters of this book and for their encouragement. I am further indebted to Peter Stone, Stefan Markschläger, Richard Wild, Roger Brownsword, Mary Hayes, John Birds, Maurice Sunkin and Ken Lidstone, who have supported me at various stages of this book. As always, special thanks go to Jürgen Wellner who has provided invaluable academic and moral support.

Table of Cases

Table of Legislation

List of Abbreviations

A.2d	Atlantic Reporter, Second Series
AC	Appeal Cases
AJDA	Actualité Juridique Droit Administratif
ALD	Actualité Législative Dalloz
All ER	All England Law Reports
App.	Court of Appeals
App.Div.	Appellate Division
Ariz.	Arizona; Arizona Supreme Court Reports
Ark.	Arkansas; Arkansas Supreme Court Reports
ARS	Arizona Revised Statutes
Art.	Article
Arts	Articles
Bay ObLG	Bayerisches Oberstes Landesgericht
BGH	Bundesgerichtshof
BGHR	Bundesgerichtshof Rechtsprechung Strafsachen
BGHSt	Entscheidungen des Bundesgerichtshofs in Strafsachen
BGHZ	Entscheidungen des Bundesgerichtshofs in Zivilsachen
BL	Basic Law
BMA	British Medical Association
BMJ	British Medical Journal
BMLR	Butterworths Medical Law Reports
BT	Deutscher Bundestag
Bull.	Bulletin
BVerfGE	Entscheidungen des Bundesverfassungsgerichts
C.3d	California Reports, Third Series
CA	Cour d'Appel; Court of Appeal
Cal.	California
Cal.App.3d	California Appellate Reports, Third Series
Cal.Rptr.	California Reporter
Cal.Rptr.2d	California Reporter, Second Series
Cass. Civ.	Arrêt de la Chambre Civile de la Cour de Cassation
CFLQ	Child and Family Law Quarterly
Ch	Law Reports, Chancery Division
Ch. civ.	Chambre Civile
Ch. corr.	Chambre Correctionnelle
Ch. crim.	Chambre Criminelle
Ch D	Chancery Division
chron.	chronique
Cir.	U.S. Court of Appeal ... Circuit

CJ	Chief Justice
C.L.R.	Commonwealth Law Reports
Cmnd.	Command Papers
Colo.	Colorado; Colorado Reports
Comm.	Commentaire
Comp. State	Compiled Statutes
Conn.	Connecticut
Cr App R	Criminal Appeal Reports
Crim LR	Criminal Law Review
Ct App.	Court of Appeal
CYS	Children and Youth Services
D.	District Court (Federal); Recueil Dalloz Sirey
DC	District of Columbia; District Council; District Court; Divisional Court
Dist.	District
DNotZ	Deutsche Notarzeitschrift
doct.	doctrine
D.P.	Recueil Dalloz Périodique et Critique
DPA	Data Protection Act 1998
DRiZ	Deutsche Richterzeitung
ECHR	European Convention on Human Rights
ECJ	European Court of Justice
ECR	European Court of Justice, Reports of Cases (European Court Reports)
Ed.	Edition; editor
E.D.	Eastern District
E.H.R.R.	European Human Rights Reports
EJHL	European Journal of Health Law
EMLR	Entertainment and Media Law Reports
Ent.L.R	Entertainment Law Review
F.2d	Federal Reporter, Second Series
F.3d	Federal Reporter, Third Series
Fam	Law Reports, Family Division
Fam Law	Family Law
FCR	Family Court Reporter
FD	Family Division
Fed.Reg.	Federal Register
Fla.	Florida
FLR	Family Law Reports
FRD	Federal Rules Decisions
FRE	Federal Rules of Evidence
FSR	Fleet Street Reports of Patent Cases
F.Supp.	Federal Supplement
F.Supp.2d	Federal Supplement, Second Series
GA	Goltdammer's Archiv für Strafrecht

Ga.	Georgia
Gaz.Pal.	Gazette du Palais
Gen. State.	General Statutes
GMC	General Medical Council
G.S.	General Statutes
HL	House of Lords
HRA	Human Rights Act 1998
ICLQ	International and Comparative Law Quarterly
Id.	Idaho
Ill.	Illinois
Ind.	Indiana
J	Justice
JA	Juristische Arbeitsblätter
J.C.P.	Juri-classeur périodique (Semaine juridique)
JMBINW	Justizministerialblatt für das Land Nordrhein-Westfalen
JME	Journal of Medical Ethics
JOAN	Journal Officiel de l'Assemblée Nationale
JR	Juristische Rundschau
JZ	Juristenzeitung
Kan.	Kansas
KG	Kammergericht
La.	Lousiana
LG	Landgericht
LJ	Lord Justice
LSA-C.E.	Lousiana Statutes Annotated – Code of Evidence
Ltd	Limited
Mass.	Massachusetts
Md.	Maryland
M.D.	Middle District
MDR	Monatschrift für Deutsches Recht
Med Law Int	Medical Law International
Med L Rev	Medical Law Review
MedR	Zeitschrift für Medizinrecht
Med. Sci. Law	Medicine, Science and the Law
Mich.	Michigan
Minn.	Minnesota
Misc.2d	New York Miscellaneous Reports, Second Series
MLR	Modern Law Review
Mo.	Missouri
MR	Master of the Rolls
N.C.	North Carolina
N.D.	Northern District; North Dakota
N.D.R.Evid.	North Dakota Rules of Evidence
N.E.2d	North Eastern Reporter, Second Series
Neb. Rev. State.	Revised Statutes of Nebraska

N.H.	New Hampshire; New Hampshire Supreme Court Reports
NHS	National Health Service
N.J.	New Jersey
N.J. Super.	New Jersey Superior Court; New Jersey Superior Court Reports
NJW	Neue Juristische Wochenschrift
NLJ	New Law Journal
N.M.	New Mexico
n°	number
NStZ	Neue Zeitschrift für Strafrecht
N.W.2d	North Western Reporter, Second Series
N.Y.	New York; New York Reports
N.Y.2d	New York Court of Appeals Reports, Second Series
N.Y.S.2d	New York Supplement, Second Series
Ohio St.	Ohio State Reports
Okl.	Oklahoma
OLG	Oberlandesgericht
Or.	Oregon
P	President of the Family Division
P.2d	Pacific Reporter, Second Series
Pa.	Pennsylvania
PACE	Police and Criminal Evidence Act
para.	paragraph
PC	Privy Council
PN	Professional Negligence
QB	Law Reports, Queen's Bench Division
QBD	Queen's Bench Division
R	Rule; Receuil des Décisions du Conseil d'Etat; Regina, Rex
RCW	Revised Code of Washington
Rec.	Recueil des Décisions du Conseil Constitutionnel
Rev. Stat. Ann.	Revised Statutes Annotated
RGSt	Entscheidungen des Reichsgerichts in Strafsachen
RPC	Reports of Patent Cases
RSA	Revised Statutes Annotated
RSC Ord	Rules of the Supreme Court Ordinance
S.	Recueil Sirey; Scotland
s.	section
S.C.	South Carolina
S.D.	Southern District; South Dakota
S.E.2d	South Eastern Reporter, Second Series
Sec.	Section
S.W.2d	South Western Reporter, Second Series
So.2d	Southern Reporter, Second Series

Sol J	Solicitors Journal
somm.	sommaire
ss.	sections
St	Statutes
Stat. Ann.	Statutes Annotated
StPO	Strafprozeßordnung
StV	Strafverteidiger
Sup. Ct.	Supreme Court
Supp.	Supplement
Trib. civ.	Tribunal Civil
Trib. corr.	Tribunal Correctionnel
U.S.	United States Supreme Court Reports
Va.	Virginia
V-C	Vice-Chancellor
Vol.	volume
Vt.	Vermont; Vermont Reports
Wash.	Washington
W.D.	Western District
Wis.	Wisconsin
wistra	Zeitschrift für Wirtschaft, Steuer, Strafrecht
WLR	Weekly Law Reports
Wyo.	Wyoming
ZStW	Zeitschrift für die gesamte Strafrechtswissenschaft

Chapter 1

Introduction

Medical confidentiality lies at the very heart of the physician-patient relationship and is relevant to all areas of medical law. It is universally recognised as a value worth protecting, and there is widespread agreement that physicians should not, in principle, announce to the world that which the patients have confided in them. This principle was already recognised by the Hippocratic Oath which provided that:

> Whatsoever things I see or hear concerning the life of men, in my attendance on the sick or even apart therefrom, which ought not to be noised abroad, I will keep silence thereon, counting such things to be as sacred secrets.

The concept of medical confidentiality is now an integral part of International Conventions, such as the Declaration of Geneva of 1994, and an obligation to maintain medical confidentiality is imposed on physicians by the rules of their profession. Many legal systems guarantee the protection of medical confidentiality in various ways. At the European level, the importance of medical confidentiality was recently confirmed by the European Convention on Human Rights and Biomedicine, and by the Data Protection Directive 1995 addressing the particular threats to the confidentiality of personal (including medical) data which are being processed by automatic or non-automatic means; in the U.S., the significance of patient privacy has been stressed by the Privacy Rule.[1]

As with many other areas in which there is a general consensus that a particular interest deserves protection, the principle of medical confidentiality is uncontroversial as long as it does not conflict with other interests. Such conflicts, however, frequently arise where the physician holds confidential patient information which may be relevant for the purposes of crime prevention or criminal prosecution. A physician may, for example, receive information in confidence that the patient has committed a serious crime, or that the patient intends to commit such a crime. It is also possible that the physician holds confidential information that would exonerate a person who is accused in criminal proceedings, or at least assist that person's defence. In these cases, the interest in medical confidentiality can compete with a number of other interests: that of finding the truth in the course of criminal proceedings; the general public interest in crime prevention and criminal prosecution; the interests of parties who are wrongly accused in criminal proceedings; and defence rights. To resolve such conflicts of interests, a balance

---

[1] Standards for Privacy Protection of Individually Identifiable Health Information (65 FR 82462).

must be struck to decide how to accommodate the competing interests. The outcome of such a balancing exercise is largely based on policy considerations and deeply rooted moral concepts. In order to resolve these conflicts of interests, it is thus essential to be clear about the reasons for which the various interests that are at stake receive legal protection.

Despite the general agreement that medical confidentiality should, in principle, be guaranteed, opinions differ when it comes to explaining why exactly medical confidentiality should be protected. Is medical confidentiality mainly protected in the interests of the patient, and if so, how, exactly, can the patient's interest in medical confidentiality be defined? Or is medical confidentiality mainly protected in the interests of the physician? The physician's job may be made much easier if he/she has the right to refuse any disclosure of confidential patient information, as many patients will only be willing to reveal all information necessary for diagnosis and treatment if they can rely on the physician's silence. Alternatively, is medical confidentiality mainly protected in the public interest, as patients might, for example, be deterred from seeking medical advice and treatment if they fear the disclosure of their medical secrets? It can easily be seen that the answers to these questions are of more than academic relevance, as the approach adopted towards potential conflicts depends largely on the reasons for which the different interests receive protection. If, for example, the main emphasis were to be placed on the protection of the physician's interests, it would be sensible to give the physician discretion in deciding whether or not to disclose certain confidential patient information, regardless of the wishes of the patient. If, on the other hand, medical confidentiality is mainly protected to pay heed to the interests of the patient, the existence or absence of the patient's consent to disclosure would have a decisive role to play. If the public interest were to be the most significant consideration behind the protection of medical confidentiality, the scope and limits of confidentiality protection would mainly depend on an analysis of how these public interests could best be secured.

The idea for this book was born when the author, who had trained as a German lawyer and took it for granted that confidential patient information should receive protection from disclosure in criminal proceedings, realised that English lawyers find it just as natural that the interests in the administration of justice in principle prevail over medical confidentiality. This raised academic questions about the reasons behind such a difference in approach, such as whether this can be explained by a different legal tradition, a divergence in moral thinking, or whether it is just accidental that the two systems have developed differently. Moreover, it raises the question of which of the approaches, if any, reflects sounder legal and moral principles. From a German perspective, the main interest in comparing different approaches to medical confidentiality in the context of crime prevention and criminal prosecution would be to identify better and more consistent ways of balancing the competing interests in certain problem areas. From an English perspective, until the coming into force of the Human Rights Act 1998, a discussion of the potential merits of introducing a medical privilege in criminal court, giving the physician the right to remain silent about confidential patient information and the right to refuse the production of medical records, might have seemed like a pointless exercise. The legal situation was clear – no such privilege existed for confidential information which is relevant to the proceedings.[2] However, English law nevertheless has to resolve conflicts, particularly where confidential patient information is to be disclosed outside of court proceedings. No clear legal principles exist to deal with this problem apart from the provisions of the Police and Criminal Evidence Act 1984 which govern the specific question of the search for and seizure of medical records. A comparative analysis can thus assist in identifying criteria for the solution of such problems. Furthermore, in the light of the HRA, it needs to be reconsidered whether the recognition of the right to private life under Article 8(1) of the ECHR requires a difference in approach to medical privilege in court, and if not, whether changes are nevertheless desirable.

This book has the threefold aim of (1) describing different legal approaches to medical confidentiality, in general, and to the conflict between medical confidentiality and competing interests in the context of crime prevention and criminal prosecution, in particular; (2) identifying the factors which might cause these differences; and (3) suggesting criteria for an ethically and legally convincing approach to the different conflicts of interests. Given that at the outset of the study fundamental differences in approach between Germany and England had already been identified, it seemed undesirable to restrict the comparison to these two countries. It would have been too easy to explain arising differences based on the fact that one of the countries has a civil law tradition, the other being a common law country, and that one country has a written constitution and a rights-based culture while the other does not. To avoid this risk, two more countries have been chosen as comparators. Two common law countries (England and the U.S.) and two civil law countries (France and Germany) will be examined to see whether and how the fundamental differences between those two types of legal systems influence the approach in the area under examination. At the same time, two systems providing extensive constitutional protection for privacy (the U.S. and Germany) will be compared with two systems that do not provide such protection (England and France). These differences among the legal systems under examination will help to identify the factors influencing the approach towards the protection of medical confidentiality and to the resolution of conflicts between medical confidentiality and other interests. Given its importance for three of the four legal systems under examination, the relevant law of the European Union and of the Council of Europe will also be examined briefly.

A comparative study faces many problems, not the least of which is that of how to structure the outline of the different legal systems so as to make a comparison possible, without losing the authenticity of each legal system. The resolution of conflicts between medical confidentiality and competing interests in the context of

---

[2] *Attorney-General v Mulholland* [1963] 2 QB 477 (CA), at 489 per Lord Denning; *Nuttall v Nuttall and Twynan* [1964] 108 Sol J 605, per Edgedale J; *Hunter v Mann* [1974] 2 All ER 414, at 417 per Boreham J; *Goddard v Nationwide Building Society* [1986] 3 All ER 264, at 271 per Nourse LJ.

criminal proceedings and crime prevention requires that a balancing exercise be performed. To understand how the different legal systems approach the balancing test, it is essential to undertake a detailed analysis of the law of each legal system, and, in particular, of the interplay of different legal provisions and concepts within each system. Even though all legal systems are faced with similar problems and therefore have to consider comparable conflicts, they all start from very different premises. The legal protection of medical confidentiality in France, for example, is mainly based on the provisions of the Criminal Code, and the conflicts arising are mostly dealt with by the provisions of the Code of Criminal Procedure. The approach is thus determined by principles and concepts of criminal law. In German law, the main focus equally lies on the provisions of the Code of Criminal Procedure and of the Criminal Code. However, the German approach cannot be understood without reference to constitutional principles which have a decisive influence on the interpretation and application of the legal provisions by German courts. In the U.S., medical confidentiality similarly has a strong constitutional basis which has widely influenced the legal approach towards the conflict of interests in the context of crime prevention and criminal prosecution. However, in the U.S. medical confidentiality is not protected by substantive criminal law, but rather by particular statutes conferring privilege and providing very detailed provisions expressly regulating many of the conflicts between medical confidentiality and the interests of justice. Complicating the inquiry is the fact that the content of these statutes will vary from State to State, and even identically worded statutes may be interpreted differently in different States. In England, on the other hand, the protection of medical confidentiality is a creature of case-law and has been mainly developed in the context of private law actions for breach of confidence. It is therefore based on private law principles and concepts. Because of these conceptual differences, a meaningful comparison of the different legal systems can only be performed once the relevant law of each country has been explained comprehensively. This approach, as opposed to an entirely problem-based comparison, has the advantage that in addition to providing a comparative analysis of specific problems, this book also presents a detailed description and analysis of the relevant law of four different countries.

The examination of each legal system which takes place in separate chapters will adopt, as far as practicable, the same structure, in order to facilitate the subsequent comparative analysis. The analysis of each legal system will be divided into two parts. The first part of each of these chapters will examine the way in which the interest in medical confidentiality is protected. This includes, for example, the question of whether only embarrassing or otherwise particularly sensitive information deserves legal protection, whether the protection is limited to confidences expressly communicated to physicians by their patients, or whether everything the physician learns in the course of the physician-patient relationship is covered by medical confidentiality. The legal mechanisms used to guarantee this protection will also be looked at, for example by examining whether medical confidentiality is protected by private law and/or criminal law provisions; whether it is a constitutional right; and what remedies are available in case of a breach of medical confidentiality. The author by no means claims to present a complete picture of the legal protection of medical confidentiality in each country. The first part of each chapter rather concentrates on those features of confidentiality protection encountered in each country which might help to explain the approach adopted towards the balancing of interests. Important aspects of the legal protection of medical confidentiality which did not seem relevant for this particular purpose, for example the approaches to the protection of medical data in the different Data Protection Acts, have therefore been neglected.

The second part of these chapters will focus on conflicts between medical confidentiality and the interests in crime prevention and criminal prosecution. Different questions will be discussed, such as that of whether the physician has a right or is even under an obligation to refuse to give testimony in court regarding confidential patient information; and whether or not he/she can be justified when disclosing confidential patient information outside of court proceedings. Particular emphasis will be placed on the resolution of conflicts between medical confidentiality, on the one hand, and the interest in the administration of justice; the interest in criminal prosecution; the interests of a person who is wrongly accused in criminal proceedings, be it the physician or a third party; the interest in the guarantee of defence rights; and the interest in crime prevention, on the other. Specific problems regarding the disclosure of medical records will also be introduced. In this context, it is of particular importance whether the police can lawfully seize such material for the purpose of criminal prosecution, whether it must be made available as evidence in criminal proceedings, and whether the physician has the right voluntarily to submit material to the police or the court for the purposes of criminal investigations or prosecutions. While an attempt will be made to discuss the same issues from the perspective of each of the four legal systems, this will not always be appropriate. Frequently, a problem which is of particular importance for one legal system and requires a detailed discussion, does not cause any specific difficulties in another legal system and therefore does not merit detailed attention.

It cannot be overlooked that the law in the area of medical confidentiality is largely based on policy considerations and ethical principles. Resolutions of a conflict between different interests require a balancing of the interest involved which can only be carried out satisfactorily if the interests at stake and their respective values are clearly defined. Therefore, the weight to be accorded to the principle of medical confidentiality as well as the importance of the competing interests will have to be assessed. For a critical assessment of the law's approach to medical confidentiality in general, and to the protection of medical confidentiality in the context of crime prevention and criminal prosecution in particular, it is therefore essential to introduce philosophical principles which justify or even demand the protection of medical confidentiality, and which affect the weight to be given to the competing interests that need to be balanced. This is particularly important in the context of a comparative study, since moral conflicts are the same in all legal systems, and philosophical debate considers these problems in an attempt to find a universally acceptable moral solution, detached from the constraints of any one legal system. Before the law of the different legal systems is explained in chapters three to seven, chapter two will therefore introduce the theoretical and philosophical discussion of the different values, interests and conflicts involved by the two predominant approaches to medical ethics: the deontological and the utilitarian schools of thought. Based on this theoretical outline, chapters three to seven which contain the analysis of the law of the different legal systems will examine to what extent the law of each country is influenced by deontological or utilitarian considerations, and identify the impact of the philosophical approach endorsed by each country on the legal solutions favoured.

The ethical and legal analyses will be followed by comparative reflections in chapter eight. Selected legal problems that were introduced in the preceding chapters will be discussed from a comparative perspective, and the solutions promoted by different legal systems will be evaluated. The main emphasis is placed upon a comparison of the practical solutions reached in each legal system, rather than on theoretical differences in approach. This is important for an assessment of whether or not apparent similarities will lead to similar results, and apparent differences to different results. The comparative analysis of the different approaches will help to identify the strengths and weaknesses of different legal approaches, and to develop a more objective and satisfactory attitude towards the balancing of interests. Comparative and ethical reflections will be combined in order to develop workable and ethically justifiable criteria to resolve the conflicts between medical confidentiality, on the one hand, and the interests in criminal prosecution, defence rights and crime prevention, on the other.

Chapter 2

Ethical Considerations

Medical confidentiality is the term commonly used to describe the concept that a relationship of trust exists between physicians and their patients, generating an expectation that all communications taking place in the course of this relationship remain confidential. Medical privilege, on the other hand, refers to the specific situation that physicians are exempt from giving testimony in court with regard to confidential patient information and from submitting medical records of their patients in evidence. In a broader sense, the term medical privilege is sometimes used to encompass, in addition, the right or obligation of the physician not to disclose confidential patient information to the police for the purposes of crime prevention. When trying to answer the general question of whether and to what extent the law should protect medical confidentiality, and the more specific question of whether or not medical privilege should be recognised, the importance of policy considerations is obvious. Particularly with regard to medical privilege, where a conflict of interests must be resolved, the solutions favoured in different legal systems are, at least to some extent, based on the respective value systems. The outcome of legal disputes will therefore in great measure be determined by the significance accorded to the different interests at stake. Even though in the context of the legal debate, values are rarely expressed with reference to philosophical thought, it is nevertheless clear that the policy decisions, though often only intuitively, reflect philosophical ideas and ethical principles.

In the context of medical ethics, two approaches, that of the utilitarian and that of the deontological school of thought, are of particular importance. While it is conceded that a discussion of these two approaches by no means conveys the full spectrum of philosophical debate in this area, any attempt to summarise all different philosophical schools with regard to their attitude towards medical confidentiality would far exceed the scope of this work. As Mason and McCall Smith remind us: 'Contemporary medical ethics is a tapestry in which an array of philosophical theories interweave with one another.'[1]

It is not the purpose of this chapter to resolve the conflicts between the different ethical approaches or the inconsistencies inherent in each of them. Instead, this chapter aims at establishing the theoretical background necessary for a comparative analysis of the law. Ethical thought can be used as a tool for an assessment of the law as it stands. In particular, it can assist in the examination of whether the balancing of interests performed in each legal system and the results thus achieved can be justified by reference to the predominant ethical theories. As the balancing

---

[1] At 5.

of interests depends largely on ethical and policy considerations, ethical reasoning can contribute to a more coherent approach to the balancing process.

1 Main schools of medical ethics

1.1 Utilitarianism

For utilitarians, an action is right not because it is inherently good, but because it maximises 'utility', that is produces the maximal positive value, or the best consequences. So-called 'act-utilitarianism' focuses on the utility of every action and holds that actions are right if they promote the best consequences in the individual case. This means that an agent must assess the consequences of his/her acts in a specific situation before pursuing a course of action. 'Rule-utilitarianism', on the other hand, is based on more general considerations when concentrating on the consequences of a rule, rather than on the consequences of an individual act. For a rule-utilitarian, the right act is that which is in accordance with a rule that conforms with the principle of utility, i.e. a rule that is thought to achieve the best consequences for an indeterminate number of cases. To abide by such a rule is more important than to achieve the best result in a particular case. This is because it is thought by rule-utilitarians that the good that may result from a certain course of action in an individual case may lead to bad consequences in an unpredictable number of cases, if to achieve the good result, a good rule must be disregarded. A rule-utilitarian, when deciding on a course of action, will therefore be guided by general rules that are based on the principle of utility. Bentham and Mill, the early promoters of utilitarianism, defined utility exclusively by reference to pleasure and happiness,[2] notions which are not unambiguous in their meaning. More recent utilitarians have recognised additional values such as autonomy.[3]

The principle of utility could be summarised as a principle of striving for the greatest happiness for the greatest number. This means that utilitarian theory to some extent favours the public good over that of the individual. It claims to be objective, in that the determination of whether or not an act or a rule is good or bad depends on a calculation of the pain and pleasure thereby caused. If the pleasure outweighs the pain, then the act or rule is good. However, utilitarian theory is faced with the problem of how to decide what are good or bad consequences and how to measure what are the best consequences to be achieved. If the good of a rule or an act is to be decided according to its consequences, this presupposes an antecedent system of judging and ranking consequences, and thus a pre-existing 'vision of the good'.[4] Another problem which will become apparent in the context of a discussion of medical confidentiality and medical privilege is that of whether only certain and direct consequences are to be taken into account, or whether and to

---

[2] Bentham, at 59.
[3] Griffin, at 67.
[4] Engelhardt Jr., at 46.

what extent possible long-term or indirect consequences might weigh in the cost-benefit analysis.

1.2 Deontological theories

1.2.1 A duty-based approach

Deontological theories focus on the rightness or wrongness of an act in itself. They are not concerned with the consequences an act may have, but instead with identifying those features of the act which make it morally right, and they suggest that some acts have an intrinsic value. According to Kant, for example, an agent acts morally only when acting from a sense of duty. This makes it necessary to identify the duties of the individual. Kant promotes that the individual ought to behave as if the behaviour were to become a universal law, so that only an act that passes the test of universalisability qualifies as a moral act.[5] Kant demonstrates this principle by giving the example of a person who, because of financial problems, borrows money, promising to pay it back, but knowing that this will not be possible. The maxim on which this act was based, that is that it is morally permissible in times of need to make promises one knows one cannot keep, could not become a universal law, because it would subvert the whole concept of promises by undermining the trust in promises being kept. Applied to the concept of medical confidentiality, this would, for example, mean that if a physician induces the patient to share confidences with him/her, but when doing so knows that he/she is going to disclose the information thus obtained, the very concept of medical confidentiality would be impaired. Another important feature of Kantian ethics is that it is immoral to use others merely as a means to an end. Rather, every person must be treated as an end in him/herself, and have his/her integrity as an individual respected. In the example of the person borrowing money by making a false promise, he/she uses the lender merely as a means to his/her ends. In the words of Kant:

> This violation of the principle of humanity in other men is more obvious if we take in examples of attacks on the freedom and property of others. For then it is clear that he who transgresses the rights of men intends to use the person of others merely as a means, without considering that as rational beings they ought always to be esteemed also as ends, that is, as beings who must be capable of containing in themselves the end of the very same action.[6]

One important problem medical ethics, based on Kantian views, would have to face is how to resolve conflicts of interests. As, according to Kant, a person's duties are absolute there is no room for conflict resolution or for the balancing of two competing duties. Given the realities of medical practice where conflicts frequently arise, this approach is ineffectual for practical medical ethics.[7]

---

[5] Kant, at 44.
[6] Ibid., at 52-3.
[7] Beauchamp, Childress, at 354; Davies, at 6.

Other deontologists have tried to overcome this problem. Ross, for example, who argued that 'if there are things that are intrinsically good, it is *prima facie* a duty to bring them into existence rather than not to do so, and to bring as much of them into existence as possible', nevertheless recognised that a conflict of these duties may arise. According to him:

> When I am in a situation, as perhaps I always am, in which more than one of these *prima facie* duties is incumbent on me, what I have to do is to study the situation as fully as I can until I form the considered opinion (it is never more) that in the circumstances one of them is more incumbent on me than any other; then I am bound to think that to do this *prima facie* duty is my duty *sans phrase* in the situation. [8]

Ross, like Kant, defines morality in terms of obligations. But unlike Kant, he acknowledges that duties are not absolute and can be overridden by more urgent duties, depending on an assessment of all the circumstances in a given case. Even if it avoids the absoluteness of Kantian obligations, this theory nevertheless raises two fundamental problems. First, how is one to determine which of the competing duties is the more urgent one and therefore the duty that will prevail in a given conflict of duties? More importantly, there is the problem of the moral justification of which duties are to be regarded as *prima facie* duties. Ross identifies three qualities that are intrinsically good: virtue, knowledge and pleasure. However, even though he attempts to give a moral justification of this particular choice of values, for those who do not share his value system the determination of certain acts or values as intrinsically good seems to be no more than the announcement of personal preferences,[9] even though they might be widely shared in society, a criticism that can be made equally of other deontological approaches.

1.2.2 A rights-based approach

Rights-based theories rest on the assumption that morality primarily aims at protecting the interests of individuals, and that rights are the most effective instrument to achieve such protection. If an interest is given the status of a right, the individual has an enforceable claim that his/her interest not be violated. According to Ronald Dworkin, a prominent promoter of the rights-based approach to ethics, to talk of a right means to give an individual interest, in principle, priority over collective goals. Individual rights are thus 'trumps' which cannot be restricted in order to pursue ordinary public or community interests.[10] This is because the concept of individual rights only makes sense if rights cannot be overridden simply by referring to some potential utilitarian gain, as individual rights would then not confer any special protection. Moreover, rights cannot be infringed in the interest of the majority, unless there is a case of special urgency, as individual rights are of particular importance to achieve the protection of the most vulnerable, a purpose which would be completely undermined if majority interests could routinely

---

[8]   Ross, at 16-29.
[9]   Engelhardt Jr., at 65.
[10] Dworkin, at 92 and 191.

outweigh these rights. However, the language of rights with its emphasis on the interests of the individual, cannot avoid the problem that even rights may have to yield when they are in conflict with other, more important rights, either of third parties or of the public.[11] Thus, rights-based theories need to decide which right has to yield and which right will prevail in case of conflict. Dworkin suggests that a balancing of rights is appropriate where individual rights compete with each other, and that the outcome of the balancing will then depend on the facts of the individual case. An individual right can also be outweighed by a public interest, but only if the costs of respecting the individual right in the case at issue go far beyond the general costs of recognising such an individual right.[12] Rights-based theories are faced with the problem that the abstract recognition that an individual's interests should sometimes have the force of a right says nothing about which interests are important enough to justify the recognition of a right. Rights-based moral theories are thus confronted with problems similar to those faced by duty-based ethics in that they have to defend the choices made when according an interest the status of a right, and when deciding that in a given conflict one right should prevail over the other. However, unlike duty-based theories, they propose a framework for the resolution of potential conflicts and the weighing of competing rights.

1.2.3 A principle-based approach

In contemporary medical ethics, more and more writers have come to realise the inadequacies of traditional ethical theories. In addition to the particular problems inherent to each theory, there is the fundamental problem that monistic theories which are based on a particular vision of the good can only be regarded as binding by those who share the same basic beliefs. However, they do not deliver sufficient moral justification to be convincing to every individual in a pluralistic society.[13] Furthermore, traditional ethical theories are so complex, and the full understanding and application of any of them requires such an immersion in philosophical ideas, that professionals who are faced with ethical conflicts, such as medical practitioners, will frequently not have an adequate philosophical background to approach these conflicts on the basis of the particular ethical theory which suits them best. Nor would such an approach necessarily be justifiable, given the possibility that their patient may subscribe to a completely different set of beliefs.[14] Therefore, rather than trying to develop a comprehensive ethical theory, an alternative approach starts from the assumption that workable medical ethics should be based on what Beauchamp and Childress call common morality or shared beliefs. Promoters of this approach allege that certain beliefs are shared by different ethical theories.[15] Principles which are acceptable to the adherents of rival moral theories could be developed on the basis of these beliefs, without any need

---

[11] Ibid., at 191–4.
[12] Ibid., at 200.
[13] Engelhardt Jr., at 65-6.
[14] Schöne-Seifert, at 564.
[15] Beauchamp and Childress, at 394-408.

first to resolve the fundamental philosophical disagreements about the very basis of moral justification. This approach emphasises and combines the strengths of different moral theories when searching for justifiable ethical principles to be used as guidelines for the resolution of conflicts of interests. It acknowledges that moral principles and practical experience are interdependent and that a constant mutual assessment of principles and experience is needed to develop new and to improve existing principles and approaches. Once principles are thus derived from common morality, they will be *prima facie* binding, but can be overridden by other principles.

This approach, of course, raises the problem of which interests can be identified as being recognised by common morality. While Engelhardt, for example, only works with two principles, permission and beneficence,[16] and holds that the principle of permission is the principle on which all moral authority is based,[17] Beauchamp and Childress identify four principles, autonomy, beneficence, non-maleficence and justice, without giving one of them precedence over the other.[18]

2 Autonomy, privacy and confidentiality

2.1 Principle of autonomy

While most contemporary moral theories accept the importance of the principle of autonomy and agree that the individual's autonomy deserves protection, the exact scope and meaning of autonomy is far from clear. Autonomy means self-rule, which indicates that autonomy refers to a person's ability of self-determination, that is of choosing his/her acts and life plan. Autonomy thus understood presupposes freedom from controlling influences and a capacity to make one's own decisions. If these conditions are met, a person is an autonomous agent. According to some moral theories, autonomy is an intrinsic value and as such deserves protection. Deontological theories state that every individual is under the obligation to respect the autonomy of others;[19] the principle-based approach regards the principle of autonomy as one of the fundamental principles of medical ethics;[20] and according to rights-based theory, the autonomous agent even has a right that his/her autonomy be respected.[21] However, while some utilitarians recognise that respect for autonomy may promote happiness,[22] utilitarian thought nevertheless predominantly maintains that autonomy only requires respect as long

---

[16] Engelhardt Jr., at 119.

[17] Ibid., at 69.

[18] Beauchamp, Childress, at 12.

[19] See, for example, Kant, at 52-3, although it needs to be emphasised that Kant himself used the term autonomy in a different sense.

[20] See, for example, Beauchamp, Childress, at 57.

[21] See, for example, Dworkin, at 277.

[22] Griffin, at 67.

as this will produce the best possible consequences. According to utilitarian theory, autonomy is therefore only of instrumental value.

Respect for autonomy is required in different ways. The individual must be given space to make autonomous decisions and, consequently, respect for autonomy dictates the principle of non-interference with the individual's autonomous affairs. In the light of the growing importance of personal autonomy, positive action may also be required, as the individual will often only be able meaningfully to exercise his/her autonomy with the assistance of others or of the state.[23] It has been argued that to respect an autonomous agent requires at a minimum to acknowledge that person's right to hold views, to make choices, and to take actions based on personal values, beliefs and preferences.[24]

2.2 Privacy

When looking at the use of the term privacy by courts and by different writers, it can easily be seen that the term is not given a single meaning, but is used to describe different phenomena. The importance of the right to privacy was already emphasised by Warren and Brandeis in an influential article published in 1890.[25] When the notion of a right to privacy first emerged, the main focus lay on the protection of the individual from unwarranted disclosure of private information. However, this perspective is too narrow, as privacy refers to the entire private sphere of the individual, so that a person's privacy could be defined as the inaccessibility of this person's private sphere to others. In that respect, privacy refers to the physical as well as to the mental sphere as it includes a person's body and bodily products, but also a person's thoughts, and intimate and confidential relationships.[26] This embraces, but is not restricted to, the protection of personal information. It is now widely recognised that privacy is closely linked with autonomy.[27] Privacy is said to be one aspect of the principle of autonomy, as without privacy, the guarantee of personal autonomy would be incomplete.[28]

In the context of contemporary medical ethics, the concept of privacy is sometimes divided into four different categories of cases: (1) informational privacy regarding access to personal information; (2) physical privacy regarding access to persons and personal space, a category of privacy that requires, for example, that medical treatment of a competent patient is not administered without the patient's consent; (3) decisional privacy regarding personal choices, which excludes governmental and other third-party interference with such intimate decisions as health care and family planning; and (4) proprietary privacy regarding the appropriation and ownership of interests in human personality.[29] In the context of a

---

[23] Herman, at 601; O'Neill, at 354-5.
[24] Beauchamp, Childress, at 58.
[25] Warren, Brandeis, at 193-220.
[26] Beauchamp, Childress, at 295.
[27] See, for example, Westin, at 33-4; Fried, at 219; Henkin, at 1425; Gostin, at 513-4.
[28] Beauchamp, Childress, at 296.
[29] Allen, at 33.

study of medical confidentiality, the first three privacy categories are of particular importance.[30]

With regard to the individual's interest in informational privacy, the connection between privacy and autonomy focuses on the concept of control over personal information. Informational privacy goes beyond the interest that no information be spread about the individual. It additionally justifies a feeling of security because the individual is in control of his/her private and intimate information. Respect for privacy is essential for developing a sense of self and personhood, as the individual needs private space to develop and formulate autonomous preferences.[31] Control over personal information is thus of fundamental importance to individuals. It not only enables persons to avoid the shame of having embarrassing intimate information disclosed publicly, but it also ensures that they can engage in unconventional behaviour without having to fear negative consequences. Consequently, if the principle of autonomy is recognised and respected, then the privacy of the individual must equally be protected, as it must be left to the individual's autonomous choice whether, to whom and to what extent to disclose personal information.[32] Informational privacy could thus be defined as an expression of the right to self-determination in respect of personal information, as the individual retains control over what will be known about him/her.[33] However, it is important to stress that informational privacy is not mainly concerned with shielding potentially embarrassing facts from public scrutiny. Rather, privacy is valuable regardless of how the information is viewed by others, as it does not aim at protecting the content of information, but rather at giving the individual the power to control the extent to which others can participate in his/her life.[34] Or, to express this thought differently, the unwanted disclosure of private data can in itself cause harm, so that respect for a person's privacy can be seen as a recognition of the desirability that the individual should be protected against the insult to dignity and the lack of respect for the person such unwanted disclosure might entail.[35] Another important aspect of privacy is to guarantee intimate relationships. Only if individuals are secure in the knowledge of their privacy will they be comfortable to share their confidences with others, and without privacy, intimate human relationships could thus not develop.[36] This is significant for the physician-patient relationship, as privacy protection gives the individual the space to form a confidential relationship with his/her physician in which he/she can disclose medical secrets without the fear that such confidences will be disclosed beyond that relationship. Some distinguish this aspect of privacy protection from

---

[30] In the context of this book, the particular problems of property in personal information is not relevant and will therefore not be discussed.
[31] Gostin, at 514.
[32] Bok, at 120.
[33] Moore, at 190.
[34] Orentlicher, at 79.
[35] Gostin, at 490.
[36] Francis, at 135.

informational privacy by introducing a separate category of physical privacy, that is the privacy to be given the personal space to form relationships with others.[37]

Decisional privacy is also linked to the principle of autonomy, as the principle of autonomy includes the right to decide what will happen to one's person and one's body. In that sense, it concerns a person's liberty as well as privacy, as what is at stake is the person's freedom to make decisions which, because of their nature, are private and therefore involve a person's privacy.[38] Privacy shields the individual's decisions and actions from the view of others, thereby preventing interference, control, and adverse reactions which could restrict decisional freedom,[39] as in private matters, freedom to make choices depends on the security that others will not, without the person's consent, be given access to the decision-making process or influence the outcome of the decision. This category of privacy is important for the physician-patient relationship, as without privacy, the patient would not have the opportunity to choose freely whether or not to seek medical advice and treatment and to make autonomous health care decisions without giving up the privacy of all information thus made known to the physician. It can be seen that in the context of medical confidentiality, informational, physical and decisional privacy are closely linked aspects of the patient's autonomy.

This leaves the question of how to determine what exactly is meant by 'personal' information or decisions and by the 'private' sphere that receives privacy protection. Some argue in favour of an objective approach when suggesting a reasonable person standard to define what is or is not personal.[40] However, while at least within a given society an agreement can frequently be identified regarding some areas of life that are viewed as particularly sensitive and private, this objective approach neglects the autonomy aspect of privacy. If privacy is to protect the individual's autonomy, then the definition of what is private needs to have a subjective focus and leave space to accommodate the particular sensitivities of individuals which the majority does not share.[41] Furthermore, an objective approach is not only complicated by the plurality of views in modern societies, but also by the fact that the sensitivity of information might depend on the circumstances. For example, information regarding the patient's medical condition which is in itself not regarded as embarrassing and therefore not deemed sensitive might nevertheless become sensitive if disclosed to a person's employer or insurance company.

For deontologists who see privacy as a part of the principle of autonomy, privacy is a fundamental right which is closely linked to the dignity of human persons.[42] Utilitarians also value privacy, but for different reasons. For them, privacy does not possess any intrinsic value. However, it is acknowledged that privacy promotes personal development and fosters personal or intimate relationships. Privacy is thus

---

[37] Allen, at 33; Beauchamp, Childress, at 295.

[38] Wagner DeCew, at 164-5 and 170.

[39] Gavison, at 450.

[40] Wagner DeCew, at 168.

[41] See also Parent, at 307.

[42] Francis, at 141.

said to be of instrumental value in achieving certain personal goals. In the context of the physician-patient relationship, the benefits of privacy protection are that it enhances autonomy, prevents embarrassment and promotes effective communication between physician and patient. It therefore promotes health and thereby happiness. Thus, utilitarians recognise that privacy may be important for its consequential effects.[43]

2.3 Medical confidentiality

Although medical confidentiality and privacy are closely linked, some writers stress that they are distinct concepts. Privacy refers to the general interest in control of one's private sphere. Confidentiality, in contrast, presupposes a relationship of confidence and can occur, for example, in the commercial setting, so that it does not necessarily relates to private information. Privacy and confidentiality may overlap where a person is given access to an individual's private sphere in the context of a confidential relationship, that is where the confidant makes a promise of confidentiality, or where the person is under an obligation, legal or ethical, not to disclose the other person's secrets.[44] If this distinction between privacy and medical confidentiality is accepted, medical confidentiality concerns a small part of privacy in that a claim for medical confidentiality can only exist in the confined setting of the physician-patient relationship. However, as information related to a person's physical or mental health is regarded as private, confidential medical information is already protected by the general guarantee of privacy. Privacy in its connection with personal autonomy also protects intimate personal relationships, so that privacy includes the right to form a relationship with one's physician and have the privacy of this relationship protected. This raises the question of whether, in the context of the physician-patient relationship, the particular protection of medical confidentiality can add anything to the general privacy protection. Additional protection stems from the fact that confidentiality imposes an obligation on the person who obtained information in confidence not to disclose this information. Furthermore, the confidential nature of a relationship stresses that the degree of privacy involved differs from, and usually surpasses that existing in non-confidential settings.

What, then, are the moral justifications for a protection of medical confidentiality? It could be argued that the confidentiality of the physician-patient relationship does not deserve any protection, as patients usually voluntarily grant their physicians access to their private sphere and thereby voluntarily surrender some degree of privacy. Warwick, for example, argues that confidentiality is not a necessary component of the physician-patient relationship, but that the physician's obligations to maintain the patient's confidences and the patient's expectation of medical confidentiality are rather only artificially created by the physician's promise to that respect. Without this promise, the moral justification for medical confidentiality would disappear. As the argument goes, privacy considerations

---

[43] Gostin, at 514.
[44] Beauchamp, Childress, at 306; Gillon, at 1635.

cannot justify medical confidentiality, as the patient has a free choice between keeping his/her medical secrets to him/herself by not revealing them to the physician and by not allowing the physician to examine him/her, or choosing to disclose such information, thus giving up privacy protection. According to Warwick, it is acceptable that patients must thus decide between privacy and health interests, as 'their health is sacrificed in good cause - that of their individual autonomy', and as 'it would seem that ill-health may be a reasonable price to pay for the maintenance of autonomy'.[45] However, it is submitted that this argument takes a too narrow view of personal autonomy. As was already explained, autonomy protects the self-determination of autonomous agents and requires respect for their free and voluntary choices. An important feature of respecting the individual's autonomy is that the private sphere be protected from unwanted access to as well as from interference with personal choices. At least personal autonomy in the form of decisional privacy is inadequately protected by the model suggested by Warwick. While without medical confidentiality, the individual still has a choice between privacy and health, the argument neglects the point that free and autonomous health-care decisions are one important expression of the person's privacy and autonomy. Thus, rather than achieving the alleged purpose of strengthening the patient's autonomy, this opinion gives the patient no more than a choice between exercising one element of autonomy to the detriment of the other, which is not necessarily the best way to enhance autonomy.

One justification for the protection of medical confidentiality is based on the premise that it seeks to guarantee respect for a patient's autonomy and privacy when entering a professional relationship with a physician.[46] Physicians and psychotherapists incessantly emphasise the importance of frankness and candour in the course of the medical encounter both for the purpose of a correct diagnosis and for the purpose of effective treatment. A patient who seeks medical or psychological help will regularly have to reveal intimate personal information to the physician or psychotherapist, and whenever a patient allows a medical or psychological examination to take place he/she necessarily grants the physician or psychotherapist access to his/her personal sphere. Only if the patient can rely on medical confidentiality and knows that the information will not be accessible to third parties or the state beyond the therapeutic relationship, will the patient be free to seek medical or psychological advice and treatment.[47] Without medical confidentiality, the patient will not have a true choice, as he/she then has to sacrifice one aspect of his/her autonomy and privacy for another. An element of trust is therefore said to be essential in order for patients to feel secure when confiding their secrets in the physician.[48] Given the close link between the concept of medical confidentiality and the principles of privacy and autonomy, some of the arguments listed in support of a right to privacy equally justify the recognition of medical confidentiality, and many writers, when trying to give a moral justification

---

[45] Warwick, at 184.
[46] Siegler, at 1519.
[47] Kottow (1994), at 475.
[48] See, for example, Siegler, at 1519; Orentlicher, at 84; Gostin, at 511.

for the protection of medical confidentiality, content themselves with the statement that medical confidentiality is based on the patient's privacy interests which are protected as part of the principle of autonomy.[49] Others specify this further. Siegler, for example, argues that medical confidentiality serves a dual purpose. First, it acknowledges respect for the patient's sense of individuality and privacy, as the patient's most personal physical and psychological secrets are kept confidential in order to avoid shame and vulnerability. Secondly, medical confidentiality plays a role in improving the patient's health care. As Emson explained the interplay between autonomy, privacy and medical confidentiality:

> In the contemporary ethics of Western societies primacy is accorded to autonomy, to the right of the patient to dispose of his or her own body according to personal wishes. Various rights devolve from this and confidentiality is one of them; the right to autonomy includes the right to privacy. The patient, disclosing all freely to the physician, has the right to have the privacy of this information respected by the confidentiality afforded to it.[50]

Deontologists who accept the significance of the principle of autonomy will thus usually assert that respect for medical confidentiality is necessary in order to achieve the protection of autonomy and privacy in the health care setting.

For utilitarians, medical confidentiality only deserves protection if, on balance, such protection has beneficial consequences. What, then, are the beneficial consequences that can be promoted by respecting medical confidentiality? The main justification for the principle of medical confidentiality voiced by utilitarians is that confidentiality is thought to encourage patients to disclose fully their symptoms and all confidential and intimate information needed by the physician in order to make a diagnosis and to provide effective medical advice and treatment. Gillon summarised the beneficial consequences resulting from a protection of medical confidentiality as people's health, welfare, the overall good and overall happiness. All of these consequences are more likely to be attained if doctors are fully informed by their patients which in turn is more likely if physicians will not disclose their patient's medical secrets to the state or third parties.[51] As the value of medical confidentiality depends on the consequences the respect for such a principle might entail, the utilitarian justification accordingly rests on the assumption that without a guarantee of medical confidentiality, large numbers of patients would fail to make sufficient disclosure, thereby endangering their own, as well as public, health. Empirical proof would therefore be needed to decide whether or not medical confidentiality is a principle worth protecting. However, no empirical evidence exists to support this assumption, and it is rather questionable whether most patients are even aware of the physician's legal and ethical obligations in the area of medical confidentiality.[52] Utilitarian philosophers

---

[49] See, for example, Moore, at 190.
[50] Emson, at 87.
[51] Gillon, at 1635.
[52] Shuman, at 664-5.

nevertheless seem to agree that the mere possibility of deterring a patient from seeking adequate medical advice and treatment is a sufficient justification for the principle of medical confidentiality, given the significance of individual and public health.[53] Some utilitarians emphasise, in addition, that medical confidentiality promotes the creation and maintenance of socially valuable relationships.[54] Medical confidentiality would then have to be protected because of the societal value of the physician-patient relationship and the potential injury to that relationship if its confidentiality were not protected. In her summary of the utilitarian view, Hogan states that this theory, which she calls public function theory, is not concerned with the individual suffering that a failure of the relationship might cause, but that it focuses instead on the societal harm caused by such a failure.[55] It is problematic whether utilitarians will also accept that medical confidentiality deserves protection because it enhances patient autonomy and privacy. Utilitarians rarely seem to discuss this question. It is submitted that it is not at all evident that a utilitarian perspective would dismiss this consideration, as a course of action that promotes the individual's autonomy could arguably promote happiness. Gillon introduces this idea when stating that patients who decide to disclose confidential information to their physicians despite a lack of medical confidentiality might feel anxious and unhappy at the prospect of their secrets being made known and their autonomy being undermined.[56]

Deontological and utilitarian approaches to medical confidentiality are not mutually exclusive. Nor is it true that every writer who attempts to find a moral justification for the recognition of the principle of medical confidentiality adheres to either a pure deontological or a pure utilitarian approach. Instead, many writers borrow deontological and utilitarian thoughts and combine elements from both philosophies in order to explain the importance of medical confidentiality. Thus, writers who stress the overriding importance of medical confidentiality for an adequate protection of the patient's autonomy and privacy sometimes acknowledge that medical confidentiality also lies in the public interest. It is argued, for example, that without medical confidentiality, society will deter precisely those patients from seeking medical advice and treatment whom it is trying to bring under control, for example people displaying deviant and possibly dangerous behaviour, or persons suffering from illnesses such as venereal diseases, that may be regarded as embarrassing.[57] It is also argued that public health can best be promoted if medical confidentiality is upheld and people are therefore encouraged to seek medical advice and treatment.[58] Sissela Bok suggests that medical confidentiality rests on four premises: (1) individual autonomy over personal information; (2) the legitimacy of sharing personal secrets and the assumption of

---

[53] Moore, at 188.
[54] Weisberg, at 971.
[55] Hogan, at 420-421.
[56] Gillon, at 1635; see also 'Developments in privileged communications', (1985) 98 Harvard Law Review, at 1555.
[57] Kottow (1994), at 478.
[58] Vickery, at 1435.

respect for intimate relationships; (3) respect for a promise of confidentiality; and (4) the utility of professional confidentiality for individuals and society.[59] While the first three justifications are based on deontological thought, the last consideration clearly refers to utilitarian theory.

It can be seen that in spite of the significant conceptual differences between the deontological and the utilitarian approaches to medical confidentiality, both have much in common. Both agree that medical confidentiality serves important functions in that it enhances patient frankness. For the purpose of establishing an initial justification for medical confidentiality, the differences between the two approaches do not seem overly important. This, however, will not necessarily be true in the context of developing a moral justification for the recognition of medical privilege.

3 Conflicts of interests in the context of criminal prosecution and crime prevention

In the context of criminal prosecution or crime prevention, the value to be attached to medical confidentiality must be reassessed in the light of the conflict between medical confidentiality, on the one hand, and the interests of justice, the interest in criminal prosecution and the interest in crime prevention, on the other. While the different moral theories introduced above agree that the protection of medical confidentiality is, in principle, morally justified, this does not necessarily imply that medical confidentiality is an absolute principle that must be upheld, even in case of a conflict, under all circumstances and at all costs.

3.1 Strict confidentiality?

Utilitarians mostly promote the view that medical confidentiality should only be protected as long as a cost-benefit analysis favours this protection, and deontologists usually argue that medical confidentiality can sometimes be outweighed by other interests of overriding importance. Thus, both philosophical schools agree that medical confidentiality is not an absolute principle that will prevail under all circumstances and trump all other interests. Such relativist views of medical confidentiality make it necessary to define exceptions to the general principle and thereby create their own problems. From a utilitarian perspective which argues that medical confidentiality is needed to promote frankness in the physician-patient relationship and which therefore rests on the assumption that without medical confidentiality, a patient may be reluctant openly to reveal all the information that enables the physician adequately to advise and treat the patient, every exception to the principle risks undermining its very purpose. If the patient knows that the privilege is fraught with exceptions, he/she may react by withholding information or by avoiding therapy, just as if no privilege existed at

---

[59] Bok, at 119-22.

all, as the reassuring function of a privilege loses its value if exceptions are admitted.[60]

From a deontological perspective, pleas for absolute confidentiality could equally be made. Where a patient is enticed to frankness by the assurance that his/her confidences will be kept secret, and that he/she will therefore keep control over confidential information that was shared with the physician, it seems unfair to alter the initial conditions of the physician-patient relationship on the grounds that the content of the information requires disclosure, once the act of confiding has occurred.[61] Exceptions to the principle of medical confidentiality accordingly undermine the patient's autonomy.

However, it will be seen that in some situations, it would be equally, if not more problematic strictly to adhere to medical confidentiality, as it might conflict with interests of equal or even overriding importance. Even Kottow who is frequently quoted as promoting an absolute nature of the principle of medical confidentiality therefore concedes that the principle cannot be absolute, but should instead only be respected as far as possible.[62] However, if exceptions cannot be avoided, they should at least be clearly established, so that every patient knows in advance what to expect.[63] More importantly, exceptions need a moral justification, as they constitute an inroad in a value which is recognised as morally important both by deontological and utilitarian ethics. The following discussion will therefore assess the moral basis and justification of exceptions to medical confidentiality in the context of criminal prosecution and crime prevention.

3.2 Medical confidentiality and the administration of criminal justice

Medical privilege protects medical confidentiality in the context of judicial proceedings, in that physicians are exempt from the obligation to give testimony in court. A testimonial privilege thus demonstrates the value accorded to the principle of medical confidentiality, as it gives medical confidentiality precedence over the countervailing interests of justice.[64] The recognition of medical privilege accordingly expresses the idea that the possible impairment of the interests of justice is a price worth paying for the protection of the confidentiality of the physician-patient relationship.[65] As the resolution of a conflict of interests is typically based on policy considerations, it is interesting to analyse the problem of medical privilege from a philosophical perspective to develop a better understanding of the ethical concerns at issue.

Criminal proceedings have many different functions. They aim at reaching a just decision as to the guilt or innocence of a person who is accused of having committed a criminal offence. As the state has the monopoly in punishing criminal

---

[60] Kendrick, Tsakonas, Smith, at 7-10.
[61] Kottow (1986), at 118.
[62] Kottow (1994), at 478.
[63] Ibid., see also Kottow (1986), at 118.
[64] Vickery, at 1435.
[65] Peiris, at 301.

offenders, it is essential that it performs this function effectively in order to fulfil the obligation owed to all citizen that they be safe from criminal offences, and the obligation owed to the victims of crime that an offender be brought to justice. To achieve these purposes, it is essential that the truth be established in criminal court, and this is most likely if all relevant evidence is made available to the court. Medical privilege, in contrast with other exclusionary rules such as the privilege against self-incrimination, aims at the exclusion of evidence, not for the purpose of enhancing the truth-finding function of criminal proceedings, but rather for extra-judicial purposes.[66] Seen in this light, testimonial or communication privileges such as the privilege of a physician or a psychotherapist conflict with the smooth operation of the criminal justice system. As privileges result in withholding evidence from the fact-finder, they can lead to grossly incorrect results and as a consequence, miscarriages of justice may occur.[67] The question must therefore be asked:

> whether acknowledgement of privilege in respect of confidential communications to members of the medical profession is defensible on the basis of considerations of policy which are sufficiently compelling to relegate the negative effect of exclusion of relevant evidence in judicial proceedings.[68]

Only if the ethical analysis shows 'that there is something of merit that requires protection in these communications, something more valuable than the needs of "the law"'[69] can medical privilege be morally justified.

3.2.1 Utilitarian approaches

At first sight, the costs of medical privilege for criminal proceedings seem clear: if medical privilege is recognised, certain information will not be available to the court for the purpose of criminal proceedings if the physician invokes medical privilege and refuses to give testimony. The main benefit arising from medical privilege, on the other hand, is that it encourages frank communication between patient and physician.

From a utilitarian perspective, the recognition of a medical privilege depends on the outcome of a cost-benefit analysis which must examine to what extent medical privilege causes the loss of relevant information, and whether or not this potential loss is outweighed by the rationale behind granting medical privilege. As both medical confidentiality and the efficient administration of criminal justice can promote good consequences, it must therefore be decided which of the two interests should prevail in case of a conflict, that is which of the two interests promotes greater happiness. Sometimes the utilitarian approach conversely focuses on the minimisation of harm, and medical privilege would then only be justified if the possibility of disclosure of confidential information did in fact deter patients

---

[66] Hogan, at 418-20.

[67] Snyder, at 200-201.

[68] Peiris, at 306.

[69] Oppenheim, at 619.

from divulging to their physicians all information that is necessary to obtain adequate medical advice and treatment, and if the benefits arising from non-disclosure outweighed the harm thereby caused.[70] No empirical evidence exists in support of the view that medical confidentiality promotes the physician-patient relationship. It is rather doubtful whether patients are aware of the applicable law of privilege and consider that law before consulting a physician.[71] Indeed, empirical studies seem to suggest that patients do not necessarily know whether or not their legal system endorses medical privilege, and what exceptions to such privilege are recognised.[72] Some utilitarians consequently argue that without such evidence, medical privilege cannot be justified. This opinion rests on the assumption that it is certain that a privilege will impair the fact-finding function of judicial proceedings, while it is not at all established whether and to what extent the physician-patient relationship will be harmed by compelled disclosure of confidential medical information in court. It is therefore suggested by promoters of this view that medical privilege cannot be justified given the uncertainty of the benefits thereby obtained, and given the costs its recognition entails.[73]

Other utilitarians come to a different result when proposing that the outcome of the cost-benefit analysis should not be determined generally and for all cases, but should be performed on a case-by-case basis, depending on the harm inflicted by disclosure, on the one hand, and the significance of the potential loss of evidence, on the other. It has been argued that, in principle, medical privilege is not highly significant for the physician-patient relationship, as most patients will disclose the same information to a physician whether or not a privilege exists.[74] However, even if most communications were made to physicians in the absence of medical privilege, it is possible that some communications would not take place if no privilege is in place. On the other hand, not all litigation would suffer from the recognition of medical privilege.[75] Therefore, even if in most cases the balance did strike in favour of disclosure, a different result might be reached in cases in which the information the disclosure of which is sought is not of particular relevance to the proceedings. In such cases, the costs of recognising a privilege would not be high. If little or no relevant evidence were lost, and if the physician-patient relationship were seriously impaired by disclosure, the overall balance would lead to a recognition of medical privilege in that particular case. While there is a presumption in favour of disclosure,[76] exceptional circumstances may thus occur in which the protection of medical confidentiality in criminal court is more important than the interest in the administration of justice.

The utilitarian approaches to medical privilege that have been introduced thus far start from the premise that in principle, the interests of justice should prevail over

---

[70] Moore, at 192; see also Wigmore, at 829-30.

[71] Shuman, at 664-5.

[72] Snyder, at 172.

[73] Wigmore, at 829-30.

[74] Watson, at 1131.

[75] Saltzburg, at 619 note 74.

[76] Ibid., at 648.

the interest in medical confidentiality. However, this opinion is not uncontroversial among utilitarians. It has, for example, been argued that the value of promoting open relations between patients and their doctors outweighs the cost of judicial decisions that are reached without a full disclosure of all relevant facts.[77] Thus, even though medical privilege entails high costs in that it creates a risk of miscarriages of justice, the protection of the confidentiality of the physician-patient relationship is viewed by some as important enough to justify incorrect results in individual cases, as society cannot afford to deter people from seeking medical advice and treatment.[78] For the health of the community, 'medical treatment is so valuable that few would lose it to prevent facts from coming to light in court'.[79]

With regard to the special case of the psychotherapist-patient privilege, it is sometimes suggested that the cost-benefit analysis differs from that to be performed in the context of the ordinary physician-patient relationship, as frankness is even more important for the psychotherapist-patient relationship. Without the patient's willingness to share openly even his/her most secret thoughts and feelings with the psychotherapist, effective psychotherapy would be impossible. Also, the matters discussed in psychotherapy, for example drug abuse, sexual problems or violent tendencies will frequently make the patient particularly anxious about later courtroom disclosures.[80] Among physicians, psychotherapists are therefore particularly adamant that medical confidentiality should be respected.[81] If accepted, these special features would give medical confidentiality more weight in the context of the psychotherapist-patient relationship, as the costs of a disclosure by a psychotherapist would then be higher than the costs a disclosure by a physician might entail. However, it has been countered that no psychotherapist-patient privilege exists in the UK and some parts of Canada, and that no evidence points to adverse consequences for effective therapy.[82]

It can be seen that utilitarian thought does not result in a clear and unequivocal attitude towards medical privilege. Rather, the outcome of the utilitarian cost-benefit analysis largely depends on the weight accorded to the benefits and harms following from a recognition or a rejection of medical privilege. As the cost-benefit analysis seems to be based on empirical evidence, the utilitarian approach conveys the impression of a certain objectivity. However, it should be borne in mind that the utility of medical privilege is not supported by any empirical evidence. It is difficult to assess the consequences of this lack of empirical evidence for utilitarian theory. Does it necessarily mean that medical privilege is not beneficial for the physician-patient relationship, and for the patient's and the public welfare? More importantly, are the benefits arising from a rejection of medical privilege really as certain as frequently purported? Arguably, the costs of a

---

[77] Kendrick, Tsakonas, Smith, at 7-8.

[78] Snyder, at 201.

[79] Chafee, at 609; see also Peiris, at 304.

[80] Kendrick, Tsakonas, Smith, at 7-9 to 7-10.

[81] Advisory Committee's Notes on the Proposed Federal Rules of Evidence, (1972-73) 56 FRD 183, at 242.

[82] Shuman, Weiner, at 895.

medical privilege are not necessarily equal to the value of the evidence thereby excluded from judicial proceedings, as some evidence presumably exists only because a privilege encouraged its creation.[83] There is at least a possibility that without medical privilege, the communications between patient and physician might change,[84] so that without medical privilege, the physician might not obtain the information the disclosure of which is sought in court. The unavailability of such evidence can then not be regarded as a cost of medical privilege. Thus, any assessment of the costs of medical privilege must take into account the extent to which people would communicate in the absence of the privilege and depends on the same empirically unverified factor that determines the benefits flowing from the privilege. Therefore, even if the proponents of medical privilege fail to offer empirical proof in support of their assumption that medical privilege promotes patient frankness and ultimately individual and public health, the costs that privileges purportedly impose on the truth-finding function of the courts are just as uncertain as the asserted benefits. The whole basis of the utilitarian approach is thus problematic and not very helpful in the context of medical privilege, as neither the costs nor the benefits of medical privilege are amenable to empirical proof. Absent empirical proof supporting the cost-benefit analysis, the analysis does not weigh the objective consequences of rules or acts, but rather merely the presumed consequences. As the different opinions among utilitarians show, the importance accorded to certain consequences, and the assessment of what is harmful, what is beneficial and how to balance harm and benefits in case of a conflict largely depends on the value attached to the different interests at stake.

The case-by-case approach to medical privilege that has been suggested by some utilitarians is also problematic. If the patient cannot be certain whether in his/her individual case the balance will be struck in favour of or against disclosure, the main purpose of medical confidentiality according to utilitarian thought, i.e. to encourage the patient to receive medical treatment and to disclose all relevant information to the physician, can hardly be achieved.[85]

3.2.2 Deontological approaches

According to the deontological approach, the disclosure of confidences revealed in certain relationships is regarded as wrong because it would violate the patient's privacy and autonomy. Medical privilege is then the legal device through which these interests can be protected in the context of judicial proceedings. But is medical confidentiality important enough to outweigh the public interest in truth-finding in criminal proceedings? For deontologists, the patient's privacy interests are of sufficient significance to justify a presumptive right against disclosure. Understood in this way, medical confidentiality has the status of a *prima facie* right which has to be respected unless weightier considerations justify an exception.

---

[83] 'Developments in privileged communications', (1985) 98 Harvard Law Review, at 1513; see also Slovenko, at 49 for the psychotherapist-patient relationship.

[84] Saltzburg, at 602.

[85] Kendrick, Tsakonas, Smith, at 7-10; Thomas-Fishburn, at 194 regarding the attorney-client privilege; Gurfein, at 733 also regarding the attorney-client privilege.

This means that medical confidentiality must be protected even in criminal court provided that this interest is not exceptionally overridden by a more important right or interest.[86] Accordingly, the recognition of a medical privilege requires a value judgment, as it must be decided whether medical confidentiality or the interest in the unhindered administration of criminal justice is the more important interest and therefore deserves precedence in case of conflict. As deontologists do not place great weight on the consequences of value decisions, the value judgment that needs to be made does not depend on empirical evidence, but rests, instead, on moral beliefs. If privacy is regarded as the overriding interest, medical privilege is morally justified, and the potential exclusion of relevant evidence is then 'merely a secondary and incidental feature of the privilege's "vitality"',[87] but does not influence the value judgment as such.

It is striking that for most deontologists the outcome of the value judgment so clearly turns in favour of a recognition of medical privilege that hardly any attempts are made to justify this result. Rather, it seems sufficient to stress the importance of medical privilege for the patient's autonomy and privacy,[88] and to state that the threat to the ascertainment of truth resulting from the recognition of medical privilege is not too high a price to pay for the preservation of medical confidentiality.[89] In the absence of a moral justification of medical privilege that goes beyond emphasising its importance for privacy and autonomy, it is difficult to predict with certainty how the conflict between medical confidentiality and the interests in the administration of criminal justice will be approached in specific cases. It has been argued, for example, that exceptions to medical privilege should be made where the prosecution of serious crimes is at stake,[90] at least where medical information is likely to be central to a successful prosecution, as in most drunk driving and child abuse cases. While a presumption exists in favour of protecting the patient's privacy, the proposed exception would ensure that information is available to the courts where the loss of information entails particularly high costs.[91] This argument combines deontological and consequential elements, as it justifies exceptions to medical confidentiality on the basis of the consequences of a recognition of medical privilege, rather than on the basis that the conflicting interests, here the interest in the prosecution of serious crimes, outweigh the interest in medical confidentiality. It seems to suggest that interests do not necessarily have a fixed value, but that the value of an interest must rather, in case of conflict, be determined with reference to all the circumstances of the individual case, including the consequences of the value decision. This approach, while making it possible to adopt a more fine-tuned balancing test, is nevertheless problematic, unless morally justified criteria are developed on the basis of which the balancing can be performed.

---

[86] Moore, at 191-4.

[87] Shuman, at 664.

[88] Krattenmaker, at 90.

[89] Louisell, Crippin, at 414.

[90] Kendrick, Tsakonas, Smith, at 7-35.

[91] 'Developments in privileged communications', (1985) 98 Harvard Law Review, at 1553.

One attempt to argue generally against the recognition of medical privilege in criminal proceedings was made by Sissela Bok who argued that with regard to criminal prosecution, medical confidentiality must be weighed against interests of social justice and restitution.[92] According to her, medical confidentiality must find its limits where it contradicts the very respect for persons and for human bonds that it was meant to protect.[93] The validity of this argument is questionable. Where confidences of victims or other third parties are concerned, it cannot be said that the patient has disregarded the respect owed to others and thereby forfeited his/her claim to medical confidentiality. However, even where the confidence is that of the criminal offender, this argument is problematic, as it presupposes that the accused did in fact disregard the values behind a protection of medical confidentiality. In the course of criminal proceedings this is impossible to know, as the guilt of the accused will only be established at their very end. David Black seems to be right when stating that:

> Most people might see the disclosure of confidential information for the purpose of criminal prosecution as a matter of degree, giving preference to autonomy for trivial offences, but becoming skewed to non-maleficence in case of terrorism or other serious crime.[94]

This demonstrates the main problem of the deontological approach towards medical privilege, that is the difficulty of how to resolve conflicts of interests, as generally agreed upon criteria for establishing priorities among the conflicting interests or for determining when generally accepted priorities must give way to extreme interests do not appear to exist.[95] Instead, the outcome of the balancing exercise seems to depend to a large extent on personal preferences and intuition. The rights-based approach at least offers some help when deciding how the balancing of interests should be performed. Medical confidentiality forms part of the right to privacy and is thus an individual right. The interests behind criminal prosecution are societal, rather than individual interests. Given that individual rights cannot normally be outweighed by communal interests,[96] medical confidentiality would have to be given precedence over the interest in criminal prosecution, and the recognition of medical privilege would seem to be the logical conclusion of acknowledging a right to medical confidentiality. The result would only be different if it could be shown that criminal prosecution and proceedings also aim at protecting individual rights of other citizens, for example of the victim of the offence. However, the right of the victim is mainly a right to be protected from the crime before its commission as well as from repeat victimisation, but these are questions of crime prevention, not of the prosecution of the offender. Even if it were conceded that the victim in addition not only has an interest in the

---

[92] Bok, at 131.
[93] Ibid., at 135.
[94] Black, at 487.
[95] Moore, at 195.
[96] Dworkin, at 92 and 191-4.

prosecution of the offender, but also a right to that effect, that right does not go beyond the right that the state provide a system of effective criminal prosecution. As long as this is guaranteed, the actual design of the procedure, including what privileges the state decides to implement, will not affect the individual rights of the victim. Individual rights of the victim therefore do not stand in the way of the recognition of medical privilege.

With regard to the special case of the psychotherapist-patient privilege, it has been argued that such communications deserve more protection than those between patients and physicians, as matters disclosed in psychotherapy are often much more personal than matters discussed in the course of consultations for physical illnesses.[97] Therefore, the patient's privacy interests are said to have more weight in the context of the psychotherapist-patient relationship.[98] Others reject this distinction, arguing that physicians today cannot focus solely on one aspect of a person's problems, either physical or psychological, as the increase in psycho-somatic illnesses clearly demonstrates.[99] The same need for trust would then exist in both relationships. Given that confidentiality is protected mainly to respect the patient's autonomy, the distinction also seems to overlook that it should be left to the patient to determine which information, whether physical or psychological, he/she regards as particularly sensitive and in need of most protection.

3.3 Medical confidentiality and the interests of third parties

Another conflict which frequently arises is that between medical confidentiality, on the one hand, and the protection of third parties, on the other. In the context of medical privilege, this may embrace cases in which the patient threatens to inflict harm on third parties, and cases in which physicians hold confidential information that might be beneficial to a person who is accused in criminal proceedings.

3.3.1 Crime prevention
Many argue that the disclosure of confidential patient information aimed at preventing a criminal offence is justified, at least where it may help prevent violent crime. For utilitarians, a justification of disclosure seems at first sight rather compelling, as the prevention of violent crime averts significant harm from the potential victim as well as from society, while most utilitarians regard the harm prevented by the maintenance of medical confidentiality as uncertain. Some writers nevertheless question this approach, arguing that it is difficult to assess whether more lives will be saved by disclosure than by respect for medical confidentiality, as violent patients could be deterred from seeking medical and, in particular, psychological advice and treatment.[100] This, once more, brings to light the problem of how to weigh uncertain and long-term costs and benefits. Engelhardt, for example, argues that:

---

[97] Kendrick, Tsakonas, Smith, at 7-9 to 7-10.

[98] Slovenko, at 49.

[99] Saltzburg, at 621.

[100] Moore, at 193.

The fact that a particular disclosure of a patient's dangerousness could have saved the life of a particular third party should not obscure the fact that a general rule requiring disclosure may in fact lead to the deaths of more individuals.[101]

And Kottow equally opposes the utilitarian argument that disclosure would produce the better consequences in such cases. According to him, a violation of medical confidentiality results in certain harm, as it brings suspicion into the physician-patient relationship, thereby undermining patient frankness and lowering the standard of medical care. At the same time, it seems difficult to perform an adequate risk assessment and to predict with sufficient certainty the harm caused by the threat of violent behaviour. First, there is a possibility that threats of violence issued by patients may never materialise. How can the physician or psychotherapist assess whether the risk is real, potential or fictitious?[102] The threat may only be the expression of a patient's violent fantasy in the course of psychotherapy. Secondly, if disclosure for the purpose of crime prevention were allowed, this would not necessarily help to avert harm, as preventive arrest is not lawful, and as other preventive measures will often not be available to ensure that the threat may not be carried out.[103] Also, if individual freedom were regarded as a benefit, the outcome of the cost-benefit analysis in such cases may not be so obvious, given that the breach of medical confidentiality to avert a hypothetical danger entails a certain infringement of individual freedom.[104] Therefore, it was argued that as long as a plausible risk-benefit analysis is lacking, the utility of disclosure is not sufficiently demonstrated so as to justify a breach of confidentiality.[105] Others, in contrast, argue that the imponderability of the harm prevented or caused by a disclosure should not prevent the physician from nevertheless attempting to assess the value of the interests at stake in every given case.[106]

Deontologists also frequently hold disclosure to be justified where it can prevent violent crime. This attitude is mainly based on two arguments. First, it is often argued that an individual's bodily integrity and life are more important values than privacy, so that the balancing of the competing interests would come down in favour of disclosure.[107] However, the conflict could also be regarded differently. If medical confidentiality promotes a patient's decisional privacy, in that it gives the patient the freedom to make autonomous health care decisions, then medical confidentiality serves the patient's interest in bodily integrity. The overriding importance of the competing third party interest is then no longer obvious where only the physical integrity but not the life of the potential victim is at risk. When others argue that the third party interests should at least prevail where there is a

---

[101] Engelhardt Jr., at 339.
[102] Kottow (1986), at 120.
[103] For a critical view see Adshead, at 1619.
[104] Kottow (1994), at 477.
[105] Ibid., at 475.
[106] Emson, at 90.
[107] Shuman, at 667; Turkington, at 888; Watson, at 1144.

risk of serious harm which could not otherwise be prevented,[108] this shows, again, that consequences of actions can be of importance for the balancing of interests. While the patient's autonomy interests may be more important than the avoidance of a very remote risk of slight impairments of a third party's bodily integrity, the outcome of the balancing test might change where the risk is less remote and the potential harm more serious, as the weight of the interest harmed by non-disclosure might be influenced by the potential consequences of non-disclosure. Others focus on the fact that the interest to be impaired by disclosure is the patient's interest in privacy and autonomy. It is argued that a person's autonomy is limited by the autonomy of others and can therefore not go as far as putting others at risk of bodily harm or even risks to their lives.[109] 'Just as no one is granted autonomy when it comes to *doing* violence to others, so there is no reason to concede such autonomy and control for *plans* to do so, once divulged.'[110] It is submitted that this argument in itself cannot be conclusive when deciding whether or not disclosure is justified. It can hardly be said that the patient, particularly when it is a psychiatric patient revealing thoughts during therapy, waives the right to privacy when uttering threats. While the patient's autonomy might have to yield in these cases, it would nevertheless be violated by disclosure. Therefore, for disclosure to be justified it would need to be demonstrated that it protects a more important interest, which, again, requires a balancing of the competing interests at stake.

Engelhardt suggests a different approach when emphasising that the patient's dangerousness is not increased by the fact that a physician knows about it and that it is not the physician's silence that injures the potential victim.[111] However, this argument seems to miss the point, as it does not assess the value of the different interests at stake, but rather exclusively concentrates on the question of whether or not additional injury is caused by the fact of non-disclosure. The question, however, is not whether non-disclosure causes additional harm, but whether it prevents harm that would be more significant than the injury contained in disclosure. If that is the case, disclosure will be justified.

It can be seen that regarding the conflict between medical confidentiality and the interest in the prevention of crime, both utilitarian and deontological ethicists have difficulties in defining the criteria according to which the interests at stake should be balanced. Again, the rights-based approach, while not providing an abstract answer as to the value to be attached to the conflicting rights in each case, nevertheless seems to provide the most workable framework in clarifying that if it is accepted that medical confidentiality is an individual right, a careful assessment in each case of conflict needs to take place in order to justify disclosure. It is submitted that in addition to demonstrating that the right protected by disclosure outweighs the right violated thereby, it also needs to be shown that the interest at risk could in fact be protected by disclosure. This will not always be the case, for example where a patient makes an unspecified threat.

---

[108] Beauchamp, Childress, at 426.
[109] Moore, at 194-5.
[110] Bok, at 128-129.
[111] Engelhardt Jr., at 337.

3.3.2 Defence rights
With regard to the conflict between medical confidentiality and defence rights, the utilitarian cost-benefit analysis would probably come down in favour of disclosure. Given that most utilitarians favour disclosure even where medical confidentiality merely conflicts with the interests in the administration of criminal justice, the reasons supporting disclosure are even more compelling where the defence rights of an accused are at stake. In that case, medical privilege might impose the additional costs of an impairment of the defence rights of the accused, which might lead to unjust results, and, in the worst case, to a criminal conviction of an innocent person and to a loss of faith in the criminal justice system. However, those utilitarians who think that a miscarriage of justice is not too high a price to pay for the protection of medical confidentiality would maybe equally argue in favour of medical privilege where confidentiality conflicts with defence rights. From a deontological perspective, all depends on the weight accorded to the competing interests, and it is highly likely that most deontologists would argue in favour of disclosure, as the defendant's freedom, an interest of very high rank, is at stake.

4 Conclusion

The preceding analysis has demonstrated the similarities of and differences between the utilitarian and the deontological approaches to medical confidentiality. Both approaches accept that medical confidentiality is important. While utilitarians justify the importance of the principle by reference to the consequences of its recognition, deontologists argue that medical confidentiality is a value to be protected because it is closely linked with personal autonomy and privacy. From these different starting points, both theories provide an initial justification for the principle of medical confidentiality. However, the differences in approach come to light in the context of medical privilege, where conflicts of interests must be resolved. While according to the utilitarian approach, in case of conflict it must be positively demonstrated that medical confidentiality produces better consequences than disclosure, the deontological approach starts from a presumption in favour of medical confidentiality, and each exception to this principle must be justified by the overriding importance of the value which outweighs medical confidentiality. This fundamental difference may explain why, in the context of medical privilege, most utilitarians favour disclosure while most deontologists favour the upholding of medical confidentiality. Consequently, the protection awarded to medical confidentiality according to deontological thought is much stronger than its protection by utilitarian theory.

Both theories have their strengths and weaknesses. Utilitarianism has to face the problem that consequences can frequently not be determined with any certainty, particularly not in the area of medical confidentiality and medical privilege, where a variety of factors interact. A theory that decides on right and wrong according to the consequences of acts or rules will hardly be able to produce satisfactory results where these consequences cannot be adequately determined. More importantly, however, it is problematic that the utilitarian cost-benefit analysis favours the best consequences, which seems to require value judgments about right and wrong independent of the consequences themselves. If happiness is the only value that is accepted, this is rather vague and can be subject to many different interpretations, as it is neither clear whether the focus should lie on individual or societal happiness, nor what exactly is meant by happiness in the first place. Therefore, utilitarian theory is not free from the reproach that its results in case of conflict resolution are arbitrary, depending on the personal preferences of the respective philosopher. Utilitarian thought as applied by many of its promoters has the additional problem that it seems to be too heavily focused on communal interests to the detriment of individual freedom.

Deontological theory promotes individual freedom by emphasising the intrinsic value of personal autonomy and privacy. However, this approach also seems to be of limited value for the resolution of moral conflicts, as the judgment on the hierarchy of values seems to be based on personal preferences, and not on a coherent system of morally justified considerations. While the importance of autonomy is clearly established, neither the value of conflicting interests, nor guidelines on how to balance competing interests are determined with sufficient clarity to assist with the resolution of moral problems. What, for example, should be the place of general considerations of welfare[112] in the context of the deontological balancing exercise? And should consequences of a decision be completely omitted from the balancing process? If so, how can the value of conflicting interests be determined in a given case if the consequences of the decision for each interest cannot be taken into account? If, on the other hand, consequences can be of importance for the outcome of the balancing process, this could be seen as a limited convergence of deontological and utilitarian thought. The two approaches could also be brought more closely together if happiness or beneficial consequences were understood as including individual freedom. At least in liberal societies, individual freedom is of overriding importance not only for the individual concerned, but also for a democratic society as such. Utilitarian analysis would then have to accommodate personal autonomy and privacy when assessing the costs and benefits of certain acts or rules.[113]

In the light of the inadequacies of both theories, it is hardly surprising that neither has succeeded in presenting a satisfactory framework for the resolution of all conflicts of interests. Nancy Moore has therefore rightly remarked that: 'Given the difficulties in applying both utilitarian and deontological theories, it is obvious that philosophers have by no means solved the problems now confronting the medical profession.'[114] This is not to say that reference to moral theory will not be useful for an analysis of the law regarding medical confidentiality and medical privilege. The principal questions arising in the context of medical privilege, that is whether or not medical confidentiality is important enough to outweigh conflicting interests in the context of judicial proceedings, are moral, not legal questions. Accordingly,

---

[112] For the importance of welfare considerations in the context of criminal law and criminal prosecution see, for example, Ashworth, at 30-31.

[113] 'Developments in privileged communications', (1985) 98 Harvard Law Review, at 1555.

[114] Moore, at 196.

they cannot be addressed without reference to moral principles. However, predictability is an essential feature of legal principles, so that the abstract and often vague guidelines to be derived from philosophical concepts can be no more than a tool when formulating legal responses to the problems discussed.

Chapter 3

European Law

As France, Germany and the UK are Members of the Council of Europe as well as of the European Union, the relevant law of both of these bodies dealing with medical confidentiality will briefly be outlined in this chapter.

PART 1 – PROTECTION OF MEDICAL CONFIDENTIALITY

1 European Convention on Human Rights

France, Germany and the UK have ratified the European Convention on Human Rights and in all three countries, legislation must be interpreted so as to be compatible with Convention rights. Therefore, it is important to be clear about the protection of the principle of medical confidentiality under the Convention. The relevant article of the ECHR is Article 8 which states that:

> (1) Everyone has the right to respect for his private and family life, his home and his correspondence.

With regard to the scope of the right to private life, the European Commission of Human Rights stated[1] that the right to respect for private life is the right to privacy, the right to live as far as one wishes, protected from publicity. This rather general delineation of the scope of the privacy right under Article 8 of the ECHR was clarified in subsequent decisions in which the European Court of Human Rights held that the right to private life protects health related data of the individual.[2] Even though the ECJ's interpretation of the ECHR is not binding, it seems worth mentioning that the ECJ has confirmed that Article 8 of the ECHR awards the right to keep one's health condition secret.[3] It is thus clear that Article 8 of the ECHR protects health related information from compelled disclosure. This, however, does not answer the question of whether the protection awarded by Article 8 of the ECHR embraces information that the patient has confided in the physician or

---

[1] Application No. 6825/74, Decision of 18 May 1974.
[2] *M.S. v Sweden,* Judgment of 27 August 1997, (1997) 3 BHRC 248, at para.26; *Z v Finland,* Judgment of 25 February 1997, (1998) 25 E.H.R.R. 371, at para.95.
[3] Case C-62/90 *Commission v Germany* [1992] ECR I-2575, at para.23; Case C-404/92P *X v Commission* [1994] ECR I-4737, at para.17.

which the physician observed in the course of his/her profession, as in such a case, the patient voluntarily releases private medical information from his/her personal sphere by disclosing it to a third party. In *Niemitz v Germany*,[4] the European Court of Human Rights stated to that effect that:

> The Court does not consider it possible or necessary to attempt an exhaustive definition of the notion of 'private life'. However, it would be too restrictive to limit the notion to an 'inner circle' in which the individual may live his own personal life as he chooses and to exclude therefrom entirely the outside world not encompassed within that circle. Respect for private life must also comprise to a certain degree the right to establish and develop relationships with other human beings.[5]

In that case, the Court had to decide whether the search of a law firm violated the lawyer's right to private life under Article 8(1) of the ECHR and came to the conclusion that it did. Thus, the mere fact that someone has communicated information to a third party does not exclude this information from the protection of 'private life' and the lawyer's interest in the confidentiality of his/her files is now protected by Article 8(1) of the ECHR. But does this mean that the physician-patient relationship is equally protected by Article 8 of the ECHR? This question was, for example, at issue in *M.S. v Sweden*.[6] In that case, the Court had to decide whether a patient's medical records were protected from disclosure to the Social Insurance Office. The European Court of Human Rights emphasised that the medical records in question contained highly sensitive and personal information about the applicant, including information about an abortion, and that these records were protected under Article 8 of the ECHR.[7] This case thus seems to suggest that the protection of medical records is warranted if the information concerned has a particularly sensitive and personal character. In such a case, even the disclosure of medical confidences to other public authorities that are equally under an obligation of confidentiality amounts to a violation of the right to private life.[8]

A broader discussion of the protection of confidential medical information took place in *Z v Finland*.[9] In that case, the Court was concerned with the compatibility of court orders with Article 8 of the ECHR. The court orders at issue forced the physicians of the applicant to give evidence in court regarding the applicant's medical condition, *inter alia* relating to her HIV infection, and ordered the seizure of the applicant's medical records. The Court held that:

> The protection of personal data, not least medical data, is of fundamental importance to a person's enjoyment of his or her right to respect for private and family life as guaranteed by Article 8 of the Convention. Respecting the confidentiality of health data is a vital principle in the legal systems of all the Contracting Parties to the Convention. It is crucial

---

[4] Judgment of 16 December 1992, Series A, No.251-B.
[5] Ibid., at para. 29.
[6] Judgment of 27 August 1997, (1997) 3 BHRC 248.
[7] Ibid., at para.26.
[8] Ibid., at para.35.
[9] Judgment of 25 February 1997, (1998) 25 E.H.R.R. 371.

not only to respect the sense of privacy of a patient but also to preserve his or her confidence in the medical profession and in the health services in general. Without such protection, those in need of medical assistance may be deterred from revealing such information of a personal and intimate nature as may be necessary in order to receive appropriate treatment and, even, from seeking such assistance, thereby endangering their own health and, in the case of transmissible diseases, that of the community. The domestic law must therefore afford appropriate safeguards to prevent such communication of disclosure of personal health data as may be inconsistent with the guarantees in Article 8 of the Convention.[10]

The Court went on to stress the particular sensitivity of information relating to a person's HIV status and concluded that interferences with the protection of the confidentiality of such information can only be compatible with Article 8 of the ECHR if justified by an overriding requirement in the public interest.[11] This decision thus confirms the view that the extent of protection awarded to personal medical data depends on the sensitivity of the information in question. The particular significance of the decision, however, lies in the fact that it discusses the reasons behind the protection of medical data by Article 8 of the ECHR. According to the Court, the protection is based on the patients' interest in keeping their health information secret. Article 8 thus aims at the protection of the individual's interest in the confidentiality of sensitive personal data. In addition, the patient's confidence in the members of the medical profession is guaranteed. This demonstrates that the protection goes beyond the patient's interest in secrecy, as this interest could be achieved simply by not forcing the patient to reveal his/her medical secrets to a physician. Given that the right to private life guarantees the development of relationships with others, the relationship between physician and patient itself receives protection, and it is recognised that this relationship may be adversely affected if the physician is forced to disclose confidential patient information to the state. The Court goes even further in acknowledging that the protection of medical data is also based on the patients' health interest, as patients, without a guarantee of confidentiality, may be deterred from seeking medical advice and treatment. The reasons thus far summarised demonstrate that the protection of medical confidentiality is based on deontological considerations that the patient's informational and decisional privacy deserve respect. However, the Court also stresses that community interests are at stake, as public health may be adversely affected if patients with transmissible diseases do not seek medical advice or treatment. This demonstrates that the protection is also based on utilitarian concerns.

In *Z v Finland* the Court went beyond an interpretation of Article 8(1) of the ECHR as protecting the individual from state interference, as the state is not merely prevented from forcing the individual to disclose medical information. The Court rather in addition stated that Article 8 of the ECHR imposes an obligation on the state appropriately to protect medical information the patient confided in the

---

[10] Ibid., at para.95.
[11] Ibid., at para.96.

physician.[12] However, given the limited amount of European case-law on questions of medical confidentiality, it is not at all clear to what extent confidential medical information is protected by Article 8 of the ECHR and how far the Court will be prepared to go in imposing a positive obligation on the States to protect a patient's confidences.[13]

Article 8 is also applicable to the storage of personal, for example confidential medical, data, without the individual's consent.[14]

2 European Convention on Human Rights and Biomedicine

It should be noted that medical confidentiality is now also protected under Article 10(1) of the European Convention on Human Rights and Biomedicine, stating that:

> Everyone has the right to respect for private life in relation to information about his or her health.

It thus expressly guarantees the right to respect for medical confidentiality. However, the European Convention on Human Rights and Biomedicine has not yet been ratified by France, Germany and the UK and it therefore currently only enjoys persuasive rather than legal authority.

3 Data Protection Directive 95/46/EC

In 1995, the European Parliament and the Council of the European Union issued the Data Protection Directive the twofold aims of which are identified in its Article 1 as the protection of fundamental individual rights and freedoms, particularly the right to privacy with regard to the processing of personal data, on the one hand, and the prevention of barriers to the free flow of personal data between Member States, on the other. The provisions of the Directive apply to the processing of personal data by automatic means, and to non-automatic processing of data that form part, or are intended to form part, of a filing system (Article 3). This means that medical records are protected under the Directive, as long as they are computerised or part of a manual filing system that meets the definition of Article 1(c). Medical data receive special protection under Article 8 which applies to data concerning the health of the individual. It has been suggested that the Data Protection Directive will have the effect that the processing of medical data, given

---

[12] This view has recently been confirmed in *Botta v Italy*, 24 February 1998, (1998) 26 E.H.R.R. 241, at para.34.

[13] For a discussion of the impact of Article 8 of the ECHR on the physician-patient relationship, see Hondius, (1997) 4 EJHL 361-388.

[14] See, for example, *Leander v Sweden*, Judgement of 26 March 1987, Series A, No 116, at para.48; *Amann v Switzerland*, Application No. 27798/95, Judgment of 16 February 2000, at para.48.

their highly sensitive nature, is likely to be subject to particularly careful monitoring by the supervisory authorities.[15]

4 European Charter of Fundamental Rights

At the Nice summit in December 2000, the European Council proclaimed the European Charter of Fundamental Rights. The Charter has not come into force and is therefore only of authoritative value without binding the Member States. According to Article 52(3) of the Charter, insofar as the Charter contains rights which correspond to rights guaranteed by the ECHR, the meaning and scope of those rights shall be the same as that of the Convention rights. This means that case law of the European Court of Human Rights interpreting the provisions of the ECHR will be highly relevant for the interpretation of the corresponding Charter provisions.

The right to respect for private and family life in Article 7 is based on Article 8 of the ECHR and should therefore, according to the Explanatory Notes to the Charter,[16] be given the same scope and interpretation. However, the Charter in Article 8(1) expressly protects personal data, by stating that 'everyone has the right to the protection of personal data concerning him or her'; and that 'such data must be processed fairly for specified purposes and on the basis of the consent of the person concerned or some other legitimate basis laid down by law' (Article 8 (2)). It is based both on Article 8 of the ECHR and on the Data Protection Directive. Article 8 of the Charter goes beyond Article 8 of the ECHR in that it expressly protects personal information of the individual. However, given that case law of the European Court of Human Rights includes confidential patient information and medical records in the protection of Article 8(1) of the ECHR, it is not to be expected that the Charter will add to the protection already existing under the ECHR and the Data Protection Directive.

PART 2 – DISCLOSURE IN THE CONTEXT OF CRIME PREVENTION AND CRIMINAL PROSECUTION

It now needs to be examined whether the different provisions guaranteeing medical confidentiality at the European level, that is Article 8 of the ECHR, Article 10 of the European Convention on Human Rights and Biomedicine, Articles 7 and 8 of the European Charter and the provisions of the Data Protection Directive, allow for, require or stand in the way of a recognition of medical privilege.

---

[15] Bainbridge, at 172.
[16] CHARTE 4471/00 CONVENT 48 of September 20, 2000.

1 Criminal prosecution

None of the above mentioned provisions guarantee medical confidentiality in an unlimited way. The Data Protection Directive provides in Article 13 that the Member States may adopt exceptions to the obligations and rights created by the Directive for the purpose of the detection and prosecution of criminal offences. This implies that medical privilege need not be guaranteed in order to comply with the provisions of the Directive. As far as possible limitations to the right to private life under Article 8(1) of the ECHR are concerned, Article 8(2) determines that:

> There shall be no interference by a public authority with the exercise of this right except such as is in accordance with the law and is necessary in a democratic society in the interests of national security, public safety or the economic well-being of the country, for the prevention of disorder or crime, for the protection of health or morals, or for the protection of the rights and freedoms of others.

Article 8(2) of the ECHR does not expressly state that the right to private life can be restricted for the purpose of criminal prosecution. However, case law of the European Court of Human Rights has clarified that Article 8(2) of the ECHR is to be interpreted so as to allow for exceptions to the right to private life in order to guarantee effective criminal proceedings. In *Z v Finland*,[17] a case in which the Court had to assess the compatibility with Article 8 of the ECHR of court orders forcing the applicant's physicians to give evidence in court regarding the applicant's medical condition, including her HIV infection, the Court held that:

> Such interference cannot be compatible with Article 8 of the Convention unless it is justified by an overriding requirement in the public interest. ... At the same time, the Court accepts that the interests of a patient and the community as a whole in protecting the confidentiality of medical data may be outweighed by the interest in investigation and prosecution of crime and in the publicity of court proceedings.[18]

The Court's holding in *Z v Finland* thus determines that the interest in criminal prosecution forms part of the interests listed in Article 8(2) of the ECHR. States will therefore not violate Article 8 of the ECHR when giving the interest in the investigation and prosecution of criminal offences precedence over the interests in medical confidentiality, even though the interest in criminal prosecution is not explicitly mentioned in Article 8(2) of the ECHR. However, the interest in criminal prosecution can only trump the right to medical confidentiality if this is necessary, that is proportionate. With regard to the proportionality analysis, the decision in *Z v Finland* adopted a broad approach, thereby allowing for far-reaching restrictions to the right to medical confidentiality. In that case, the physician's evidence served the purpose of establishing at what time X, who had been accused of a number of sexual offences and who was found to be HIV positive, had known of his infection, as this knowledge was essential for a conviction for attempted manslaughter in

---

[17] (1998) 25 E.H.R.R. 371.
[18] Ibid., paras 96-97.

addition to a conviction for rape. Given that the applicant, X's wife, was also an HIV carrier, it was important to find out at what time she had known of her infection, as this could give some indication as to when the accused must have become aware of the risk of his own infection. With regard to the significance of the physician's evidence, the Court argued:

> Their evidence had the possibility of being at the material time decisive for the question whether X was guilty of sexual offences only or in addition of the more serious offence of attempted manslaughter in relation to two offences ... . There can be no doubt that the competent national authorities were entitled to think that very weighty public interests militated in favour of the investigation and prosecution of X for attempted manslaughter in respect of all of the five offences concerned and not just three of them.[19]

Thus, even in cases in which the physician's testimony in criminal court was not necessary for the prosecution of an offender as such, but rather only served the purpose of facilitating the prosecution for more serious offences, this interest can still outweigh medical confidentiality. The Court then emphasised the exceptional circumstances under which Finnish law allows for ordering the physician to give evidence (only in connection with serious criminal offences for which at least 6 years of imprisonment was prescribed) and that the questioning took place *in camera*, that all relevant files were ordered to be kept confidential, and that all those involved in the proceedings were under a duty to treat the information as confidential. This led the Court to conclude that:

> The various orders requiring the applicant's medical advisers to give evidence were supported by relevant and sufficient reasons which corresponded to an overriding requirement in the interests of the legitimate aims pursued. [The Court] is also satisfied that there was a reasonable relationship of proportionality between those measures and aims.[20]

It is difficult to predict whether the non-existence of medical privilege would be tolerated in the absence of specific procedural safeguards that allow for some protection of confidential medical information in the context of criminal proceedings. It is interesting to note that the Court saw no reason to question the extent to which the applicant's physicians were ordered to give evidence, as this was a matter to be primarily decided by the national authorities. The Commission had taken a different stance and questioned the proportionality of the measures, arguing that even if the violation of the privacy right was, in principle, justified, the measures were not proportionate, as no attempt had been made to limit the disclosure of confidential information to what was strictly necessary for the purpose of the criminal investigation and proceedings. It seems as if the Court gives a lot of leeway to the national authorities when determining whether or not disclosure of confidential information was necessary and therefore proportionate.

---

[19] Ibid., para.102.
[20] Ibid., para.105.

A recognition of medical privilege is thus not required by Article 8 of the ECHR. In that respect, Article 10(1) of the European Convention on Human Rights and Biomedicine does not add any protection, as according to Art 26(1) of that Convention:

> No restrictions shall be placed on the exercise of the rights and protective provisions contained in this Convention other than such as are prescribed by law and are necessary in a democratic society in the interest of public safety, for the prevention of crime, for the protection of public health or for the protection of the rights and freedoms of others.

Article 10(1) of the European Convention on Human Rights and Biomedicine can thus be restricted under the same circumstances as Article 8(1) of the ECHR. The Explanatory Report points out with regard to Article 10(1) that a breach of medical confidentiality would, for example, be justified in order to identify the author of a crime. This result was reached with reference to the exception relating to the prevention of crime. While it is submitted that the identification of the author of a crime relates to the investigation and prosecution of an offence already committed, and not to the prevention of a future crime, a distinction between the two situations was clearly not envisaged by the drafters of the Convention.

It can thus be seen that all of the provisions guaranteeing medical confidentiality at the European level either expressly qualify that right for the purpose of criminal prosecution, or have been interpreted so as to allow for such a qualification. Consequently, medical privilege does not need to be recognised based on any of these provisions. This leaves the question of whether any of the European provisions prohibit medical privilege in the course of criminal investigations and proceedings. It could be argued that medical privilege stands in the way of the effective investigation and prosecution of crime. The European Court of Human Rights has consistently held that at least where a crime led to a person's death:

> the obligation to protect the right to life under Article 2 of the Convention, read in conjunction with the State's general duty under Article 1 of the Convention to 'secure to everyone within [its] jurisdiction the rights and freedoms defined in [the] Convention', also requires by implication that there should be some form of effective official investigation when individuals have been killed as a result of the use of force.[21]

While the form of the investigation can vary according to the circumstances, 'it must be effective in the sense that it is capable of leading ... to the identification and punishment of those responsible'.[22] However, the authorities must do no more than take 'reasonable steps'. There have been no cases discussing whether the recognition of medical privilege could be regarded as a violation of the

---

[21] *Avsar v Turkey*, Application No. 25657/94, Judgment of 10 July 2001, at para.393. See also *Akkoc v Turkey*, Application No. 22948/93, Judgment of 10 October 2002, at para.97; *McKerr v UK*, Application No.28883/95, Judgment of 4 May 2001, at para.111; *Kelly v UK*, Application No. 30054/96, Judgment of 4 May 2001, at para.94.

[22] *Avsar v Turkey*, Application No. 25657/94, Judgment of 10 July 2001, at para.394; *Kelly v UK*, Application No. 30054/96, Judgment of 4 May 2001at para.96.

requirement of an effective investigation. It is submitted, however, that a violation of Article 2 of the ECHR was only found in cases of a total failure by the relevant State to pursue effective investigations. This case law can therefore not be interpreted to require the investigation of a crime by all possible means, and to go as far as prohibiting certain procedural rules which give effect to the protection of the right to private life under Article 8(1) of the ECHR in the course of criminal investigations.

2 Conflicting defence rights

If a State decides to recognise medical privilege, a conflict between medical confidentiality, on the one hand, and defence rights of an accused person, on the other, may arise. Article 6 of the ECHR guarantees the right to fair trial and, as part of that right, Article 6(3)(d) specifies that a person charged with a criminal offence has the right:

> To examine or have examined witnesses against him and to obtain the attendance and examination of witnesses on his behalf under the same conditions as witnesses against him.

It can be inferred from existing case law that Article 6 of the ECHR does not award the right to examine witnesses regardless of existing privilege provisions. While no decisions of the European Court of Human Rights directly address the issue of medical privilege, the Court has had to discuss the privilege granted to close relatives under Austrian law. In *Unterpertinger v Austria*,[23] the European Court of Human Rights held that while the relevant provision of the Austrian Code of Criminal Procedure prevented the trial judge from hearing and the defence and the prosecution from examining the defendant's wife and daughter as witnesses:

> As such, the provision is not incompatible with Article 6(1) and (3)(d) of the Convention: it makes allowances for the special problems that may be entailed by a confrontation between someone 'charged with a criminal offence' and a witness from his own family and is calculated to protect such a witness by avoiding his being put in a moral dilemma; furthermore, there are comparable provisions in the domestic law of several member States of the Council of Europe.[24]

Thus, defence rights are not absolute and when conflicting with other interests, a balancing exercise must take place. In *Unterpertinger*, both the prosecution and the defence were barred from access to certain information or the examination of certain witnesses, so that the principle of equality of arms, which is protected by Article 6 of the ECHR and means that 'each party must be afforded a reasonable

---

[23] (1986) 13 E.H.R.R. 434.
[24] Ibid., at para.30.

opportunity to present his/her case in conditions that do not place him at a disadvantage vis-a-vis his opponent',[25] will not be affected.

A slightly different situation arises if a witness was examined by the prosecution or a judge prior to the trial stage but refuses to give testimony in court based on a privilege. In that situation, the European Court of Human Rights has consistently held that if statements made by witnesses during the investigatory stage of the proceedings were treated as proof in a criminal trial without the defendant being given the opportunity to question the witnesses at any stage of the proceedings, defence rights would be violated.[26] Similarly, if the prosecution refuses to disclose documents to the defence which are important for the case, for example information that could possibly shed doubt on the credibility of a prosecution witness, this might result in a violation of the defence rights guaranteed under Article 6(1) and Article 6(3) of the ECHR, particularly where the decision not to disclose the information was not brought to the attention of the trial judge, so that there is no judicial control of the impact of the non-disclosure on the rights of the accused.[27]

None of these cases concerned the situation that the prosecution had access to and withheld from the defence information on the grounds that otherwise an individual's interest in medical confidentiality might be adversely affected. However, given the importance of the right to private life under Article 8(1) of the ECHR, similar considerations to those that made the privilege in *Unterpertinger*[28] acceptable, would apply to medical privilege which is recognised in several Member States of the Council of Europe. In *Doorson v Netherlands*,[29] the European Court of Human Rights has made it clear that where interests of the witness, for example those coming within the ambit of Article 8 of the ECHR, are at stake, the Contracting States need to organise their criminal proceedings in such a way that those interests are not unjustifiably imperilled. Accordingly, 'interests of fair trial also require that in appropriate cases the interests of the defence are balanced against those of witnesses or victims called upon to testify'.[30] However, this only applies if the conviction is not solely or to a decisive extent based on privileged information.[31] Defence rights therefore do not exclude the recognition of medical privilege. They are equally not violated if in a State in which such a privilege exists a conviction is based on inadmissible privileged evidence, as long as this evidence is not the sole basis of the conviction. This follows from decisions

---

[25] *Foucher v France*, Judgment of 18 March 1997, (1998) 25 E.H.R.R. 234, at para.34.

[26] See, for example, *Lüdi v Switzerland*, Judgment of 15 June 1992, Series A, No.238, at paras 49-50; *Luca v Italy*, Application No. 33354/96, Judgment of 27 February 2001, at para.40; *P.S. v Germany*, Application No. 33900/96, Judgment of 20 December 2001, at paras 28 and 309.

[27] *Rowe and Davis v UK*, Application No. 28901/95, Judgment of 16 February 2000, at para.66; see also *P.G. and J.H. v UK*, Application No. 44787/98, Judgment of 25 September 2001, at para.71.

[28] *Unterpertinger v Austria*, Judgment of 24 November 1986, (1986) 13 E.H.R.R. 434.

[29] Application No 20524/92, 26 March 1996.

[30] Ibid., at para.70.

[31] Ibid., at para.76.

such as *P.G. and J.H. v UK*[32] and *Khan v UK*[33] in which the European Court of Human Rights has held that the Court is not concerned with specific questions such as the use of inadmissible evidence, but is rather only concerned with the fairness of the proceedings as a whole.

As Article 6(1) of the ECHR inter alia guarantees the right to a public trial, another question that might be of relevance is that of the compatibility with Article 6 of *in camera* proceedings where these are resorted to in order to examine sensitive evidence, for example medical information of an individual. The relevant part of Article 6(1) states that:

> the ... public may be excluded from all or part of the trial in the interest of morals, public order or national security in a democratic society, where the interests of juveniles or the protection of the private life of the parties so require ...

Thus, Article 6(1) of the ECHR provides for an exception to the principle of a public trial based on privacy considerations, and *in camera* proceedings aiming to protect the medical confidences of an individual would therefore, in principle, be acceptable. This view finds support in *Z v Finland*, where *in camera* proceedings were regarded not only as acceptable, but also as a good compromise between the interests of justice and the privacy interests of the witness.[34] However, the Court has held in *Diennet v France*,[35] in the context of disciplinary proceedings against a medical practitioner, that 'while the need to protect professional confidentiality and the private lives of patients may justify holding proceedings *in camera*, such an occurrence must be strictly required by the circumstances'.[36] In that case, a violation of the right to a public trial was confirmed. As the trial was concerned with the methods of practice employed by a medical practitioner, there was only a very slight likelihood that confidential patient information would be introduced during the trial. The decision to conduct the hearing *in camera* was therefore disproportionate, as it would have been sufficient to resume the trial *in camera* when and if confidential patient information was referred to.

3 Crime prevention

Art.8(2) of the ECHR, Article 26 of the European Convention on Human Rights and Biomedicine and Article 13 of the Data Protection Directive allow for exceptions to the protection of medical confidentiality for the purpose of crime prevention. However, no clear guidelines exist concerning the possible extent and application of these exceptions. The principle of proportionality needs to be taken

---

[32] Application No 44787/98, Judgment of 25 September 2001, at para.76.

[33] Application No.35394/97, Judgment of 12 May 2000, at para.38.

[34] Judgment of 25 February 1997, (1998) 25 E.H.R.R. 371, at para.105.

[35] Judgment of 26 September 1995, (1996) 21 E.H.R.R. 554.

[36] Ibid., at para.34.

into account, so that the disclosure of confidential information will only be justified as long as it was necessary for the protection of the rights of others and no less intrusive means were available to achieve that purpose. This means that a careful balancing of the conflicting interests needs to be performed in each case to determine whether or not a violation of medical confidentiality would be proportionate.

While these exceptions are concerned with the question of possible justifications, that is with the permissibility of violations of the right to medical confidentiality for the purpose of crime prevention, another problem is whether there can be an obligation to reveal confidential medical information if such a disclosure could protect the rights of an individual. Such an obligation could follow from Article 2 of the ECHR, the right to life, as the European Court of Human Rights has frequently held that Article 2 imposes on the state the obligation to protect the citizens' right to life by having in place an effective law-enforcement machinery for the prevention of offences that put the individual's life at risk, and to take preventive measures to protect an individual whose life is at risk from the criminal acts of other individuals.[37] However, the Court has qualified this obligation by stating that it does not impose an impossible or disproportionate burden on the state. Rather:

> For a positive obligation to arise, it must be established that the authorities knew or ought to have known at the time of the existence of a real and immediate risk to the life of an identified individual or individuals from the criminal acts of a third party and that they failed to take measures within the scope of their powers which, judged reasonably, might have been expected to avoid that risk.[38]

It is difficult to predict how these principles would be applied to situations concerning medical confidentiality. If, for example, a public authority was in possession of confidential medical information regarding the commission of a homicide offence, it could be argued that it is under an obligation to disclose this information. However, even though in rare cases such as that of a psychiatric patient professing to kill a specific individual, there might be an immediate danger to an identified victim, an obligation to warn does not necessarily follow. In *Osman*, the Court has held that:

> Another relevant consideration is the need to ensure that the police exercise their powers to control and prevent crime in a manner which fully respects the due process and other guarantees which legitimately place restraints on the scope of their action to investigate crime ... including the guarantees contained in Articles 5 and 8 of the Convention.[39]

---

[37] See, for example, *Mahmut Kaya v Turkey*, Application No.22535/93, Judgment of 28 March 2000, at para.85.

[38] Ibid., at para.86; see also *Osman v UK*, Judgment of 28 October 1998, (2000) 29 E.H.R.R. 245, at para.116.

[39] *Osman v UK*, Judgment of 28 October 1998, (2000) 29 E.H.R.R. 245, at para.116.

This could be interpreted to mean that a State's positive obligation under Article 2 of the ECHR is qualified by other Convention rights, and that the State cannot be reasonably expected to prevent crime by the means of a breach of the right to private life under Article 8(1) of the ECHR. On the other hand, it could be argued that at least in cases in which the life of an individual can clearly be saved by disclosure of confidential information, a duty to disclose might exist, as the right to life is of higher rank than the right to private life.

4 Summary

It can be seen that the recognition of medical privilege is not mandated by the provisions of the ECHR, the European Convention on Human Rights and Biomedicine, the European Charter and the Data Protection Directive, as all of these documents provide for exceptions to the protection of privacy and medical confidentiality for the purposes of criminal prosecution and crime prevention. In principle, defence rights do not stand in the way of medical privilege. Some problems such as that of a possible obligation of disclose confidential medical information in order to save the life of a person have not yet been resolved.

Chapter 4

French Law

This chapter will in a first part examine how French law protects medical confidentiality by the means of constitutional, private and criminal law. In the second part it will be demonstrated how the provisions of the Criminal Code and of the Code of Criminal Procedure deal with the various conflicts between medical confidentiality and the interests in crime prevention and criminal prosecution.

PART 1 – PROTECTION OF MEDICAL CONFIDENTIALITY

1 Medical confidentiality as a fundamental right

Two possible sources for awarding medical confidentiality the status of a fundamental right must be examined: the French Constitution, and the European Convention on Human Rights.

1.1 Constitutional right

The French Constitution does not expressly protect the right to privacy. In 1992, the Advisory Committee on the Revision of the Constitution suggested that a new paragraph to art.66 of the Constitution be added, stating that: 'Everybody has the right to respect for his/her private life and dignity'.[1] This suggestion has not been acted upon. The French Constitutional Court (Conseil Constitutionnel), however, has stressed in various decisions that the Preamble to the 1958 Constitution, together with the Declaration of 1789 and the Preamble to the 1946 Constitution, guarantees individual freedom. In a decision concerning the constitutionality of a statute giving the police broad rights to search vehicles, the Constitutional Court held for example:

> Considering that individual freedom constitutes one of the fundamental principles guaranteed by the laws of the Republic, and proclaimed in the Preamble to the Constitution of 1946, and confirmed by the Preamble to the Constitution of 1958;

---

[1] See Favoreu, Philip, at 891.

Considering that art. 66 of the Constitution,[2] in reaffirming that principle, entrusts its safeguard in the judicial authorities.[3]

The reference to art.66 could at first sight be taken to mean that the constitutional protection of individual liberties is limited to the specific situation of detention and does not include the guarantee of a general right to privacy. According to a commentary to this decision,[4] however, the Constitutional Court adopts a broad interpretation of the concept of individual liberty which includes the protection of private life. This view is supported by a decision[5] of the Constitutional Court concerning the constitutionality of a statutory provision giving fiscal agents, assisted by police officers, rights of search and seizure in the course of the investigation of tax offences. In that case, the Constitutional Court stated:

Considering that ... such investigations can only be carried out in accordance with art.66 of the Constitution which entrusts all aspects of the safeguard of individual liberty and, in particular, those concerning the inviolability of the home, in the judiciary.

The constitutional protection of individual freedom goes thus beyond safeguards in the case of detention, and embraces the protection of individual liberty as such. In 1995, the Constitutional Court has confirmed that privacy is a constitutional principle.[6] And in a recent case dealing with the constitutionality of a system of health insurance and the introduction of electronic cards containing patient information, the Constitutional Court interpreted art.2 of the Declaration of 1789 which states that:

The aim of all political association is the preservation of the natural and imprescriptible rights of man. These rights are liberty, property, security, and resistance to oppression;[7]

to mean that the freedom protected under that article includes respect for private life.[8] Even though the Constitution does not explicitly mention the right to privacy, it is now nevertheless regarded as having constitutional rank.[9] This coincides with a change in the French constitutional debate which has only recently recognised the

---

[2] Art.66 of the Constitution of 1958: No person may be detained arbitrarily. The judiciary, the guardian of individual liberty, ensures respect for this principle in circumstances provided for by law.

[3] Conseil Constitutionnel 12 January 1977, AJDA 1978, 215; see also the decision of 16 July 1971, Rec. 29.

[4] Favoreu, Philip, at 341-52.

[5] 29 December 1983, Rec. 67.

[6] Decision of 18 January 1995, Rec. 170.

[7] Le but de toute association politique est la conservation des droits naturels et imprescriptibles de l'Homme. Ces droits sont la liberté, la propriété, la sûreté, et la résistance à l'oppression.

[8] Decision 99-416 DC of 23 July 1999.

[9] Picard, at 75-6.

notion of fundamental rights.[10] These new developments seem to put an end to the controversy on whether or not privacy is constitutionally protected.[11] It is, however, not clear whether medical confidentiality is included in the protection of privacy as a fundamental right. Given the rather narrow scope of constitutional review in France, even if medical confidentiality were protected as a constitutional principle the main effect of that protection would be that new parliamentary legislation would have to accord with that guarantee, and that French courts could control the compatibility of executive acts with this constitutional principle.

1.2 European Convention on Human Rights

The European Convention on Human Rights was ratified according to Act 73-1227 of 31 December 1973 and published by decree of 3 May 1974. Once an international treaty is ratified and published, it is incorporated into domestic law. In 1981 France accepted the individual right of petition to the Commission. Art.55 of the Constitution of 4 October 1958 states that international conventions are of higher rank than ordinary statutes.[12] According to the *Nicolo* decision of the Conseil d'Etat,[13] the highest French Court dealing with administrative matters, international conventions are not only of higher rank than domestic law enacted prior to their ratification, but they are also superior to subsequent national legislation. In its *Confédération nationale des associations familiales catholiques* decision,[14] the Conseil d'Etat applied this principle to the European Convention on Human Rights, stating that all legislation, whether enacted prior or subsequent to the ratification of the ECHR, must be in accordance with the Convention. Even though superior to ordinary statutes, international treaties nevertheless do not have constitutional status, and judicial review examining the compatibility of the challenged statute with an international treaty will be exercised by ordinary courts, not by the Conseil Constitutionnel.[15] This means that French judges who cannot review the constitutionality of legislation, can control the compatibility of a parliamentary statute with the ECHR.[16] In France, therefore, the protection of medical confidentiality under the ECHR to some extent compensates for the rather weak protection awarded by the French Constitution.

---

[10] See various articles in AJDA 1998, numéro spécial – les droits fondamentaux.

[11] See for example Rivero, Tome 1, at 153; and Steiner, at 281.

[12] Art.55: Traités et accords internationaux, régulièrement ratifiés ou approuvés, ont, dès leur publication, une autorité supérieure a celle des lois, sous réserve, pour chaque accord ou traité, de son application par l'autre partie.

[13] 20 October 1989, R.190.

[14] Conseil d'Etat 21 December 1990, R.369.

[15] Rivero, Tome 1, at 150; Turpin, at 109.

[16] Steiner, at 281.

2 Protection under criminal law

In France, the discussion of the duty of medical confidentiality mainly focuses on the relevant provisions of the Criminal Code (code pénal), as in French law, a breach of the duty of medical confidentiality is a criminal offence (art.226-13 of the Criminal Code). This criminal offence was first laid down in art.378 of the Criminal Code of 1810. Art.378 of the old Criminal Code stated that:

> Physicians, surgeons and other health officers as well as pharmacists, midwives and all other persons being by their status or their profession or by their temporary or permanent position depositories of secrets confided in them, when revealing these secrets outside those cases in which the law obliges or authorises such a denunciation, will be punished with imprisonment of one month to six months and a fine of 500 F to 15,000 F.[17]

Most members of the medical profession were thus expressly mentioned in art.378 as being under a duty, sanctioned by criminal law, to maintain medical confidentiality. Art.378 of the old Criminal Code was replaced by art.226-13 when the new Criminal Code came into force in 1994. In the new Criminal Code, the provision was formulated differently. Art.226-13 of the new Criminal Code states that:

> The disclosure of any secret information confided in a person in connection with his/her social position or profession or on the grounds of a temporary office or mission, will be punished with imprisonment of one year and a fine of 15,000 Euros.[18]

The new provision no longer expressly states that it applies to the members of the medical profession. However, it is uncontroversial that art.226-13 applies to those professionals who had been listed in art.378 of the old Criminal Code, including medical professionals.[19]

For art.226-13 of the Criminal Code to apply, different requirements have to be fulfilled. First, the disclosure must refer to 'information confided in a person in connection with his/her social position or profession or on the grounds of a temporary office or mission' (art.226-13 of the Criminal Code). In this respect, art.226-13 of the Criminal Code and art.378 of the old Criminal Code adopted a similar approach, so that case-law developed under the old Criminal Code,

---

[17] Art.378 of the old Criminal Code:
Les médecins, chirurgiens et autres officiers de santé, ainsi que les pharmaciens, les sages-femmes et toutes autres personnes dépositaires, par état ou profession ou par fonctions temporaires ou permanentes, des secrets qu'on leur confie, qui, hors le cas où la loi les oblige ou les autorise à se porter dénonciateurs, auront révélé ces secrets, seront punis d'un emprisonnement d'un mois à six mois et d'une amende de 500 à 15 000 F.
[18] Art.226-13:
La révélation d'une information à caractère secret par une personne qui en est dépositaire soit par état ou par profession, soit en raison d'une fonction ou d'une mission temporaire, est punie d'un an d'emprisonnement et de 15 000 Euros d'amende.
[19] Chomienne, Guéry, ALD.1995.comm.85.

establishing that the obligation to medical confidentiality was not limited to what the patient had confided in the physician, but included everything the physician heard, saw or observed in the course of the exercise of his/her profession[20] is still valid. This clarification of the extent of the protection of medical confidentiality is based on the view that it seems appropriate to protect confidential patient information in cases in which the patient has not expressly shared his/her secret with the physician, but in which the physician nevertheless, in the course of the exercise of his/her profession, gained knowledge of confidential information concerning his/her patient. The Cour de Cassation, the highest French court in civil and criminal matters, for example, had to decide a case in which a physician, acting in his capacity as adviser of an insurance company, had obtained access to the hospital records of a road accident victim and later revealed the content of those records to his employer. The Court held that the physician's disclosure of the victim's confidential medical information to the insurance company violated medical confidentiality. Even though the victim had not confided any medical information in the physician, the physician had obtained access to the medical records by presenting himself as a member of the medical profession. The Court argued that the patient's medical confidences had therefore come to the physician's knowledge in the course of exercising his profession and concluded that he was thus under an obligation not to reveal what he heard, saw or inferred, even in the absence of confidences made by the patient.[21] Another example is a case in which a physician who happened to be at the site of a road accident applied first aid to an accident victim and later submitted the medical certificate regarding the victim's injuries to the police. According to the court, in doing so, the physician violated his duty of confidentiality.[22] Even though the patient had not confided any medical information in the physician, the physician, in his capacity as a medical practitioner, obtained some knowledge about the patient's health condition, and thus the patient's intimate sphere. This expansion of the scope of medical confidentiality has been welcomed by legal scholars[23] and seems uncontroversial. Some explain this approach by arguing that if the patient's trust in the physician is protected where the patient expressly confides in the physician, the same principle should be applied to the situation that he/she allows the physician to obtain information and to draw certain conclusions by examining the patient.[24] However, this view rests on the assumption that medical confidentiality depends on the patient's express wishes and comes into existence only by virtue of a patient's consent to a medical examination. This cannot explain the example of the accident victim, as unconscious and incompetent persons who are not in a position to give their consent to a necessary medical examination would then remain unprotected. The approach adopted by the French courts rather seems to be based on the

---

[20] See, for example, 17 May 1973, Ch. crim., D.1973.583; 23 January 1996, Ch. crim., Bull. n°37.

[21] 17 May 1973, Ch. crim., D.1973.583.

[22] 14 February 1952, JCP.1952.II.7030.

[23] See for example Légal, JCP.1948.II.4141; Véron, at 153.

[24] Rassat, D.1989.chron.107.

consideration that a patient's confidences should be protected regardless of how the physician has come to know them, as long as this knowledge was gained in a professional capacity. In this context, the patient's consent to the examination is irrelevant.

The information must have come to the knowledge of the person who is bound by the professional secret in the exercise of his/her profession. This raises the question of whether a distinction must be made between confidential information gained directly during the exercise of the medical profession, and confidential information otherwise obtained. With regard to the comparable situation of a priest, it has been argued, for example, that information confided in a priest was only acquired in the course of the exercise of his/her profession and protected by his/her obligation to confidentiality if it was confided in him/her in his/her role as a priest, but not, for example, if it was confided in him/her by a friend at a social gathering.[25] Others reject this distinction as unworkable, as in the example of the priest, it seems impossible to establish whether or not the secret was shared with this friend on the grounds of his/her role as a friend, and/or that of a priest. For the physician, this means that it is controversial whether or not medical information confided in a physician outside the formal framework of his/her professional activity is protected by the obligation to maintain medical confidentiality.

In addition, the fact revealed by the physician must have been a secret. An interpretation of the notion of a 'secret' encounters two different problems: (1) does all information gathered by the physician in the course of his/her profession necessarily qualify as a secret, or does the information have to be of particular sensitivity to deserve secrecy? And (2) does information merely qualify as secret as long as only the physician knows about it, or is it still a secret even though it might have become known, partly or even in its entirety, to third parties outside the physician-patient relationship? With regard to the first aspect of the question of secrecy, different approaches have been suggested. Some have argued that the information must have a certain quality to it to be considered confidential. Savatier, for example, voiced the opinion that the admission of a patient to a hospital has nothing secret about it and is therefore not protected by the obligation to medical confidentiality.[26] But others, to the contrary, argue that the very fact that the patient has consulted a physician must be covered by medical confidentiality,[27] as often the mere knowledge that a patient has attended a certain medical practice as well as the frequency of attendance may allow for conclusions as to the purpose behind the visits, the medical condition of the patient and the illness he/she is suffering from.[28] Another argument brought forward in favour of limiting the scope of protected information is that only information which in itself has a medical aspect deserves confidentiality. Facts without medical significance which every person without any medical knowledge could have observed in the same way as the physician, such as the destruction of a will in the room of a patient, would then not be protected as

[25] Ch. crim. 11 May 1959, D.1959.312.
[26] Savatier, JCP.1970.II.16306.
[27] Mazen (1988), at 44.
[28] Pradel, Danti-Juan, at 232.

confidential.[29] Others object, however, that all information obtained in relation with the exercise of the medical profession should be kept secret, regardless of whether the information has medical aspects or not,[30] as the distinction between medical and non-medical information will sometimes be very difficult to make. Also, it is possible that some information that very obviously does not have a medical aspect, such as the place of refuge of a fugitive criminal in need of medical care,[31] will be made known to the physician exclusively for the purpose of enabling him/her to exercise his/her profession and treat the patient. Even though the information is therefore not as such related to the medical condition of the patient, it was nevertheless obtained by the physician in the course of his/her profession, and the trust placed in the physician when revealing this information was based on the patient's medical needs.

Some argue that the changes in the perception of illness, that is that an illness in itself is no longer perceived as something shameful that has to be hidden, require a new definition of medical confidentiality, in that it no longer seems appropriate for the duty of medical confidentiality to embrace all information relating to the patient's health, given that patients will not feel any need to keep most medical information confidential.[32] But others object that while the perception of illness might have changed, even a benign illness that according to most people does not have anything indecent attached to it, can nevertheless have an aspect that the patient might want to hide for personal reasons, for example the way in which he/she contracted the illness.[33] It should be added that if privacy protection is one of the reasons underlying medical confidentiality, the view that only sensitive or potentially embarrassing information be covered by medical confidentiality is problematic. The disclosure of private medical information as such then reduces the patient's control over the dissemination of such information, regardless of the information's content.

With regard to the second requirement of a secret, i.e. the question of whether information can still be regarded as secret even if it is public knowledge, the courts have decided in several cases that it does not matter that the information had already been made public before any disclosure by the physician, because a physician's disclosure will often serve as confirmation of what until then was only a rumour,[34] and the physician's disclosure can add a scientific basis to the knowledge of the public. In one case, a physician who had been threatened by a patient over the telephone brought charges, stating that the patient was mentally ill and had aggressive tendencies. According to the physician, these tendencies had manifested themselves for example in the fact that the patient had often threatened his wife. The Cour d'appel of Lyon held that these revelations violated the physician's duty to maintain medical confidentiality, as the patient's aggressive

---

[29] Reboul, JCP.1950.I.825.

[30] Savatier, D.1957.445.

[31] Example given by Savatier, ibid.

[32] Ibid.

[33] Ryckmans, Meert-Van de Put, at 131.

[34] 23 January 1996, Ch. crim., Bull. n°37; Véron, at 153.

tendencies, though notorious, were discovered by the physician only in the exercise of his profession.[35] And in another case regarding the obligation of a police officer to maintain the professional secret, the Cour de Cassation held that the obligation applied even to facts that, in all likelihood, were already publicly known.[36]

To comprehend art.226-13 of the Criminal Code and the scope and limits of medical confidentiality, it is essential to understand whose interests the principle of medical confidentiality is aiming to protect. As was already indicated, the French Criminal Code does not award protection against the revelation of every confidence. Rather, only information confided in the members of certain professions is protected by criminal law. The reason behind this concept is clear: the confidence placed in so-called necessary confidants, i.e. persons to whom the individual must in some situations reveal confidential information, is seen as important enough to deserve special protection,[37] even protection by the means of criminal law. However, it is not at all clear why this confidence is important enough to justify special protection. While it is widely accepted that medical confidentiality exists in the interest of the patient,[38] it is controversial how exactly the patient's interests can be determined. Some argue that the duty of medical confidentiality protects the interests of those who, when in need of having recourse to the service of someone else, confide information in him/her which they would have kept to themselves but for the need to inform the professional whose help they are seeking.[39] There seems to be widespread agreement that the patient has an interest in being assured that the physician will never reveal any confidential patient information without the patient's consent,[40] as otherwise the patient might not feel confident to share all relevant information with his/her physician.[41] For some, this interest is merely psychological: patients would find it undesirable to see their medical secrets revealed.[42] Others argue that the patient's interest in his/her bodily integrity is concerned, as patients, when holding back essential information,[43] endanger the efficiency of their medical treatment. Some authors suggest that the right to medical confidentiality is part of the patient's personality rights which protect the individual's private and intimate sphere.[44] They argue that the patient's interest in medical confidentiality is comparable to the interest in one's own picture, voice and letters, and they conclude that everybody has the right to consider his/her health and all health related information as confidential. The fact that art.226-13 of the Criminal Code is part of the book on 'crimes and

[35] 17 January 1980, CA Lyon, Gaz. Pal. 1981.2.491.
[36] 8 February 1994, Gaz. Pal.1994.somm.298.
[37] 19 November 1985, Bull n° 364; Waremberg-Auque, 237-56.
[38] Waremberg-Auque, at 251; Mazen (1988), at 42; Rassat, D.1989.chron.107.
[39] Gulphe, D.1947.109.
[40] Légal, JCP.1948.II.4141; Savatier, D.1957.445.
[41] Albucher, JCP.1954.II.8107; Combaldieu, D.1967.122.
[42] Honnorat, Melennec, JCP.1979.I.2936.
[43] Gulphe, D.1947.109.
[44] Mazen (1988), at 28; the same, Gaz. Pal. 1981.2.491; Melennec, Gaz. Pal. 1980.doct.145.

misdemeanours against the individual', and within that book part of the chapter on 'offences against the personality', also supports the view that the right to medical confidentiality is part of the personality rights.[45] If that is accepted, it follows that the provision aims at ensuring that an individual who is obliged to reveal intimate details when seeking the advice and help of a medical practitioner does not have to fear indiscretion and a violation of his/her private and intimate sphere.[46] Art.226-13 of the Criminal Code could then be seen as imposing an obligation on the physician that corresponds to the patient's right under art.9 of the Civil Code to keep his/her medical information secret.[47] It has also been suggested that the principle of medical confidentiality, in addition to a protection of the patient's privacy rights, aims at respect for the patient's dignity.[48] All these considerations seem of deontological, rather than utilitarian origin, as they are not concerned with the consequences of a lack of medical confidentiality, but rather recognise that medical confidentiality must be protected in order to guarantee the patient's informational and decisional privacy.

With regard to the question of whether the principle of medical confidentiality also intends to protect the individual physician or the medical profession as such, again many different opinions exist. Some infer from the wording of art.378 of the old Criminal Code that the physician is only the depository of the patient's secret, and that therefore not the physician, but only the patient can be the master of confidential medical information referring to him/her.[49] In the domain of medical confidentiality, physicians would then only have duties, but not rights.[50] Many argue, however, that the members of the medical profession have themselves an interest in the maintenance of medical confidentiality, as the exercise of their profession would be seriously impaired if patients, when not being sufficiently assured of confidentiality, held back important information.[51] Physicians could then no longer efficiently fulfil their professional tasks, so that without a protection of medical confidentiality, the interest in the functioning of the medical profession would be adversely affected.[52] Another argument is that since the members of the medical profession see confidentiality as a sacred duty,[53] they accordingly have an interest in not being forced to reveal confidential patient information.[54]

In addition, some argue that the interests of the members of the patient's family in the protection of their intimate sphere as well as in their honour and reputation are protected by art.226-13.[55]

---

[45] Mazen (1988), at 27.

[46] Thouvenin (1997), Art.378, note 1.

[47] Mazeau, Chabas, at 394-5.

[48] Flécheux, JCP.1982.II.19721; Mémeteau, Gaz.Pal 1996, at 755.

[49] Savatier, JCP.1967.II.15126.

[50] Melennec, Gaz. Pal. 1980.doct.145.

[51] Gulphe, D.1947.109; Saury, at 248.

[52] Combaldieu, D.1967.122.

[53] Albucher, JCP.1954.II.8107.

[54] Roujou de Boubée, Bouloc, Fancillon, Mayaud, at 399.

[55] Albucher, JCP.1954.II.8107; Combaldieu, D.1967.122.

For many authors, society as a whole has an interest in the protection of medical confidentiality.[56] This view is mainly promoted by those who fear that without medical confidentiality, patients would no longer openly reveal all their medical secrets to their physicians, which could have an adverse effect on public health,[57] as efficient medical treatment would then no longer be guaranteed.[58] They argue that the protection of medical confidentiality mainly lies in the public interest, as the criminal offence of revealing confidential information is not a 'délit privé', but a charge can rather be brought directly by the public prosecutor,[59] even if no individual feels harmed and is interested in pressing charges.[60] Others, however, question whether medical confidentiality really has any significance for the patient's readiness to receive medical advice and treatment, as no evidence supports the view that in countries without a protection of medical confidentiality the patient's behaviour in this respect differs from that of a French patient.[61] This debate equals the utilitarian discussion of whether or not sufficient evidence exists to justify the assumption that a protection of medical confidentiality produces beneficial consequences.

Medical confidentiality could also lie in the public interest if the right to respect for one's private life were regarded as a general principle that lies within the public interest.[62] This view could be based on the consideration that society has an interest in the protection of the individual and of the freedom of the individual.[63] Furthermore, it could be argued that the mere fact that medical confidentiality is protected by a criminal provision shows that the legislature considers the principle as being in the public interest.[64] Understood in this way, the public interest argument in favour of medical confidentiality is based on deontological considerations as it promotes that the public has an interest in preserving individual interests that are worth protecting. At the same time, it could also reflect utilitarian thought, if it were accepted that the promotion of individual privacy as such produces beneficial consequences.

To summarise, the predominant opinion promotes the view that the protection of medical confidentiality by the Criminal Code is mainly guaranteed in the interests of the patient, which are identified as the interest in keeping confidential medical information secret, the interest in bodily integrity, and the interest in respect for human dignity. However, some argue that medical confidentiality mainly or additionally aims at protecting the interests of the physician or of the medical profession, the interests of the patient's family and the interests of society as a whole.

---

[56] Combaldieu, D.1967.122.

[57] Gulphe, D.1947.109.

[58] Honnorat, Melennec, JCP.1979.I.2936; Savatier, Auby, Savatier, Péquignot, at n° 304.

[59] Gulphe, D.1947.109.

[60] Ryckmans, Meert-Van de Put, at 131.

[61] Mazen (1988), at 22 and 28.

[62] Mazen, Gaz. Pal. 1981.2.491.

[63] Mazen (1988), at 26.

[64] Flécheux, JCP.1982.II.19721; Mazen, Gaz. Pal. 1981.2.491.

Law 2002-303 concerning the rights of patients and the quality of the health care system[65] has introduced an additional criminal offence. In art.L.1110-4, a patient's right to private life and to medical confidentiality is recognised:

Every person under the care of a health care professional, institution, organisation, or any other organism that participates in the prevention and care has a right to respect for his/her private life and for the confidentiality of all information regarding him/her.

Except in cases of exemptions expressly provided for by law, confidentiality covers all information regarding the person which has come to the knowledge of the health care professional, of any member of the personnel of these institutions and organisations and any other person related to these institutions or organisations by their activities. It is imposed on every health care professional and on all professionals intervening in the health care system.[66]

This provision which has become part of the Code of Public Health (Code de santé publique), provides for criminal sanctions in case someone obtains the communication of such information in violation of this provision. It therefore extends the criminal law's protection of medical confidentiality which had been limited to the disclosure of confidential information by health care professionals (art.226-13) to the receipt of such information.

3 Protection under private law

3.1 Article 9 of the Civil Code

The right to the protection of one's private life as guaranteed under art.9 of the Civil Code, is also of importance in the context of medical confidentiality. According to art.9 of the Civil Code:

Everybody has the right to respect for his private life.

Courts can, without prejudice to the reparation of damage suffered, prescribe all measures, such as sequestration, seizure and others, suitable to prevent or stop an attack on

---

[65] Loi 2002-303 du 4 mars 2002 relative aux droits des malades et à la qualité du système de santé.

[66] Toute personne prise en charge par un professionnel, un établissement, un réseau de santé ou tout autre organisme participant à la prévention et aux soins a droit au respect de sa vie privée et du secret des informations la concernant. Excepté dans les cas de dérogation, expressément prévus par la loi, ce secret couvre l'ensemble des informations concernant la personne venues à la connaissance du professionnel de santé, de tout membre du personnel de ces établissements ou organismes et de toute autre personne en relation, de par ses activités, avec ces établissements ou organismes. Il s'impose à tout professionnel de santé, ainsi qu'à tous les professionnels intervenant dans le système de santé.

the inviolability of the private life. In case of urgency, these measures can be ordered by temporary injunction.[67]

Art.9 of the Civil Code was introduced by an Act of 17 July 1970 as a reaction to new threats to the inviolability of private life, for example through new technologies.[68] It enables the courts to protect a person's private life by measures such as injunctive relief, sequestration of printed material etc. so as to prevent the violation of an individual's private life.[69] Under this provision, every person has the right to control the dissemination of personal information and to exclude others from his/her private sphere of life.[70] This includes the protection of the secrecy of one's health condition and of personal medical information.[71]

3.2 Obligation under contract and tort law

In French law, the physician-patient relationship is usually governed by contract law. The physician is then under a contractual[72] duty to maintain medical confidentiality, and the legal consequences will be dealt with by art.1147 of the Civil Code, which allows for compensation for any loss, including non-pecuniary loss, suffered as a consequence of the breach of a contractual duty. In principle, a violation of medical confidentiality by a physician could also constitute a tortious act under art.1382 of the Civil Code and thereby give rise to a claim for damages under tort law. However, in French law, contractual and delictual responsibility cannot co-exist.[73] A case in which compensation is at issue is either governed by the principles of contract law or by the principles of tort law. This means that in the case of a breach of a contractual obligation, delictual responsibility for the same act is excluded.[74] Given that the physician's obligation to maintain medical confidentiality is usually based on the contract existing between physician and patient, it follows that a breach of that duty can normally only give rise to a claim for compensation under contract law, but not for compensation under art.1382 of

---

[67] Art.9: Chacun a droit au respect de sa vie privée.

Les juges peuvent, sans préjudice de la réparation du dommage subi, prescrire toutes mesures, telles que séquestre, saisie et autres, propres à empêcher ou faire cesser une atteinte à l'intimité de la vie privée; ces mesures peuvent, s'il y a urgence, être ordonnées en référé.

[68] Rivero, Tome 2, at 85.

[69] See for example CA Paris, 13 March 1996, JCP.1996.22632, a decision regarding the distribution of the book *Le grand secret* revealing details of the late President Mitterand's medical condition.

[70] Mazeau, Chabas, at 397.

[71] Rivero, Tome 2, at 77.

[72] Honnorat, Melennec, JCP.1979.I.2936; Savatier, Auby, Savatier, Péquignot, at 303; but according to Anzalec, Gaz. Pal. 1971.113, the obligation to medical confidentiality is not based on a contract, but is rather a legal obligation based on 'l'ordre public'.

[73] Terré, Simler, Lequette, at 771.

[74] Ch. civ., 20 May 1936, D.P.1936.1.88; S.1937.1.321; Ch. Civ., 9 June 1993, JCP 1994.II 22264.

the Civil Code. A claim for compensation under tort law is normally only available if there is no contract between the patient and the physician, for example in the case of a medical examination of an accident victim by a physician at the site of the accident.

It should be noted that in civil matters, French courts often do not specify the provision the successful action was based upon, but rather justify their decisions by a general reference to the different Civil Code provisions mentioned. Arts 9, 1147, 1382 of the Civil Code, and also art. 226-13 of the Criminal Code are being used to deduce the general principle that medical confidentiality is legally protected.[75]

4 Professional obligation

The Code of Medical Ethics 1995 (code de déontologie médicale) issued by the medical profession states in art.4(1):

The professional secret established in the interest of the patient is imposed on every physician according to the conditions stated by law.

Thus, a French physician is under an ethical duty to maintain medical confidentiality. The scope of this obligation is specified in art.4(2) of the Code of Medical Ethics, stating that:

The secret covers everything that came to the knowledge of the physician in the course of his profession, that is it not only covers what was confided in him, but also what he has seen, heard or understood.

The extent of protection awarded to medical confidentiality under the professional regulations therefore coincides with the legal protection as developed by the courts.

5 Summary

Even if the protection of confidential medical information could be seen as part of the constitutionally protected right to personal freedom, this protection would only be of limited effect, given the narrow system of constitutional protection of fundamental rights in France. Protection of confidential medical information in accordance with Article 8 of the ECHR is guaranteed, and every court can control the compatibility of statutes and executive acts with that provision. Medical confidentiality is also protected under private law, and injunctive relief is available where a violation of this interest is to be feared. Compensation can be claimed under art.1147 of the Civil Code for a violation of the contractual obligation of medical confidentiality, or, in the absence of a contract between physician and patient, under art.1382 of the Civil Code. Physicians are also under an ethical

---

[75] Agostini, D.1996, chron.58.

obligation to respect their patients' medical secrets, and the violation of that obligation can give rise to disciplinary sanctions. The strongest protection of medical confidentiality, however, is achieved by the means of criminal law, as a violation of the obligation to maintain medical confidentiality by the physician is a criminal offence under art.226-13 of the Criminal Code. The significance of medical confidentiality has recently been reconfirmed by art.L.1110-4 of Law 2002-303.

The academic debate of the scope of medical confidentiality which mainly takes place in the context of criminal law, favours a deontological perspective in emphasising the importance of medical confidentiality for the protection of the patient's privacy rights. However, the significance of medical confidentiality for the integrity of the physician-patient relationship has also been stressed. Utilitarian considerations based on public health arguments are advanced, but seem of only subordinate significance.

PART 2 – DISCLOSURE IN THE CONTEXT OF CRIME PREVENTION AND CRIMINAL PROSECUTION

Consistent with the fact that medical confidentiality is primarily protected by the criminal law, questions of medical privilege mainly refer to the interplay of various provisions of the Criminal Code, and of the link between those provisions and the relevant articles of the Code of Criminal Procedure. This part will therefore introduce the relevant provisions of both codes, examine their interpretation by the courts and legal academics, and analyse how consistency between the numerous provisions can best be achieved.

1 General and absolute obligation of medical confidentiality

To understand the French approach to the resolution of conflicts between medical confidentiality and other interests, it is essential to be familiar with the concept of the 'general and absolute' nature of medical confidentiality. The formula of the 'general and absolute' nature of the principle of medical confidentiality is a fundamental feature of the French approach to medical confidentiality and has mainly been promoted by the criminal courts. The Chambre criminelle of the Cour de Cassation, for example, stated in its decision of 22 December 1966 that the duty to maintain confidentiality as imposed on physicians by the provisions of the Criminal Code, is general and absolute and that no one can relieve the physician from it.[76]

Several arguments have been advanced in favour of this approach. Combaldieu, for example, promotes the view that even though there can sometimes be good and

---

[76] D.1967.122; this formula was used more recently by the Cour de Cassation on 7 March 1989, Bull n° 109; on 8 February 1994, Gaz. Pal.1994.somm.298; and on 8 April 1998, *Dr. pén.* 1998, comm. 11.

even imperative reasons for revealing the secret, it is still true that every exception bears the risk that the duty will be annihilated. To allow for exceptions would require a case by case rather than an absolute approach and would have the inconvenience of blurring the content of the duty to maintain confidentiality. He therefore concludes that it is preferable to declare the obligation to be of a general and absolute nature, as this concept, though being rigid and inflexible, nevertheless has the merit not only of relying on tradition and precedents, but also of regulating behaviour in a precise manner.[77] It has also been argued that a relativist concept of medical confidentiality is dangerous for physicians, because it leaves them with a choice of whether or not to disclose the confidential information. If this choice does not find the approval of the judges, they risk a conviction and disciplinary sanctions. Accordingly, it has been maintained that physicians who find themselves confronted with a criminal provision must know where they stand and need a rule that leaves no room for doubts.[78] The theory seems partly to be based on the rather pragmatic view that the imposition of an absolute duty of medical confidentiality has been of surprising efficiency and has been rigidly respected by physicians.[79] While this interpretation of the 'general and absolute' formula thus suggests that the principle of medical confidentiality should always prevail without allowing for any exceptions, others object that this concept is too rigid, as it can sometimes lead to results that are contrary to morals or to the requirements of justice.[80] A different approach has therefore been proposed, submitting that the theory of an absolute secret does by no means imply that confidences cannot be revealed under any circumstances. Rather, according to this approach, the theory of the general and absolute obligation merely entails that confidential patient information can only be disclosed in accordance with general legal principles and within the framework of the known legal justifications.[81] Thus, medical confidentiality, while in principle deserving absolute protection, could nevertheless in some cases be outweighed by overriding interests.

Others reject the theory of the absolute nature of medical confidentiality altogether and argue that the relative nature of the medical secret is confirmed by legislation imposing on the physician a duty to disclose certain sensitive health information, for example with regard to venereal diseases.[82] If exemptions are possible, it is argued, the secret cannot be absolute.

It will be seen below how the concept of the general and absolute nature of the obligation to maintain medical confidentiality influences the approach towards the different conflicts arising in the context of criminal proceedings.

---

[77] Combaldieu, D.1967.122.

[78] Flécheux, JCP.1982.II.19721.

[79] Monzein, D.1984.chron.9.

[80] Anzalec, Gaz. Pal. 1971.113.

[81] Rassat, D.1989.chron.107.

[82] Le Roy, D.1963.280; Pradel, JCP.1969.I.2234.

2 Obligation to give testimony

In a criminal trial, the testimony of a witness is an important means to achieve the purpose of such proceedings: finding the truth and ensuring that the offender will be convicted without risking a wrongful conviction of the innocent. This interest is undoubtedly a public interest.[83] Therefore, art.109 of the Code of Criminal Procedure creates a duty for every citizen to give testimony in court. But the provision contains an exemption for those persons who are under an obligation of professional confidentiality, the violation of which is punishable under arts.226-13 and 226-14 of the Criminal Code. Art.109 states:

> Every person who was subpoenaed to be heard as a witness is under a duty to appear, to swear an oath, and to testify, subject to the dispositions ... of arts.226-13 and 226-14 of the Criminal Code.[84]

When a physician is called to give testimony concerning confidential patient information, a conflict between the public interest in finding the truth and the interest in medical confidentiality arises. As art.226-13 of the Criminal Code (obligation to medical confidentiality) and art.109 of the Code of Criminal Procedure (obligation to give testimony) impose conflicting duties, it is important to establish how this conflict should be resolved. Should the physician always give testimony, as finding the truth in criminal proceedings is more important than upholding medical confidentiality? Alternatively, should the physician always refuse to give testimony, as medical confidentiality is more important than finding the truth? Or should the physician have the choice to decide the conflict in every individual situation according to the facts of the case and the dictates of his/her conscience?

As art.109 of the Code of Criminal Procedure expressly exempts persons who are under an obligation to professional confidentiality from the obligation to give testimony, art.109 must be interpreted as imposing a general duty on a physician to give testimony in court when called as a witness only if the interrogation does not involve confidential information protected by the duty of medical confidentiality.[85] Under art.109, the physician is thus not under an obligation to give testimony in court with regard to confidential patient information. This, however, leaves the question of whether it follows that the physician is not allowed to give testimony, or whether it only means that the physician, while under no obligation to give testimony, can choose to do so and will then be exempt from his/her duty of medical confidentiality under art.226-13 of the Criminal Code. Art.109 of the Code of Criminal Procedure has mostly been interpreted so as to prohibit any testimony

---

[83] Gulphe, D.1947.109.

[84] Art.109: Toute personne citée pour être entendue comme témoin est tenue de comparaître, de prêter serment et de déposer, sous réserve des dispositions ... des articles 226-13 et 226-14 du Code pénal.

[85] Damien, Gaz. Pal.1982.doct.136.

that might violate the obligation to maintain medical confidentiality.[86] As art.109 exempts the physician from the obligation to give testimony, while art.226-13 does not provide for an exemption in the case of testimony in court, the legislature has clearly demonstrated how to resolve the conflict between the two competing duties. According to this interpretation, a physician who decides to give testimony in court will thereby commit the criminal offence of art.226-13, unless, exceptionally, a legal justification in his/her favour applies.

Some suggest, however, that case-law leaves the physician a choice between the two obligations,[87] but there are no cases directly on this point.[88] Rather, the existing case-law refers to the question of whether the physician has the right or even the obligation to give testimony if the patient has consented to the disclosure of confidential information.[89] In that situation, the courts took the stance that it was up to the physician to choose which obligation to fulfil in the particular case. Given the rather narrow scope of this case law, it is thus not at all clear whether the courts would give the physician a choice between giving testimony or maintaining medical confidentiality where the patient has not consented to the disclosure.

It can be seen that the debate in France mainly concentrates on finding a coherent approach to the interplay between art.226-13 of the Criminal Code and art.109 of the Code of Criminal Procedure. As the provisions do not seem to leave much scope for interpretation, it is not surprising that no reference is made to ethical principles.

3 Defence rights of the physician

A problem arises if a physician is accused of professional irregularities and wants to testify about confidential patient information to exonerate him/herself. In such a case, we are no longer merely concerned with a conflict between the interest in medical confidentiality and the general public interest in establishing the truth in criminal proceedings. Rather, in addition to the latter, the physician's interest in the unobstructed exercise of his/her defence rights is at stake. Given that defence rights are regarded as fundamental human rights,[90] there is wide agreement that the physician's defence rights outweigh the interest in medical confidentiality.[91] In a case in which a physician was accused of medical malpractice leading to the death of a patient, and where the physician submitted to the court photos which he had taken in the course of the medical examination and which were useful for his defence, the court for example held that: 'one cannot deny defence rights to

---

[86] Mazen (1988), at 130; Vouin, at 367.

[87] Chomienne, Guéry, ALD.1995.comm.85.

[88] Loiret, at 162; Vouin, at 367.

[89] See for example 8 May 1947, D.1947.109; 5 June 1985, Bull N° 218.

[90] Champeil-Desplats, D.1995.chron.323.

[91] See, for example, Damien, at 36; Décheix, D.1983.chron.133; Mazen (1988), at 147; Pradel, JCP.1969.I.2234; Reboul, JCP.1950.I.825; Thouvenin, at 99-100.

anybody, and this fundamental freedom cannot be limited by the principles relating to medical confidentiality.'[92]

In the famous case of the 'King of the Gypsies', the court went even further. In that case the leader of a gypsy community had manipulated two female members to make them act as follows: after having had car accidents, they misled their physicians as to the seriousness of their resulting medical condition and, as a consequence, the physicians certified serious and persistent medical problems. The drivers who had caused the accidents were then asked to pay high amounts of damages. When the grave errors made by the physicians were discovered, they were, in the course of criminal proceedings against the community leader, asked for an explanation. The physicians indicated that they had been influenced by statements made by persons who were close to the victims, and by the victims' simulations. The Cour de Cassation held that:

> The Court of Appeal was right to state that even though the duty of confidentiality was a strict principle, it could not prevent the physician who had been turned into the accessory of a fraud because he delivered a wrong medical certificate from clearing himself in the course of judicial proceedings concerning this fraud, by revealing the details that had led to the delivery of the medical certificate at issue. This is particularly true given that art.160 of the Criminal Code makes the delivery of a certificate falsely certifying the existence of illnesses a criminal offence.[93]

Some commentators thought that the Court's decision was justified, given that the physicians could not otherwise have cleared themselves from the suspicion of having participated in the fraud.[94] Others went even further and argued that as the case concerned a physician who was being accused in court or at least seriously threatened of being accused, the principle of respect for defence rights applied, allowing the accused to reveal in court all information necessary for his defence.[95] However, in this case the physicians had not been accused of any illegal or unprofessional conduct, as they were asked for the explanation as witnesses in the course of criminal proceedings against third parties. It was also clear from the outset that the physicians had acted in good faith. In this case, it is thus rather difficult to justify the result by reference to the physician's defence rights which were not affected. The decision suggests that the simple eventuality of a charge being brought against a physician is sufficient to justify a disregard of art.226-13 of the Criminal Court.[96]

The courts based their decisions on rather general considerations regarding the conflict between the interest in medical confidentiality and the physician's interest in defending him/herself when accused in criminal proceedings, without any reference to the legal basis of a possible justification. Nevertheless, a short examination of the applicability of legal justifications seems in order. French law

---

[92] 26 October 1951, CA Douai (4e Ch. corr.), Gaz.Pal. 1951.2.425.

[93] 20 December 1967, D.1969.309.

[94] Lapointe, D.1969.309.

[95] Rassat, D.1989.chron.107.

[96] Lapointe, D.1969.309.

mainly offers two different legal justifications that could apply in this context, the first of which is that of self-defence (légitime défense), set out in art.122-5 of the Criminal Code:

> A person who, in the face of an unjustified attack against himself or a third party, commits, at the same time, an action commanded by the necessities of self-defence or the defence of a third party, is not responsible in criminal law, unless there is disproportionality between the defence measures employed and the seriousness of the attack.[97]

And the necessity defence (état de nécessité) as regulated by art.122-7 of the Criminal Code, applies under the following conditions:

> A person who, in the face of a present or imminent danger to himself, a third party or an object, commits an action necessary to safeguard the person or the object, is not responsible in criminal law, unless there is disproportionality between the measures employed and the seriousness of the threat.[98]

The opinions are split as to whether the prerequisites of self-defence will be fulfilled where criminal charges are brought against a physician and the physician, as part of his/her defence, discloses confidential patient information. Self-defence presupposes an aggression emanating from the victim who has to accept the reaction because he/she tried to harm another. In the case of disclosure of confidential medical information, this means that the information may only be revealed in cases of an attack emanating from the patient, and only to the extent necessary for the refutation of such an attack.[99] Moreover, it will frequently be difficult to allege that the charge against the physician was unjustified, another prerequisite of self-defence, so that in many cases, the requirements of the justification of self-defence will not be fulfilled.[100]

It has also been argued that the necessity defence can be invoked as it justifies revelations that are necessary in the social interest, and it seems to some to be the most appropriate defence, as it is the most flexible one.[101] The supporters of this view suggest that the harm caused by the physician when disclosing confidential information is not punishable because he/she is trying to avert a more serious danger from him/herself. However, the requirement of an immediate and imminent

---

[97] Art.122-5: N'est pas pénalement responsable la personne qui, devant une atteinte injustifiée envers elle-même ou autrui, accomplit, dans le même temps, un acte commandé par la nécessité de la légitime défense d'elle-même ou d'autrui, sauf s'il y a disproportion entre les moyens de défense employés et la gravité de l'atteinte.

[98] Art.122-7: N'est pas pénalement responsable la personne qui, face à un danger actuel ou imminent qui menace elle-même, autrui ou un bien, accomplit un acte nécessaire à la sauvegarde de la personne ou du bien, sauf s'il y a disproportion entre les moyens employés et la gravité de la menace.

[99] Honnorat, Melennec, JCP.1979.I.2936.

[100] Waremberg-Auque, at 252.

[101] Pradel, Danti-Juan, at 241; Rassat, D.1989.chron.107.

danger can be problematic. Some argue that this requirement will often not be met as the simple threat of a prosecution does not constitute an imminent danger.[102] Others, in contrast, argue that the requirement of an imminent danger is obviously fulfilled, given that in such a situation the physician is exposed to harm.

The problem at hand does not fit neatly into the framework of the legal justifications recognised by French law. This is why the courts and most legal writers have never referred to the justifications known in criminal law and instead restrict themselves to confirming that the right to defend oneself is a fundamental right outweighing medical confidentiality,[103] without trying to establish the prerequisites of either self-defence or necessity. However, two principles are here in conflict with each other: if confidentiality were given priority over the right to defend oneself, it would mean to accept the risk that an innocent person who was not given the possibility to exculpate him/herself might be convicted, or to give a guilty person the prerogative of not having to take responsibility for his/her actions. But to give the physician's defence rights priority over medical confidentiality would constitute an inroad in the principle of medical confidentiality and a disloyalty on the part of the physician. It is thus difficult to find a solution.

Some have tried to reconcile and optimise both interests, by stating that it seems normal not to deny a physician defence rights, i.e. rights enjoyed by everybody else; but that this does not mean that the physician can divulge everything and under all circumstances. Rather, the disclosure must be strictly limited to the needs of the defence.[104] It has also been suggested that the physician can only reveal the confidential information once an action is started against him, and only if the action was commenced by the patient, as it is only the patient, master of the secret, who can relieve the physician from his/her duty to maintain medical confidentiality.[105] If the patient accuses the physician of an irregularity, some writers suggest that the patient should not be allowed to invoke medical confidentiality, as he/she has dragged his/her medical secrets into the public sphere.[106] But it is not clear whether this consideration is limited to civil litigation, or whether it also applies to criminal law, as it is then not the patient, but the public prosecutor who brings charges. It has also been suggested that the impact of the breach of confidentiality could possibly be mitigated by conducting in chamber proceedings.[107]

The resolution of this conflict of interests can be viewed differently. Some say that the interests of the physician can never legitimise an exception from medical confidentiality, even where the silence requires heroic efforts, as only the law can provide for exceptions to the principle of confidentiality, and as such exceptions can only be justified with reference to the protection of overriding public interests.

---

[102] Waremberg-Auque, at 252.
[103] See, for example, Monzein, D.1984.chron.107.
[104] Anzalec, Gaz. Pal. 1971.113.
[105] Pradel, JCP.1969.I.2234.
[106] Mazen, Gaz. Pal. 1981.2.491; Honnorat, Melennec, JCP.1979.I.2936; Peytel, Gaz. Pal. 1952.2.doctr.13; but see Monzein, D.1984.chron.9.
[107] Loiret, at 121-2.

Therefore, in the absence of such express legislative exceptions in favour of the physician's defence rights, no breach of medical confidentiality by the physician would be justified.[108] A medical practitioner cannot lawfully breach the professional secret on the grounds of trying to avoid moral harm, e.g. protecting his professional integrity or honour, or to avoid a criminal conviction.[109] This is how the conflict has sometimes been decided in the past, when some courts have held that the physician, when being accused of a criminal offence, did not have the right to disclose confidential information necessary for his defence.[110] Others do not go this far but argue instead that only revelations for the mere purpose of avoiding potential liability or for other purely economic interests of the physician should be punished.[111]

Another opinion states that the physician generally has the right to defend him/herself in court with regard to accusations made by his/her patient without being bound to maintain medical confidentiality, as the opposite conclusion would violate the rights of the parties to court proceedings.[112] The principle of defence rights has a legal foundation in art.171-1 of the Code of Criminal Procedure and in the European Convention on Human Rights. As a fundamental right, defence rights justify a violation of the medical secret.[113]

It can be seen that many different theories are promoted with regard to the question of whether or not the physician's defence rights outweigh the patient's interests in medical confidentiality. While the courts have adopted a very broad interpretation of defence rights and justify a disclosure whenever the physician is asked to give an explanation for potential misconduct, the positions of legal scholars mainly fall into three different categories. For some, defence rights always trump medical confidentiality, and this seems so clear that the promoters of this view did not perceive any need to justify their view other than by referring to the human rights status of defence rights. This, however, can hardly be a sufficient explanation, given that medical confidentiality is equally protected as a fundamental human right, for example by the European Convention on Human Rights. For defence rights to outweigh medical confidentiality, it would therefore be necessary to present reasons why defence rights are of a higher rank. Others take the opposite view and argue that the physician's defence rights can under no circumstances justify a disclosure of confidential patient information. This opinion is based on the rather formalistic view that the Criminal Code does not expressly provide for an exception to the principle of medical confidentiality where it is in conflict with the physician's defence rights. Again, this opinion is difficult to justify on that basis alone, as it is at least arguable that in some cases the breach of medical confidentiality could be justified by the legal justifications of self-defence

---

[108] Savatier, Auby, Savatier, Péquignot, at 304.
[109] Légal, JCP.1948.II.1582.
[110] Trib corr. d'Amiens, 12 March 1902, D.1902.2.493; CA d'Aix, 19 March 1902, D.1903.2.451.
[111] Anzalec, Gaz. Pal. 1971.113.
[112] Mazen, Gaz. Pal. 1981.2.491.
[113] Thouvenin, at 99-100.

or necessity, or by overriding fundamental interests of the physician. Given that under French law, in such cases two fundamental interests clash, the third approach which suggests some balancing seems most in line with traditional legal principles. However, such a balancing approach would require an identification of the conflicting interests involved as well as a determination of their respective values. The discussion as outlined above seems to suggest that such an analysis or any agreement on the outcome of such a balancing is lacking, and that most writers base their arguments on personal preferences and values, without any reference to ethical principles and theories. The courts, when allowing the physician's defence rights to outweigh the obligation to medical confidentiality,[114] seem to contradict their own view of the absolute nature of the duty to maintain medical confidentiality.

4 Effects of the patient's consent

Situations can arise in which a physician is called as a witness and in which the patient consents to the disclosure of his/her confidential medical information by the physician in court. The patient may be the accused and may want to prove certain medical facts beneficial to his/her defence, or the patient could be the victim of a criminal offence and may want the physician to give testimony regarding his/her injuries. Even if the patient is neither accused of having committed a crime nor victim of a criminal offence, medical information concerning this patient can still be important for the outcome of a criminal case, and the patient might want it to be available to the court through the testimony of his/her physician. Two questions can arise in this context: (1) can the patient validly exempt the physician from his/her obligation to medical confidentiality so as to enable the physician to give testimony with regard to confidential patient information without being subjected to the punishment laid down in art.226-13 of the Criminal Code; and (2) if the first question is answered in the affirmative, can the physician invoke medical confidentiality and refuse to disclose confidential patient information if the patient has consented to or even required that disclosure?

With regard to the question of the effect of the patient's consent, the opinions are split. To understand the debate, it seems important to mention that in French criminal law, consent of the victim normally does not provide a legal justification for the criminal offence.[115] The reason behind this is that criminal law does not primarily intend to safeguard individual interests, but rather aims at maintaining the social and public order, even though this may indirectly promote individual interests.[116] However, in respect of a criminal offence protecting interests that are at the free disposition of the victim, the victim's consent omits one of the constituent elements of the crime, so that the criminal offence cannot be committed

---

[114] 20 December 1967, D.1969.309; see also Damien, at 36.

[115] See, for example, Desportes, Le Gunehec, at 621; Saury, at 251.

[116] Stefani, Levasseur, Bouloc, at 343.

where the victim has consented to it.[117] Thus, if medical confidentiality were at the free disposition of the patient, the patient's consent could have the effect of negating a constituent element of the offence of art.226-13 of the Criminal Code. If, on the other hand, medical confidentiality were not at the free disposition of the patient, the patient's consent could not exempt the physician from the obligation of medical confidentiality, and a physician, disclosing confidential patient information with the patient's consent, would still be guilty of the criminal offence under art.226-13 of the Criminal Code. The attitude of the criminal courts is clear:

> The duty to maintain confidentiality, established and sanctioned by art.378 [of the old Criminal Code] to guarantee the confidence necessary for the exercise of certain professions, is imposed on physicians as a duty in relation with their position, it is general and absolute and no one can relieve the physician from it.[118]

French courts have made it clear that the notion of 'no one' includes the patient him/herself. The physician's obligation to medical confidentiality is not at the disposition of the patient and the patient cannot exempt the physician from his/her duty of medical confidentiality. An important consequence of the principle of the general and absolute nature of the obligation to maintain medical confidentiality is therefore that the criminal offence of breach of confidentiality can be committed even if the patient gave his/her consent to the physician's disclosure. In this respect, the criminal courts do not make any distinction between cases in which the patient was accused in criminal proceedings and called the physician as a defence witness, and all other cases including those in which the patient was the victim of a criminal offence.

In its decision of 8 May 1947, the Cour de Cassation had to decide the case of a physician who refused to give testimony in court with regard to observations already laid down in a medical certificate that had been handed out to the victim. A physician had been called by the parents of a girl, victim of an indecent assault, to examine their daughter. Upon the parents' request, he delivered a medical certificate with regard to his diagnosis and findings, but refused to give testimony in court about the same observations. The Cour de Cassation held that given the general and absolute nature of the physician's obligation to medical confidentiality, he did not have to give testimony even though the victim's parents had consented to the disclosure.[119] This has been confirmed in a more recent decision in which the Cour de Cassation decided that a physician who had examined a rape victim under the age of fifteen, was, when being called as a witness to give testimony with regard to the diagnosis and the medication prescribed, free to decide whether or not to give testimony even though the victim or the victim's parents had consented to

---

[117] Légal, JCP.1948.II.4141; Mazen, Gaz. Pal.1981.2.491; Waremberg-Auque, at 246.

[118] See, for example, 8 May 1947, JCP.1948.II.4141; 22 December 1966, D.1967.122; 7 March 1989, Bull n° 109 ; 16 December 1992, Bull n° 424; 8 February 1994, Gaz. Pal.1994.somm.298.

[119] JCP.1948.II.4141.

the disclosure.[120] Critics of these decisions argue that if the requested testimony is no more than a repetition of observations contained in a medical certificate, the physician should not be allowed to refuse to give testimony with regard to the same facts on the grounds that he/she was bound by an obligation to medical confidentiality,[121] particularly bearing in mind that the patient has a right to demand the delivery of such a certificate.[122] It seems here that different problems are being mixed up: the critique seems to be based on the assumption that the information in such a situation is no longer confidential, rather than supporting the view that the physician is under an obligation to give testimony where the patient has relieved him/her from the duty of medical confidentiality.

Another case which the Cour de Cassation had to decide was that of a woman who was accused of having stabbed her husband to death. She called her treating physician as a defence witness and gave her consent to a revelation of the confidential details regarding her medical treatment. When the physician refused to give testimony, invoking his obligation to medical confidentiality, the court repeated its formula of the general and absolute nature of the obligation to maintain medical confidentiality and concluded that the patient's consent to the revelation could not relieve the physician from this obligation.[123] In yet another decision in which a physician was called as a defence witness and in which the accused patient had consented to the physician's testimony about confidential medical facts, the Cour de Cassation stated that:

> The court cannot determine for the physician in which cases the disclosure of confidential information is appropriate. Consent of the accused cannot be seen as a justification taking away the criminal nature of a disclosure of confidential information. The refusal of the instance court to force a physician called as a defence witness by the accused to give testimony with regard to confidential information referring to the accused, when the physician invoked the medical privilege, was a correct application of the law. The principle that medical confidentiality is general and absolute ... applies to everybody without any distinction between witnesses of the prosecution and witnesses of the defence.[124]

An analysis of this decision shows that the Cour de Cassation again confirmed the principle of the general and absolute nature of the medical secret, and that it inferred from this principle that medical confidentiality cannot be at the disposition of the patient, so that the patient cannot validly relieve the physician from this obligation. More importantly, however, the first sentence of the quote could be read as giving the physician a choice to decide whether or not to give testimony in a situation in which the patient has consented to the disclosure of his/her confidential medical information or even requested it to assist with his/her defence. Thus, the court seemed to indicate that disclosure would under these circumstances

---

[120] 16 December 1992, Bull n° 424; see also 8 April 1998, *Dr. pén.* 1998, comm. 11.

[121] Légal, JCP.1948.II.4141.

[122] Savatier, JCP.1967.II.15126.

[123] 22 December 1966, D.1967.122.

[124] 5 June 1985, Bull n° 218.

not be regarded as a violation of the principle of medical confidentiality, and that the decision of whether or not to give testimony was exclusively in the hands of the physician.[125] Legal scholars approving of this case law and trying to explain the reasoning behind it argued that as the protection of medical confidentiality is not exclusively based on the interest of the patient, it follows that the patient cannot have the right to exempt the physician from an obligation that is imposed on him/her in the public interest.[126] If the obligation to medical confidentiality exists in the public interest of protecting the confidence of the public in the secrecy of the medical profession, it does not seem appropriate that the patient can relieve the physician from his/her obligation to confidentiality, as potential patients could be worried when seeing a physician disclose confidential patient information in court.[127] But how can it then be explained that the physician is given the choice between maintaining confidentiality and disclosure? It must certainly be more worrying for patients if it is left to the physician to decide whether or not to disclose information.

Another argument supporting the view that the patient's consent cannot relieve the physician from his/her duty of confidentiality is that valid consent must be informed and freely given. Therefore, one can only validly exempt someone from a duty of confidentiality with regard to confidential information the content of which one knows perfectly well. However, sometimes, for humanitarian reasons, the physician will not reveal the whole truth to the patient so that the patient who relieves the physician from his/her duty of confidentiality cannot fully appreciate the range of this consent.[128] But this problem could be avoided if the physician, when relieved by his/her patient from the duty of medical confidentiality, interpreted this authorisation as only including what is known to the patient.[129] It should also be noted that this rather paternalistic argument loses a lot of force when bearing in mind that the patient has a right of access to his/her medical records, and a right to be informed by the physician about his/her medical condition.

Yet another worry of the opponents of the patient's right to exempt the physician from his/her obligation to medical confidentiality is that it would follow from such a right that a patient's refusal to consent to a disclosure could raise suspicions regarding his/her guilt. As a consequence, a patient might feel forced into waiving his/her right to medical confidentiality and allow a revelation just to avoid negative conclusions a court could draw from his/her reluctance to consent to disclosure.[130] Others, admitting this risk, demand that the courts and the law ensure that the patient be free from any pressure to consent to the disclosure of his/her medical confidences. They suggest that in situations where the patient is the accused, only the patient him/herself but not the prosecution should have the right to call the physician as a witness. To deny the accused patient to call the physician as a

---

[125] In favour of such an interpretation see, for example, Penneau, D.1999.381.

[126] Combaldieu, D.1967.122.

[127] Rassat, D.1989.chron.107.

[128] Combaldieu, D.1967.122; Mazen (1988), at 57.

[129] Fénaux, D.1988.106; Mazen (1988), at 91.

[130] Loiret, at 105.

witness, it is argued, would be a violation of his/her defence rights. If, on the other hand, the prosecution or a third party could call the physician as a witness, this would subject the patient to an inadmissible dilemma: either to refuse to consent to the disclosure, which could give rise to suspicions on the part of the judge or the jury, or to relieve the physician from the obligation of medical confidentiality to avoid this risk, thus exposing him/herself to a disclosure of information which was covered by a promise of secrecy.[131] It is submitted that the problem could also be resolved by clarifying that no negative conclusions may be drawn from the exercise of the patient's right not to have his/her medical secrets disclosed in court.

A totally different argument brought forward is that even if as a result of the patient's consent, the criminal offence of breach of confidence disappeared and the confidant, who decided to speak, could not be penalised, consent would nevertheless not free the physician from the moral duty of medical confidentiality. The supporters of the view that this moral dilemma justifies the physician's refusal to give testimony submit that only the physician, in accordance with his/her conscience, can judge whether or not to give testimony, and that, as a consequence, the patient's consent cannot force the confidant into a breach of his/her silence.[132] When called upon to give testimony, the physician must assess the patient's interests according to his/her conscience. If his/her testimony conforms with these interests, the physician should give testimony under the twofold condition that free and voluntary consent of the patient exists and that in the given case medical confidentiality exclusively promotes a private interest. In the opposite case, the physician has to remain silent.[133] However, the whole argument seems dubious. The possible moral dilemma here seems to stem from a very paternalistic view of the physician's role, as it implies that the physician knows better than the patient what the patient's interests are.

Those who support the opinion that medical confidentiality is a principle that aims at protecting the interests of the patient think that the patient must be given the right to exempt the physician from the obligation of medical confidentiality. As the patient can always reveal his/her confidential facts, the patient is the master of his/her medical confidences and the only judge of his/her interests. The interest in medical confidentiality is therefore at the free disposition of the patient.[134] It seems to follow that the patient can release the physician from the obligation to medical confidentiality.[135] Furthermore, as art.226-13 of the Criminal Code sees the physician as a trustee of the patient's secret, the patient has the right to require from the physician respect for the ownership of his/her confidence.[136] Some therefore conclude that the patient's consent not only authorises the physician to disclose confidential information, but also obliges him/her to do so, so that the physician no longer has the right to refuse to give testimony once the patient has

---

[131] Savatier, JCP.1967.II.15126; Savatier, Auby, Savatier, Péquignot, at 303.
[132] Légal, JCP.1948.II.4141.
[133] Pradel, JCP.1969.I.2234.
[134] Waremberg-Auque, at 246.
[135] Légal, JCP.1948.II.4141; Savatier, Auby, Savatier, Péquignot, at 303.
[136] Savatier, JCP.1967.II.15126.

consented to the disclosure.[137] According to this view, there is then no longer a duty of confidentiality, and not even a right to maintain medical confidentiality, as there is no longer a confidence to be silent about.[138] This approach has also been adopted by a civil court that decided on 7 June 1955:

> The considerations justifying the general and absolute nature of the medical secret as being in the public interest apply to the relations between the physician and everybody apart from the patient, so that they cannot be invoked with regard to the physician-patient relationship.[139]

The civil chamber of the Cour de Cassation and also the Conseil d'Etat recognise that the patient may give consent to a disclosure of his/her own medical secrets by the physician. To prove medical facts in front of these courts, the patient can either produce a medical certificate or call the physician as a witness who then does not have the right to hide behind medical confidentiality.[140]

The decisions of the criminal courts, by contrast, have the effect that medical confidentiality is turned directly against the patient instead of working in his/her favour. Not only does this application of the provisions protecting medical confidentiality deny the patient any autonomous decision regarding his/her confidences. This case-law also stands in direct conflict with the case-law that upholds the physician's defence rights. Thus, the Cour de Cassation has denied the patient the right to prove his own medical condition with the help of the physician, while allowing the physician to defend him/herself by disclosing someone else's confidences. Given the fundamental value of defence rights, it is surprising that the promoters of the general and absolute nature of medical confidentiality seem to think that the interests thereby protected are not adversely affected if the physician reveals the secrets to defend him/herself, but that the assessment changes dramatically where the patient wants to defend him/herself with the help of the physician. If medical confidentiality is mainly aimed at a protection of the patient's privacy or health care interests, it is difficult to see a good reason for denying the patient the right to compel the physician to testify in favour of the accused patient regarding the patient's own medical confidences. The patient's privacy and health care interests will only be adversely affected where the physician discloses the patient's medical secrets without the patient's consent. If medical confidentiality intends to protect the public interest in promoting health, it is not obvious how society or individual patients could lose their trust in the secrecy of members of the medical profession where they disclose confidential information with the patient's consent. And if medical confidentiality aims to assist the physician in fulfilling his/her role, as without a guarantee of confidentiality, patients may be reluctant to seek advice and help or fully to reveal the information necessary for effective treatment, it is not easy to understand how this interest can be harmed where the

---

[137] Fénaux, D.1988.106.

[138] Mazen (1988), at 90.

[139] Trib. civ. de la Seine, D.1955.588.

[140] Honnorat, Melennec, JCP.1979.I.2936.

physician discloses confidential information with the patient's consent. The reason behind the courts' rulings seems to be the paternalistic view that physicians know better than their patients when to disclose confidential facts and when to refrain from doing so. If this were true, it would make sense to give the physician the choice between protecting medical confidentiality even where the patient has waived his/her interest in keeping the information secret, while the patient should not be in a position to compel the physician to disclose medical confidences. It has been argued, however, that one can expect from the physician, in addition to caring for the body of the patient and to refrain from harming the patient by indiscreet disclosures, to protect the patient when at risk and therefore to serve, if need be, as the patient's witness with regard to the patient's secrets. If the confidence is turned against the patient, this constitutes a real breach of trust on the part of the physician.[141] Some have thus concluded that this case-law very clearly demonstrates the inhuman and unacceptable consequences of attaching a 'general and absolute' nature to medical confidentiality.[142] The case-law mainly creates two problems: it applies different standards to the defence rights of the physician and to those of the patient, and it disregards the patient's right to decide whether his/her medical secrets should be kept confidential or be disclosed.[143]

5 Obligation to disclose certain information

Under certain circumstances, citizens are under a legal obligation, the contravention of which constitutes a criminal offence, to disclose certain facts to the judicial or administrative authorities. In the context of criminal proceedings, three different situations can be of relevance: disclosure for the purpose of crime prevention; disclosure in cases of child neglect and abuse; and disclosure of information regarding the innocence of a person who is under arrest or has been convicted for a crime. Where a physician has received such information in the course of exercising his/her profession, a conflict between the obligation to disclose and the obligation to maintain medical confidentiality arises.

5.1 Crime prevention

Art.434-1 of the Criminal Code determines the circumstances under which the non-disclosure of information for the purpose of crime prevention amounts to a criminal offence, in stating that:

> A person who has information about a crime the commission of which can still be prevented or the effects of which can still be limited, or the authors of which are likely to commit future crimes that could be prevented, and does not inform the judicial or

---

[141] Pradel, JCP.1969.I.2234.
[142] Savatier, JCP.1967.II.15126; see also Mazen (1988), at 90; Merle, Vitu, at 183.
[143] Pradel, JCP.1969.I.2234; Waremberg-Auque, at 249-51.

administrative authorities will be punished with three years of imprisonment and a fine of Euros 45,000. ...

The persons subjected to the professional secret by art.226-13 are exempt from the dispositions of the first paragraph.[144]

It can thus be seen that every citizen is, in principle, under an obligation to disclose information about a criminal offence to the police if its commission or its effects can be averted. The Criminal Code provision introducing this obligation, however, expressly exempts physicians from this duty to disclose. What, then, is the relationship between the obligation to maintain medical confidentiality, on the one hand, and the obligation to disclose, on the other? Given that art.434-1 of the Criminal Code exempts the physician from the obligation to disclose, while art. 226-13 of the Criminal Code does not exempt the physician from the obligation to maintain medical confidentiality where a disclosure is necessary for the purposes of crime prevention, one could think that, similar to the relationship between art.226-13 of the Criminal Code and the obligation to give testimony in criminal court under art.109 of the Code of Criminal Procedure, there is no real conflict of duties and the obligation of medical confidentiality to which no exemption applies should therefore prevail. However, this is not the solution suggested for this particular conflict. In 1973, the Secretary of Justice, when asked about the application of art.62 of the old Criminal Code (which laid down an obligation to disclose information for the purposes of crime prevention and in cases of child abuse), declared that:

> The legislation wanted to leave it to the person bound by the secret to decide, according to his conscience, which conduct to adopt in every individual case, and to decide whether the obligation to disclose justifies or does not justify the disclosure of confidential information. An imperative solution could, in some cases, put at risk the necessary trust in those who receive secrets or confidences, and, in other cases, prevent the denunciation of facts that endanger third parties or the patient himself.[145]

However, art.62 of the old Criminal Code did not exempt physicians from the general obligation to disclose, so that the situation differed from the current situation in that under the old Criminal Code, there was in fact a conflict of duties for which a solution had to be found. In his report to the Assemblée Nationale,[146] François Colcombet voiced the opinion that under the new regime of arts.434-1, 434-3 and 434-11 of the Criminal Code it was still desirable to leave the

---

[144] Art.434-1: Le fait, pour quiconque ayant connaissance d'un crime dont il est encore possible de prévenir ou de limiter les effets, ou dont les auteurs sont susceptibles de commettre de nouveaux crimes qui pourraient être empêchés, de ne pas en informer les autorités judiciares ou adminstratives est puni de trois ans d'emprisonnement et de 45 000 Euros d'amende.

Sauf lorsque la loi en dispose autrement, sont exceptées des dispositions qui précèdent les personnes astreintes au secrets dans les conditions prévues par l'article 226-13.

[145] Quoted from Chomienne, Guéry, ALD.1995.comm.85.

[146] JOAN 26 September 1991, at 2244.

professional the choice to decide according to his/her conscience, in every individual case, which conduct to adopt.[147] At the moment, in the absence of case-law regarding the conflict between the two obligations under the new Criminal Code, it is difficult to assess whether or not the courts would agree and give the physician the free choice between the obligation to maintain the patient's confidence and the obligation to disclose. It is submitted that formalistically, the only consistent solution would be to accept the legislature's decision that the obligation of medical confidentiality to which no exemption has been provided, should have precedence over the obligation to disclose information for the purpose of crime prevention. Any disclosure for this reason would then have to be assessed according to the normal criteria, that is it would have to be established whether or not a criminal justification applies. However, such a formalistic interpretation of the interplay of the different provisions at issue might lead to unfortunate results. If one were to argue that the legislative opinion clearly favoured the interests in medical confidentiality over the interests in crime prevention, neither self-defence nor necessity could apply, as this would circumvent the legislative decision expressed in art.434-1. It is difficult to see that the legislature intended to exclude disclosure of confidential medical information in all situations in which crimes could be prevented, no matter how serious the intended offence and how valuable the interests at risk. On the other hand, the predominant French approach of giving the physician a choice between disclosure and secrecy in all cases of potential crime prevention is equally unsatisfactory, as it does not require any balancing of interests, does not impose proportionality considerations, and does not provide any guidelines as to how such discretion should be exercised.

With regard to disclosure for the mere purpose of criminal prosecution, it was argued that it cannot be the role of the physician to hand the patient over to the police, whatever his/her crime. Every individual must have the possibility of receiving medical treatment without having to fear to be denounced to the police by his/her physician.[148] If the physician holds information regarding the consequences of a crime that has already been committed, he/she has to maintain confidentiality.[149]

5.2 Child abuse

Art.434-3 of the Criminal Code imposes an obligation on every citizen to disclose information about abuse of children or other vulnerable persons to the relevant authorities. Again, there is an exemption from this obligation for medical professionals. The provision states as follows:

A person who has knowledge about ill treatment of or hardship inflicted on a child of less than fifteen years of age or on a person who is not able to take care of him/herself because of his/her age, illness, handicap, physical or mental defect, or pregnancy, and does not

---

[147] See also Alt-Maes, at 306; Lepage, JCP.1999.4.

[148] Mazen (1988), at 121.

[149] Pradel, JCP.1969.I.2234.

inform the judicial or administrative authorities will be punished with three years of imprisonment and a fine of Euros 45,000.

The persons subjected to the professional secret by art.226-13 are exempt from the dispositions of the first paragraph, unless otherwise stated by law.[150]

This provision must be seen together with art.226-14 of the Criminal Code which lists certain situations in which a physician is free to disclose confidential information without being subjected to the punishment foreseen in art.226-13. Art.226-14 states to that effect that:

Article 226-13 is not applicable in cases where the law requires or authorises the disclosure of the secret. In addition, it is not applicable:
  1. to a person who informs the judicial, medical or administrative authorities of any abuse or neglect which has come to his/her knowledge and which was inflicted upon a minor of less than 15 years or upon a person incapable of protecting him/herself on the grounds of his/her age, or physical or mental condition.[151]

The conflict thus differs from that between the obligation to disclose for the purpose of crime prevention and the obligation of medical confidentiality, as the physician is here exempted from both obligations. In this situation, it cannot be said that the obligation to maintain confidentiality was regarded as more important by the legislature, and that any disclosure of confidential patient information related to child abuse will constitute a violation of the duty of confidentiality. All authors who have discussed the conflict between arts.226-14 and 434-3 of the Criminal Code seem to agree that in this case of a real conflict of duties, one should refer to the case-law concerning the provisions of the old Criminal Code[152] and leave the physician the choice as to which obligation to fulfil in each case.[153] Thus, if the physician decides to disclose confidential information, he/she will not commit the offence under art.226-13; and if he/she decides to remain silent, he/she will not commit the offence of breaching an obligation to disclose under art.434-3.

---

[150] Art.434-3: Le fait, pour quiconque ayant eu connaissance de mauvais traitements ou privations infligés à un mineur de quinze ans ou à une personne qui n'est pas en mesure de se protéger en raison de son âge, d'une maladie, d'une infirmité, d'une déficience physique ou psychique ou d'un état de grossesse, de ne pas en informer les autorités judiciaires ou administratives est puni de trois ans d'emprisonnement et de 45 000 Euros d'amende.
Sauf lorsque la loi en dispose autrement, sont exceptées des dispositions qui précèdent les personnes astreintes au secrets dans les conditions prévues par l'article 226-13.

[151] Art.226-14: L'article 226-13 n'est pas applicable dans les cas où la loi impose ou autorise la révélation du secret. En outre, il n'est pas applicable:
1. A celui qui informe les autorités judiciares, médicales ou administratives de sévices ou privations dont il a eu connaissance et qui ont été infligés à un mineur de quinze ans ou à une personne qui n'est pas en mesure de se protéger en raison de son âge ou de son état physique ou psychique.

[152] See, for example, 28 February 1963, CA Aix en Provence, Gaz. Pal. 1963.2.122.

[153] 8 October 1997, Bull. n°329; 8 April 1998, *Dr. pén.* 1998, comm. 11; Rassat (1999), at 410.

While disclosure serves as a justification for a violation of confidentiality, the obligation of confidentiality serves as a justification for non-disclosure.[154] Some reach this conclusion by interpreting art.226-14 Criminal Code as giving an authorisation to disclose information, not an order to do so, so that the physician remains free to decide according to his/her conscience whether to speak up or to keep quiet.[155] The decision of giving the physician the free choice between the two competing obligations has been explained by arguing that it is the sole solution that is in conformity with the intention of the legislature and that it is justified by the concern that otherwise the authors of these cruelties might not consult a physician to seek medical treatment for the victim for fear of risking a prosecution. On the other hand, it must be borne in mind that it is in the interest of the victim that the physician has the right to intervene if he/she thinks that it is necessary.[156] Again, the physician is given discretion without any guidance as to the situations that might justify disclosure and without any requirement of a balancing of the competing interests and of the proportionality of disclosure.

5.3 Protection of the innocent

Another obligation to disclose information exists in the following situation. Art.434-11 of the Criminal Code states:

> A person who has evidence regarding the innocence of a person who is under arrest for investigation or has been convicted of a crime or misdemeanour, and voluntarily refrains from immediately informing the judicial or administrative authorities will be punished with three years of imprisonment and a fine of Euros 45,000. ...
> The persons subjected to the professional secret by art.226-13 are exempt from the dispositions of the first paragraph.[157]

The legal situation regarding the conflict between medical confidentiality, on the one hand, and the interests of someone who is under arrest for investigation, or has been convicted of a criminal offence he/she did not commit, is similar to that of the conflict between medical confidentiality and disclosure for the purpose of crime prevention. While the physician is exempt from the obligation to disclose information to protect the innocent person, he/she is not for that purpose exempt from the obligation of medical confidentiality. Therefore, here again the legislature has unequivocally favoured medical confidentiality and does not seem to leave the

---

154 Roujou de Boubée, Bouloc, Fancillon, Mayaud, at 767.
155 Pradel, Danti-Juan, at 237 and 239; Véron, at 155.
156 Roujou de Boubée, Bouloc, Fancillon, Mayaud, at 404-5.
157 Art.434-11: Le fait pour quiconque connaissant la preuve de l'innocence d'une personne détenue provisoirement ou jugée pour crime ou délit, de s'abstenir volontairement d'en apporter aussitôt le témoignage aux autorités judiciares ou administratives est puni de trois ans d'emprisonement et de 45 000 Euros d'amende. ... Sont également exceptées des dispositions du premier alinéa les personnes astreintes au secret dans les conditions prévues par l'article 226-13.

physician any choice.[158] However, while the courts did not as yet have to deal with that question, most scholars agree that the balancing of the interests involved very clearly comes down in favour of the interests of the innocent and that the obligation to maintain medical confidentiality cannot be used as a justification for the criminal offence of refusing to give testimony in favour of an innocent person. Pradel, for example, argued in his commentary to a decision involving the professional secret of social workers that the only situation in which social workers do not have a choice but rather have to give testimony is where their testimony would allow to establish the innocence of a person unfairly detained or convicted.[159]

Even those promoting the view that exceptions to the principle of medical confidentiality can never be justified by the countervailing interests of third parties, not even where silence requires heroic efforts, submit that the only exception acceptable for the benefit of an overriding public interest is the situation where the physician breaches medical confidentiality in favour of an innocent who was wrongly detained and suggest that in such a case, the physician is under no duty of medical confidentiality.[160] Some distinguish: if the patient is the real perpetrator, the disclosure is less acceptable than where the perpetrator is a third party, given that a disclosure is then particularly harmful to the patient and, accordingly, cannot be justified.[161] On the other hand, it has been conceded that the physician's silence manifestly violates good morals and l'ordre public and that in order to reconcile the competing interests, the physician would have to disclose the facts that establish the innocence of the detainee, without exposing the real perpetrator, at least where the patient objects to the disclosure of his/her identity.[162] This solution may not always lead to satisfactory results, as the physician's allegation is then not amenable to any proof.

The opinions voiced with regard to the resolution of the conflict between the protection of the innocent and the medical secret of a patient seem hardly convincing. First, most of the arguments ignore the fact that the physician is not under conflicting legal obligations which allow for a balancing of interests to take place. Secondly, the discussion shows that most commentators are not entirely clear about the value of the conflicting interests at stake. While it is understandable that some people may value the freedom of a wrongly accused person more than medical confidentiality, it is difficult to comprehend why it makes a difference whether or not it is the patient who committed the crime for which the innocent person has wrongly been detained. This view seems to be based on the fear that the physician-patient relationship may be harmed more where the physician denounces the patient than where the physician denounces a third person who stands outside of the physician-patient relationship. But it is submitted that this does not necessarily have to be the case, as the patient may be as interested in protecting a

---

[158] Rassat (1999), at 412.
[159] Pradel, D.1978.354; see also Mazen(1988), at 131.
[160] Savatier, Auby, Savatier, Péquignot, at 306.
[161] Pradel, JCP.1969.I.2234.
[162] Anzalec, Gaz. Pal. 1971.113.

close friend or relative from criminal prosecution as in his/her own protection. This solution also seems to suggest that the reason behind medical confidentiality is not the patient's interest in controlling the dissemination of confidential personal information, as this interest is as affected where the patient is the perpetrator as it is where the perpetrator is a third person. Nor can it be the purpose of medical confidentiality to protect the public interest in encouraging patients to seek medical treatment to enhance public health, as again, the interest the physician has violated is the same in both cases. It could only make a difference who committed the offence if medical confidentiality were to protect the physician from having to breach medical confidentiality where the disclosure might harm the patient. This demonstrates a rather paternalistic approach, as it is then not the patient who decides what will or will not harm him/her. It is submitted that if one is of the opinion that the interests of the innocent are more important than the interests in medical confidentiality, and that French law leaves scope for a balancing of interests to take place, it cannot make a difference whether the patient or someone else committed the offence.

The offence of Art.434-11 must be committed with intent, which presupposes perfect knowledge of the innocence of the accused.[163]

6 Admissibility of the physician's testimony

Courts usually recognise that if the physician's testimony constitutes a breach of the duty of confidentiality, it must be disregarded.[164] Thus, if the physician surpasses the limits of a permissible disclosure, the judge can neither accept it as evidence nor use evidence already collected this way, as a classic principle of criminal law excludes all evidence acquired in an illegitimate way.[165] Nevertheless, in a decision of 15 December 1942, the Cour de Cassation accepted medical testimony of a physician because the accused had not voiced any opposition to the interrogation of the witness in the course of the preliminary proceedings.[166]

Not every statement made by a witness who is under an obligation to medical confidentiality violates art.226-13 of the Criminal Code and entails the nullity of the record of the statement and of the proceedings. Rather, this consequence only applies if the statement consists of the disclosure of protected information.[167]

7 Search for and seizure of medical records

The search for and seizure of confidential patient documents are governed by the provisions of the Code of Criminal Procedure. According to art.56 of the Code of

---

[163] Roujou de Boubée, Bouloc, Fancillon, Mayaud, at 779-80.
[164] Légal, JCP.1948.II.1582.
[165] Pradel, JCP.1969.I.2234; Thouvenin, at 117-8.
[166] Thouvenin, ibid.
[167] 15 September 1987, JCP.1988.II.21047.

Criminal Procedure, the domicile of third parties to the crime under investigation can be searched by officers of the criminal investigation department for papers, documents and other objects relating to the incriminating facts. He/she is, however, under the obligation to observe all measures necessary to ensure that the professional secret be respected. Given that this provision is aimed at searches at the residence of persons, it is difficult to imagine that it will frequently be of relevance in cases of a search for a physician's medical records.

The Code also contains provisions specifically designed to regulate the search of a physician's surgery. Thus, art.56-1 of the Code of Criminal Procedure states in paragraph 2:

> A search in a surgery ... is executed by a magistrate in the presence either of a responsible member of the professional order or organisation to which the person concerned belongs, or of his representative.[168]

And art.97 of the Code of Criminal Procedure provides:

> If, in the course of the investigation, there is a good reason to search for documents, subject to the needs of the investigation and to the respect, if relevant, for the obligation laid down in paragraph three of the preceding article, the examining magistrate or the officer of the criminal investigation department determined by him are the only persons who have the right to take knowledge of the content before conducting the seizure.[169]

Art.96(3) of the Code of Criminal Procedure to which art.97 refers states:

> However, [the examining magistrate] is under the obligation first to observe all reasonable measures to ensure that the professional secret be respected.[170]

The legal situation can thus be outlined as follows: If access to confidential medical information is sought in the course of police investigations, the police can seize confidential medical documents outside the physician's surgery under the conditions mentioned in art.56, i.e. only persons of a certain status can read through the confidential papers and documents. Also, the officer, before performing the search and seizure, must take all measures that are necessary for the respect of medical confidences (art.56(3)). But it is difficult to know what exactly these measures consist of. If search and seizure take place in a surgery, art.56-1

---

[168] Art.56-1: Les perquisitions dans le cabinet d'un medecin ... sont effectuées par un magistrat et en présence de la personne responsable de l'ordre ou de l'organisation professionnelle à laquelle appartient l'intéressé ou de son représentant.

[169] Art.97: Lorsqu'il y a lieu, en cours d'information, de rechercher des documents et sous réserve des nécessités de l'information et du respect, le cas échéant, de l'obligation stipulée par l'alinéa 3 de l'article précédent, le juge d'instruction ou l'officier de police judiciare par lui commis a seul le droit d'en prendre connaissance avant de procéder à la saisie.

[170] Art.96(3): Toutefois, il a l'obligation de provoquer préalablement toutes mesures utiles pour que soit assuré le respect du secret professionnel et des droits de la défense.

applies, and the operation must be executed by a magistrate in the presence of a member of the professional organisation the physician belongs to. If access to confidential medical documents is sought in the course of investigations of the examining magistrate, he/she is under the obligation to observe all measures necessary for the respect of professional confidentiality (art.96(3)), and the examining magistrate him/herself or the officer of the criminal investigation department specifically determined by him/her are the only persons who have the right to read through the confidential documents before conducting the seizure. Thus, confidential medical documents can be seized in the course of investigations by the police or by the examining magistrate, and the relevant provisions of the Code of Criminal Procedure, apart from making special provisions as to who can conduct the search and examine the material, do not protect such information from state access through search and seizure.

Of course, if confidential patient records can be seized and used in the course of criminal investigations, the state will thereby violate the principle of medical confidentiality. The problem mainly arose in three different situations: (1) the investigation was directed against the patient, and the examining magistrate sought access to confidential medical documents of the accused patient to establish the truth and to use it as evidence against him/her; (2) the patient was not the accused, but the victim, and confidential medical information was needed as evidence against the accused; (3) the investigation was directed against the physician, and access to confidential patient information was needed in the course of this investigation, mainly with regard to fraud or tax offences.

Some case-law sheds light on the courts' attitude towards the seizure of confidential medical documents of the accused. In the case of a man who was accused of having killed his wife and who pretended that he had lost consciousness during the efforts of saving her from drowning and who had been hospitalised immediately after the event, the examining magistrate ordered the seizure of the hospital records to establish whether the accused had in fact been unconscious, or whether he had only simulated unconsciousness. With regard to the question of the lawfulness of the seizure, the Court held that:

> Under the circumstances, the seizure does not constitute a violation of the law or of defence rights. The duty of confidentiality does not prevent the examining magistrate from the seizure of all documents or objects needed to establish the truth. The powers of the examining magistrate under art.81 of the Code of Criminal Procedure[171] are in principle unrestricted.[172]

---

[171] Art.81: The examining magistrate conducts, in conformity with the law, all investigative acts he thinks are necessary to establish the truth. (Le juge d'instruction procède, conformément à la loi, à tous les actes d'information qu'il juge utiles à la manifestation de la verité.)

[172] 24 April 1969, JCP 1970.II.16306.

This holding very clearly demonstrates the attitude of French courts which is generally approved of by legal scholars.[173] As the Code of Criminal Procedure does not restrict the examining magistrate's rights to search for and seize confidential medical documents, courts refuse to read these limitations into the code. However, the Court of Appeal of Aix en Provence somewhat mitigated the effects of this case-law. An examining magistrate had, after the refusal of hospital directors to hand over the list of women who had stayed in the gynaecological clinic, himself collected these lists for the purpose of investigating women for illegal abortions. The examining magistrate did not have a more specific suspicion against the women than the fact that they had attended a gynaecological clinic. The Court held that the examining magistrate had illegally obtained information which was outside the scope of his mission, as not every woman staying in a gynaecological clinic has necessarily had an abortion. More importantly, the court continued that the examining magistrate was under an obligation to undertake all measures necessary to respect professional confidentiality and that this obligation had been violated when the magistrate proceeded despite the legitimate objections to the seizure voiced by the hospital directors on the grounds of medical confidentiality.[174]

In a decision regarding confidential medical information of a victim rather than of an accused, the Cour de Cassation has held that judges, when introducing hospital records as evidence in court, necessarily expose facts that are covered by medical confidentiality. Therefore, instead of introducing the records as such, the court argued that it would be more protective of medical confidentiality if judges gave medical experts who have to examine the injured person the mandate to inspect the hospital records.[175] This case-law has been criticised. Melennec, for example, stated that the court does not have the power to authorise a medical expert to consult the medical records of his/her colleagues, as a simple mission of expertise could then result in circumventing the principle of medical confidentiality, as well as the safeguards provided by the Code of Criminal Procedure. According to him, the only solution for a judge who wants access to confidential documents would therefore be a seizure of the documents.[176] Pradel suggests a different approach, arguing that the procedure promoted by the courts can be lawful, but only if limited to situations in which the court could also obtain the information directly from the treating physician. Under those circumstances, it is argued, the recourse to an expert is justified because the magistrate does not have the technical knowledge to assess the evidence. However, Pradel limits these restrictions to cases in which medical information of someone other than the accused is concerned, as he thinks that if the investigation is directed against the patient, search and seizure are always legitimate.[177] However, no principles seem to support this view.

---

[173] See, for example, Chappart, D.1969.637.
[174] 28 February 1963, CA Aix en Provence, Gaz. Pal. 1963.2.122.
[175] 20 January 1976, Bull n° 23; 16 November 1976, Bull n° 327.
[176] Melennec, Gaz. Pal. 1980.doct.145.
[177] Pradel, JCP.1969.I.2234.

The approach adopted towards searches for and seizures of confidential patient records seems to depend largely upon the interpretation of art.96(3) of the Code of Criminal Procedure. This article could be interpreted as supporting the argument that an invocation of medical confidentiality against measures by the examining magistrate restricts his/her powers, given that he/she is under an obligation to take all necessary preliminary measures to guarantee respect for medical confidentiality. But this is not how art.96(3) is normally understood. Instead, that provision is interpreted to impose upon the examining magistrate the restriction that a search of a physician's practice can only lawfully be performed in the presence of a member of the Medical Council, but not as prohibiting all searches in surgeries. This interpretation is widely accepted, as many agree that in order to establish the truth, the examining magistrate must be able to have recourse to all means the law puts at his/her disposal. Therefore, no restrictions on the examining magistrate's powers that were not mentioned in the Code of Criminal Procedure should be tolerated.[178] Chappart came to the same conclusion, arguing that the law does not guarantee absolute protection of medical confidentiality, and that the necessity to determine the truth justifies an exception from that protection.[179] It has been suggested that if confidential patient records could not be seized, the physician would be given too much power. Sometimes confidential information will be exclusively known to the physician, and if no search powers existed it would be entirely in the hands of the physician whether or not truth-finding was possible in a specific case.[180] As the argument goes, the interests of society, and the interests of the individual imperatively request that criminal justice can be accomplished. Even though the search of surgeries is sometimes met with indignation, some authors promote that it is difficult to argue that the protection of medical confidentiality by the Criminal Code could be interpreted so as to allow for an impairment of the interests of criminal justice. If medical confidentiality were to prevail over the interests of justice, medical confidentiality would be placed above the law, when it is the law that has institutionalised medical confidentiality in the first place.[181]

However, it is also in the interest of society and the individual that the powers of the examining magistrate are strictly confined to those granted by the law. These two imperatives are reconciled, in that while search and seizure are possible in physicians' surgeries, rigid safeguards apply. The physician cannot object to the search and seizure in his/her surgery. The judge, however, cannot indiscriminately seize all confidential records he/she finds, but the seizure must rather be limited to that which is necessary in the circumstances. Waremberg-Auque has argued, however, that the right to establish the truth cannot prevail over medical confidentiality, as the search for the truth can never legitimise the use of unfair means of collecting evidence. The interests of justice and of society can never paralyse the exercise of primordial human rights such as the right to medical

---

[178] Thouvenin, at 118-9.
[179] Chappart, D.1969.637.
[180] Thouvenin, at 135.
[181] Mazen (1988), at 144; Melennec, Gaz. Pal. 1980.doct.145.

confidentiality.[182] It thus seems as if the interpretation of the scope and limits of search powers depends on the value accorded to medical confidentiality, on the one hand, and to the interests of justice, on the other.

In cases in which the investigation is directed against the physician, slightly different considerations apply. In one case, a physician had tried to use medical confidentiality to escape accountability by unnecessarily entering non-anonymised patient data into medical records so that, besides the facts relevant for bookkeeping, they also contained the name and the diagnosis of the patients. When asked to make his records available, he refused to do so, invoking his obligation to medical confidentiality. The Court decided that the seizure of the records or the examination of the records by tax officers did not constitute the disclosure of confidential medical information.[183] In his commentary, Savatier reasoned:

> The secret belongs exclusively to the patient, as do all other details of his intimate life. The court seems to have misjudged the respect owed to the autonomous freedom of the patient who is the only master of his confidences when allowing a disclosure of the confidences to the administration and the court as a consequence of a concealment by the physician, even though it was unlawful. In this context, the physician's behaviour is of little importance. One should not treat medical confidentiality as being dependent upon the sanctions which the physician is trying to avoid, given that the confidence which is part of the patient's intimate sphere, does not belong to the physician, but rather to the patient, and given that it is based on the public interest. Confidences are therefore not sufficiently protected by ensuring that they will only be revealed to the closed circle of administrators.[184]

Savatier continued that the boundaries of medical confidentiality should be insurmountable, and that the judge should reject the admission of medical records, denying that tax fraud committed by the physician could justify a different approach. He concluded that the prosecution should always refuse to collect as evidence those documents that refer to confidential patient information, as medical confidentiality requires that the patient be given the guarantee that his confidences, when revealed to a qualified confidant, will never be transmitted to any third party. Strangely, in the end Savatier nevertheless approved of the outcome of the decision because the information at issue did not concern the patient's intimate sphere. Pradel suggests a different approach. According to him, if a seizure of confidential information takes place in the course of an investigation directed against the physician, the right to seizure is uncontested, but it is limited where the patient has expressly requested that his/her data will not be disclosed, as search and seizure must stop in front of the intimate sphere the protection of which is a right of the patient. As search and seizure can only be effected where it is essential for the investigation, they should only be allowed under exceptional circumstances.[185]

---

[182] Waremberg-Auque, at 253 and 256.

[183] 11 February 1960, JCP.1960.II.11604.

[184] Savatier, JCP.1960.II.11604.

[185] Pradel, JCP.1969.I.2234.

Melennec, on the other hand, argued that it is obvious that a physician cannot invoke medical confidentiality to cover his/her own irregularities, as medical confidentiality was not introduced for the benefit of the physician, but rather as a right aimed at the protection of the patient's personality rights.[186] It is submitted that this argument can only justify a seizure of confidential patient records where the patient has consented to this measure, as otherwise the patient's personality rights are at risk.

Another question is whether a physician can voluntarily submit medical certificates containing confidential patient information. In that respect, it has been decided on 14 February 1952 that:

> With the exception of cases in which a physician acts as an expert witness, he cannot, without failing his professional obligation, deliver a medical certificate containing observations about his patient's condition to a third party, given that the patient is the only person who can legitimately claim the issuance of a medical certificate about his condition to use it according to his own wishes. Therefore, a physician who applies first aid to an accident victim and then delivers the medical certificate regarding the victim's injuries to the police station in charge of the inquiry violates his obligation of medical confidentiality.[187]

When comparing case-law with regard to the physician's testimony in court with that concerning the seizure of confidential patient records, it seems justified to observe that art.96 of the Code of Criminal Procedure gives the judge the possibility to circumvent the prohibition of forcing the physician to give testimony in court, by seizing the relevant patient records instead. In the realm of investigative measures under the Code of Criminal Procedure, a balancing of the interest in medical confidentiality and the interests of justice is performed, and the predominant opinion in France very clearly favours the interests of justice. This is rather surprising when compared to the situation of a physician's testimony in criminal court. As outlined above, where the physician's testimony regarding confidential patient information is sought in criminal proceedings, the law has exempted the physician from the obligation to testify. This demonstrates the legislature's view that in case of a conflict between the obligation to testify in the interests of justice, and the obligation to maintain patient confidences, the latter prevails. The Criminal Code thus contains a value decision favouring the interest in medical confidentiality over the interests of justice. In the light of this, the argument that in the context of the seizure of medical records the interests in medical confidentiality cannot outweigh the interests of justice is inconsistent and unconvincing. However, it is possible that this approach is based on the thought that the interest in medical confidentiality is affected more seriously when the physician is forced to testify in court, as this involves an active participation of the physician in the disclosure of the medical secret, while in the case of a seizure of

---

[186] Melennec, Gaz. Pal.1980.doct.145.
[187] JCP.1952.II.7030.

medical records, the state obtains access to pre-existing records by the use of compulsion, so that it is at least arguable that the harm done to the physician-patient relationship differs in the two situations under examination. This could also explain why medical records can be seized, but the physician cannot voluntarily hand over the very same records without committing a criminal offence. This protects the physician rather than the patient, as the physician does not actively have to breach the medical secret, while the patient's medical information is still available through the means of search and seizure.

8 Summary and conclusion

The Courts as well as the majority of legal writers promote the view that the physician's obligation to maintain medical confidentiality is absolute and that no one can exempt the physician from that duty. However, the protection of medical confidentiality is not as absolute as it may seem. First, the law itself has created exemptions from the physician's obligation to keep the patient's medical secrets. Art.226-14 of the Criminal Code, for example, provides for an exemption in cases of child abuse and the abuse of other vulnerable persons. Where the physician obtains knowledge of such abuse in the course of his/her profession, he/she is free to decide whether or not to report his/her findings or to maintain medical confidentiality. With regard to the physician's role as a witness in criminal court, art.109 of the Code of Criminal Procedure exempts the physician from the obligation imposed on all citizens to give testimony in court. Thus, the legislature has clearly demonstrated that in the case of a general conflict between the interest in medical confidentiality and the interests of truth-finding in criminal proceedings, the interest in medical confidentiality prevails. Therefore, the physician is only allowed to testify in criminal court where a legal justification applies to justify the breach of medical confidentiality. However, the situation is entirely different where the physician's defence rights are at stake. In that case, the courts and the predominant opinion among legal scholars give the physician the right to breach medical confidentiality, as defence rights are regarded as more important than medical confidentiality. It is interesting that the discussion only focuses on the defence rights of the physician, while the defence rights of the patient or of third parties are not considered. With regard to the patient, the situation is dominated by the view that the patient cannot, by giving consent to the physician's testimony, relieve the physician from the obligation to medical confidentiality. As the physician's obligation to maintain medical confidentiality is absolute, no one, not even the patient can relieve the physician from this obligation. Therefore, the patient's consent will not have the effect of negating the physician's criminal responsibility for a breach of medical confidentiality. As case-law shows, this is so even where the patient wants to use the physician's testimony for defence purposes. Thus, medical confidentiality is more important than the patient's defence rights, but not more important than the physician's defence rights.

Arts.434-1, 434-3, and 434-11 of the Criminal Code create obligations to disclose information about crimes the effects of which can still be prevented or mitigated, about the innocence of a person under arrest or already convicted, and about child abuse. All three provisions contain an exemption from this obligation for physicians. In the case of child abuse, the physician is thus neither under an obligation to maintain medical confidentiality, as art.226-14 of the Criminal Code contains an exemption from that duty in such a case, nor under an obligation to disclose the information. The physician is then given a choice as to which obligation to fulfil in the individual case. In the cases of disclosure for the purpose of crime prevention or protection of an innocent detainee, the physician is under an obligation to maintain medical confidentiality, as no exemption applies, but not under an obligation to disclose. While this would seem to make clear the legislature's intention to demonstrate that priority has been given to medical confidentiality, this is not the conclusion drawn by legal writers. The predominant opinion rather promotes the view that the physician should be allowed to decide which obligation to fulfil, and that a breach of one of the obligations should be justified by the conflicting obligation the fulfilment of which caused the breach. It can be seen that while the patient cannot relieve the physician from the obligation to maintain medical confidentiality, the physician's decision to disclose based on his/her conscience can in certain situation justify a breach of this obligation.

Where a patient's medical records are sought in the context of criminal investigations, the physician is not allowed to hand them over to the police voluntarily. However, they are not exempt from search and seizure. The sole protection medical confidentiality receives in that context is that some safeguards apply to make sure that only certain designated persons can seize and take knowledge of such records. It is interesting to contrast the almost unlimited powers to seize medical records with the fact that the physician cannot even be forced to testify in criminal court at the patient's request. This means that the patient's medical records can be used by the prosecution against the patient. Where the prosecution's case is thus based on the patient's confidential medical information, the patient cannot compel the physician to testify in order, for example, to give explanations of his/her notes that may be favourable to the accused patient.

It is interesting to note that statutory law very clearly outlines the obligations of the physician, including, in most cases of conflict, which obligation should prevail, and that it is always, with the exception of cases of child abuse, the obligation of medical confidentiality that is given precedence. However, courts as well as legal scholars are far from accepting this approach. Indeed, the predominant interpretation of these statutes confers upon the physician the power to decide how to reconcile the conflict between fundamental individual and public interests, even though these conflicts have been addressed by the legislature. While a formalistic approach excluding disclosure in all cases of crime prevention or of the protection of the innocent from wrongful convictions does not take sufficient account of the interests to be protected, to leave a decision of whether or not to disclose patient information, thereby violating a patient's fundamental right to privacy, to the physician without imposing any conditions, such as the proportionality of the disclosure in a given case, does not adequately protect the interests of the patient.

Case-law as well as the academic discussion point towards a very paternalistic approach to the physician's role in the physician-patient relationship as well as in society. Only where the physician thinks that the particular physician-patient relationship, the reputation of the medical profession or the interests of society demand that in a given case respect for medical confidentiality is more important than the competing interests of justice, will the patient's confidences be protected. On the other hand, where the patient does not have an interest in keeping his/her medical information secret and therefore authorises the physician to disclose such information, this decision will not bind the physician and the physician remains free to decide whether or not disclosure is the best approach to adopt in that specific situation. French law of medical confidentiality thus aims less at the protection of the patient's privacy interests and more at the protection of the integrity of the physician-patient relationship as defined from the physicians' perspective.

Chapter 5

German Law

In this chapter, a first part will introduce how medical confidentiality is protected as part of the constitutional personality right and by criminal, contract and tort law. The second part will analyse how courts resolve conflicts between medical confidentiality and the interests in crime prevention and criminal prosecution by interpreting the relevant provisions of the Criminal Code and the Code of Criminal Procedure in the light of the constitutional protection of medical confidentiality.

PART 1 – PROTECTION OF MEDICAL CONFIDENTIALTY

1 Medical confidentiality as a fundamental right

In German law, fundamental rights are protected both under the German Constitution (Basic Law - BL) and under the European Convention on Human Rights.

1.1 Protection under the German Constitution[1]

The right to medical confidentiality is not expressly guaranteed by the German Constitution; neither is the right to privacy. However, the Federal Constitutional Court (Bundesverfassungsgericht), the highest German court dealing exclusively with constitutional questions, inferred the constitutional protection of personality rights, including the right to privacy, from Arts 2(1) and 1(1) BL, stating as follows:

> Art.2(1) BL: Everyone has the right to the free development of his personality, insofar as he does not violate the rights of others or the constitutional order or the moral law.[2]
> Art.1(1) BL: The dignity of the human person is inviolable. It is the duty of all state authority to have regard to it and to respect it.[3]

---

[1] The translation of Federal Constitutional Court decisions is partly based on Michalowski, Woods, at 117-9.

[2] Art.2(1): Jeder hat das Recht auf die freie Entfaltung seiner Persönlichkeit, soweit er nicht die Rechte anderer verletzt und nicht gegen die verfassungsmäßige Ordnung oder das Sittengesetz verstößt.

[3] Art.1(1): Die Würde des Menschen ist unantastbar. Sie zu achten und zu schützen ist Verpflichtung aller staatlichen Gewalt.

The Federal Constitutional Court argued that freedom of self-determination as guaranteed by Art.2(1) BL could only be exercised effectively if the state refrained from interfering with the private sphere of the individual. The Court also stressed the importance of respecting the individual's intimate and private sphere to preserve his/her human dignity. This reference to Art.1(1) BL considerably strengthens the protection of the personality right, as human dignity is accorded the highest value under the German Basic Law. According to the Federal Constitutional Court, the personality right following from Art.2(1) in conjunction with Art.1(1) BL protects every individual's interest that certain personal and intimate information be kept secret and need not be disclosed. As the Court held in its *Personal Diary Decision*:[4]

> The personality right as protected by Art.2(1) in conjunction with Art.1(1) BL guarantees in principle the right of the individual to decide him/herself when and to what extent to disclose personal facts, a right which follows from the principle of autonomy.[5]

With regard to the question of what information is protected by the personality right, the Federal Constitutional Court included, *inter alia*, medical records[6] and medical-psychological reports.[7] In its *Medical Records Decision*,[8] the Federal Constitutional Court explained the operation of the constitutional protection of the right to privacy as follows:

> The Basic Law grants every individual an inviolate sphere of private life which is free from state encroachment. The constitutional tenet for respect of the intimate sphere of the individual is based on the right to the free development of one's personality which is guaranteed by Art.2(1) BL. When determining the content and scope of that right, the fact that, according to Art.1(1) BL, human dignity is inviolate and must be protected by all state authority must be taken into consideration. ... However, not the entire private sphere falls under the absolute protection of the basic right under Art. (1) in tandem with Art.1(1) BL. The individual as a part of a community rather has to accept state interventions which are based on an overriding community interest under strict application of the principle of proportionality, as long as they do not affect the inviolate sphere of private life.[9]

The Federal Constitutional Court has thus developed a system whereby the private life of the individual is divided into different spheres, and the extent of protection awarded to the individual's private life depends on the sphere affected by the state intrusion. While the intimate sphere of the individual is inviolate, and can thus not be intruded upon by the state under any circumstances, other spheres of private life,

---

[4] BVerfGE 80, 367 (1989).
[5] Ibid., at 373; see also the *National Census Case*, BVerfGE 65, 1, 42 (1983).
[6] BVerfGE 32, 373 (1972).
[7] BVerfGE 89, 69 (1993).
[8] BVerfGE 32, 373 (1972).
[9] Ibid., at 379.

though constitutionally protected, are open to restrictions if the intervention aims at the protection of an overriding community interest. To understand the degree of constitutional protection awarded to medical confidentiality, it is thus important to know which sphere within the realm of private life confidential medical information belongs to. The Federal Constitutional Court clarified this point in the above-cited decision by holding that:

> As medical records contain statements regarding the case history, the diagnosis and therapeutic measures, even though they do not concern the inviolate intimate sphere, they nevertheless concern the private sphere of the patient. As such, they are protected against state access by the basic right of Art. 2(1) in conjunction with Art. 1(1) BL. This applies in particular to knowledge of the patient's medical condition that the physician gained in the course of his professional duty and which he laid down in writing. It is not important whether these notes refer to illnesses, ailments or problems the disclosure of which would incriminate the patient, would otherwise embarrass him or would be detrimental to his social reputation. Rather, the wish of the individual to keep free from the view of third parties such highly personal matters as the assessment of his physical condition by a physician in general deserves protection.[10]

The personality right thus not only guarantees that the individual does not have to disclose embarrassing or detrimental information, but further respects the interest of the individual to keep all personal information to him/herself. This is important, as it demonstrates that the constitutional protection of medical confidentiality in Germany aims to protect the patient's interest in keeping private information to him/herself, regardless of the information's content. The protection thus guarantees the patient's autonomy in deciding which private information to disclose or not to disclose. Even the fact that the patient is suffering from a cold, normally not in itself giving rise to any embarrassment of the patient, is protected by the patient's privacy right, as it is up to the patient to decide whether or not to disclose this information to anyone.

In the more recent *Medical-Psychological Reports Decision*,[11] the Federal Constitutional Court had to decide a case in which the complainant's ability to drive motor vehicles was at doubt after he had been caught smoking cannabis. The Road Traffic Authority threatened that his driving licence be withdrawn unless he agreed to a medical-psychological examination and submitted a report to the effect that his ability to drive a motor vehicle was not diminished. In that case, the Federal Constitutional Court summarised the protection awarded by the personality right as follows:

> This right protects generally against the collection and transmission of results regarding [a person's] medical condition, mental condition or character ... . This protection is the more intense, the closer the data are linked with the person's intimate sphere which, as an inviolate sphere of private life, requires respect by and protection against all state authority ... . The report requested by the Road Traffic Authorities presupposes the

---

[10] Ibid., at 379-80.
[11] BVerfGE 89, 69 (1993).

collection of intimate details which are protected by the personality right. This not only applies to the medical part of the examination, but even more so to its psychological part.[12]

Given that the requested report would have included the personal and medical history of the person, the Federal Constitutional Court concluded that its content was even more closely linked with the patient's intimate sphere than purely medical diagnoses and therefore received even stronger protection by Art. 2(1) and Art. 1(1) BL. It can thus be seen that even though all medical information is protected from unwanted disclosure by the personality right, the extent of protection depends on the content of the information, particularly on the degree of intimacy of the relevant information. It seems as if the Court applies an objective, rather than a subjective standard when deciding on the degree of sensitivity of personal information. It thus substitutes its own view on this matter for that of the autonomous patient.

The privacy right protects the private sphere from state interference, that is the individual is protected against forced disclosure of medical information. As the protection of medical records shows, the constitutional guarantee extends to medical information entrusted to the physician. It could of course be argued that entrusting information to a third party always carries a risk of disclosure, and that protection of confidential personal information can therefore only be ensured as long as the individual keeps this information to him/herself. It would then follow that a patient who confides certain medical secrets in his/her physician would lose the protection of the privacy right by the very fact of this disclosure to the physician, a third party. The Federal Constitutional Court, however, rejected this view, arguing that:

The right to respect for the private sphere imposes limits on the state even where the individual communicates with others. There is often an irrefutable need to attend representatives of certain healing and counselling professions. Efficient help can frequently only be expected if the individual totally reveals himself and makes them accessories of private areas of his life. On the other hand, he has an interest that those facts will not come to the knowledge of third parties. The principal preservation of this interest in secrecy is the necessary prerequisite for the trust, which he must place in the physician for his own sake, and it is also the basis for the successful work of those whose help he requires. Otherwise he would only have a choice between accepting a disclosure of his private sphere or to do without proper treatment and advice.[13]

In another decision, the Federal Constitutional Court added that:

All the professions [listed in S. 53(1)(3) of the Code of Criminal Procedure] have in common that their exercise typically includes services which can be characterised as individual advice in personal, legal, financial and economic matters or as immediately serving the health of the human person (counselling and healing profession). Such services

---

[12] Ibid., at 82-3.
[13] BVerfGE 33, 367, 375-6 (1972).

- more frequently and more intensely than other professional activities - touch upon areas in which confidentiality interests of the individual which are worthy of protection must be respected. They are, therefore, particularly dependent upon awarding the client or patient who enlists their help the opportunity to confide in them freely, openly and without inhibition, without having to fear the disclosure of the facts and circumstances that the other party finds out in the course of his profession.[14]

Also:

A person seeking medical treatment must and can expect that everything the physician learns about his medical condition in the course of exercising his profession will remain secret and will not come to the knowledge of unauthorised persons. Only then can the trust which forms part of the basic prerequisites of medical action, as it increases the chances of healing and therefore - on the whole - serves the purpose of maintaining efficient medical welfare services, be created between the patient and the physician.[15]

An analysis of this case law shows that according to the Federal Constitutional Court, the state does not have to respect the confidentiality of all information an individual confides in other people regardless of the circumstances. In the context of certain professional relationships including the physician-patient relationship, however, the state must respect the individual's interest in keeping confidential information he/she has entrusted to the members of these professions, given that the individual, when in need of professional help, would otherwise have to fear the disclosure of all relevant information, if for example medical records could be seized or the physician be forced to give testimony in court regarding the patient's confidential medical records. The cited case law reveals that the Federal Constitutional Court is trying to preserve a variety of interests when upholding medical confidentiality. First and foremost, the patient's autonomy is protected by this interpretation of the right to privacy. In a situation in which the patient needs medical treatment, patient autonomy would be curtailed were the patient reduced to a choice between foregoing medical treatment, or seeking treatment and risking disclosure of confidential information. Contrary to other situations in which the individual reveals intimate details to a third party without any particular need to do so, here the patient must confide this information in a third party in order to preserve his/her interest in physical or mental integrity. Under such circumstances, the state would drastically infringe upon the patient's right to safeguard his/her interests if medical confidentiality were not upheld. The interest of the patient in controlling the disclosure of personal information is also protected. Accordingly, medical confidentiality is protected to safeguard the individual's informational and decisional privacy, and the considerations on which the constitutional protection is based are mainly deontological. At the same time, the members of the medical profession have an interest in the protection of medical confidentiality, as in the view of the Federal Constitutional Court, without such a guarantee they would not be able to exercise their profession effectively. In addition, there is the public

---

[14] BVerfGE 38, 312, 323 (1975).
[15] BVerfGE 32, 373, 380 (1972).

interest in preserving public health, as there is a fear that without medical confidentiality, patients might refrain from seeking medical advice and treatment, thus putting their own health and possibly that of others at risk. This could also have adverse consequences for society. Therefore, under the German Basic Law the state has to respect the confidentiality of the physician-patient relationship as a constitutional value.

How exactly does this constitutional recognition of the confidentiality of a patient's medical information impact on the physician-patient relationship? It is important to note that all state organs, but not citizens, are bound by the basic rights.[16] It follows that physicians are not under any constitutional obligation to maintain the confidences of their patients. However, all state activity, including parliamentary legislation and court decisions, must comply with constitutional principles. Consequently, given that the state is under a constitutional obligation to protect medical confidentiality, the law governing the physician-patient relationship must conform to this constitutional tenet. The influence of constitutional principles on the provisions of criminal law and criminal procedure dealing with medical confidentiality will become obvious throughout this chapter.

1.2 European Convention on Human Rights

In Germany, the ECHR came into force on 3 December 1953. The competence of the European Court on Human Rights (Article 46 of the ECHR) and of the Commission to receive individual petitions (Article 25 of the ECHR) were recognised in 1955. According to the pre-dominant opinion, the ECHR does not enjoy constitutional status, but rather merely has the status of ordinary law.[17] This means that the incompatibility of a statute with provisions of the ECHR cannot be challenged before the Federal Constitutional Court. However, the Federal Constitutional Court takes the stance that statutes and even the Basic Law itself must be interpreted in conformity with the ECHR, as long as such interpretation does not award less protection of the basic rights as would otherwise be awarded under domestic law.[18] Statutes must be interpreted in the light of Germany's obligations under international law, regardless of whether the statutes came into force prior or subsequent to the relevant treaty. Given the extensive protection of basic rights under the Basic Law, it was long felt that the ECHR could only be of limited value in this area of law. However, the European Court of Human Rights in some cases came to the conclusion that Germany insufficiently protected certain Convention rights. In *Niemitz v Germany*,[19] for example, the European Court of Human Rights had to decide a case regarding the search of a law firm in Germany that was based on a search warrant phrased in rather broad terms. The Court came to the conclusion that a breach of Article 8(1) of the ECHR had occurred. In the same case, the German Federal Constitutional Court had declined to accept a

---

[16] BVerfGE 7, 198, 204-5 (1958).
[17] Jarass/Pieroth, 12a to Art.1.
[18] See BVerfGE 74, 358, 370 (1987).
[19] Judgment of 16 December 1992, Series A, No.251-B.

constitutional complaint for adjudication on the ground that it did not offer sufficient prospect of success. It can thus be seen that in some cases, the protection awarded by the ECHR can be wider than that enjoyed under the Basic Law. Therefore, while medical confidentiality receives protection under Arts 2(1), 1(1) BL, recourse to the ECHR may nevertheless be useful in some cases in which the European Court of Human Rights awards more extensive protection than the Federal Constitutional Court.

2 Protection under criminal law

A very important provision in the context of the protection of medical confidentiality is s.203 of the Criminal Code which makes it a criminal offence for members of certain professions to breach their duty of confidentiality:

S.203 - Breach of private confidences
(1) A person who, without authorisation, discloses a secret of another, namely a secret that belongs to the private sphere of life or a company or business secret, that was confided in him or the knowledge of which he obtained in his capacity as
1. physician, dentist, veterinary, pharmacist or member of any other healing profession the exercise or the use of the job title of which is subject to an education regulated by the state,
2. professional psychologist in the possession of an academic degree that is recognised by the state ...
will be punished with imprisonment of up to one year or with a fine.[20]

Thus, physicians and members of the other health care professions listed in s.203(1) of the Criminal Code commit a criminal offence if they reveal patient confidences under the circumstances mentioned in s.203 of the Criminal Code. For s.203(1) of the Criminal Code to apply, the disclosure must concern a secret. Facts are secret if they are only known to a limited number of people. If a rumour exists regarding the confidential fact, that is if, for example, several people suspect that a patient might be infected with HIV, and if they gossip about this, the patient's HIV status is still considered a secret as long as those rumours are unconfirmed. The physician's disclosure would then add credibility to the rumour.[21] However, facts

---

[20] S.203:
(1) Wer unbefugt ein fremdes Geheimnis, namentlich ein zum persönlichen Lebensbereich gehörendes Geheimnis oder ein Betriebs- oder Geschäftsgeheimnis, offenbart, das ihm als
1. Arzt, Zahnarzt, Tierarzt, Apotheker oder Angehörigen eines anderen Heilberufs, der für die Berufsausübung oder die Führung der Berufsbezeichnung eine staatlich geregelte Ausbildung erfordert,
2. Berufspsychologen mit staatlich anerkannter wissenschaftlicher Abschlußprüfung, ...
anvertraut worden oder sonst bekanntgeworden ist, wird mit Freiheitsstrafe bis zu einem Jahr oder mit Geldstrafe bestraft.
[21] RGSt 26, 5, 7 (1894).

are no longer secret if they have been made known publicly.[22] Information is only protected as a 'secret' by s.203 of the Criminal Code if the person the facts relate to has a reasonable interest in keeping it secret.[23] But this requirement is interpreted extensively, to exclude only situations in which a desire to keep facts confidential seems totally arbitrary.[24] It is therefore not necessary that the information is potentially embarrassing, but it is rather sufficient that the patient wants it to remain confidential.

The physician must have learned about the secret in his/her position as a medical professional. S.203 of the Criminal Code expressly includes the protection of facts that were confided in the physician, and of facts the physician found out about in the course of his/her profession. The protection is not restricted to medical facts. Thus, if a patient for example confides in the physician more general facts about his/her private life that are not directly linked to the patient's medical problem, these confidences are still protected by s.203, as they indirectly support the physician-patient relationship and help create the trust necessary for medical treatment.[25] Facts are protected without having been confided in the physician by the patient, if they came to the physician's knowledge in the exercise of his/her profession. Thus, if a physician who was called to the home of a patient overhears a conversation between the patient's relatives, the obligation to medical confidentiality applies, as this knowledge was obtained by the physician in the course of his/her profession. Medical confidentiality is thus not only protected with regard to observations concerning the patient's health, but all other observations linked with the exercise of the medical profession are protected, too, so that for example information related to the car in which a patient came to the doctor, or to the identity of the person who accompanied the patient, is covered by medical confidentiality.[26]

The obligation of medical confidentiality begins with the initiation of the physician-patient relationship and embraces the name of the patient and the very fact that the patient saw the physician and why.[27] Medical confidentiality not only encompasses secrets relating to the patient, but also confidences of third parties, if the physician gained knowledge of this information in the course of treating his/her patient. Therefore, if a physician is told by his patient that his wife is an alcoholic or that she is having an affair, this information is protected by medical confidentiality, and a revelation will constitute a criminal offence under s.203 of the Criminal Code.[28]

---

[22] Schönke/Schröder-Lenckner, 6 to s.203.

[23] OLG Düsseldorf JMBlNW 1990, 153.

[24] KG NJW 1992, 2771; Schönke/Schröder-Lenckner, 7 to s.203.

[25] Schönke/Schröder-Lenckner, 14 to s.203.

[26] BGH NJW 1985, 2203, 2204.

[27] Ibid.; BGH JZ 2000, 683, 684; Gramberg-Danielsen, Kern, NJW 1998, at 2710; Laufs/Uhlenbruck-Ulsenheimer, at 550; but see LG Oldenburg NJW 1992, 1563, stating that the disclosure of data showing that a person had received dental treatment was not a violation of medical confidentiality.

[28] Müller-Dietz, at 42.

For a breach of medical confidentiality to be a criminal offence, the disclosure must be made without authorisation or legal justification. Thus, no criminal offence can be committed if the patient has waived his/her right to medical confidentiality, as medical confidentiality is only protected by the Criminal Code as long as the person the information relates to, that is in most cases the patient, has an interest in keeping the information confidential.[29]

The opinions as to the purpose behind the protection of medical confidentiality and, in particular, behind s.203(1) no.1 of the Criminal Code are split. While some argue that s.203(1) of the Criminal Code exclusively[30] or at least mainly[31] aims at the protection of the privacy rights of the individual, others support the view that the main purpose behind s.203(1) of the Criminal Code is the protection of the public interest in the general trust in members of the medical profession. Medical confidentiality, it is argued, is significant for society, given that if the patient cannot rely on the discretion of his/her physician, public health might be endangered, as patients will then be reluctant to seek medical advice and treatment.[32] There is thus a utilitarian argument favouring medical confidentiality. However, the privacy argument is more important. When the current version of s.203(1) of the Criminal Code was enacted in 1974, the legislature included it in a newly introduced chapter called 'Violation of the personal sphere of life and intimacy', in which different provisions aiming at the protection of the personal sphere were brought together. This demonstrates that the legislative intent behind the protection of the professional secret was to guarantee the patient's personal and intimate sphere, and it underlines the significance attached to privacy.[33] The Parliamentary debates also show that the legislative purpose behind s.203(1) of the Criminal Code was the protection of the constitutional privacy interests of the patients guaranteed by Arts 2(1), 1(1) BL.[34] In addition, according to s.205(1) of the Criminal Code, the offence will be prosecuted exclusively upon request of the person concerned. This only makes sense if the provision is mainly aimed at the protection of the individual interests of the patient, as the protection of public interests that go beyond the interests of the individual cannot be left at the discretion of the individual, but will rather normally be prosecuted *ex officio*.[35] While it can be seen that the argument that s.203(1) of the Criminal Code serves the protection of the patient's privacy rights is more convincing than the public health argument, the pre-dominant opinion in Germany adopts the view that s.203(1) of the Criminal Code protects both the patient's privacy interest and the

---

[29] Schönke/Schröder-Lenckner, 22 to s.203.
[30] Leipziger Kommentar-Schünemann, 14-15 to s.203; Nomos Kommentar-Jung, 3 to s.203; Ostendorf, JR 1981, at 448; Schünemann, ZStW 90 (1978), at 57.
[31] BGH (Civil Senate) JZ 1994, 46; Bay ObLG NJW 1987, 1492, 1493; OLG Oldenburg NJW 1992, 758, 759; Kreuzer, ZStW 100 (1988), at 804; Laufs, NJW 1975, at 1434.
[32] Schönke/Schröder-Lenckner, 3 to s.203.
[33] Laufs, NJW 1975, at 1433.
[34] BT-Drucksache 7/550, at 235.
[35] Kreuzer, ZStW 100 (1988), at 803-4; Ostendorf, JR 1981, at 446; Schmitz, JA 1996, at 772.

public interest in preserving public health.[36] Accordingly, the pre-dominant opinion promotes a combination of deontological and utilitarian ideas.

Since s.203 of the Criminal Code does not sanction the violation of confidences in general, but instead only applies to the members of the professions especially listed, it follows that the provision is not intended to protect the personal and intimate sphere comprehensively against any intrusion, but only awards protection against indiscretions committed by the members of certain professions. When trying to understand the reason behind the special protection awarded to confidences made within the physician-patient relationship, several considerations are possible. One could argue that the physician-patient relationship deserves particular protection, as patients place a special trust in physicians. However, this argument is problematic, as it cannot explain why s.203 of the Criminal Code applies, for example, to the relationship between a prison doctor and his/her patient, a relationship which is not necessarily based on any particular trust in the physician. It seems more convincing to explain the special protection by the need to reveal personal, intimate facts to a physician as otherwise effective medical treatment might not be possible. S.203 of the Criminal Code can thus be seen as a reaction of the criminal law to the protection of the patient's privacy interests under Arts 2(1), 1(1) BL. Given that the constitutional protection is only available against state intrusions, s.203 of the Criminal Code adds to this protection by guaranteeing that the physician keeps the medical confidences of his/her patient. Without this additional safeguard, the protection of medical confidentiality would be incomplete, and the patient would still have to fear a disclosure of his/her medical secrets. The protection of medical confidentiality under s.203 of the Criminal Code can thus be seen as the protection of intimate facts that had to be revealed to a necessary confidant. It has been argued that in addition to guaranteeing the privacy interests of the patient, s.203(1) of the Criminal Code also protects the interests the patient pursues when consulting the physician, i.e. the patient's health interests.[37]

3 Protection under contract and tort law

In German law, the physician-patient relationship is normally based on a contract for services (s.611 of the Civil Code).[38] The physician's obligation to medical confidentiality is a contractual duty in the framework of this contract,[39] and a violation of that obligation can result in an obligation to pay compensation, if the prerequisites of the remedy for breach of contract are satisfied.

Medical confidentiality is also protected under tort law by s.823(1) and (2) of the Civil Code.

---

[36] See, for example, Bay ObLG NJW 1987, 1492, 1493; Fischer, 1b to s.203; Kreuzer, ZStW 100 (1988), 786, at 804; Ulsenheimer, at 270.

[37] Schmitt, at 124.

[38] Palandt-Putzo, 18 to s.611.

[39] Timm, at 37.

S.823 (Duty to compensate for harm)

(1) A person who intentionally or negligently injures the life, body, health, freedom, property or other right of another unlawfully is obliged to compensate the other for the harm arising therefrom.

(2) The same obligation applies to a person who offends against a statutory provision which has in view the protection of another.[40]

Under s.823(1) of the Civil Code, compensation for a violation of medical confidentiality is available if the revelation has caused economic harm. Even though a violation of the right to privacy is not specifically listed in s.823(1) of the Civil Code as giving rise to a claim for compensation, the civil courts have interpreted the reference to 'any other rights' in s.823(1) of the Civil Code so as to include the right to privacy.[41] This protection of the privacy right under private law was developed as a consequence of the constitutional protection of privacy. It is now well-established that information about a person's health belongs to the intimate sphere that is protected by s.823(1) of the Civil Code,[42] so that an unauthorised breach of medical confidentiality amounts to a tort under that provision if the other prerequisites are equally present. To give the constitutional privacy right adequate protection, the courts even award, in circumvention of the provisions of the Civil Code,[43] compensation for non financial harm.[44] It can thus be seen that the protection of privacy as a constitutional right has strengthened its protection under private law.[45] Compensation under tort law is also available under s.823(2) of the Civil Code. The requirements of s.823(2) of the Civil Code are met in particular where the physician has violated s.203(1) of the Criminal Code, as the provisions of the Criminal Code are statutory provisions having in view the protection of another in the meaning of s.823(2) of the Civil Code.

4 Professional obligation

The duty to maintain medical confidentiality is a professional duty and as such is laid down in the Code of Medical Ethics issued by the medical profession. S.2 of

---

[40] S.823 (Schadensersatzpflicht)

(1) Wer vorsätzlich oder fahrlässig das Leben, den Körper, die Gesundheit, die Freiheit, das Eigentum oder ein sonstiges Recht eines anderen widerrechtlich verletzt, ist dem anderen zum Ersatze des daraus entstehenden Schadens verpflichtet.

(2) Die gleiche Verpflichtung trifft denjenigen, welcher gegen ein den Schutz eines anderen bezweckendes Gesetz verstößt.

[41] BGHZ 26, 349 (1958); BGH NJW 1965, 685; BGHZ 39, 124 (1963).

[42] BGH NJW 1988, 1984; Palandt-Thomas, 178 to s.823.

[43] See s.253 of 3the Civil Code.

[44] See, for example, BGH NJW 1965, 685. This has been confirmed by the Federal Constitutional Court, see BVerfGE 34, 269 (1973).

[45] To see how German case law has developed the protection of privacy rights under tort law see, for example, Markesinis, at 412-478.

the Model Professional Regulations which formed the basis for the Codes of Medical Ethics of the different German States, provides that:

> (1) The physician has to keep silent about everything confided in him or having become known to him in the exercise of his profession. This includes written statements of the patient, patient records, x-rays and other examination results.[46]

It can thus be seen that the professional duty is not limited to information which the patient expressly confided in the physician. A violation of the professional duty to respect patient confidentiality can give rise to disciplinary sanctions.

5 Summary

The constitutional protection of medical confidentiality as part of the personality right must be the starting point for any examination of medical confidentiality. Protected is the individual's interest in keeping personal medical information secret as well as the interest in being able to make an autonomous choice as to whether or not to disclose confidential information to the physician. In the light of this constitutional protection which is not all that different from the protection available under Article 8 of the ECHR, the impact of the ECHR in this area is rather limited. The breach of medical confidentiality by the physician also amounts to a criminal offence. This offence predated the German Basic Law, but it needs to be interpreted in the light of constitutional provisions. Thus, in the context of criminal law, the constitutional protection strengthens the protection of confidentiality that was already in existence under ordinary criminal law. S.203 Criminal Code mainly aims at protecting the patient's privacy interests against disclosure by the physician, but also at protecting the public interest in the preservation of public health.

The constitutional privacy protection has also improved the protection of medical confidentiality under private law, as the civil courts have interpreted s.823(1) of the Civil Code so as to protect the right to personality. Compensation for a violation of the right to medical confidentiality is available in tort law according to s.823(1) of the Civil Code and, under certain circumstances, also under s.823(2) of the Civil Code. An unauthorised disclosure of medical secrets can also give rise to an action in breach of contract. Furthermore, physicians are under an ethical obligation to maintain medical confidentiality imposed by their professional authorities and the violation of that ethical duty can result in disciplinary sanctions.

---

[46] S.2(1) Berufsordnung für die deutschen Ärzte:
Der Arzt hat über das, was ihm in seiner Eigenschaft als Arzt anvertraut oder bekannt geworden ist, zu schweigen. Dazu gehören auch schriftliche Mitteilungen des Patienten, Aufzeichnungen über Patienten, Röntgenaufnahmen und sonstige Untersuchungsbefunde.

PART 2 – DISCLOSURE IN THE CONTEXT OF CRIME PREVENTION AND CRIMINAL PROSECUTION

This part will give an overview of how German law deals with questions of a physician's testimony about confidential information in criminal proceedings and of state access to medical records for purposes of criminal investigations. It will introduce the relevant provisions of the Code of Criminal Procedure and examine case law and legal doctrine to demonstrate how these provisions have been interpreted and applied. Given that a breach of medical confidentiality amounts to a criminal offence under s.203 of the Criminal Code, it needs to be discussed whether the law provides for justifications if the physician discloses confidential patient information for the purposes of crime prevention or criminal prosecution.

1 A physician's testimony in criminal court

S.53 of the Code of Criminal Procedure providing for a medical privilege in criminal proceedings states as follows:

> (1) Also entitled to refuse to give testimony are
> 1. priests ...
> 2. criminal defence lawyers ...
> 3. ... physicians, dentists, psychological psychotherapists, psychotherapists for children and juveniles, pharmacists and midwifes about what has been confided in them or what came to their knowledge in this capacity ... .
> (2) The persons listed in subsection 1 Numbers to 2 to 3b are not entitled to refuse to give testimony when they have been released from their obligation to remain silent.[47]

The Code of Criminal Procedure in s.53 awards physicians the right to refuse to testify in court about confidential information obtained in the course of their profession. In principle, the extent to which information is protected from disclosure in criminal court coincides with the protection awarded by s.203 of the Criminal Code.[48] This means that the physician does not have to give testimony about information that has come his/her knowledge, or about observations, including those of non-medical facts, which he/she has made in the context of the physician-patient relationship. Recently, the German Supreme Court has added that

---

[47] S.53

> (1) Zur Verweigerung des Zeugnisses sind ferner berechtigt
> 1. Geistliche ...
> 2. Verteidiger ...
> 3. ... Ärzte, Zahnärzte, Psychologische Psychotherapeuten, Kinder- und Jugendpsychotherapeuten, Apotheker und Hebammen über das, was ihnen in dieser Eigenschaft anvertraut worden oder bekanntgeworden ist ... .
> (2) Die in Absatz 1 Nr. 2 bis 3b Genannten dürfen das Zeugnis nicht verweigern, wenn sie von der Verpflichtung zur Verschwiegenheit entbunden sind.

[48] See supra, part 1, 2.

in the context of s.53 of the Code of Criminal Procedure, the physician's right not to give testimony extends to the question of whether or not the accused was in fact a patient of the physician. The Court argued that if the physician were only allowed to refuse to testify if the accused was a patient, but had to answer the same question if the accused was not a patient, then the very fact that the physician decides to refuse to give testimony about this issue allows for the inference that a physician-patient relationship existed between him/her and the accused. This was regarded as a circumvention of the principle of medical confidentiality.[49]

With regard to the interests protected by a recognition of medical privilege, it could at first sight be thought that medical privilege serves exactly the same purposes as the general protection of medical confidentiality under s.203 of the Criminal Code, and that s.53 of the Code of Criminal Procedure does no more than clarify that this protection extends to criminal proceedings. However, the legal discussion in Germany is far from unanimous in accepting this view. Most authors as well as the courts recognise that the protection of the patient's privacy rights is at least one important interest behind granting medical privilege in criminal proceedings.[50] However, some arguments have been submitted in support of the view that medical privilege might aim at different objectives than s.203(1) of the Criminal Code. A first argument focuses on the wording of s.53 of the Code of Criminal Procedure. The provision gives the physician the right not to testify in court when called as a witness with regard to confidential patient information, without imposing a corresponding obligation. It could be inferred from this that the protection of the patient's privacy interests cannot be the main concern behind medical privilege, as such protection could only be guaranteed effectively if the physician were placed under an obligation not to testify, instead of being given a choice between testifying and refusing to testify.

Some have inferred that s.53 was enacted in the interest of the medical profession.[51] This view is based on the case law of the Federal Constitutional Court stressing that the members of the medical profession must necessarily rely on medical confidentiality for an unfettered exercise of their profession, as it is typical for their profession that they are entrusted with confidential information.[52] Without medical privilege, the members of the medical profession could not exercise their profession successfully, so that medical privilege according to this view is recognised to guarantee the right of occupational freedom guaranteed by Art.12(1) BL.[53] However, it is difficult to accept that the interests of the members of the medical profession in the exercise of their profession are of such overriding

---

[49] BGH JZ 2000, 683, 684.

[50] BVerfGE 32, 373, 380 (1972); Baier, at 57; Klöhn, at 15-16; Schmitt, at 122.

[51] Rengier, at 13-14.

[52] BVerfGE 38, 312, 323 (1975).

[53] See Baier, at 56. It should be noted that Baier promotes the view that medical privilege exists to protect the interests of the medical profession as well as the privacy interests of the patient. Art.12(1) BL states that: All Germans have the right freely to choose their occupation or profession, their place of work, study or training. (Alle Deutschen haben das Recht, Beruf, Arbeitsplatz und Ausbildungsstätte frei zu wählen.)

importance that they should prevail over the state interest in criminal prosecution. The exercise of the medical profession can only be hindered by the non-existence of medical privilege if without medical privilege, patients are more reluctant to seek medical advice and are less forthcoming with information that is essential for effective medical treatment. However, this primarily has an impact on the interests of the patients, while the interests of the medical profession are in that respect only indirectly affected. It would be unconvincing to argue that the indirectly affected interests of the medical profession deserve more protection than the directly affected interests of the patient and can outweigh the interest in the administration of justice.

It must be admitted, however, that historically medical privilege had the purpose of protecting the physician from conflicts between the ethical duty to maintain medical confidentiality, and a legal duty to testify about confidential patient information.[54] As physicians were traditionally obliged by the Hippocratic Oath to keep their patients' confidences, an obligation which at present forms part of several International Conventions, as well as of the codes of medical practice, the obligation to testify in court would have put physicians in the position either to disregard their professional or their legal obligation. Thus, one reason behind medical privilege is that it protects physicians from this type of conflict.[55]

Another aspect sometimes raised is that medical privilege serves the protection of the *nemo tenetur* principle which has constitutional rank and states that no one can be forced to incriminate him/herself. The argument is that freedom from self-incrimination is circumvented if the patient's right not to testify with regard to confidential facts were undermined by the possibility of calling the physician to the witness stand and examine him/her about the same confidential facts.[56] The strength of the argument is mitigated by the fact that s.53 of the Code of Criminal Procedure not only grants medical privilege with regard to a patient who is accused in criminal proceedings, but that it extends to all patients, for example to victims of criminal offences. Freedom from self-incrimination cannot explain the existence of medical privilege in respect of confidential information concerning other persons than the accused.[57]

As can be seen, s.53(2) of the Code of Criminal Procedure expressly provides that the physician is no longer free to refuse to testify in criminal court if the patient has exempted him/her from the obligation of confidentiality. German law is thus based on the premise that medical privilege is no longer justified if the patient has no interest in keeping his/her confidential information secret in the context of criminal proceedings. S.53(2) could support the impression that medical privilege only exists in the patient's interest, as it could be argued that the patient can only waive his/her own privacy rights, but not the physician's or the state interest in maintaining confidentiality. This argument must fail, however, because the only interest either the patient, the physician or the state can have in the protection of

---

[54] Schmitt, at 131.
[55] BGHSt 9, 59, 61 (1956).
[56] Klöhn, at 46.
[57] Schmitt, at 122.

medical confidentiality is that the doctor is not forced to disclose confidential information against the patient's wish.[58] Thus, where the patient has authorised the physician to testify about confidential information, the physician is no longer in a moral conflict, and the state interest in respecting the privacy right of the patient and also the confidential nature of the physician-patient relationship in order to promote public health are no longer affected.[59] Where the patient has consented to the disclosure of information by the physician, the doctor has no choice and must testify.[60]

It is thus recognised that medical privilege serves different purposes: according to case-law and the predominant opinion among legal writers, it protects the privacy rights of the patient, the professional integrity of the physician, the integrity of the physician-patient relationship and the public interest in respecting the individual's basic rights and in promoting public health. However, some conclusive remarks about the main purpose behind medical privilege seem appropriate. The different legal provisions and concepts in Arts 2(1) and 1(1) BL, s.203(1) of the Criminal Code and s.53 of the Code of Criminal Procedure only add up to a coherent system if the medical privilege recognised by s.53 of the Code of Criminal Procedure is interpreted as giving effect to the patient's privacy rights in the context of criminal proceedings. The Federal Constitutional Court has held that:

> As far as the right to refuse to testify concerns facts regarding the citizen's private sphere, the protection of the private sphere of the individual was accorded precedence over the public interest in fully establishing the truth in criminal proceedings.[61]

The Federal Constitutional Court thus clearly took the stance that the interests outweighing the state interest in the administration of criminal justice in the context of professional privilege are the constitutionally protected privacy interests of the patient. Only this interpretation of the intention behind s.53 of the Code of Criminal Procedure is compatible with the purposes identified as underlying s.203 of the Criminal Code, and with the significance of the patient's right to privacy. Medical privilege may incidentally serve the interests of the members of the medical profession and the public interest in the preservation of public health. However, at the heart of medical privilege lie the privacy interests of the individual patient, and only these interests are regarded as important enough to outweigh the interest in the administration of justice.

1.1 Refusal to testify - right or obligation?

If the privacy interests of the patient are one of the purposes underlying medical privilege, or even its main justification, it is rather surprising that, according to the

---

[58] Lenckner, NJW 1965, at 323; Petry, at 48.
[59] See also Schmitt, at 133.
[60] Karlsruher Kommentar-Senge, 51 to s.53.
[61] BVerfGE 33, 367, 378 (1972).

predominant opinion of German courts and legal writers,[62] physicians are said to have a discretion in deciding whether or not to testify in court about confidential patient information. At first sight, this opinion seems convincing as it is in conformity with the wording of s.53 ('entitled to refuse to give testimony'). But this literal interpretation of s.53 of the Code of Criminal Procedure focuses on the physician and his/her protection from a possible conflict between the obligation of confidentiality and the obligation to testify in court and therefore only makes sense if the protection of the physician's interests were the main purpose behind s.53 of the Code of Criminal Procedure, a view that has already been discussed and rejected above. As the physician's testimony concerns confidences of the patient, a disclosure of this information at the physician's discretion would not give adequate protection to the patient's privacy interests.

Instead, the patient's privacy interests can only be sufficiently protected if s.53 were interpreted so as to impose upon the physician the obligation not to testify about confidential patient information without the patient's consent.[63] It is important to note that only this interpretation is consistent with s.203 of the Criminal Code. As s.53 of the Code of Criminal Procedure awards the right to refuse to testify, it is uncontroversial that s.203 of the Criminal Code also applies to testimony in court. The fact that a physician discloses confidential information in the court room can, therefore, not in itself justify a breach of medical confidentiality.[64] This means that a physician who exercises his/her 'right' under s.53 of the Code of Criminal Procedure and decides to give testimony about confidential patient information without the patient's consent commits the offence of breach of confidentiality under s.203 of the Criminal Code.

To interpret s.53 of the Code of Criminal Procedure as imposing an obligation on the physician not to give testimony only at first sight seems to contradict the wording of the provision. S.53 of the Code of Criminal Procedure is phrased as awarding a right, rather than as imposing an obligation, because not all persons who are exempt from testifying in criminal court according to s.53 of the Code of Criminal Procedure are under an obligation of confidentiality imposed by s.203 of the Criminal Code. Priests, like physicians, can refuse to testify about penitents' confidences under s.53 of the Code of Criminal Procedure. Unlike physicians, however, they will not commit a criminal offence if they decide to give testimony, as their profession is not listed in s.203 of the Criminal Code. It therefore makes sense to give them the right to decide freely whether or not to testify. Furthermore, the right to refuse to testify in court is broader than the obligation to maintain medical confidentiality under s.203(1) of the Criminal Code, as s.203(1) only protects 'secrets', while s.53 of the Code of Criminal Procedure awards the right to remain silent even with regard to confidential patient information that does not qualify as a secret in the meaning of s.203(1) of the Criminal Code. The

---

[62] See, for example, BGHSt 9, 59, 61 (1956); 15, 200, 202 (1960); 42, 73, 76 (1996); BGH MedR 1997, 270; Karlsruher Kommentar-Senge, 7 to s.53 with further references; Kleinknecht/Meyer-Goßner, 6 to s.53; Laufs/Uhlenbruck-Ulsenheimer, at 554.

[63] Fezer, at 203.

[64] Roxin, at 213.

physician's 'right' under s.53 could thus be interpreted as merely referring to the choice of whether or not to testify in court about confidential patient information that is not a secret protected by s.203(1) of the Criminal Code and the disclosure of which would therefore not amount to a criminal offence.[65]

This interpretation of s.53 of the Code of Criminal Procedure avoids the unconvincing result of the predominant opinion that the physician can freely decide whether or not to testify, but when exercising this choice in favour of giving testimony, he/she will as a consequence be held liable under s.203 of the Criminal Code for breach of confidentiality. The predominant opinion, while pertaining to protect the physician, has the undesirable consequence that the physician is given a choice the exercise of which might result in a criminal prosecution. This opinion adds nothing to the protection of the physician. With regard to a possible conflict between the legal and ethical obligation to maintain patient confidences and the obligation to testify, the physician is protected comprehensively by the existence of s.53 of the Code of Criminal Procedure which exempts the physician from the duty to give testimony in criminal court. If the physician in certain exceptional situations feels that the disclosure of confidential medical information in criminal court is desirable, for example where it may help a person who is wrongly accused in criminal proceedings, this conflict cannot be resolved with reference to the procedural provision of s.53 of the Code of Criminal Procedure, as the question of whether or not such a disclosure is permitted will have to be resolved according to the provisions of substantive law which decide questions of possible legal justifications.

Even if the main purpose behind medical confidentiality were not the protection of the patient's privacy rights, but rather the protection of the public interest in promoting public health, or the physician's interest in the exercise of his/her profession, these interests would equally be undermined if the physician had a choice as to whether or not to breach medical confidentiality in court. The patient then cannot rely on the physician's secrecy. Only if s.53 of the Code of Criminal Procedure is interpreted as creating an obligation, rather than a right to refuse to testify, can consistency between s.203 of the Criminal Code and s.53 of the Code of Criminal Procedure be achieved. The interests behind medical confidentiality can only be satisfactorily safeguarded where the physician has no right to divulge the information without the patient's consent.[66]

The whole discussion may seem somewhat theoretical, as it could be thought that from the point of view of the patient, it does not make any difference whether the physician is only under the general obligation of medical confidentiality imposed by s.203 of the Criminal Code, or whether s.53 of the Code of Criminal Procedure creates an additional obligation for the physician not to testify in court, as long as s.203 of the Criminal Code is applicable to evidence given as a witness in criminal proceedings. However, the interpretation of s.53 of the Code of Criminal Procedure has an important impact on the admissibility of the physician's testimony. Criminal courts have taken the stance that as the physician has the right to testify, this

---

[65] Welp, JR 1997, at 37-8.
[66] Lenckner, NJW 1965, at 326; Schmitt, at 145.

testimony is admissible evidence, regardless of whether or not the disclosure in the specific case constitutes a criminal offence.[67] This situation is problematic as it permits the admission of evidence that has possibly come about through the means of a criminal offence.[68] The restoration of peace and justice after the commission of a crime, one of the purposes of criminal proceedings, cannot be achieved if the witness, in testifying, commits a new criminal offence and, consequently, an additional breach of peace and justice occurs.[69] This problem could be avoided if the physician were not allowed to testify in court regarding confidential patient information.

1.2 Effects of the patient's consent

According to s.53(2) of the Code of Criminal Procedure, the physician can no longer refuse to testify if the patient has waived his/her right to medical confidentiality and consented to disclosure. In such a case, no criminal offence under s.203 of the Criminal Code will be committed by the physician if he/she discloses confidential patient information. What causes legal problems in this context is the question of who has the right to waive medical confidentiality, and under which conditions such a waiver is valid. With regard to the first question, the answer is easy where the confidential information at issue exclusively relates to the patient. In such a case, it is clear that only the patient can have the right to consent to the disclosure of confidential information. However, the problem is more complex where the information confided in the physician by the patient relates to a third party, for example where the patient tells the physician confidential details relating to his/her spouse. In such a case, some argue that only the person the information relates to has the right to relieve the physician from the obligation to medical confidentiality.[70] Even though there is no physician-patient relationship between the physician and the third party, the protection of s.203 of the Criminal Code still applies, as the physician has learned confidential information of another in the course of his/her profession.[71] It seems rather surprising that a third party can consent to the disclosure of confidential information obtained by the physician in the course of a professional relationship with the patient, while the patient him/herself cannot validly consent to the disclosure of such information. Even where the third party's consent exclusively concerns his/her own confidences, it is difficult to reconcile this view with any of the purposes behind the protection of medical confidentiality. As no physician-patient relationship exists between the physician and the third party, the physician only owes the patient, but not the third

---

[67] BGHSt 9, 59, 62 (1956); 18, 146, 147 (1962); BGHR-Schweigepflicht I zu StPO §53 (1995); Karlsruher Kommentar-Senge, 9 to s.53; Löwe/Rosenberg-Dahs, 11-14 to s.53; for a further discussion see Alternativkommentar-Kühne, 3-6 to s.53.

[68] For a discussion see Kleinknecht/Meyer-Goßner, 6 to s.53 with further references.

[69] Freund, GA 1993, at 63-4; Lenckner, NJW 1965, at 327; Nomos Kommentar-Jung, 35 to 203; Roxin, at 213.

[70] Karlsruher Kommentar-Senge, 46 to s.53; Göppinger, NJW 1958, at 243.

[71] OLG Hamburg NJW 1962, 689, 691.

party an obligation to maintain medical confidentiality, and it is then difficult to accept that the third party can validly relieve the physician from an obligation not owed to him/her. The courts seem to share these doubts when stating that the third party can have no right that his/her confidential data be protected by someone else's physician, so that the patient's consent should be sufficient to waive medical confidentiality even with regard to information not relating to him/her.[72]

Valid consent presupposes capacity. This capacity is not subject to any age limits, but rather exclusively refers to the ability to understand the general nature and scope of the act consented to and the faculty to assess the consequences of giving consent at least in a general manner.[73] This means that for example an eleven-year-old child could validly consent to the breach of medical confidentiality as long as it understands the general features of this waiver. Consent must also be given freely and voluntarily. Voluntariness is not excluded merely because the patient feels in a real dilemma and consents to the disclosure only to avoid an even more serious disadvantage. Rather, to exclude voluntariness, the patient must be under such pressure that he/she no longer has any meaningful choice between consenting and refusing to consent.

It is problematic whether the patient's consent is only valid with regard to information he/she is aware of, as it is possible that the physician has not fully informed the patient about his/her health condition. Thus, if a patient consents to the physician's testimony in court, he/she might not be able to predict the content of such testimony with certainty. The Higher Regional Court of Hamburg argued that it should be sufficient that the physician indicates the possibility that the patient might not be aware of the full extent of the physician's knowledge. If the patient then still consents to the disclosure, this consent is valid.[74]

1.3 Disclosure for the purpose of criminal prosecution

It has already been established that a physician who discloses confidential patient information either in court or in the context of police investigations commits the criminal offence of s.203(1) of the Criminal Code, except where a legal justification applies. Unless the patient consented to the disclosure, the most important legal justification applicable to cases of a breach of professional confidentiality is the necessity defence. S.34 of the Criminal Code provides in that respect:

A person who commits an offence in present danger, that cannot be otherwise averted, to life, body, freedom, honour, property or another legal interest, in order to protect himself or another from that danger, does not act unlawfully if, on balancing the conflicting interests, particularly the legal interests concerned and the degree of the dangers to them,

---

[72] OLG Köln NStZ 1983, 412, 413; Schönke/Schröder-Lenckner, 23 to s.203; Göppinger, NJW 1958, at 243.

[73] BGHSt 12, 379, 382 (1959); 23, 1, 4 (1969).

[74] OLG Hamburg NJW 1962, 689, 690.

the protected interest significantly outweighs the interest impaired. This only applies insofar as the offence is an appropriate means to avert the danger.[75]

For the necessity defence to apply in the context of a breach of medical confidentiality, the physician's disclosure of confidential patient information must be aimed at protecting the physician him/herself or a third party from a present or imminent danger. This means that the testimony cannot be justified if it is merely given for the purpose of a criminal prosecution, as in that case, the danger has already materialised and there is no longer any present or imminent harm to an individual. Even where the most serious crimes are under investigation, the violation of the victim's rights is already complete, and there is no longer a present danger as required by s.34.[76] The general risk that someone who has committed a crime might do so again is not sufficient to justify a breach of confidence under the necessity defence.[77] If the physician wants to testify because he/she thinks that the perpetrator is likely to commit future crimes, a breach of confidence would not serve the purpose of prosecuting the relevant crime, but rather the purpose of crime prevention which is a different problem dealt with below.[78]

A breach of medical confidentiality can thus not be justified under the necessity defence for the mere purpose of criminal prosecution. The legislature, when introducing the right not to testify, did not distinguish between different offences according to their seriousness, but rather awarded this right independent of the nature of the crime at trial. This means that the legislature, when resolving the conflict between the public interest in criminal prosecution and truth-finding, on the one hand, and the private and public interests in medical confidentiality, on the other, balanced the competing interests as required by s.34 of the Criminal Code and came to the conclusion that the interest in medical confidentiality generally outweighed the interests in criminal prosecution.[79] Consequently, a physician who breaches medical confidentiality in the interest of criminal prosecution does not protect an interest that significantly outweighs the interest impaired, as required by s.34 of the Criminal Code. In addition, the necessity defence could only apply where the violation of medical confidentiality would be an adequate means to

---

[75] S.34 (Rechtfertigender Notstand): Wer in einer gegenwärtigen, nicht anders abwendbaren Gefahr für Leben, Leib, Freiheit, Ehre, Eigentum oder ein anderes Rechtsgut eine Tat begeht, um die Gefahr von sich oder einem anderen abzuwenden, handelt nicht rechtswidrig, wenn bei Abwägung der widerstreitenden Interessen, namentlich der betroffenen Rechtsgüter und des Grades der ihnen drohenden Gefahren, das geschützte Interesse das beeinträchtigte wesentlich überwiegt. Dies gilt jedoch nur, soweit die Tat ein angemessenes Mittel ist, die Gefahr abzuwenden.

[76] Baumann, Weber, Mitsch, at 332; Haffke, GA 1973, at 69.

[77] Leipziger Kommentar-Schünemann, 141 to s.203.

[78] But see Laufs/Uhlenbruck-Ulsenheimer, at 557, who argues that the danger that a person who has committed serious crimes might possibly commit serious future crimes justifies disclosure under s.34.

[79] BVerfGE 33, 367, 378 (1972); Baier, at 117; Haffke, GA 1973, at 69; Kramer, NJW 1990, at 1763; Ostendorf, DRiZ 1981, at 11; Schilling, JZ 1976, at 620; Steinberg-Copek, at 60; Sydow, at 115.

achieve the intended purpose, i.e. to ensure criminal prosecution. The confidential information the physician can testify about will frequently not in itself be sufficient for a successful prosecution, so that this requirement of the necessity defence would then not be fulfilled.

As can be seen, the necessity defence is for various reasons not available as a legal justification for a violation of medical confidentiality when the physician gives testimony in court. Some authors find it hard to accept that as a consequence, a breach of medical confidentiality for the purpose of criminal prosecution will always amount to a criminal offence. To avoid this result, it has been suggested that a justification of conflicting duties should be recognised, so that in every case of a breach of medical confidentiality by a physician the duty to protect the intimate sphere of the patient should be balanced against the public interest in an effective administration of justice, an interest which is equally of constitutional rank as it follows from the constitutional principle of the rule of law. This is, however, problematic. First, the physician is not under any legal duty to assist the state in the prosecution of crime. The only legal duty imposed on individuals in this context is the duty to give testimony in criminal court, an obligation from which s.53 of the Code of Criminal Procedure exempts the physician. It is thus incorrect to speak about a conflict of duties which could justify the breach of one of these obligations. It seems as if the promoters of the view that a breach of medical confidentiality can be justified by a conflict of duties rather have a conflict of interests in mind, when they argue that this justification should only apply to the prosecution of serious offences, as the public interest in such cases is said to outweigh medical confidentiality.[80] However, given that the legislature has not created any exemptions from the obligation to keep the medical secret for the purpose of assisting the prosecution of serious offences, there is no legal basis for such a balancing of interests outside of the necessity defence.[81]

1.4 Testimony to establish the innocence of an accused

A different problem arises where the physician has information about the innocence of an accused person, for example where the real perpetrator is a patient of the physician and has confessed his/her guilt to the doctor in the course of medical treatment, or where the physician has made observations regarding his/her patient's guilt. First, it should be noted that under German law, the accused does not have a right to compel the physician to give testimony in his/her favour, as such a right is barred by medical privilege, unless the accused is the patient and consents to the disclosure of his/her own medical secrets according to s.53(2) of the Code of Criminal Procedure.

The only controversial problem is whether or not the physician can lawfully volunteer his/her testimony. In this situation, again, the breach of confidentiality can only be justified if all requirements of the necessity defence are met. The first question therefore must be whether or not a present and imminent danger exists in

---

[80] Kohlhaas, GA 1958, at 74.
[81] Schmitz, JA 1996, at 953.

such a scenario. This is not problematic where the innocent person has already been convicted and the punishment is currently being executed or its execution is imminent, but the danger is no longer imminent where the execution of punishment is already terminated, for example where a person who was wrongly sentenced to imprisonment has been released. The danger is imminent where the proceedings have reached a stage approaching a conviction. The situation is problematic, however, if the evidence does not unequivocally point to the guilt of the accused, as it is then more difficult to decide at which point there is an imminent danger to the liberty of the wrongly accused. Even where a conviction is not imminent so that an imminent danger exists neither with regard to the assets nor with regard to the liberty of the innocent person, it could be argued that there is an imminent risk that he/she is subjected to unwarranted criminal prosecution.

If the requirement of a present or imminent danger is met, the justification depends on the outcome of a balancing of interests, as the necessity defence only applies where the interests pursued with the criminal offence at issue outweigh the interests violated thereby. The criteria to be applied to the balancing process depend on whether the innocent person is the patient, a third party or the physician him/herself. If the physician possesses confidential information about his/her patient which could establish the patient's innocence when being accused in criminal proceedings, for example information that the patient was in hospital at the time when the crime had been committed, or that a certain physical condition of the patient excludes him/her as the perpetrator, the physician's testimony to that regard can never be justified. This is because in such a situation, the patient, when wishing evidence to be made available to the court, could easily release the physician from his/her duty of confidentiality with the consequence that the physician, according to s.53(2) of the Code of Criminal Procedure, would be obliged to testify. If the patient does not want to do this, either because he/she wants to protect a third party, or because he/she values privacy more than his/her liberty, it is not up to the physician to disregard the patient's preferences and to substitute his/her judgment for that of the patient.

If the physician's testimony could exonerate a third party who is wrongly accused in criminal proceedings, many scholars argue that the necessity defence should apply to justify a breach of confidentiality. They argue that the interests of the wrongly accused not to be convicted outweigh the interests of the perpetrator in the protection of his/her medical confidences.[82] Others reject such a justification completely, because a doctor is bound only by the patient's well-being, without owing any obligation to a third party or to the public to prevent incorrect court decisions.[83] This is not convincing, as in the context of the necessity defence, it is not important whether or not the physician has an obligation to protect the interests at issue. Once the physician has decided to violate medical confidentiality to protect the interests of an innocent third party, the only consideration can be

[82] OLG Celle NJW 1965, 362, 363; Baier, at 117; Fischer, 31 to s.203; Flor, JR 1953, at 368-9; Schmitt, at 153; Schönke/Schröder-Lenckner, 1 to s.203.
[83] Woesner, NJW 1957, at 692.

whether the protected interest outweighs the violated interests as required by s.34 of the Criminal Code.

In that respect, some argue that only issues of liberty rank higher than the maintenance of professional confidentiality so that a breach of confidentiality would only be justifiable where the accused is at risk of imprisonment.[84] The importance of the loss of money after a conviction to a fine will probably differ according to the special circumstances of each case and it is questionable whether financial interests can prevail over the privacy interests of the patient. However, other interests also have to be taken into account. A criminal conviction or even the threat of a criminal conviction can entail a loss of reputation as well as bring about consequences in respect of the exercise of certain professions. To decide whether or not a breach of confidentiality can be justified under s.34 of the Criminal Code, it thus has to be decided in each case whether these consequences affect interests of such overriding importance that the interest in medical confidentiality will have to yield. A case-by-case approach seems thus most appropriate, and also conforms with the objectives of the necessity defence which aims at enabling a just and fair decision in a particular case. The generalised approach in favour of upholding medical confidentiality which has been suggested above in the context of the conflict between medical confidentiality and the interests in criminal prosecution cannot be applied to this situation, as the latter is a conflict between an individual right and a general interest of the public which the legislature has resolved in favour of the interest of the individual. The conflict between the patient's interest in medical confidentiality and the interests of a person not to be wrongly convicted in criminal proceedings, on the other hand, is a conflict between individual rights which can only be fairly resolved when looking at the specific circumstances of each case.[85]

If it is the physician who is wrongly accused in criminal proceedings, in addition to the considerations made in the context of the prosecution of an innocent third party, the physician's defence rights are also at issue. Defence rights are of constitutional rank and many argue that they must prevail over the interest in medical confidentiality.[86] When others suggest that the physician must wait for a conviction before being allowed to reveal confidential information,[87] it should not be forgotten that the danger is already imminent before the actual conviction takes place, and that the physician's defence rights can no longer be exercised effectively once the conviction has occurred. This argument cannot thus be sustained in the context of the necessity defence.

---

[84] Müller, MDR 1971, at 970.

[85] Leipziger Kommentar-Schünemann, 142 to s.203, who seems to argue that these interests can never justify disclosure.

[86] BGHSt 1, 366, 368 (1951); KG JR 1985, 161, 162; Fischer, 31 to s.203; Schönke/Schröder-Lenckner, 33 to s.203.

[87] Systematischer Kommentar-Samson, 45 to s.203.

2 Crime prevention

Another question is whether a breach of confidentiality can be justified where there is a risk that someone will commit a crime. In this context, it is first of all important to look at ss.138 and 139 of the Criminal Code which impose an obligation to disclose to the relevant authorities information for the purpose of crime prevention.

S.138 of the Criminal Code states that:

(1) A person who has plausible knowledge regarding the plan or the carrying out of
1. preparations for a war of aggression ...
2. high treason ...
3. treason or an endangerment of the external security ...
4. counterfeiting of money or bonds ... or counterfeiting of credit or bank cards or of forms for Eurocheques ...
5. aggravated trafficking in human beings ...
6. murder, manslaughter or genocide ...
7. an offence against personal freedom ...
8. robbery ... or
9. a criminal offence endangering the public safety ...
at a time when the commission of the offence or its consequences could still be averted, and omits timely to inform the authorities or the potential victim, will be punished with imprisonment of up to five years or with a fine.
(2) Similarly will be punished every person who plausibly learns about the plan or the carrying out of an offence under s.129(a) [forming of a terrorist organisation] at a time when the commission can still be prevented and omits to inform the authorities immediately.[88]

---

[88] S.138 (Nichtanzeige geplanter Straftaten):
(1) Wer von dem Vorhaben oder der Ausführung
1. einer Vorbereitung eines Angriffskrieges ...
2. eines Hochverrats ...
3. eines Landesverrats oder einer Gefährdung der äußeren Sicherheit ...
4. einer Geld- oder Wertpapierfälschung ... oder einer Fälschung von Zahlungskarten und Vordrucken für Euroschecks ...
5. eines schweren Menschenhandels ...
6. eines Mordes, Totschlags oder Völkermordes ...
7. einer Straftat gegen die persönliche Freiheit ...
8. eines Raubes oder einer räuberischen Erpressung ... oder
9. einer gemeingefährlichen Straftat ...
zu einer Zeit, zu der die Ausführung oder der Erfolg noch abgewendet werden kann, glaubhaft erfährt und es unterläßt, der Behörde oder dem Bedrohten rechtzeitig Anzeige zu machen, wird mit Freiheitsstrafe bis zu fünf Jahren oder mit Geldstrafe bestraft.
(2) Ebenso wird bestraft, wer von dem Vorhaben oder der Ausführung einer Straftat nach § 129a zu einer Zeit, zu der die Ausführung noch abgewendet werden kann, glaubhaft erfährt und es unterläßt, der Behörde unverzüglich Anzeige zu erstatten.

And s.139 of the Criminal Code states:

> (3) A person who omits to make a report on a relative, remains free from punishment if he seriously endeavoured to prevent him from committing the offence or to avert its consequences, unless the offence in question was
> 1. murder or manslaughter (ss.211 or 212),
> 2. genocide in the cases of s.220(a)(1) No.1, or
> 3. kidnapping (s.239(a)(1)), hostage-taking (s.239(b)(1)) or an assault on air or sea traffic (s.316(c)(1)) by a terrorist organisation (s.129(a)).
> Under the same conditions, a solicitor, criminal defence lawyer or physician is under no obligation to report that which was confided in him in his professional capacity.[89]

Thus, while individuals are normally under an obligation to report all of the offences listed in s.138 of the Criminal Code for the purpose of crime prevention, physicians are under a more limited obligation and only have to report those offences that are listed in s.139(3) of the Criminal Code, but do not have to disclose information regarding the other offences listed in s.138 of the Criminal Code, provided that they seriously tried either to prevent the commission of the offence or to avert its consequences. Even if these attempts fail, the physician cannot be held criminally liable for omitting to report the planned commission of the offence. A physician who reports a planned criminal offence to the relevant authorities in accordance with his/her obligations under ss.138 and 139 of the Criminal Code will not be liable for a breach of his/her obligation to medical confidentiality.[90] For a small number of criminal offences, the legislature has thus made the decision that the interest in medical confidentiality is outweighed where such offences can be prevented by a breach of confidence.

In all other cases, the conflict between medical confidentiality and crime prevention must be resolved according to the criteria of the necessity defence. The necessity defence can, as was explained above, only be invoked successfully if the danger of harm to other individuals is present or imminent. Even then, necessity only applies where the balancing of all interests involved points towards a precedence of the interest protected by the breach of confidentiality, and where no less intrusive means are available to prevent the commission of the crime. It thus needs to be examined how these requirements relate to the disclosure of confidential medical information in the context of crime prevention.

---

[89] S.139 (Straflosigkeit der Nichtanzeige geplanter Straftaten):
(3) Wer eine Anzeige unterläßt, die er gegen einen Angehörigen erstatten müßte, ist straffrei, wenn er sich ernsthaft bemüht hat, ihn von der Tat abzuhalten oder den Erfolg abzuwenden, es sein denn, daß es sich um
1. einen Mord oder Totschlag (§§ 211 oder 212),
2. einen Völkermord in den Fällen des § 220a Abs. 1 Nr.1 oder
3. einen erpresserischen Menschenraub (§ 239a Abs. 1), eine Geiselnahme (§ 239b Abs. 1) oder einen Angriff auf den Luft- und Seeverkehr (§ 316c Abs. 1) durch eine terroristische Vereinigung (§ 129a)
handelt. Unter denselben Voraussetzungen ist ein Rechtsanwalt, Verteidiger oder Arzt nicht verpflichtet anzuzeigen, was ihm in dieser Eigenschaft anvertraut worden ist.
[90] Schönke/Schröder-Cramer, 23 to s.138.

Danger is defined as a situation in which the likelihood with which the violation of a right can be expected exceeds the general risks of life.[91] The 'imminent danger' requirement can be problematic. It is without doubt fulfilled if the patient tells his/her physician that he/she will commit a crime the details of which are already specified. However, it is difficult to draw the line between an imminent danger and the mere possibility that the patient might commit a crime, the latter not being sufficient to justify a breach of medical confidentiality under the necessity defence. It is questionable whether an imminent danger exists when the patient informs the physician about his/her intentions to commit a future crime without any specifications with regard to time, place, intended victims etc., or where the mental condition of the patient gives rise to general worries that the patient might commit a crime. While some would answer this question in the affirmative, arguing that a danger in the meaning of s.34 exists in a situation in which the permanent dangerousness of a person could at any time lead to the commission of a criminal offence,[92] in none of the above-mentioned cases exists a danger that exceeds the general risks of life. In most cases, even if the prerequisite of an imminent danger is met, the necessity defence will still not succeed, as a breach of medical confidentiality will often not be a suitable means to avert the danger, given that the disclosure of such information will only rarely prevent the commission of the crime.

In those cases in which exceptionally all of the other prerequisites of the necessity defence are met, the success of the necessity defence depends on the outcome of a balancing exercise. The patient's interest in medical confidentiality has to be balanced against the interests of the potential victims and the state interest in crime prevention. Factors to be taken into account when balancing the competing interests are, for example, the seriousness of the intended criminal offence and the value accorded to the endangered rights. Thus, the result of the balancing test may be influenced by factors such as whether the patient intends to commit a serious assault with a weapon, or whether he/she merely wants to utter a verbal threat. It is also important whether there is a risk to the life or health of another, or a risk to property or financial interests, and whether the patient plans to cause considerable damage. Not many cases exist to shed light on these questions. In a recent case, the Higher Regional Court of Frankfurt a.M. has decided that at least where the life of the victim is at risk, the balancing very clearly comes down in favour of disclosure, as the protection of the victim's life is more important than the protection of the interests behind medical confidentiality.[93]

---

[91] Jakobs, at 415.

[92] Schönke/Schröder-Lenckner, 17 to s.34.

[93] OLG Frankfurt a.M. MedR 2000, 196, 197-8. In this decision which concerned an action in tort by the wife of an HIV positive patient against the physician of both husband and wife for a failure to disclose her husband's HIV status to her which allegedly resulted in her infection, the Court even decided that s.34 of the Criminal Code created a duty to disclose confidential information where the interest in disclosure outweighed the interest in confidentiality. Such a duty was welcomed by Spickhoff, NJW 2000, at 848-9, and by Vogels, MDR 1999, at 1445-6.

Given these rather vague considerations, the question arises whether some general criteria should be developed to facilitate the balancing exercise. One possibility could be to borrow the criteria provided by the legislature in ss.138 and 139 of the Criminal Code for the conflict between the state interest in the prevention of certain serious crimes and the interest in medical confidentiality. It has been suggested that it follows from these provisions that the legislature values medical confidentiality more than the prevention of intended crimes that are not listed in s.139. Some go even further and argue that the disclosure by the physician of an intended criminal offence can never be justified under the necessity defence unless the physician is under an obligation to disclose pursuant to ss.138 and 139.[94] However, it is rather problematic to interpret ss.138 and 139 of the Criminal Code, the purpose of which is to create an obligation to disclose intended serious criminal offences, as excluding the application of the necessity defence which aims at the resolution of specific conflicts of interests and requires to take into account all the circumstances of the individual case. The legislature is reluctant to impose obligations on the citizen, so that it does not seem appropriate to interpret the rather narrow obligations imposed on the physician by ss.138 and 139 of the Criminal Code so as to limit his/her right to refer to the necessity defence in the case of a conflict between the obligation to maintain confidentiality and the necessity to prevent a criminal offence by the way of disclosure. Ss.138 and 139 should therefore not be seen as strict rules for the balancing process in the context of s.34 of the Criminal Code, but rather only as guidelines concerning the value of the rights protected by different criminal provisions. Consequently, the disclosure of criminal offences that are not listed in ss.138 and 139 of the Criminal Code will normally not be justified, but a justification of a breach of medical confidentiality under the necessity defence with regard to such offences remains possible under exceptional circumstances.[95]

3 Confidential material exempt from search and seizure

Police access to confidential patient information is governed by s.97 of the Code of Criminal Procedure stating that:

(1) Are exempt from seizure
1. written communications between the accused and persons entitled to refuse to give testimony under s.52 or s.53(1) numbers 1 to 3b;
2. documents prepared by the persons listed in s.53(1) numbers 1 to 3b relating to information confided in them by the accused or relating to other information the right to refuse to give testimony refers to;
3. other material, including the results of medical examinations, the right to refuse to give testimony awarded to the persons listed in s.53(1) numbers 1 to 3b refers to.
(2) These restrictions only apply if the material is in the custody of the person who has the right to refuse to give testimony. ... The restrictions to seizure do not apply when the

---

[94] Kielwein, GA 1955, at 231.
[95] Schönke/Schröder-Lenckner, 31 to s.203; Maurach/Schroeder/Maiwald, at 293.

person who has a right to refuse to give testimony is suspected of aiding and abetting, of acting as an accessory after the fact, of obstruction of criminal prosecution, or of handling or receiving stolen goods ...[96]

It can be seen that patient information is comprehensively protected, in that not only written patient communications and documents are exempt from seizure, but also other material the physician holds in confidence, which, for example, includes bullets removed from the patient's body.[97]

S.97 of the Code of Criminal Procedure must be seen in the context of the protection of confidentiality. If the physician could be forced to hand over confidential patient material, the right not to testify in criminal court would lose much of its protective effect, as the information which is protected by s.53(1) of the Code of Criminal Procedure would then be available to the state by the means of seizure. S.97 of the Code of Criminal Procedure thus aims at preventing a circumvention of the physician's right under s.53(1) of the Code of Criminal Procedure to refuse to give testimony in criminal court about confidential patient information.[98] The provision accordingly intends to guarantee the same rights s.53 of the Code of Criminal Procedure is designed to protect, i.e. mainly the privacy right of the patient.[99] This conforms with the Federal Constitutional Court's holding that medical records, as they contain information on anamnesis, diagnosis and therapeutic measures, belong to the private sphere of the patient, and are protected by Art.2(1) and Art.1(1) BL against state access.[100] In addition, s.97 of the Code of Criminal Procedure serves the protection of the physician's interest in an unimpeded exercise of his/her profession and in not having to contribute to the patient's criminal conviction.[101] Moreover, s.97 of the Code of Criminal Procedure

---

[96] S.97:

(1) Der Beschlagnahme unterliegen nicht

1. schriftliche Mitteilungen zwischen dem Beschuldigten und den Personen, die nach § 52 oder § 53 Abs. 1 Nr. 1 bis 3b das Zeugnis verweigern dürfen;

2. Aufzeichnungen, welche die in § 53 Abs. 1 Nr. 1 bis 3b Genannten über die ihnen vom Beschuldigten anvertrauten Mitteilungen oder über andere Umstände gemacht haben, auf die sich das Zeugnisverweigerungsrecht erstreckt;

andere Gegenstände einschließlich der ärztlichen Untersuchungsbefunde, auf die sich das Zeugnisverweigerungsrecht der in § 53 Abs. 1 Nr. 1 bis 3b Genannten erstreckt.

(2) Diese Beschränkungen gelten nur, wenn die Gegenstände im Gewahrsam der zur Verweigerung des Zeugnisses Berechtigten sind. ... Die Beschränkungen der Beschlagnahme gelten nicht, wenn die zur Verweigerung des Zeugnisses Berechtigten einer Teilnahme oder einer Begünstigung, Strafvereitelung oder Hehlerei verdächtig sind

... .

[97] Karlsruher Kommentar-Nack, 14 to s.97.

[98] BVerfGE 32, 373, 385 (1972); BGHSt 38, 144, 145 (1991); OLG Frankfurt StV 1982, 64, 65; Karlsruher Kommentar-Nack, 1 to s.97.

[99] BVerfGE 44, 353, 373 (1977); BVerfGE 32, 373, 380 (1972); Klöhn, at 331; Lorenz, MDR 1992, at 315-6; Rengier, at 15-16; Schmitt, at 122.

[100] BVerfGE 32, 373, 380 (1972).

[101] BVerfGE 38, 312, 323 (1975); LG Koblenz MDR 1983, 779, with regard to the lawyer-client relationship; Schlüchter, at 289; Weyand, wistra 1990, at 5-6.

aims at a protection of the confidential physician-patient relationship,[102] and at promoting public health.[103] It can thus be seen that the purpose behind s.97 of the Code of Criminal Procedure accords with the purpose behind s.53 of the Code of Criminal Procedure and s.203 of the Criminal Code.

3.1 Protection of the accused

S.97(1) and (2) of the Code of Criminal Procedure expressly refer to the protection of a patient who is accused in criminal proceedings. This gave rise to the controversial debate on whether only confidential information of an accused patient is protected from seizure, and how the non-accused patient can be protected. While a small minority of legal scholars argue that s.97 of the Code of Criminal Procedure not necessarily must be interpreted so as to apply exclusively to information relating to the patient who is accused in criminal proceedings,[104] this view seems inconsistent with the express wording of s.97 of the Code of Criminal Procedure, which only refers to the accused and does not mention the protection of other persons.[105] S.97 of the Code of Criminal Procedure thus leaves witnesses' or victims' confidential medical documents without protection from search and seizure. This is difficult to explain, given that the predominant opinion sees a protection of the patient's privacy rights as one, if not the most important rationale behind s.97 of the Code of Criminal Procedure. If s.97 of the Code of Criminal Procedure is designed to prevent a circumvention of s.53, this goal cannot be achieved if the protection is limited to accused patients, because s.53 of the Code of Criminal Procedure gives the physician a right not to testify regardless of whether the confidential information concerns an accused, a witness or a third party not at all related to the criminal proceedings.[106] The restriction of s.97 of the Code of Criminal Procedure to the protection of confidential medical documents of an accused patient is thus inconsistent with s.53 of the Code of Criminal Procedure and with s.203 of the Criminal Code.[107]

Some therefore argue that s.97 of the Code of Criminal Procedure only serves the purpose that evidence gained in the course of the confidential physician-patient relationship should not be used against the accused and relate this purpose to the privilege against self-incrimination.[108] If this were the purpose behind s.97 of the Code of Criminal Procedure, confidential material would have to be protected from seizure regardless of whether it is in the possession of the patient, or the physician.

---

[102] LG Köln NJW 1959, 1598.

[103] Amelung, DNotZ 1984, at 198-9; Rengier, at 22-3.

[104] Amelung, DNotZ 1984, at 207; Krekeler, NStZ 1987, at 201.

[105] OLG Celle NJW 1965, 362, 363; LG Hildesheim NStZ 1982, 394, 395; LG Hamburg NJW 1990, 780; LG Fulda NJW 1990, 2946, 2947; Löwe/Rosenberg-Schäfer, 3a to s.97; Schmitt, at 117; Welp, JZ 1974, at 423.

[106] Amelung, DNotZ 1984, at 207; Alternativkommentar-Amelung, 14-15 to s.97.

[107] OLG Celle NJW 1965, 362, 363; LG Hildesheim NStZ 1982, 394, 395.

[108] Rudolphi, NStZ 1998, at 473; Welp, JZ 1974, at 423.

However, s.97(2) of the Code of Criminal Procedure clarifies that the protection from seizure only applies to material that is in the possession of the physician.[109]

It is difficult to accept that a victim's or other third party's interest in the confidentiality of medical information deserves less protection than the privacy interests of the accused. As a way around the insufficient protection of medical records of the non-accused patient from seizure under s.97 of the Code of Criminal Procedure, courts increasingly refer to constitutional principles as a basis for a prohibition to seize patient records. Under German constitutional law, every statute and every act by a state authority must be compatible with the provisions of the Basic Law. Given the constitutional protection of medical confidentiality and of medical records, the courts therefore have to examine whether the seizure of confidential patient information that is in the possession of a physician is compatible with the patient's right to privacy. The Federal Constitutional Court has held that there are different spheres of intimacy which deserve different degrees of protection. While the core of the intimate life of the individual is inviolate, private spheres outside of this core are also constitutionally protected, but can be subject to restrictions. If a state act violates the private sphere, a balancing act between the interests pursued by the state and the privacy interest of the individual has to take place, and only if the state pursues a legitimate interest, which cannot be achieved by less intrusive means and which is not outweighed by the privacy interest, is the act compatible with the Basic Law.

As medical records do not belong to the core of the intimate sphere, but rather form part of the private sphere which can be restricted subject to the requirements mentioned, in the case of a seizure of confidential medical records, the public interest in criminal prosecution must be balanced against the privacy interests of the patient. According to the Federal Constitutional Court, the interest in the prosecution of a crime is, in principle, not sufficient to justify a violation of the privacy right.[110] Recent case law of the German Supreme Court, the highest court in criminal and civil matters, seems to suggest that this court now uses the constitutional balancing test for a broad interpretation of s.97 of the Code of Criminal Procedure. In a case of rape in which the victim had consented to the physician's testimony regarding her physical examination after the event, and the defence wanted access to other medical records of the victim to establish that she had alcohol and psychological problems, the court rejected this motion on the grounds that it was not supported by a sufficient showing that the victim's medical records were material to the case. The Court continued:

> The Senate can leave open the question of whether medical records which do not concern the accused but a witness, are in general protected by the prohibition of seizure under s.97 of the Code of Criminal Procedure and are therefore inadmissible in court ... or whether such a principal exemption from seizure which would correspond with the general right to refuse to testify under s.53 of the Code of Criminal Procedure cannot be considered. ... Under the circumstances of this case, a seizure and use of medical records through

---

[109] Weinmann, at 208.
[110] BVerfGE 32, 373, 381 (1972).

procedural measures against the wishes of the victim and against the wishes of the physician must be ruled out ... as a disproportionate intrusion upon a particularly sensitive area of the private sphere.[111]

In another case, however, in which a regional court had decided that the seizure of a victim's medical records was unlawful as it disproportionately interfered with the victim's personality rights, the Supreme Court disagreed and held that:

> The prohibition of a seizure which is not unlawful according to the provisions of the Code of Criminal Procedure can follow directly from the Basic Law, if ... it intrudes upon the constitutionally protected sphere and violates the principle of proportionality. ... However, the intrusion upon the personality right of the person concerned by a seizure for the purpose of securing evidence is only disproportionate if the personality right outweighs the needs of effective criminal prosecution and crime prevention, following from the principle of the rule of law. ... The patient's personality right does not necessarily exclude the seizure of third parties' medical records. ... Rather, the seriousness of the offence must be considered in the balancing process ... so that in cases of serious crime the seizure of third parties' medical records can be lawful.[112]

The Court then excluded the seizure on other grounds.

This case law is interesting, as the Federal Supreme Court in both decisions left open the question of whether or not s.97 of the Code of Criminal Procedure protects the medical records of the non-accused patient. Given that until very recently, those who interpreted s.97 of the Code of Criminal Procedure as protecting the medical records of all patients were in a small minority, the express reference to this minority opinion and the statement that this controversy does not have to be decided in the specific case suggests that the minority opinion gains some weight with the courts. The case law also shows that the Supreme Court is willing to protect medical records of a victim at least as long as the materiality of their content was not sufficiently established by the defence. Furthermore, the Court now expressly holds that in the case of medical records of a non-accused patient, a balancing test has to be performed. According to the Supreme Court the patient's personality rights will not automatically prevail over the state interest in criminal prosecution. Rather, the personality rights may have to yield in cases concerning the prosecution of serious offences.[113] The Regional Court of Hamburg, on the other hand, decided that where the privacy interest of a witness conflicted with the state interest in establishing facts which could potentially incriminate the accused, the privacy interest of the witness had to prevail and the seizure of the witness' medical records was unconstitutional, even though not prohibited under s.97 of the Code of Criminal Procedure.[114]

While the recent developments in the Federal Supreme Court's case law are to be welcomed, it is nevertheless submitted that the protection awarded to medical

---

[111] BGH NStZ 1997, 562.

[112] BGH NStZ 1998, 471, 472.

[113] See also LG Fulda NJW 1990, 2946.

[114] LG Hamburg NJW 1990, 780, 781.

records of non-accused patients does not go far enough and that the view of the Regional Court of Hamburg is preferable. If a patient's confidences are protected by the provisions of the Criminal Code, the provisions of the Code of Criminal Procedure and by constitutional principles, and if in other cases of conflict between the right to medical confidentiality and the state interest in criminal prosecution for various reasons the latter has to yield, regardless of the seriousness of the offence under investigation, it seems inconsistent to allow the seriousness of the crime to be determinative in deciding whether or not the medical records of a non-accused patient may lawfully be seized. Rather, the balancing process now performed by the courts should follow the principles outlined above in the context of a breach of medical confidentiality by the physician.

Another problem sometimes arising in this context is that of whether or not the patient's interest in medical confidentiality outweighs the interest in an effective exercise of defence rights. The Higher Regional Court of Celle[115] had to decide a case in which a physician was accused of negligently causing the death of a patient. The court held that the interest of the physician in presenting exonerating evidence should prevail over the privacy interest of the deceased patient. The court considered whether it was less intrusive and more appropriate to reconcile the competing interests by maintaining medical confidentiality and assuming the truthfulness of the assertions of the defence, but rejected this solution on the grounds that even if this procedure were to result in the acquittal of the physician, without full exploration of the evidence he would still be tormented by doubts as to whether his behaviour had contributed to the patient's death. While it is at least arguable that the interest of the accused in not being subjected to a criminal penalty without having the possibility of presenting exonerating evidence can be important enough to outweigh the privacy interests of a patient, it is submitted that moral quandaries of the physician cannot be of higher value than constitutionally guaranteed privacy rights.

In this context another problem is caused by seizures of confidential patient records in the course of investigations against the physician, for example investigations for tax fraud or for medical malpractice. As s.97 of the Code of Criminal Procedure is only applicable where the patient is accused in criminal proceedings, in such a situation s.97 of the Code of Criminal Procedure will not provide any protection against a search for and seizure of confidential patient records.[116] In its famous *Memmingen* decision, the German Supreme Court held that the seizure of patient records in the course of criminal investigations against a physician for illegal abortions was lawful.[117] In support of this view it has been argued that in such a situation the physician-patient relationship is no longer worthy of protection,[118] and that otherwise the physician could abuse the confidential physician-patient

[115] NJW 1965, 363.
[116] Karlsruher Kommentar-Nack, 6 to s.97.
[117] BGHSt 38, 144, 146 (1991).
[118] Schlüchter, at 289.

relationship for committing crimes without having to fear discovery.[119] It is submitted, however, that the confidentiality of the physician-patient relationship is mainly protected to guarantee the patient's privacy rights and that those rights do not deserve less protection just because the physician has abused this relationship as a cover for criminal activities.[120] If, as already demonstrated, the patient's interest in medical confidentiality always outweighs the state interest in criminal prosecution, this must also apply to the criminal prosecution of physicians. As a way around the fact that the physician does not have to fear discovery, the police could seek the patient's consent to the seizure of his/her medical records, which will in many cases probably be given, particularly if a considerate use of these data were guaranteed.

It is submitted that the current legal situation regarding the application of s.97 of the Code of Criminal Procedure to the seizure of medical records of non-accused patients needs clarification, given that there is a lack of clear guidelines as to the operation of the balancing test and the weight to be accorded to the principle of medical confidentiality within that process.[121] The privacy rights of the patient who is not accused in criminal proceedings are not sufficiently safeguarded under present law. The situation needs to be changed, in that the restriction of the protection of s.97 of the Code of Criminal Procedure to the accused should be abolished, and all patients should be protected against disclosure of their confidential medical records for the mere purpose of criminal prosecution.[122] This is the only way to reconcile the law with the objectives underlying s.97 of the Code of Criminal Procedure, and to put an end to the existing inconsistencies between s.97 of the Code of Criminal Procedure, on the one hand, and s.53 of the Code of Criminal Procedure and s.203 of the Criminal Code, on the other.

3.2 Custody requirement

S.97(2) of the Code of Criminal Procedure limits the protection of confidential medical documents to records that are in the possession of the physician, thus excluding medical documents that are in the possession of the patient him/herself. It follows that medical records of an accused patient cannot be seized at the physician's surgery, but a copy of the same documents can be seized when found in the patient's possession. It is difficult to find a justification for this restriction. The rationale behind the custody requirement seems to be that if protection is awarded to information obtained in the framework of a protected relationship, for example that of physician and patient, there is no longer a justification for this

---

[119] Weyand, wistra 1990, at 6.

[120] See also Lorenz, MDR 1992, at 316, who argues that the fact that the seizure violates the patient's privacy rights is an important factor in the context of the balancing exercise.

[121] For an example of how difficult it is for German courts to make sense of this confusing situation see most recently LG Bielefeld StV 2000, 12, and the commentary by Samson, StV 2000, 55-6.

[122] See also Krekeler, NStZ 1987, at 201; Muschallik, at 138; Schmitt, at 128.

protection when the material has left the confidential context. Thus, where confidential material is no longer in the possession of the physician and third parties have access to this information, the purpose behind the protection of medical confidentiality can no longer be achieved, and, most importantly, the information is no longer confidential. But where the material is in the possession of the patient, it is still within the confidential setting of the physician-patient relationship, and it is as worthy of protection as if it were in the physician's possession.[123] Of course one could object that s.97 of the Code of Criminal Procedure only wants to protect the physician-patient relationship insofar as it would be seriously undermined if the patient were to fear that all information given to the doctor, and no longer under the patient's exclusive control, might be available to the police. It could thus be said that patient documents in the hand of the patient do not need extended protection, as they are under the patient's control. But this leads to the unfortunate result that a physician must be conscious of the danger involved when handing documents or copies of documents over to patients. As the patient has a right of access to his/her medical records, this means that the doctor has to draft those documents very carefully. This could result in sketchy, incomplete or even inaccurate records, as physicians might want to ensure that the confidential information obtained will not leave the confidential sphere. To prevent these unfortunate results, it has been suggested that s.97 of the Code of Criminal Procedure should be interpreted so as to protect medical records from search or seizure regardless of whether they are in the possession of the physician or of the patient, as this is the only way to ensure that the inviolability of a patient's medical confidences is guaranteed.[124] Others, while being of the opinion that s.97(2) of the Code of Criminal Procedure does not leave room for such an interpretation, demand an amendment of the provision to this effect.[125]

3.3 Effect of the patient's consent

Yet another question is that of the effect of the patient's consent in the context of s.97 of the Code of Criminal Procedure. As the purpose behind s.97 of the Code of Criminal Procedure is to prevent a circumvention of s.53 of the Code of Criminal Procedure, it has been widely argued that medical documents are no longer exempt from seizure once the patient has consented to the physician's testimony in respect of confidential information, as according to s.53(2) of the Code of Criminal Procedure such consent excludes the physician's right to refuse to testify.[126]

---

[123] See also Schmitt, at 154-7; Welp (1973), at 416, for the lawyer-client privilege.
[124] Bandisch, NJW 1987, at 2201.
[125] Muschallik, at 138; Petry, at 53.
[126] OLG Hamburg NJW 1962, 689, 690; Karlsruher Kommentar-Nack, 5 to s.97.

3.4 The physician's right to submit confidential material

Another question is whether the physician is allowed voluntarily to submit the material protected by s.97 of the Code of Criminal Procedure to the police or the court, a question which the predominant opinion answers in the affirmative. As according to the predominant opinion, the physician can freely decide to give testimony with regard to the patient's confidences, the same should apply to s.97 of the Code of Criminal Procedure which aims at preventing a circumvention of s.53 of the Code of Criminal Procedure.[127] The voluntary submission of medical records is seen as a waiver of the physician's right, and the material is admissible in court even where the doctor's behaviour constitutes a breach of confidence under s.203 of the Criminal Code,[128] which will always be the case unless a legal justification applies. This approach must be rejected for the same reasons for which it has been argued that the physician does not have a right to decide to give testimony in court about confidential patient information.

4 Summary and conclusion

As medical confidentiality is protected as part of the constitutional personality right, medical privilege equally serves this purpose, though it is argued that medical privilege additionally aims at protecting the physician's interest in the exercise of his/her profession and the state interest in preserving public health. The wording of s.53 of the Code of Criminal Procedure gives the physician the right, rather than imposing upon him/her an obligation, to refuse to testify in criminal court. The predominant opinion concludes that it lies in the physician's discretion whether or not he/she exercises this right. If the physician decides to give testimony, however, he/she will commit the criminal offence of breach of confidentiality, unless the patient has consented to the disclosure of the confidential information, or the prerequisites of the necessity defence are fulfilled. The predominant interpretation of s.53 of the Code of Criminal Procedure thus leads to the unconvincing result that the physician is given a choice the exercise of which will regularly amount to a criminal offence. Given the interplay of s.53 of the Code of Criminal Procedure with s.203 of the Criminal Code, and in the light of the purpose behind medical confidentiality and medical privilege, it seems compelling to argue that no such right can exist and that the physician is rather under an obligation not to testify in criminal court.

S.97 of the Code of Criminal Procedure further complicates the situation, in that it prohibits the seizure of medical documents, but restricts this protection to the patient who is accused in criminal proceedings and to material that is in the possession of the physician. As s.97 of the Code of Criminal Procedure intends to prevent a circumvention of s.53 of the Code of Criminal Procedure, it would seem consistent to interpret both provisions the same way and to extend the protection

---

[127] Karlsruher Kommentar-Nack, 2 to s.97.
[128] BGHSt 18, 227, 230; Kleinknecht/Meyer-Goßner, 5 to s.97.

under s.97 of the Code of Criminal Procedure to all patients. The courts, while leaving open whether or not in the future they might be willing to interpret s.97 of the Code of Criminal Procedure extensively, adopt the approach that a seizure of medical documents relating to non-accused patients is admissible only subject to a balancing test which is based on the principles of constitutional law. Even if a seizure is not prohibited under s.97 of the Code of Criminal Procedure, it is thus only admissible if the privacy right is in the particular case outweighed by a competing interest.

A breach of medical confidentiality can only be justified if a legal justification applies. The only justification sometimes available in cases of such a breach is the necessity defence of s.34 of the Criminal Code which requires, *inter alia*, that the interest promoted by the breach must considerably outweigh the interest which is thereby impaired. While this can never be the case where medical confidentiality conflicts with the interest in criminal prosecution, as the existence of a statutory privilege shows the legislative intent that the interest in medical confidentiality is prevalent, the situation can be different where medical confidentiality conflicts with the interest in crime prevention, with defence rights or with the interests that the innocent will not be prosecuted and convicted, as medical confidentiality then stands in conflict with third party rights. Which interest prevails then depends on a balancing exercise, assessing the competing interests on a case-by-case basis.

The situation in Germany is characterised by the attempt to create a coherent system of protecting privacy and medical confidentiality. However, it can be seen that many inconsistencies exist, and that one of the main problems the German system is faced with is that of trying to interpret and apply all the provisions relevant in this context consistently. Most of the relevant provisions of the Criminal Code and the Code of Criminal Procedure predate the development of the constitutional right to privacy and medical confidentiality. The courts have reacted to the constitutional protection of privacy and medical confidentiality by interpreting statutes according to these principles and by extending the already far-reaching protection provided by ordinary statutes if this is necessary to give effect to constitutional principles. The German experience demonstrates that the existence of statutory provisions does not make reference to broader principles and a balancing of interests superfluous. On the contrary, both the relevant provisions of the ordinary law (for example the necessity defence pursuant to s.34 of the Criminal Code) and the relevant constitutional principles require a balancing exercise and the proportionality of all legal acts and decisions.

The inconsistencies identified in this chapter show that the goal of creating a coherent and consistent system has not been altogether accomplished.

Chapter 6

English Law

In its first part, this chapter will explain how English courts have developed equitable remedies for the protection of confidences, including medical confidentiality, and how the Human Rights Act 1998 has influenced the law in this area. The second part will address the case law regarding medical privilege in criminal court and the physician's disclosure of confidential medical information for the purposes of crime prevention and criminal prosecution. It will also introduce the statutory provisions regulating the search for and seizure of medical records by the police.

PART 1 – PROTECTION OF MEDICAL CONFIDENTIALITY

1 Medical confidentiality as a fundamental right

The UK does not have a Bill of Rights listing fundamental rights and freedoms of the individual and providing them with constitutional rank. The Interdepartmental Working Group Concerning Legislation on Human Rights, with Particular Reference to the European Convention described the English approach to the protection of basic rights before the enactment of the Human Rights Act 1998 as follows:[1]

> The effect of the United Kingdom system of law is to provide, through the development of the common law and by express statutory enactment, a diversity of specific rights with their accompanying remedies. ... The rights that have been afforded in this way are for the most part negative rights to be protected from interference by others, rather than positive rights to behave in a particular way. Those rights which have emerged in the common law can always be modified by Parliament.

This meant that in order to determine which individual rights were protected by the English legal system, reference had to be made to the common law and to statutes.[2]

As the UK takes a dualist approach towards international law, the ratification of the ECHR by the UK did not in itself have the effect of making it part of domestic

---

[1] (1976-77) HL 81.
[2] Fenwick, at 3.

law.[3] Before the incorporation of the Convention into national law, a violation of Convention rights was therefore not actionable before an English court. In *R v Khan,*[4] for example, when deciding on the admissibility of evidence of a conversation that had been taped without the accused's knowledge, Lord Nolan stated:

> The argument that the evidence of the taped conversation is inadmissible could only be sustained if two wholly new principles were formulated in our law. The first would be that the appellant enjoyed a right of privacy, in terms similar to those of art 8 of the convention, in respect of the taped conversation. ... The objection to the first of these propositions is that there is no such right of privacy in English law.[5] ... Under English law, there is, in general, nothing unlawful about a breach of privacy.[6]

However, as the UK is under an international obligation to respect the provisions of the Convention, the ECHR had some impact on English case law. In *Derbyshire County Council v Times Newspapers Ltd,*[7] for example, the Court of Appeal held that the courts must have regard to the implications of the ECHR if a case concerned ambiguity or uncertainty in the common law.

The situation changed in October 2000 with the coming into force of the Human Rights Act 1998 under which many of the ECHR provisions now form part of English law so that they have to be applied by British courts as part of the national law. According to s.2 of the HRA, British courts, when determining a question which arose in connection with a Convention right, must take into account, inter alia, judgments and decisions of the European Court of Human Rights and opinions of the Commission. Strasbourg jurisprudence has therefore now become important for the application and interpretation of English national law. While public authorities are bound by the provisions of the HRA (s.6(1)), this does not apply to Parliament (s.6(3)). If the courts find parliamentary legislation to be incompatible with the Convention, they can issue a statement of incompatibility (s.4 of the HRA), but Parliament is not bound by this opinion and is free to enact legislation that is in violation of the provisions of the HRA. Accordingly, even though the impact of the HRA goes far beyond that of normal statutes in that it infiltrates all areas of English law, at least formally the HRA only has the status of an ordinary statute and does not confer inalienable rights.[8]

This can be demonstrated when looking at the courts' approach to the right to privacy. English courts do not seem to regard Article 8 of the ECHR, which is included in the rights listed in Schedule 1 to the HRA, as granting a new

---

[3] Gearty, at 65.
[4] [1996] 3 All ER 289.
[5] Ibid., at 297-8.
[6] Ibid., at 301.
[7] [1992] 3 WLR 28; see also *Derbyshire County Council v Times Newspapers Ltd* [1993] 1 All ER 1011 (HL), at 1020-1021, per Lord Keith, and *Reynolds v Times Newspapers Ltd and others* [1999] 4 All ER 609 (HL), at 625 per Lord Nicholls, at 635 per Lord Steyn, and at 643-4 per Lord Cooke.
[8] Fenwick, at 3.

fundamental right to private life. Instead, they continue to base their decisions on existing equitable rights and use Article 8 when determining the extent of these rights. A discussion of the impact of the HRA on this area of English law is therefore best placed in the context of the examination of the courts' approach to the equitable duty of confidentiality.[9]

2 Contractual obligation

If the physician-patient relationship is based on a contract, the doctor is under a contractual obligation to maintain the patient's secrets.[10] However, within the framework of the National Health Service (NHS), no direct contract between the physician and the patient is concluded, and a physician is therefore not under a contractual obligation to keep the medical confidences of an NHS patient.[11] Some argue nevertheless that an independent contract, to the effect that the physician owes the patient an obligation to maintain medical confidentiality, could exist between the physician and the NHS-patient, and that the provision of information to the physician by the patient could be sufficient consideration.[12] This view suggests that the provision of information is made primarily for the benefit of the physician, an interpretation that does not seem to take into account the reality of the physician-patient relationship. It is therefore submitted that the mere disclosure of information cannot be regarded as adequate consideration.[13] Thus, as far as the relationship between physicians and NHS patients is concerned, the physician is not under any contractual obligation to respect the patient's confidences. However, where patients are seeking private health care which is normally provided within a contractual relationship, the contract includes the obligation to maintain medical confidentiality, and a breach of that duty would give rise to the remedies for breach of contract.

3 Equitable duty

In English law, the most important legal basis for the protection of medical confidentiality is the equitable duty of a doctor to respect the confidences of his/her patient. Unlike most countries in which the right to confidentiality derives from the right to privacy, before the coming into force of the HRA English law did not recognise a general right to privacy.[14] Of course the distinction between privacy

---

[9] See subheading 3 in this chapter.

[10] *Parry-Jones v Law Society and Others* [1969] 1 Ch 1, at 9 per Diplock, LJ.

[11] Grubb, Pearl, at 240.

[12] Montgomery, at 101.

[13] Grubb, Pearl, at 240.

[14] See, for example, Glidewell LJ's statement in *Kaye v Robertson* [1991] FSR 62 (CA), at 66. For an overview of the different approaches to the protection of privacy in English case law see Coad, at 226-33.

and confidentiality is not clear-cut, and in some cases concerning personal confidences of an individual the courts seem to have given both notions an almost identical meaning.[15] However, English law did not protect the confidences of an individual based on the recognition that a person's private sphere deserves legal protection. The courts nevertheless acknowledged that under certain circumstances confidences might warrant the protection of the law, even in the absence of a legal right to prevent disclosure. An important case establishing the equitable protection of confidences is *Argyll v Argyll*.[16] In that case, the Duke of Argyll, the former husband of the Duchess of Argyll, had published, without her consent, articles revealing details of their married life. Ungoed-Thomas J analysed the existing case law in that area and came to the conclusion that:

> These cases, in my view, indicate ... (2) that a breach of confidence or trust or faith can arise independently of any right of property or contract other, of course, than any contract which the imparting of the confidence in the relevant circumstances may itself create; (3) that the court in the exercise of its equitable jurisdiction will restrain a breach of confidence independently of any right at law.[17]

This case thus demonstrates that the courts are willing to protect confidential relationships and situations by referring, if need be, to the instruments of equitable relief. However, the question remained under what circumstances such legal protection should materialise. In *Coco v A N Clark (Engineers) Ltd*,[18] Megarry J identified the prerequisites of a duty to maintain confidentiality as follows:

> Three elements are normally required if, apart from contract, a case of breach of confidence is to succeed. First, the information itself, in the words of Lord Greene MR in the *Saltman* case [*Saltman Engineering Co Ltd v Campbell Engineering Co Ltd* [1963] 3 All ER 413, at 415] must 'have the necessary quality of confidence about it'. Secondly, that information must have been imparted in circumstances importing an obligation of confidence. Thirdly, there must be an unauthorised use of that information to the detriment of the party communicating it.[19]

3.1 Obligation of confidence

To decide whether a physician is under an obligation to protect a patient's confidences, according to the requirements laid down in the *Coco* case it needs to be established whether information that comes to the knowledge of a physician in the course of the physician-patient relationship can be regarded as having been imparted in circumstances importing an obligation of confidence. To that effect,

---

[15] See, for example, *Prince Albert v Strange* (1849) 64 ER 293, at 312 per Knight Bruce V-C; and, more recently, *Hellewell v Chief Constable of Derbyshire* [1995] 1 WLR 804 (QBD), at 807 per Laws J.

[16] [1967] Ch 302.

[17] Ibid., at 322.

[18] [1969] RPC 41.

[19] Ibid., at 47.

Lord Keith stated in *Attorney General v Guardian Newspapers Ltd and others* (2)[20] that:

> The law has long recognised that an obligation of confidence can arise out of particular relationships. Examples are the relationships of doctor and patient. ... The obligation may be imposed by an express or implied term in a contract but it may also exist independently of any contract on the basis of an independent equitable principle of confidence.[21]

And Lord Donaldson MR held in the same case in the Court of Appeal:

> The right can arise out of a contract. ... But it can also arise as a necessary or traditional incident of a relationship between the confidant and the confider, e.g. priest and penitent, doctor and patient, lawyer and client, husband and wife.[22]

Thus, the relationship between physician and patient was expressly mentioned as a relationship giving rise to a duty of confidentiality, independent of any contractual duty to that effect. The reasons for the recognition of such an obligation can be inferred from the statement by Lord Goff that:

> A duty of confidence arises when confidential information comes to the knowledge of a person (the confidant) in circumstances where he has notice, or is held to have agreed, that the information is confidential, with the effect that it would be just in all the circumstances that he should be precluded from disclosing the information to others.[23]

The obligation is thus derived from concepts of justice and fairness, rather than being based on privacy considerations.

Given the wide-spread recognition of the principle of medical confidentiality, the physician can be said to have notice that the information imparted to him by the patient is confidential and should therefore not be disclosed to others. Thus, the physician is, in principle, under an obligation to maintain patient confidences. With regard to the protection of medical confidentiality in the context of the physician-patient relationship, therefore, the requirement of a situation of confidence will always be satisfied.

However, the condition that a relationship of confidence exists was regarded as the main hurdle for a successful action for breach of confidence in cases in which there had been an intrusion into the private sphere of an individual without a pre-existing relationship between the person whose privacy had been invaded and the intruder. This problem arose, in particular, in respect of publications of intimate details of a person's private life by the press and can relate to the disclosure of confidential medical information, as cases such as *Kaye v Robertson*[24] and *Naomi*

---

[20] [1988] 3 All ER 545.

[21] Ibid., at 639.

[22] Ibid., at 595 (CA).

[23] Ibid, at 658.

[24] [1991] FSR 62 (CA).

Campbell v Mirror Group Newspapers[25] show. Even before the Human Rights Act came into force, English courts showed some tendency to extend the action for breach of confidence to cover situations in which no prior relationship of trust existed between the parties. With regard to the unauthorised taking and publishing of photos, for example, the courts developed the view that this would constitute a breach of confidence as long as the photographer knew that the occasion at which the photos had been taken was a private one and that the scene was not intended to come to the knowledge of outsiders. In *Shelley*,[26] where a photo had been taken during the shooting of a film scene and signs had made it clear that the taking of photographs was not allowed, Martin Mann QC referred to Lord Goff's statement in *Attorney General v Guardian Newspapers Ltd and others* (2)[27] that the circumstances in which a duty of confidence may arise in equity:

> not merely ... embrace those cases where a third party receives information from a person who is under a duty of confidence in respect of it, knowing that it has been disclosed by that person to him in breach of his duty of confidence, but also ... include certain situations, beloved of law teachers, where an obviously confidential document is wafted by an electric fan out of a window into a crowded street, or where an obviously confidential document, such as a private diary, is dropped in a public place, and is then picked up by a passer-by.[28]

And in *Hellewell*, it has been held that:

> If someone with a telephoto lens were to take from a distance and with no authority a picture of another engaged in some private act, his subsequent disclosure of the photograph would, in my judgment, as surely amount to a breach of confidence as if he had found or stolen a letter or diary in which the act was recounted and proceeded to publish it. In such a case, the law would protect what might reasonably be called a right of privacy, although the name accorded to the cause of action would be breach of confidence.[29]

This shows a preparedness to expand the situations that can give rise to an obligation of confidence in order to achieve a more general protection of a person's privacy. At the same time, however, Laws LJ's statement in *Hellewell* demonstrates the limits of such an approach, as it suggests that what is protected is not the intrusion in the private sphere as such, but rather the unauthorised disclosure of personal information that has come to the knowledge of the person making the disclosure by the means of a breach of confidence. Applied to medical confidences of a patient, the invasion of the patient's privacy by obtaining confidential information about him/her, for example, by taking photos of the

---

[25] [2002] HRLR 28, 763 (QBD); [2002] All ER (D) 177 (CA).

[26] *Shelley Films Limited v. Rex Features Limited* [1994] EMLR 134 (ChD), at 146 per Martin Mann QC.

[27] [1988] 3 All ER 545.

[28] Ibid., at 658-9.

[29] *Hellewell v Chief Constable of Derbyshire* [1995] 1 WLR 804 (QBD), at 807 per Laws J.

patient through a telephoto lens during a medical examination, would be unprotected, as long as this information would not be disclosed to others. It can therefore fairly be said that actions for breach of confidence can to some extent achieve the purpose of protecting a person's privacy, but that they do not provide a means to guarantee comprehensive protection of the right to privacy.[30]

With the coming into force of the HRA, Article 8 of the ECHR was given further effect in English law.[31] Under s.6(1) of the HRA, public bodies have to act in compliance with the provisions of the HRA which means that they have to refrain from interfering with the individual's right to private life and are also to some extent under a positive obligation to protect a person's private life.[32] When deciding cases between individuals, courts as public bodies have to give effect to the Convention rights (s.6(3) of the HRA). This raised the question of how best to give the right to private life under Article 8 of the HRA the required legal protection in civil actions between two private parties. One of the cases in which the Court of Appeal had to tackle this question was *Douglas v Hello!*[33] In that case, it had to be decided whether Hello! magazine could be prevented from publishing photos taken at the wedding of Michael Douglas and Catherine Zeta-Jones at which only photographers from OK! magazine had been given the permission (and the exclusive right) to take photos. Security checks were being held at the entrance to the reception and all guests and staff were informed that they were not allowed to take photos. Sedley LJ was of the opinion that 'we have reached a point at which it can be said with confidence that the law recognises and will appropriately protect a right of personal privacy'.[34] The fact that the courts need to act compatibly with the provisions of the HRA and the ECHR 'gives the final impetus to the recognition of a right of privacy in English law'.[35] According to him, the right of privacy was grounded in the equitable doctrine of breach of confidence. However:

> what the concept of privacy does ... is accord recognition to the fact that the law has to protect not only those people whose trust has been abused but those who simply find themselves subjected to an unwanted intrusion into their personal lives. The law no longer needs to construct an artificial relationship of confidentiality between intruder and victim: it can recognise privacy itself as a legal principle drawn from the fundamental value of personal autonomy.[36]

---

[30] For a discussion of the suitability of using the action for breach of confidence in order to protect the right to privacy see, for example, Wright, at 181-2; see also the decision of the European Court of Human Rights in *Peck v UK*, Application No 4464798, Judgment of 28 January 2003.

[31] See the Preamble to the HRA.

[32] See *Venables v News Group Newspapers Ltd* [2001] Fam 430 (CA), at 446 per Butler-Sloss P.

[33] [2001] QB 967 (CA).

[34] Ibid., at 997

[35] Ibid., at 998.

[36] Ibid., at 1001.

Sedley LJ's approach in *Douglas v Hello!* is significant for two reasons. First, because it promotes that English law now recognises a right to privacy, and secondly because it determines that the way to protect this right is not through a separate action for a breach of privacy, but instead through an extension of the existing action for breach of confidence. However, the validity of Sedley LJ's proclamation that English law now recognises a right to privacy has since been questioned. In *Wainwright v Home Office*,[37] a case mainly concerned with the retrospective effect of the HRA, the Court of Appeal not only reiterated the well-known principle that a right to privacy did not exist in English law before the coming into force of the HRA but went further and argued that a general tort of invasion of privacy should not be introduced by the courts. Instead, both Mummery LJ and Buxton LJ suggested that such a decision was to be made by Parliament,[38] given the complexity of the issues involved.

The second of Sedley LJ's contentions, however, has since been confirmed. In *Venables*,[39] for example, Butler-Sloss P stated that private law actions cannot be based on the Convention. Therefore the action of Venables and Thompson, who when only children themselves had killed an infant and who wanted to secure an injunction against the newspapers to refrain them from publishing information disclosing their new identities and their location upon their release from prison, could not be based directly on the Convention, but had instead been properly brought as an action for breach of confidence.[40] She reiterated Lord Goff's statement in *Attorney General v Guardian Newspapers Ltd and others* (2)[41] that a duty of confidence may arise in equity independently of a transaction or relationship between the parties, for example where confidential information comes to the knowledge of the media in circumstances in which the media have notice of its confidentiality.[42] In *A v B*,[43] Lord CJ explained that Article 8 operates so as to extend the areas in which an action for breach of confidence can provide protection for privacy and that it requires a generous approach to the situations in which privacy is to be protected. He confirmed that a duty of confidence will arise whenever the party wanting to disclose someone else's personal information either knows or ought to know that the other person can reasonably expect his/her privacy to be protected.[44]

Thus, the impact of the HRA seems to be that while Article 8 of the HRA does not provide the basis for a new action for breach of privacy, it nevertheless gives rise to an extended application of the action for breach of confidence. To some extent, therefore, it might be justified to conclude that the reception of Article 8 ECHR into English law 'provides an impetus for the notion of respect for privacy

---

[37] [2002] QB 1334 (CA).

[38] Ibid., at 1351 and 1365.

[39] *Venables v News Group Newspapers Ltd* [2001] Fam 430 (CA).

[40] Ibid., at 447.

[41] [1988] 3 All ER 545, at 658.

[42] *Venables v News Group Newspapers Ltd* [2001] Fam 430 (CA), at 462.

[43] *A v B plc and another* [2002] 1 FLR 1021.

[44] Ibid., at 1029.

as an underlying legal value to find expression through the common law'.[45] Indeed, Lord Phillips MR proclaimed in Naomi Campbell that:

> The Human Rights Act 1998 has had a significant impact on the law of confidentiality. ... When considering what information is confidential the courts must have regard to the Article 8 right to respect for private and family life.[46]

However, as the decision in *Wainwright*[47] shows, even in the light of the HRA English courts are shying away from introducing an actionable right of privacy. Until recently it was felt that the HRA did not require the introduction of a new action for breach of privacy, as in *Spencer v UK*,[48] the European Commission of Human Rights had accepted the action for breach of confidence as a sufficient remedy for a violation of the right to private life under Article 8. It therefore seemed as if the approach of the English judiciary to protect the right of privacy under Article 8 ECHR by the means of the action for breach of confidence was compatible with Article 8. This view was reflected by Lord Woolf CJ who argued in *A v B*[49] that the question of whether or not the law requires a separate action for breach of privacy is highly theoretical, as:

> in the great majority, if not in all situations where the protection of privacy is justified, relating to events after the HRA came into force, an action for breach of confidence now will, where appropriate, provide the necessary protection.[50]

However, the recent decision in *Peck v UK*[51] shows that cases may arise in which a breach of privacy under Article 8 of the ECHR does not automatically constitute an actionable breach of confidence, for example in relation to pictures taken in public places. In such a scenario the European Court of Human Rights found the UK to be in breach of Article 13 of the ECHR, as no effective remedy existed in English law in this respect.[52] Lindsay J commented in *Douglas v Hello!*[53] that if Parliament does not introduce an action for invasion of privacy that covers cases in which no breach of confidence can be established, the courts might have to step in if such a case were to come up, despite their reluctance to do so.

Coming back to the specific subject of medical confidentiality, it is submitted that the direct impact of the recent developments under the Human Rights Act will be limited. As the physician was already under an obligation to maintain medical confidentiality before the HRA came into force, the extension of the action for

---

[45] Fenwick, at 537.
[46] *Naomi Campbell v Mirror Group Newspapers Ltd* [2003] QB 633 (CA), at 658.
[47] [2002] QB 1334 (CA).
[48] (1998) 25 EHRR CD 105.
[49] *A v B plc and another* [2002] 1 FLR 1021.
[50] Ibid., at 1027.
[51] Application No 4464798, Judgment of 28 January 2003.
[52] Ibid., at para.113.
[53] [2003] WL 1822887, at para.229.

breach of confidence will mainly be of significance if someone other than the physician has obtained knowledge of confidential patient information, as in the case of *Kaye v Robertson* where reporters took a photo revealing the medical condition of the patient, or in the *Naomi Campbell* case, in which details of her drug therapy came to the knowledge of the press. In such cases, the new approach that no longer requires a relationship of confidentiality in order to give rise to remedies for breach of confidence might enhance the protection of the patient's medical confidences.

However, the main impact of the Human Rights Act might be theoretical rather than practical. As Lord Browne-Wilkinson had explained in *Stephens v Avery*:

> The basis of equitable intervention to protect confidentiality is that it is unconscionable for a person who has received information on the basis that it is confidential subsequently to reveal that information. ... It is the acceptance of the information on the basis that it will be kept secret that affects the conscience of the recipient of the information.[54]

The focus of the law of breach of confidence therefore seemed to lie on the conscience of the person wishing to disclose information that the patient wants to keep confidential and on the trust the patient has placed in that person to keep the information confidential. A shift to the protection of a general right of privacy might give rise to the recognition that the focus should lie on the interests of the patient to have his/her private sphere protected. What is at stake for the patient is not mainly the integrity of certain relationships, but the control over who to grant access to his/her personal sphere and the decision over which information to disclose or not to disclose.

3.2 Confidential quality of the information

To conform with the first requirement set out in *Coco*,[55] it must be established whether the information the protection of which is being sought has the necessary quality of confidence about it. There does not seem to be a clear-cut definition of what exactly is required for information to be regarded as confidential. According to Lord Goff, the duty of confidence applies neither to useless information, nor to trivia.[56] What might count as trivial or useless information in the medical context is not entirely clear. Some people may regard the information that a patient has consulted a certain physician as trivial, but others might attach importance to the same information. Information referring to some illnesses that occur frequently, affect most people and are not regarded as embarrassing, for example a simple cold, may seem trivial to some people and important enough to deserve confidentiality to others. And many people might accord significance to the mere fact that a specialist clinic, such as an abortion clinic or a clinic for sexual health,

---

[54] *Stephens v Avery* [1988] 2 All ER 477, at 482 per Nicolas Browne-Wilkinson V-C (ChD).
[55] [1969] RPC 41.
[56] *Attorney General v Guardian Newspapers Ltd and others* (2) [1988] 3 All ER 545, at 659.

has been attended.[57] The problem was to some extent discussed in *Ashworth Hospital Authority v MGN Ltd.*[58] In that case, print-outs from the data recording system used at Ashworth, a secure hospital for dangerous, violent or criminal patients who are being detained under the Mental Health Act 1983, had been leaked to a journalist who published parts of the print-out in a newspaper. The print-out contained the daily reports on Ian Brady, one of the Moors murderers, including medical nursing, social work, psychology and rehabilitation matters. The extracts published in the newspaper mainly contained observations on Brady's behaviour during his hunger strike. The Court rejected the contention that this information was too trivial to be protected as confidential, quoting the first instance judge's statement that 'there must be a subjective element as to what any one patient would consider so personal that he would not wish it to be divulged'.[59] This subjective approach seems the only way adequately to protect the interests of the patient.

However, this approach is far from being uncontroversial. In *A v B,*[60] for example, the Court of Appeal had to decide an appeal against an injunction secured by a well-known married football player in order to restrain a newspaper from publishing the stories of two women with whom he had been having extra-marital affairs. Lord Woolf CJ held that:

the degree of confidentiality to which A was entitled was very modest [as unlike sexual relations within marriage at home] relationships of the sort which A had with C and D are not the categories of relationships which the court should be astute to protect when the other parties to the relationships do not want them to remain confidential. ... We do not go so far as to say the relationships of the class being considered here can never be entitled to any confidentiality. We prefer to adopt Ousley Js view[61] that the situation is one at the outer limits of relationships which require the protection of the law.[62]

It is not clear whether this statement refers to the question of whether the women owed A an obligation of confidence, or if it refers to the confidential quality of what had happened between the parties, as the Court does not distinguish clearly between those two elements of an action for breach of confidence. However, it seems more likely that Lord Woolf refers to the confidential quality of the information, as the passage he quotes from *Theakston v. MGN Limited* discusses the confidential quality of the sexual acts in question, not the existence of an obligation of confidence.

Another important case in this context is that of *Naomi Campbell.* The famous model sought damages for breach of confidentiality and compensation under s.13 of the Data Protection Act 1998 in respect of the publication of articles revealing her drug addiction and details about her attendance at meetings of Narcotics

[57] See *R v Cardiff Crown Court, ex parte Kellam* [1994] 16 BMLR 76, at 79-80.
[58] [2001] 1 All ER 991 (CA).
[59] Ibid., at 1002 per Lord Phillips MR.
[60] *A v B plc and another* [2002] 1 FLR 1021.
[61] *Theakston v MGM Limited* [2002] EWHC 137 (QB).
[62] *A v B plc and another* [2002] 1 FLR 1021, at 1040.

Anonymous, with accompanying photographs that had been taken without her consent and which showed her leaving such a meeting. Justice Morland held that 'the details of Miss Naomi Campbell's attendance at Narcotics Anonymous do have the necessary quality of confidence about them. They bear the badge or mark of confidentiality'. Citing Gleeson CJ in *Australia Broadcasting Corporation v Lenah Game Meats Pty Ltd*,[63] he argued that information relating to Naomi Campbell's therapy for drug addiction and containing details about her regular attendance at Narcotics Anonymous meetings was:

> easily identifiable as private and disclosure of that information would be highly offensive to a reasonable person of ordinary sensibilities. Or, to use the guideline test given by Lord Woolf CJ in *A v B* (CA 11 March 2002) at paragraph 11 (vii) it is obvious in my judgment that there existed a private interest worthy of protection.[64]

Both in *Naomi Campbell* and in *A v B* the courts seem to suggest that the legal protection of confidences is subject to the courts' own assessment of what interests might be worthy of the law's protection, thereby undermining the subjective approach suggested in *Ashworth Hospital Authority v MGN Ltd*.[65] It seems ironic that the Court of Appeal in *Naomi Campbell* reiterated the statement that it will usually be obvious whether there is a private interest worthy of protection, as the Court of Appeal differed from Morland J's view, stating that:

> We do not consider that a reasonable person of ordinary sensibilities, on reading that Miss Campbell was a drug addict, would find it highly offensive, or even offensive, that the "Mirror" also disclosed that she was attending meetings of Narcotics Anonymous.[66]

This was based on Lord Phillips MR's assessment that while details of a medical condition or its treatment are well recognised as confidential, Morland J erred in holding that the information that Miss Campbell was receiving therapy from Narcotics Anonymous was to be equated with disclosure of clinical details of medical treatment and in itself deserved to be protected as confidential.[67] Thus, medical information might be protected on the basis of the confidential content of the information, but the level of confidentiality is to be assessed by the courts. The danger inherent in this approach becomes apparent in *A v B* where the decision that the confidentiality of extra-marital sexual relationships does not deserve the same degree of legal protection as sexual relations within a marriage smacks of a moral judgment based on the Court's value system. It is submitted that if the Court in *A v B* had applied the first test suggested by Morland J in *Naomi Campbell*, the outcome might have been different, as it seems very unlikely that a reasonable

---

[63] [2001] H.C.A. 63, at para.42.
[64] *Naomi Campbell v Mirror Group Newspapers* [2002] HRLR 28, 763, at 771 per Morland J.
[65] [2001] 1 All ER 991 (CA).
[66] *Naomi Campbell v Mirror Group Newspapers Ltd* [2003] QB 633 (CA), at 660 per Lord Phillips MR.
[67] Ibid., at 659.

person of ordinary sensibilities would not regard such information as private and would not find it highly offensive if such information were to be disclosed. Thus, it seems far from obvious how to determine objectively whether or not certain information should be regarded as confidential. More importantly, however, approaches to confidentiality that focus on objective equitable considerations which are to be determined by the courts are difficult to reconcile with the task of an action for breach of confidence, that is to guarantee the right to privacy under Article 8 of the HRA. This objective can only be achieved if it is left to the subjective perspective of the individual whether or not personal information is to be regarded as confidential. Such an approach would still make it possible to withhold legal protection from some information that the individual wants to keep confidential when conflicting interests justify disclosure.[68]

A controversial case that had to be decided in the light of the HRA is that of *Venables*.[69] In that case, Butler-Sloss P held that the question of whether or not information falls within the confidentiality brackets, i.e. has the necessary quality of confidentiality about it and therefore deserves the protection of the law, might depend on whether or not the information 'requires a special quality of protection'. She went on to state that:

> In the present case the reasons for advancing that special quality is that, if the information was published, the publication would be likely to lead to grave and possibly fatal consequences. In my judgment, the court does have the jurisdiction, in exceptional cases, to extend the protection of confidentiality of information, even to impose restrictions on the Press, where not to do so would be likely to lead to serious physical injury, or to the death, of the person seeking that confidentiality, and there is no other way to protect the applicants other than by seeking relief from the court.[70]

Butler-Sloss P seems to have taken the stance that the positive duty of the State to protect an individual from threats to his/her life or from threats of serious injury might require the courts to extend the notion of confidence. The action for breach of confidence is thus not, as in other cases, extended to protect privacy interests but rather serves the protection of other interests of the individual.[71] It is conceded that an implication of the individual's right to life or right to physical integrity might strengthen his/her case against disclosure of confidential information. However, it can only be hoped that this case will not be interpreted to mean that the confidentiality interests of the individual as such are not important enough to deserve the law's protection.

Another recent decision relevant in the context of medical confidentiality is that of *Ann Stevens v Plymouth City Council ex parte C*.[72] The case concerned a mother's

---

[68] See the discussion in Part 2, infra.

[69] *Venables v News Group Newspapers Ltd* [2001] Fam 430 (CA).

[70] Ibid., at 462.

[71] See also *Mills v News Group Newspapers Ltd* [2001] EMLR 41, 957 (ChD), at 973 per Lawrence Collins J.

[72] [2002] 1 WLR 2583.

application to be given access to the mental health records, psychological assessments, and approved social workers' reports of her son, as well as to the minutes of case conferences and professional network meetings and summaries from staff and his keyworker at his present home. Hale LJ held that some of this information will be confidential, most obviously the medical reports and recommendations, but also parts of the records of the social workers and other professionals. However, she then went on to say that straightforward descriptions of everyday life are not normally thought to be confidential.[73] This is problematic, as these descriptions seem to be related to the mental illness of the patient and are only being made and reported because of this person's status as a patient. Accordingly, a distinction between confidential and non-confidential information in this context seems artificial and difficult if not impossible to make. At least as far as the information contained in the day to day activities has a medical content or has been observed by a medical practitioner, the case is also difficult to reconcile with well-established previous cases. Boreham J, for example, had stated in *Hunter v Mann*[74] that 'the doctor is under a duty not to disclose, without the consent of the patient, information which he, the doctor, has gained in his professional capacity'. This holding suggests that confidentiality attaches not only to information confided by the patient in the physician, but also to information that came to the knowledge of the physician by any other means, for example the physician's own observations, as long as these observations were made in the course of the physician-patient relationship.[75] This was confirmed by Bingham LJ in *W v Egdell*,[76] when stating that:

> We were referred, as the judge was, to the current advice given by the General Medical Council to the medical profession pursuant to s 35 of the Medical Act 1983. Rule 80 provides:
> 'It is a doctor's duty, except in the cases mentioned below, strictly to observe the rule of professional secrecy by refraining from disclosing voluntarily to any third party information about a patient which he has learnt directly or indirectly in his professional capacity as a registered medical practitioner ...'
> I do not doubt that this accurately states the general rule as the law now stands.[77]

Communications between patient and physician thus receive a broad protection. However, some scope for debate remains. It is not clear, for example, whether the mere attendance of a patient at a clinic is in itself confidential information. It is submitted that such information should be protected regardless of the specialty of the medical practitioner, as it should be left to the patient to determine what he/she regards as sensitive treatment.

Another question is to what extent information the physician received outside of a physician-patient relationship should be protected, for example if the patient tells

---

[73] Ibid., at 2594.

[74] [1974] 2 All ER 414, at 417.

[75] See for example Gurry, at 148.

[76] [1990] 1 All ER 835.

[77] Ibid., at 849.

a physician his/her medical secrets at a social gathering. In favour of an extension of the physician's obligation of confidence to such situations it has been argued that any information about a patient which the doctor receives should be subject to a duty of confidentiality in order to maintain the essential relationship of trust upon which the effective provision of medical treatment depends.[78] This argument may have some value as long as a physician-patient relationship exists between the two parties. If, however, no such professional relationship exists, it is difficult to see how the physician can be under any duty of confidence based on his/her profession, and how the disclosure of information confided in him at a party could undermine the trust governing a physician-patient relationship.

English law does not recognise confidence in iniquity,[79] and information about the commission of a crime therefore does not have confidential status.[80] This applies to past as well as to future crimes.[81] The exact meaning of this concept is unclear. *R v Kennedy*,[82] for example, seems to imply that psychiatrists are under no obligation of confidentiality when a patient utters threats to kill someone. Equally, Rougier J stated in *R v Harrison*[83] that no confidentiality exists for someone who expresses the intent to continue a career of murder. The case of *R v Kennedy* demonstrates the difficulties with this approach. In that case, the court accepted the trial judge's view that a distinction must be made between a 'defendant confiding in a doctor ... that he has feelings or fears that he may kill someone, and saying on the other hand that he intends to kill someone'.[84] This would have far-reaching implications for the psychiatrist-patient relationship. Not everything revealed by the patient would then be protected as confidential, and confidentiality would instead depend on a difficult distinction between intentions and mere threats and fantasies. This has the undesirable consequence that the patient needs to be careful as to how to phrase whatever he/she decides to confide in the psychiatrist, and that the psychiatrist needs to be equally careful as to how he/she phrases potential questions to the patient. If such information were not protected by confidentiality, the psychiatrist would be allowed to reveal a patient's intimate secrets without the need of testing whether or not disclosure can exceptionally be justified, as disclosure would then not constitute a breach of duty. It is submitted that it is preferable to attach confidentiality to patient information on the basis of the confidentiality of the relationship in which the information has been imparted, not on the basis of the content of the information. All information imparted in physicians or psychiatrists in the exercise of their profession would then be confidential, regardless of its

---

[78] At 499.
[79] *Initial Services Ltd. v Putterill* [1968] 1 QB 396, at 405 per Denning MR.
[80] Gurry, at 329.
[81] Ibid., at 331 with further references.
[82] [1999] 1 Cr App R 54 (CA), at 60 per Lord Bingham CJ.
[83] [2000] WL 1026999, at para.8.
[84] [1999] 1 Cr App R 54 (CA), at 58.

content, and the medical professional would have to justify every case of disclosure according to public interest criteria.[85]

Another aspect of the confidential quality of information has been mentioned by Greene MR in *Saltman Engineering Co Ltd v Campbell Engineering Co Ltd (1948)*:[86]

> The information to be confidential must ... have the necessary quality of confidence about it, namely it must not be something which is public property and public knowledge.

While this seems to be a straightforward prerequisite of a duty of confidentiality, the interpretation of what is or is not public knowledge can prove difficult and controversial. In *Stephens v Avery*,[87] for example, the plaintiff had confided details of her sex life to the first defendant and the first defendant had disclosed this information to a newspaper. The court had to decide whether the fact that the sexual conduct at issue was evidently known to the sexual partner of the plaintiff meant that it did not qualify as confidential information and held that:

> The mere fact that two people know a secret does not mean that it is not confidential. If in fact information is secret, then in my judgment it is capable of being kept secret by the imposition of a duty of confidence on any person to whom it is communicated. Information only ceases to be capable of protection as confidential when it is in fact known to a substantial number of people.[88]

This holding seems to suggest that information does not lose its confidential character merely because it was confided in or has otherwise come to the knowledge of a third party. Thus, the patient's medical information does not lose its confidential character by the fact that the physician gains knowledge of it, and it remains confidential even if the patient confides his/her medical secret in a limited number of people, for example close relatives or friends. Contrast the so-called *Spycatcher* case.[89] In that case the question arose whether information that had become widely known to the public due to the defendant's disclosure, still had the necessary quality of confidentiality to it so that the confidant remained under an obligation to maintain confidentiality. In that case, a former member of the British security service, in breach of his duty of confidentiality, wrote his memoirs. After the book had been published in the U.S. and had been disseminated in many countries, it was held with regard to whether the information still had the necessary quality of confidence:

> The reason why the duty of confidence is extinguished is that the matter is no longer secret and there is therefore no secrecy in relation to such matter remaining to be

---

[85] See also the discussion infra, part 2.

[86] [1963] 3 All ER 413, at 415.

[87] [1988] 2 All ER 477.

[88] Ibid., at 481 per Nicolas Browne-Wilkinson V-C (ChD).

[89] *Attorney General v Guardian Newspapers Ltd and others* (2) [1988] 3 All ER 545.

preserved by the duty to confidence. It is meaningless to talk of a continuing duty of confidence in relation to matters disclosed world-wide. It is meaningful only to discuss the remedies available to deprive the delinquent confidant ... of benefits flowing from the breach, or in an appropriate case to compensate the confider.[90]

And Lord Goff equally stressed that:

The principle of confidentiality only applies to information to the extent that it is confidential. In particular, once it has entered what is usually called the public domain (which means no more than that the information in question is so generally accessible that, in all the circumstances, it cannot be regarded as confidential) then, as a general rule, the principle of confidentiality can have no application to it. ... The confidential information, as confidential information, has ceased to exist, and with it should go, as a matter of principle, the obligation of confidence.[91]

Lord Donaldson MR held in the Court of Appeal:

That which has no character of confidentiality because it has already been communicated to the world, i.e. made generally available to the relevant public, cannot thereafter be subjected to a right of confidentiality. ... However, this will not be the case if the information has previously only been disclosed to a limited part of that public.[92]

The facts of this case were rather extreme, in that the information had literally been published almost world-wide. Applied to the context of medical confidentiality, the holdings seem to suggest that once the patient's medical secrets have become the subject of wide-spread publication, they cease to be confidential, and the physician can then no longer be under a duty to keep this information to him/herself. However, if it was the physician who made the information publicly known, equitable remedies might be available regarding the original breach of confidence.

This leaves the difficulty of where to draw the line between information that is so widely known as to lose its confidential status and information that is only known to a limited part of the public and therefore still confidential. In *Bunn v British Broadcasting Corporation and another*,[93] Lightman J had to decide a case in which the plaintiff sought an injunction to stop the disclosure of statements he had made during a police interview under caution. In the course of a criminal trial against the plaintiff, the judge's attention was drawn to that statement, and the judge read it to himself. Lightman J decided that even though the statement made by the plaintiff had enjoyed confidentiality, its confidential status had ended because the contents of the statement were in the public domain. To that effect, he held that:

The reading of the statement by Phillips J in open court would appear to me to be sufficient for this purpose. I do not think that it is realistic to draw a distinction between a document which the judge reads and a document which is read to the judge. The

---

[90] Ibid., at 647 per Lord Brightman.
[91] Ibid., at 660-661.
[92] Ibid., at 595.
[93] [1998] 3 All ER 552 (ChD).

distinction is artificial today when it is a matter of taste for the individual judge whether he requires a document to be read or reads it himself (consider RSC Ord 24, r 14A). But in any event Mr Suckling, referring the judge to the statement, stated its substance (the element in it for which protection is sought in these proceedings) in open court. ... [A]ny confidentiality expired when the contents of the statement were disclosed in open court.[94]

It must be questioned whether this holding is compatible with Lord Donaldson's statement in *Attorney General v Guardian Newspapers Ltd and others* (2), as it is doubtful that the fact that the substance of the statement was summarised in open court, means that it loses its confidential character.[95] The information is then still only known to a part of the public, but not to the public in general. The fact that the judge has read the statement to him/herself can hardly be used to terminate the confidential quality of the information, as then only the judge takes actual knowledge of its content. As long as other members of the public do not obtain knowledge of the content of the statement, this can hardly suffice to say that the information is now known to the public. This scepticism seems to have been shared by Eady J in *W.B. v H. Bauer Publishing Ltd*,[96] when refusing to find that information was in the public domain simply because it had been the subject of criminal proceedings which had attracted some newspaper coverage. In *R v Chief Constable of the North Wales Police and others, ex parte AB and another*,[97] it has been held that a breach of confidence can be committed by a conjunction of various facts that are all in the public domain, for example where a person is warned that the persons living on his caravan site are the sex offenders about whom a newspaper article had been published.[98]

The question of when information is so public as to lose its confidential character has recently been discussed in the context of one of the *Pinochet* decisions.[99] In the course of extradition proceedings against Senator Pinochet, the question arose whether Pinochet was unfit to stand trial. If that had been the case, according to the provisions of the Extradition Act of 1989 the Secretary of State would have had discretion as to whether or not to extradite Pinochet. In order to make this decision, the Secretary of State initiated correspondence with the solicitors representing Pinochet, inviting Pinochet to make himself available for medical examination. Pinochet agreed to the medical examination and to the condition that the Secretary of State would make the reports available to the Director of Public Prosecutions and to the Solicitor General in relation to extradition, provided that 'any medical reports would not be considered for any other purpose and would not be disclosed

---

[94] Ibid., at 557.

[95] But see *Mahon v Rahn* [1997] 3 All ER 687 (CA), a case in which Otton LJ at 708 distinguished, based on s.17 of the Criminal Procedure and Investigation Act 1996, between used and unused material and argued that no confidentiality attached to documents once they had been displayed in open court.

[96] [2002] EMLR 8, 145, at 154.

[97] [1997] 4 All ER 691 (QBD).

[98] Ibid., at 704 per Lord Bingham CJ.

[99] *R v Secretary of State for Home Department ex parte Belgium; R v Secretary of State for Home Department ex parte Amnesty International* [2000] WL 486 (QBD).

to any member of the Crown Prosecution Service in any other capacity'. Thereafter the Secretary of State selected a team of clinicians who were considered to have the required range of specialisations and who had no inappropriate personal interest in the case. The unanimous and unequivocal conclusion of all four medical experts was that following the deterioration in the state of Pinochet's health, he was not at the time of the report capable of meaningful participation in a trial, and that that was not expected to change. After receiving the report, the Secretary of State sought the advice of the Chief Medical Officer who concluded that the report was authoritative, thorough and left no doubt that Pinochet was not fit to stand trial. The Secretary of State wrote to the various interested parties to inform them of the finding of unfitness to stand trial and that no change was expected. He also stated that he was minded to decide not to extradite Pinochet and that the effect of such a decision would be that the current basis for his continuing detention would lapse. The Secretary of State asked for Pinochet's consent to the disclosure of the reports, under conditions of strict confidence, to Spain, France, Belgium and Switzerland, which was refused. In the light of this refusal, the Secretary of State felt that he could not disclose the medical reports and that he had to make his decision without giving the requesting States the opportunity to view and comment on them. Belgium and Amnesty International applied for permission to move for judicial review of the decision not to disclose the medical reports.

The question which is of interest in the current context is whether the information contained in the reports was still confidential, given that the report's conclusions, that is Pinochet's unfitness to stand trial because he would not be able to follow the proceedings, give intelligible instructions to his solicitors or give a coherent statement of his case, had already been widely disseminated to the public. According to Stephen Brown LJ, the reports nevertheless maintained their confidential status, as they contained the factual findings underlying the publicly known conclusions, so that their disclosure would have led to an additional loss of confidence. Thus, the decision clarifies that while the conclusions of the medical experts that had been widely publicised were no longer confidential so that their disclosure could not constitute a breach of confidence, all observations contained in the reports that had not been made known to the public maintained their confidential status. Interestingly, even though the decision predates the coming into force of the Human Rights Act, Stephen Brown LJ discussed the impact of Article 8 of the ECHR and stated that the protection of medical data was of fundamental importance to a person's enjoyment of his or her right for private life under Article 8 and the other two Lord Justices agreed with that approach.

3.3 Breach of duty

For an action for breach of confidence to succeed, the confidential information must have been used or disclosed without authorisation. Inherent in the definition of a breach of confidence is therefore the notion of a lack of authorisation, the authorisation usually consisting of the patient's consent. Two main problems arise when determining whether a breach of confidence has occurred: First, does a breach require disclosure of confidential information, or would a misuse of such information without disclosure be sufficient? Secondly, does the disclosure of confidential information in anonymised form amount to a breach of confidence?

In most cases of a breach of medical confidentiality, the misuse will consist in the disclosure of confidential patient information. However, it is also possible that such information is being used, without disclosure, beyond the purposes for which it had been disclosed. Take the example of the use of patient information for research purposes without the patient's consent. This could either be done by disclosing the information to a research team, or it could be done without disclosure, if the physician in whom the information has been confided uses the information for his/her own research project.[100] The answer to the question of whether a use of confidential information without disclosure would constitute a breach of confidence is controversial. It has been argued that a misuse of information without disclosure might infringe rights, for example in the context of personal information the right to privacy, but that the unauthorised use of such information would not amount to a breach of confidence.[101] This view is not convincing. First, the doctrine of breach of confidence has developed in the context of commercial transactions, where the misuse of confidential information might be just as detrimental as disclosure, and the courts accordingly have held that the misuse of information as such was sufficient to establish a breach of confidence.[102] If a breach of confidence in the context of personal information ever required disclosure, it is submitted that this can no longer be the case where an action for breach of confidence serves as the basis for the protection of the individual's right to privacy under Article 8 of the ECHR. At least if the concept of privacy is not reduced to granting a right to prevent the unauthorised dissemination of private information, but also gives the patient control over his/her confidential information, the privacy of the individual can be just as severely invaded by an unwanted use of personal information as by an unwanted disclosure of such information, for example where the information is used for a research project of which the patient disapproves.[103]

The question of the use of anonymised data arose in *Source Informatics*.[104] Source Informatics had asked pharmacists to provide against a fee certain information contained on prescription forms, namely the names of the prescribing GPs and the identity and quantity of the prescribed drugs. The Department of Health issued a policy document stating that the anonymisation of this information would not remove the duty of confidence owed to the patients. In his decision, after a comprehensive analysis of prior breach of confidence cases, Simon Brown LJ suggested that:

---

[100] For detailed guidelines on the use of confidential patient information for research purposes see GMC, *Confidentiality: Protecting and Providing Information*.

[101] Kennedy, Grubb, at 1063.

[102] See, for example, *Coco v A N Clark (Engineers) Ltd* [1969] RPC 41; *Saltman Engineering Co Ltd v Campbell Engineering Co Ltd* [1963] 3 All ER 413.

[103] For a discussion of this point see, for example, Beyleveld, Histed, at 296-7.

[104] *R v Department of Health, ex parte Source Informatics* [2000] 1 All ER 786.

[T]he clear and consistent theme emerging from all these authorities is this: the confidant is placed under a duty of good faith to the confider and the touchstone by which to judge the scope of his duty and whether or not it has been fulfilled or breached is his own conscience, no more and no less. One asks, therefore, on the facts of this case: would a reasonable pharmacist's conscience be troubled by the proposed use to be made of patients' prescriptions? Would he think that by entering Source's scheme he was breaking his customers' confidence, making unconscientious use of the information they provide?[105]

He came to the conclusion that on the facts of the case, the:

pharmacists' consciences ought not reasonably to be troubled by co-operation with Source's proposed scheme. The patient's privacy will have been safeguarded, not invaded. The pharmacist's duty of confidence will not have been breached.[106]

Thus, because according to Simon Brown LJ the privacy interests of the patient were sufficiently safeguarded by the anonymisation of the information, no interests of the patient were adversely affected by the scheme and, consequently, no breach of duty had occurred.[107] However, it could be argued that the anonymisation itself constituted a breach of confidence, as it could be qualified as a misuse of the confidential information. It is troubling that whether or not a breach of duty occurred shall depend on the conscience of the person on whom the law imposes the obligation. It seems, again, as if the courts are less concerned with the protection of the person whose confidences are at stake and focus more on the state of mind of the other party, an attitude which is not acceptable if the breach of confidence action is to guarantee privacy protection as required by Article 8 of the ECHR.

3.4 Detriment

A last requirement for an action for breach of confidence is that the confidential information has been used to the detriment of the confider. In *Attorney General v Guardian Newspapers Ltd and others* (2),[108] the court had to struggle with this requirement. Lord Keith argued:

There may be no financial detriment to the confider since the breach of confidence involves no more than an invasion of personal privacy. ... Information about a person's private and personal affairs may be of a nature which shows him in a favourable light and

---

[105] Ibid., at 796.

[106] Ibid., at 797.

[107] This was based on Bingham LJ's holding in *W v Egdell* [1990] 1 All ER 835 (CA), at 848, that a psychiatrist could not discuss the case of his patient in a learned article or in his memoirs, unless he took appropriate steps to conceal the patient's identity. For a critical analysis of this argument see Beyleveld, Histed, at 297.

[108] [1988] 3 All ER 545.

would by no means expose him to criticism. ... I would think it a sufficient detriment to the confider that information given in confidence is to be disclosed to persons whom he would prefer not to know it, even though the disclosure would not be harmful to him in any positive way.[109]

The court thus adopted a broad interpretation of detriment, as no financial harm is required. Rather, the disclosure of confidential information in itself seems to be sufficient to establish some sort of detriment, as long as the confider had an interest in keeping the information secret, regardless of whether or not the information would shed a negative light on or embarrass the confider. In *Cornelius v de Taranto*,[110] a case in which a psychiatrist who had been consulted to provide a medico-legal report forwarded that report, without the consent of the patient, to the patient's GP and another psychiatrist, Morland J decided that the very fact of a disclosure of information in breach of contract and breach of confidence amounted to a detriment.[111] In *Naomi Campbell*,[112] the Morland J accepted that the publication of details regarding her regular attendance of Narcotics Anonymous meetings was, 'viewed objectively, likely to effect adversely her attendance and participation in therapy meetings', and that was regarded as a sufficient detriment to warrant compensation. This tendency to give the notion of detriment an extensive and subjective interpretation is to be welcomed as it strengthens the interests of the person whose confidences are being disclosed.[113]

3.5 Remedies

If all of the above-mentioned prerequisites of an action for breach of confidence are met, the patient can secure an injunction to prevent disclosure. If information in relation to which an obligation of confidence existed was disclosed, the patient can in limited circumstances obtain compensation.[114] Until recently, in such cases which frequently will not involve any financial loss, only nominal damages were available.[115] In *Cornelius v de Taranto*,[116] Morland J held that Article 8 of the ECHR required that compensation in cases of breach of confidence not be restricted to nominal damages, as otherwise the right to private life would not be sufficiently protected.[117] Instead, he came to the conclusion that damages for injury

---

[109] Ibid., at 639-40.
[110] [2001] EMLR 12, 329.
[111] Ibid., at 347. This has been confirmed by the Court of Appeal, [2002] EMLR 12, 112.
[112] *Naomi Campbell v Mirror Group Newspapers* [2002] HRLR 28, 763, at 772 per Morland J.
[113] However, see *Naomi Campbell v Mirror Group Newspapers* [2003] QB 633, at 661 per Lord Phillips MR, where the Court of Appeal overturned Morland J's holding on the grounds that there was no breach of a duty of confidence.
[114] See the discussion in Kennedy, Grubb, at 1133-5.
[115] *Attorney General v Guardian Newspapers Ltd and others* (2) [1988] 3 All ER 545, at 639-40 per Lord Keith.
[116] [2001] EMLR 12, 329.
[117] Ibid., at 344.

to feelings must be made available in such cases, the assessment of which depend, inter alia, on the nature and detail of the confidential material disclosed and the extent of disclosure.[118] This approach is to be welcomed, as otherwise patients would frequently be without effective remedies in cases of breach of confidence, which would in turn limit the effectiveness of the protection of their right to private life under Article 8 of the ECHR.

3.6 Purpose behind equitable protection of medical confidentiality

Most English courts that have had to discuss problems of confidentiality have emphasised that the protection of confidentiality was granted in the public interest.[119] In *Attorney General v Guardian Newspapers Ltd and others* (2)[120] Lord Keith put it as follows:

> The right to privacy is clearly one which the law should in this field seek to protect. ... As a general rule it is in the public interest that confidences should be respected, and the encouragement of such respect may in itself constitute a sufficient ground for recognising and enforcing the obligation of confidence.[121]

And Lord Goff stated:

> The existence of this broad principle reflects the fact that there is such a public interest in the maintenance of confidences that the law will provide remedies for their protection. ... The basis of the law's protection of confidence is that there is a public interest that confidences should be preserved and protected by law. ... In the case of private citizens there is a public interest that confidential information should as such be protected.[122]

In the Court of Appeal, Lord Donaldson MR had taken a similar stance:

> There is an inherent public interest in individual citizens and the state having an enforceable right to the maintenance of confidence. Life would be intolerable in personal and commercial terms, if information could not be given or received in confidence and the right to have that confidence respected supported by the force of law.[123]

According to the different holdings in *Attorney General v Guardian Newspapers Ltd and others* (2), the protection of confidences is thus an important societal goal. However, the reasons behind the public interest in the protection of confidences are not formulated very clearly. It has already been demonstrated that the law of

---

[118] Ibid., at 248-9; see also Morland J's holding in *Naomi Campbell v Mirror Group Newspapers* [2002] HRLR 28, 763, at 790-796.

[119] See, for example, *Lion Laboratories Ltd v Evans* [1984] 2 All ER 417, at 422 per Stephenson LJ.

[120] [1988] 3 All ER 545.

[121] Ibid., at 639-40.

[122] Ibid., at 658-60.

[123] Ibid., at 596.

confidence developed in the interest of protecting the trust and integrity existing in certain relationships and certain situations. One of the main underlying considerations seems to be that of fairness, as the protection of confidences is regarded to be in the public interest where the confider had a reasonable expectation and a sufficient interest in keeping the relevant information secret, while the confidant knew that the information was disclosed to him/her in confidence.

The more general point that the preservation of a person's confidences lies in the public interest has been confirmed with regard to confidential medical information. In *X v Y and others*,[124] a case concerning medical practitioners suffering from AIDS, Rose J held that:

> Confidentiality is of paramount importance to such patients, including doctors. ... If it is breached or if the patients have grounds for believing that it may be or has been breached they will be reluctant to come forward for and to continue with treatment and, in particular, counselling. ... If treatment is not provided or continued the individual will be deprived of its benefit and the public are likely to suffer from an increase in the rate or spread of the disease. The preservation of confidentiality is therefore in the public interest.[125] ... It is in the public interest that actual or potential AIDS sufferers should be able to resort to hospitals without fear of this being revealed, that those owing duties of confidence in their employment should be loyal and should not disclose confidential matters and that, *prima facie*, no one should be allowed to use information extracted in breach of confidence from hospital records even if disclosure of the particular information may not give rise to immediately apparent harm.[126]

From this judgment, it becomes clear that the recognition of a public interest in preserving medical confidentiality is based on several considerations. According to Rose J, the public interest seems to rest on the supposition that without medical confidentiality, patients will be reluctant to seek medical advice and treatment. It follows that the absence of medical confidentiality would harm the individual's health. Society as a whole could then suffer the adverse consequences if the individual were discouraged to seek medical advice and treatment, as this might lead to a spread of disease. Medical confidentiality is thus based on utilitarian considerations. It is not entirely clear whether Rose J's holding also recognises that the protection of the individual's health and privacy lie in the public interest.

In the recent case of *H (A Healthcare Worker) v Associated Newspapers Limited* and *H (A Healthcare Worker) v N (A Health Authority)*,[127] a healthcare worker had been diagnosed as HIV positive. He ceased to practice and notified N of the reasons for this. As many of H's patients had undergone procedures which were believed to involve a risk of infection, according to the Department of Health guidelines they should have been notified that they had been treated by an HIV positive healthcare worker and offered HIV testing and advice. To be able to notify

---

[124] [1988] 2 All ER 648 (QBD).
[125] Ibid., at 656.
[126] Ibid., at 660.
[127] [2002] EMLR 23, 425 (CA).

H's former patients, N requested H to supply particulars of the patients and their medical records which H refused to do. He sought a court declaration that the proposed notification exercise was unlawful based on considerations of patient confidentiality. In addition, he applied for a court order restraining N from taking any steps which might directly or indirectly reveal H's identity and his HIV status. When the Mail on Sunday learned about this action, they wished to publish a story about it, which led H to commence an action against Associated Newspapers Limited (ANL) in order to restrain them from the soliciting and publication of any information which might directly or indirectly lead to a disclosure of the identity or whereabouts of the applicant or his patients. In particular, he asked for a prohibition on the publication of details of the applicant's specialty; details as to when he had been diagnosed as HIV positive and went off work; and a prohibition to publish the name of N. Lord Phillips MR held that:

> there is an obvious public interest in preserving the confidentiality of victims of the AIDS epidemic and, in particular, of healthcare workers who report the fact that they are HIV positive. ... [I]f healthcare workers are not to be discouraged from reporting that they are HIV positive, it is essential that all possible steps are taken to preserve the confidentiality of such reports.[128]

Again, the reasoning of the Court as to the value of medical confidentiality is mainly based on utilitarian considerations of the protection of the public from the spread of AIDS. Similarly, in the context of psychiatric treatment, it was held in *Ashworth Hospital Authority v MGN Ltd*[129] that a breach of confidentiality needs to be prevented for utilitarian reasons, as it could result in patients' reluctance openly to provide information about themselves, as well as in damage to the patient doctor relationship which rests on trust.

Another case in which the patient's interest in medical confidentiality has been discussed is that of *W v Egdell*.[130] W had been detained for shooting and killing five people and for wounding two others. After ten years of detention, his solicitors instructed Dr. Egdell, a consultant psychiatrist, to examine W and to report on his mental health with a view to using the report to support W's application to a mental health review tribunal to be discharged. In his report Dr. Egdell came to the conclusion that W should not be discharged because his long-standing interest in firearms and explosives caused a great danger to society. When the solicitors received the report, they did not forward it to the tribunal but withdrew W's application. Dr. Egdell then forwarded his report to the hospital where W was detained, and the hospital, with Dr. Egdell's prompting, sent the report to the Secretary of State who forwarded it to the tribunal. In that case, Rose J's statement in *X v Y* was embraced by the Court of Appeal, where Stephen Brown, P held that:

---

[128] Ibid., at 435-6.
[129] [2002] 1 WLR 2033 (HL), at 2037-8 per Lord Woolf CJ.
[130] [1990] 1 All ER 835 (CA).

Of course W has a private interest, but the duty of confidence owed to him is based on the broader ground of public interest described by Rose J in *X v Y*.[131]

And according to Bingham LJ:

The decided cases very clearly establish (1) that the law recognises an important public interest in maintaining professional duties of confidence. ... W of course had a strong personal interest in regaining his freedom ... . So he had a personal interest in restricting the report's circulation. But these private considerations should not be allowed to obscure the public interest in maintaining professional confidences. The fact that Dr Egdell as an independent psychiatrist examined and reported on W as a restricted mental patient under s.76 of the Mental Health Act 1983 does not deprive W of his ordinary right to confidence, underpinned, as such rights are, by the public interest.[132] ...

Counsel for W ... drew our attention to a number of features ...:

(1) Section 76 of the Mental Health Act 1983 shows a clear parliamentary intention that a restricted patient should be free to seek advice and evidence for the specified purposes from a medical source outside the prison and secure hospital system. ... The examination may be in private so that the authorities do not learn what passes between doctor and patient.

(2) The proper functioning of s.76 requires that a patient should feel free to bare his soul and open his mind without reserve to the independent doctor he has retained. This he will not do if the doctor is free, on forming an adverse opinion, to communicate it to those empowered to prevent the patient's release from hospital. ...

(5) It is contrary to the public interest that patients such as W should enjoy rights less extensive than those enjoyed by other members of the public. ...

Of these considerations, I accept (1) as a powerful consideration in W's favour. A restricted patient who believes himself unnecessarily confined has, of all members of society, perhaps the greatest need for a professional adviser who is truly independent and reliably discreet. (2) also I, in some measure, accept, subject to the comment that if the patient is unforthcoming the doctor is bound to be guarded in his opinion. If the patient wishes to enlist a doctor's wholehearted support for his application, he has little choice but to be ... frank. ... As to (5), I agree that restricted patients should not enjoy rights of confidence less valuable than those enjoyed by other patients save in so far as any breach of confidence can be justified under the stringent terms of r 81(g).[133]

This case also gives some interesting guidance for an analysis of the interests behind a protection of medical confidences. First, the holding makes it entirely clear that the fact that a patient has his/her own individual and private reasons for seeking the protection of his/her medical secrets does not mean that the patient's interest should be qualified as a private and not a public interest. Thus, the protection of the patient's private goals may very well be dictated by the public interest. In holding that the protection of the confidentiality of the physician-patient relationship in the context of an examination under s.76 Mental Health Act 1983 lies in the public interest, it becomes obvious that the public has an interest in the protection of some individual concerns, such as the concern that a person detained under the Act should have the possibility to seek independent medical advice. The

---

[131] Ibid, at 846.

[132] Ibid., at 848-9.

[133] Ibid., at 851-2.

public interest identified by Rose J in *X v Y* is of no relevance here, as the protection of medical confidentiality in the context of *Egdell* does nothing to promote public health. There is thus a public interest in the fair and equal treatment of a person detained under the Act which requires the protection of medical confidences to enable this person to pursue his/her private interests of seeking a court order to be released. This demonstrates that medical confidentiality is not only protected for utilitarian, but also for deontological reasons.

The importance of general privacy considerations in the context of medical confidentiality has recently been stressed by the Court of Appeal in *Source Informatics*,[134] when Simon Brown LJ argued in the context of the pharmacist-patient relationship that 'the concern of the law here is to protect the confider's personal privacy'; and 'his only legitimate interest is in the protection of his privacy'. This suggests that a wide range of privacy concerns, including the patient's autonomy, lie at the heart of the protection of patient confidences. Although the legal protection of medical confidentiality is placed in the context of an action for breach of confidence, it has been accepted even before the HRA 1998 came into force that medical confidentiality was not just protected in the public interest in the preservation of health, but also in the interest of the patient to have his right of privacy respected. The HRA has further increased the importance attached to the patient's privacy rights. In the context of the physician-patient relationship.[135]

A question sometimes arising is whether in addition to the patient, the treating physician and/or health authority, also have an interest in the preservation of confidential medical information. This problem became important in *Ashworth Hospital Authority v MGN Ltd.*[136] As Ian Brady himself had widely sought publicity regarding his hunger strike and had made confidential information public, the Court had some difficulty with the argument that the publication of the records violated his confidentiality interests. However, the Court accepted that the hospital had an independent interest in retaining the confidentiality of the records.[137] Equally, in *H (A Healthcare Worker) v Associated Newspapers Limited* and *H (A Healthcare Worker) v N (A Health Authority)*,[138] it was stated that the health authority had a legitimate interest in striving to protect the information, which it had obtained in confidence, that one of their employees was HIV positive. It is difficult to assess the exact meaning of these holdings. In the latter case, it could be argued that the hospital has an interest in preserving the employee's confidentiality interests as well as the confidentiality interests of the employee's patients. It is, however, difficult to see on what basis it could rely on its own confidentiality

---

[134] *R v Department of Health, ex parte Source Informatics* [2000] 1 All ER 786, at 797.

[135] See, for example, *R v Secretary of State for Home Department ex parte Belgium*; *R v Secretary of State for Home Department ex parte Amnesty International* [2000] WL 486 (QBD).

[136] [2001] 1 All ER 991 (CA); [2002] 1 WLR 2033 (HL).

[137] Ibid., at 1003-4 per Phillips MR (CA); and at 2041 per Lord Woolf CJ (HL).

[138] [2002] EMLR 23, 425 (CA).

interests. In the first case, it can hardly be said that by seeking publicity Ian Brady had entirely waived his interest in the confidentiality of his medical records.[139] It could then be argued that in trying to prevent a disclosure of his medical records the hospital was in fact protecting Brady's confidentiality interests, rather than its own. To the extent that the records contained confidential information relating to others, the hospital would be under an obligation to protect those interests. However, the hospital might also have an independent interest in protecting the confidentiality of its records, as it can be argued that the possibility of a leak of these records by an employee and their subsequent publication might inhibit the personnel from maintaining comprehensive and honest records and other patients from frankly communicating with the psychiatrists, thereby adversely affecting the physician-patient relationship. However, it needs to be stressed that only the patient's interest in the preservation of medical confidentiality is based on privacy considerations and therefore protected by Article 8 of the ECHR. Where physicians, hospitals or health authorities do not oppose the disclosure of medical records in order to protect the privacy interests of their patients, but instead pursue their independent confidentiality interests, these interests not protected as fundamental rights.

4 Statutory obligations and criminal offences

In English law, statutory duties of confidentiality are limited to special circumstances such as, for example, venereal diseases,[140] abortion,[141] and some activities under the Human Fertilisation and Embryology Act.[142] The Health Act 1999 makes it a criminal offence under certain circumstances without lawful authority to disclose information the Commission for Health Improvement has obtained in exercising its functions.[143]

A more general statutory regime concerning the processing of computerised data as well as the processing of non-computerised data that are kept as part of a qualifying filing system is provided by the provisions of the Data Protection Act 1998. Protected records include, according to s.68(2) of the Act, health records, that is records consisting of information relating to the physical or mental health or condition of an individual and which have been created by or on behalf of a health professional in connection with the care of that individual. Processing of data is a broad concept which 'includes virtually anything that is done with the personal data, such as obtaining, storing and using it in any way including disclosing it'[144] (s.1(1) DPA). Under the first principle of data protection as laid down in Schedule

---

[139] See also *C v News Group Newspapers Ltd* [2002] WL 820129, at para. 44 per Eady J (QBD).

[140] S.2 NHS (Venereal Diseases) Regulations 1974.

[141] S.5 Abortion Regulations 1991.

[142] S.33 Human Fertilisation and Embryology Act 1990.

[143] S.24 Health Act 1999.

[144] Kennedy, Grubb, at 1035.

1, personal data shall be processed fairly and lawfully. Lawful processing of data excludes the processing of data in breach of the common law doctrine confidence.[145] Thus, the above mentioned principles governing the equitable obligation of confidence are important to establish whether or not data have been processed lawfully under the DPA. Data are being processed fairly if the data controller informed the data subject, as far as practicable, at the time when the data were obtained, of the intended further use to be made of the data (Schedule 1, para.2). Data related to a person's health receive particular protection under Schedule 3 of the Act. An individual who suffers damage because of a contravention by a data controller of any of the requirements of the DPA (s.13(1)) is entitled to compensation. Furthermore, the Act makes certain abuses of computerised and manual files containing personal data a criminal offence.[146]

5 Professional obligation

The duty of medical confidentiality is imposed on every physician as a professional duty. In 2000, the General Medical Council (GMC) issued guidelines on confidentiality which provide as follows:

1. Patients have a right to expect that information about them will be held in confidence by their doctors. Confidentiality is central to trust between doctors and patients. Without assurances about confidentiality, patients may be reluctant to give doctors the information they need in order to provide good care. If you are asked to provide information about patients you should:
    a. Seek patients' consent to disclosure of information wherever possible, whether or not you judge that patients can be identified from the disclosure.
    b. Anonymise data where unidentifiable data will serve the purpose.
    c. Keep disclosures to the minimum necessary.[147]

The guidelines show that there exists a professional duty to uphold patient confidences. The reasons given for the need to protect a patient's medical information mainly seem to point towards a deontological perspective, as good care for the patient and respect for the patient's expectations seem to be the most important considerations.

According to s.36 of the Medical Act 1983, the GMC has the power to impose disciplinary measures on a physician who was judged by the Professional Conduct Committee to be guilty of serious professional misconduct. A breach of medical confidentiality can amount to serious professional misconduct and trigger disciplinary sanctions.[148] The guidelines issued by the GMC, though obviously possessing considerable authority among members of the medical profession, nevertheless do not have the force of law and therefore do not bind the courts

---

[145] See, for example, ibid., at 1038; Jay, Hamilton, at 47; Beyleveld, Histed, at 290.

[146] See, for example, s.55 Data Protection Act 1998.

[147] GMC, *Confidentiality: Protecting and Providing Information.*

[148] Kennedy, Grubb, at 1048.

which reserve the right to strike down professional regulations that are unreasonable.[149] However, as can be seen, for example, from the statement of Bingham LJ in *W v Egdell*,[150] the courts refer to those guidelines and, with regard to medical confidentiality, have decided that the rules set out by the GMC adequately reflected the law.

6 Summary

Even though the protection of medical confidentiality lies in the public interest, the legal protection of confidentiality has mainly been developed in the context of private law, in order to regulate conflicts between private parties. Thus, the state provides the individual with legal remedies where a breach of confidentiality has occurred or is about to occur, but does not normally react with the threat of criminal sanctions to a breach of the obligation of medical confidentiality. Contractual obligations to maintain a patient's confidences are of little importance, given the rare existence of contractual relationships between physicians and patients.

Medical confidentiality is not protected as an individual right of constitutional rank, and before the coming into force of the HRA, English law did not protect a general right to privacy. Medical confidentiality nevertheless received legal protection, even before the HRA came into force, as the courts developed an equitable obligation to maintain confidences in the context of certain relationships, for example the physician-patient relationship. The consideration underlying the development of the law of breach of confidence was a notion of fairness and trust, not the idea that a patient should have the right to control the dissemination of his/her confidential medical information. The legal protection focused on the patient's legitimate expectations that medical information revealed to someone under an assumption of confidentiality would not be used or disclosed against the patient's wishes. Thus, medical confidentiality was not initially protected as part of the patient's right to private life, but protection was instead granted in order to preserve the integrity of certain relationships. As a consequence, confidential medical information was protected from disclosure by the physician, but the same information was not protected from disclosure by a person who had become aware of the information outside of a situation which gave rise to an expectation of confidentiality. This situation has to some extent been remedied by case law following the coming into force of the HRA. The courts have complied with their obligation to act compatibly with the provisions of the HRA by extending the action for breach of confidence so as to include cases in which no relationship or situation of confidence exists. Thus, English courts are now willing to recognise a general right to privacy. However, the violation of that right does not give rise to an action for breach of privacy. Instead, it is actionable as a breach of confidence. This means that every action for a breach of the newly acknowledged right to

---

[149] Newdick, at 373.
[150] [1990] 1 All ER 835 (CA), at 852.

privacy needs to be fitted into the categories of the traditional action for breach of confidence, the scope of which, in turn, has been expanded. This is not entirely satisfactory. While the interest in the protection of confidences and the interest in the protection of privacy overlap, they nevertheless have distinct features, as actions for breach of confidence focus on equitable considerations, whereas the right to privacy primarily protects the individual's autonomy. In case of a breach of confidence, injunctive relief or compensation are available. In the light of the HRA, courts have now started to award more than nominal damages in cases of non-financial harm, as otherwise the right to confidentiality would not receive adequate protection.

The fact that the development of a remedy for a violation of medical confidentiality was based on equitable considerations and not on the patient's right to privacy has implications for the courts' approach to such actions. Even recent case law acknowledging the significance of Article 8 of the HRA shows a tendency to focus more on general principles of equity and less on the patient's right to control the use of and access to his/her private and confidential information. While the HRA has brought about a changed perception of the value to be attached to the right to private life, the traditional attitude necessarily impacts on the application and interpretation of the HRA. In the context of medical confidentiality, the courts' approach to breaches of confidence both under equitable principles and in the light of the HRA is decisively influenced by the predominant view that medical confidentiality is mainly protected for utilitarian reasons. It is submitted that to give adequate effect to the patient's right to private life under Article 8(1) of the ECHR, the deontological value of medical confidentiality needs to be emphasised.

The protection of medical confidentiality has recently received a lot of attention, for example through the report of the Caldicott Committee which had been established to review the transmission of identifiable patient information from one NHS body to another[151] and new legislative provisions contained in the Data Protection Act 1998, the Health Act 1999 and the Health and Social Care Act 2001.

PART 2 – DISCLOSURE IN THE CONTEXT OF CRIME PREVENTION AND CRIMINAL PROSECUTION

English law does not recognise a general medical privilege. This is not to say that confidential medical information does not receive any protection in the context of crime prevention and criminal prosecution. The problem will be approached from two perspectives. First, the powers of the state to compel the physician to disclose confidential information will be examined. It will then be discussed whether the physician can lawfully volunteer the disclosure of confidential patient information for the purposes of preventing, investigating or prosecuting crime.

---

[151] www.doh.gov.uk/confiden.htm (1997).

1 State access to confidential medical information

1.1 Medical privilege in criminal court

The first question to be discussed is whether confidential medical information is privileged in the context of criminal proceedings. The meaning of privilege was explained in *Parry-Jones v The Law Society*[152] by Diplock LJ who stated that:

> Privilege is irrelevant when one is not concerned with judicial or quasi-judicial proceedings because strictly speaking, privilege refers to a right to withhold from a court, or a tribunal exercising judicial functions, material which would otherwise be admissible in evidence.

Thus, the question of privilege can only arise in the context of judicial proceedings, and privilege can refer both to a physician's testimony or to the introduction of medical records as evidence in court. Diplock LJ's definition already points to the problem that the existence of a privilege against disclosure of information in judicial proceedings will always conflict with the interest in an unimpeded administration of criminal justice. Procedural law rests on the premise that the public interest in the administration of justice is the overriding consideration in the context of court proceedings.[153] This interest is mainly specified as an interest that the truth be established in court proceedings, a purpose which can only be achieved if, in principle, all existing evidence is available to the court when making a decision.[154] A privilege has the effect of undermining this principle by depriving the court of evidence that would otherwise be available. In the context of criminal proceedings, the interests in the administration of justice are not limited to the interest in finding the truth. Rather, they also include the unimpeded exercise of defence rights by the accused,[155] and the interest in the dissipation of unfounded suspicions against the innocent.[156] Privilege can thus be seen as an exception to the general rule that in the context of court proceedings, the interests in the administration of justice are paramount, as the existence of a privilege indicates that in the situation to which the privilege applies, the interest in the administration of justice must yield to the interest that is protected by the privilege. Therefore, privilege is only granted in very exceptional cases in which it is felt that the conflicting interests at stake are of even higher rank than the public interest in the administration of justice.[157]

---

[152] [1969] 1 Ch 1, at 9.

[153] *Home Office v Harman* [1983] 1 AC 280, at 308 per Kinkel LJ.

[154] See, for example, *Campbell v Tameside Council* [1982] 1 QB 1065 (CA), at 1076-7 per Ackner LJ.

[155] See, for example, *Re K and others (Minors) (Disclosure)* [1994] 1 FLR 377 (FD); see also Corker, at 138-41.

[156] *Re W (Minors) (Social Workers: Disclosure)* [1999] 1 WLR 205, at 215 per Butler-Sloss LJ.

[157] *Cross and Tapper on Evidence*, at 451-2.

English law has decided the conflict between the interests protected by medical confidentiality and the interests in the administration of justice in favour of the latter and does not provide physicians with a privilege in respect of the disclosure of confidential information obtained by them in the course of the professional relationship with their patients.[158] Edgedale J held in *Nuttall v Nuttall and Twynan*[159] that what a person said to his doctor in a professional consultation was not privileged and that the doctor in the witness box must either give evidence or be committed to be sent to prison for contempt of court. With regard to the disclosure of medical records in the context of criminal trials, according to s.66 of the Criminal Procedure and Investigations Act 1996, upon application the court can issue a witness summons, requiring the physician to produce the documents deemed relevant for the proceedings.

This does not mean that the physician-patient relationship does not receive any protection from disclosure in criminal proceedings. It means, however, that the physician cannot, as a matter of right, refuse to give testimony in criminal court where the testimony concerns confidential patient information. Boreham J held in *Hunter v Mann*[160] that although a doctor has no right to refuse the disclosure of confidential information in the course of judicial proceedings, in certain circumstances the judge may refuse to compel him to do so. And Lord Wilberforce held in *British Steel Corp. v Granada Television Ltd*[161] that:

> As to information obtained in confidence, and the legal duty, which may arise, to disclose it to a court of justice, the position is clear. Courts have an inherent wish to respect this confidence, whether it arises between doctor and patient ... or in other relationships. ... But in all these cases the court may have to decide, in particular circumstances, that the interest in preserving this confidence is outweighed by other interests to which the law attaches importance.

This raises the question of how the judicial discretion to exclude evidence should be exercised. Can it be said that even evidence that is relevant and necessary for a decision in criminal court can be excluded merely on the grounds that the information the disclosure of which is sought was imparted in the physician under the cloak of confidentiality? The suggestion that confidentiality should be recognised as a separate heading of privilege was expressly rejected by the House of Lords in *Alfred Crompton Amusement Machines Ltd v Commissioners of Customs and Excise (No.2)*.[162] In *D v N.S.P.C.C.*[163] the House of Lords further developed the law in this area. Lord Hailsham stated that confidentiality by itself

---

[158] *Attorney-General v Mulholland* [1963] 2 QB 477 (CA), at 489 per Lord Denning; *Hunter v Mann* [1974] 2 All ER 414, at 417 per Boreham J; *Goddard v Nationwide Building Society* [1986] 3 All ER 264, at 271 per Nourse LJ.

[159] *Nuttall v Nuttall and Twynan* [1964] 108 Sol J 605.

[160] *Hunter v Mann* [1974] 2 All ER 414, at 417.

[161] [1980] 3 WLR 774, at 821.

[162] [1974] AC 405, at 433-4 per Lord Cross.

[163] [1978] AC 171 (HL).

did not give any ground for immunity.[164] Lord Diplock confirmed that view and rejected the proposition that 'the basis of all privilege from disclosure of documents or information in legal proceedings is to prevent the breaking of confidence'.[165] Lord Simon argued similarly:

> I do not think that confidentiality of the communication provides in itself a satisfactory basis for testing whether the relevant evidence should be withheld. ... It is undesirable that exclusion should be conferred by confidentiality irrespective of the public interest. ... For the reasons I have given I do not myself think that confidentiality in itself establishes any public interest in the exclusion of relevant evidence, but rather that it may indirectly be significant where a public interest extrinsically established (for example, provision of professional legal advice or effective policing) can only be vindicated if its communications have immunity from forensic investigation.[166]

Given the broad protection of confidences in English law, it is understandable that more than the existence of a relationship of confidence is required in order to justify a privilege. However, based on this quote, it could be argued that medical confidentiality might justify a privilege. The effective provision of health care lies in the public interest and the preservation of medical confidentiality has been recognised as paramount in order to achieve that goal.[167] This public interest could be said to provide the additional ground for protecting the confidential nature of the physician-patient relationship in court. However, Lord Edmund-Davies who addressed this question more specifically and balanced the interest in the administration of justice against the interest in protecting confidentiality, came to the following conclusion:

> It is a serious step to exclude evidence relevant to an issue, for it is in the public interest that the search for truth should, in general, be unfettered. Accordingly, any hindrance to its seekers needs to be justified by a convincing demonstration that an even higher public interest requires that only part of the truth should be told. ... But it is established in our law that the mere fact that information is imparted in confidence does not, of itself, entitle the recipient to refuse disclosure of the identity of the informer. ... No reported case supports the proposition ... that a judge is entitled to direct a doctor not to disclose information regarding his patient's health.[168]

He emphasised that the physician-patient relationship cannot be treated as equivalent to the lawyer-client relationship, the only professional relationship in regard to which English law recognises a privilege,[169] and summarised the law as follows:

---

[164] Ibid., at 230.
[165] Ibid., at 220.
[166] Ibid., at 237-9.
[167] *X v Y and others* [1988] 2 All ER 648 (QBD), at 656 per Rose J; *H (A Healthcare Worker) v Associated Newspapers Limited* and *H (A Healthcare Worker) v N (A Health Authority)* [2002] EMLR 32, 425 (CA), at 435-6 per Lord Phillips MR.
[168] [1978] AC 171 (HL), at 242-4.
[169] See infra 1.2.

(I) In civil proceedings a judge has no discretion, simply because what is contemplated is the disclosure of information which has passed between persons in a confidential relationship (other than that of lawyer and client), to direct a party to that relationship that he need not disclose that information even though its disclosure is (a) relevant to and (b) necessary for the attainment of justice in the particular case. If (a) and (b) are established, the doctor or the priest must be directed to answer if, despite the strong dissuasion of the judge, the advocate persists in seeking disclosure. ...

(II) But where (i) a confidential relationship exists (other than that of lawyer and client) *and* (ii) disclosure would be in breach of some ethical or social value involving the public interest, the court has a discretion to uphold a refusal to disclose relevant evidence provided it considers that, on balance, the public interest would be better served by excluding such evidence. ...

(V) The mere fact that relevant information was communicated in confidence does not necessarily mean that it need not be disclosed. But where the subject matter is clearly of public interest, the *additional* fact (if such it be) that to break the seal of confidentiality would endanger that interest will in most (if not all) cases probably lead to the conclusion that disclosure should be withheld. ...

(VI) The disclosure of all evidence relevant to the trial of an issue being at all times a matter of considerable public interest, the question to be determined is whether it is clearly demonstrated that in the particular case the public interest would nevertheless be better served by excluding evidence.[170]

These principles have been developed in civil proceedings. However, they express general observations as to the weight to be attached to confidentiality in the context of court proceedings which are also relevant in the context of criminal trials. To summarise the principles developed in *D v N.S.P.C.C.*: a physician is not exempt from giving testimony in criminal court simply on the ground that the information he/she is called to testify upon refers to confidential patient data, as the fact that the confidentiality of the physician-patient relationship is protected outside of court proceedings is not in itself sufficient to override the competing interest in finding the truth. The judge's discretion to exempt the physician from the duty to give testimony is subject to an analysis of the relevance and the value of the information in judicial proceedings. As long as the physician's testimony is relevant and necessary to the proceedings, the judge cannot permit the non-disclosure of such information merely on the basis of its confidentiality, if the other side insists on full revelation of all relevant facts.[171] According to Lord Edmund-Davies' opinion in *D v N.S.P.C.C.*, even where information is relevant and necessary, the judge still has the discretion to direct non-disclosure if in addition to the confidentiality of the information, other reasons point towards on overriding interest in non-disclosure. *D v N.S.P.C.C.* was a case concerning public interest immunity, and in accordance with that decision, it seems now possible that a judge directs non-disclosure of confidential information if, besides the general interest in maintaining confidentiality, there is an additional interest requiring non-disclosure, for example the public interest in protecting the informants of the N.S.P.C.C. so as to enable

---

[170] [1978] AC 171, at 245-6.

[171] But see Feldman, at 628, who argues that the judge does have such a discretion.

that organisation to perform its function to protect children effectively. Only the existence of such an additional public interest can achieve what confidentiality alone could not, namely to outweigh the public interest in the administration of justice.[172] Lord Scarman expressed this thought as follows:

> The confidential nature of a document does not, by itself, confer 'public interest immunity' from disclosure. The confidential nature of a document or of evidence is no ground for a refusal to disclose the document or to give evidence, if the court requires it. I do not see the process of the decision as a balancing act. If the document is necessary for fairly disposing of the case, it must be produced, notwithstanding its confidentiality. Only if the document should be protected by public interest immunity, will there be a balancing act. And then the balance will not be between 'ethical or social' values of a confidential relationship involving the public interest and the document's relevance in the litigation, but between the public interest represented by the state and public service, i.e. the executive government, and the public interest in the administration of justice. ... It does not follow that, because we are outside the field of public interest immunity, the confidential nature of the documents is to be disregarded by the court in the exercise of its discretionary power to order discovery of documents. ... The factor of confidence ... militates against general orders for discovery and does impose upon the tribunal the duty of satisfying itself ... that justice requires disclosure.[173]

Thus, confidentiality of information the disclosure of which is sought in court proceedings does not as such give rise to a balancing of the interest in confidentiality and the interests of justice. Confidentiality is, however, protected as the courts should only order the disclosure of confidential information if it is relevant to the case at issue. This is in line with the decision in *A.G. v Mulholland*[174] where Lord Denning had tried to mitigate the effects of the lack of medical privilege by holding that judges will respect confidences and not direct a doctor to answer a question unless it is not only relevant, but in the course of justice it also is a proper and necessary question to be put and answered. Once the relevance of the information is established, the court has no discretion to allow non-disclosure merely based on the confidentiality of the information. With regard to the protection of medical confidentiality in criminal proceedings, it can therefore be stated that neither the patient nor the physician have the right to insist on non-disclosure of confidential information, and that no protection exists for confidential medical information that is relevant and necessary for judicial proceedings. In such a case, not even a balancing exercise will be performed to decide on a case by case basis whether the interest in medical confidentiality or that in the administration of justice should prevail in the individual case. Rather, the interest in the administration of justice always prevails over the interest in maintaining the secrecy of medical information that is relevant and necessary for criminal proceedings.

---

[172] See also, for example, *Campbell v Tameside Council* [1982] 1 QB 1065 (CA), at 1075 per Ackner LJ.

[173] *Science Research Council v Nassé* [1980] AC 1028 (HL (E)), at 1087-9.

[174] [1963] 2 QB 477.

The courts' reluctance to grant a privilege on grounds of confidentiality alone is understandable. English law imposes an obligation of confidence whenever information has been imparted in confidence,[175] regardless of whether the information has, for example, been confided in an individual, a business partner, or a member of the medical profession. Obviously, the public interest in the preservation of confidentiality differs significantly depending on the nature of the confidential relationship, and it can easily be argued that not every confidential relationship is important enough to outweigh the interest in the administration of justice. However, the protection of medical confidentiality serves an important public interest, the preservation of public health.[176] Therefore, in all cases in which the disclosure of confidential medical information is sought in a criminal court, two public interests are in conflict with each other. It is then difficult to see why, as required by Lord Edmund-Davies in *D v N.S.P.C.C.*,[177] an additional public interest needs to be affected in order to allow for a balancing of interests to take place.

From the utilitarian perspective mostly adopted by English courts towards medical confidentiality, the rejection of medical privilege can be partly explained by the perception that limited cases of disclosure of confidential medical information in court will not significantly undermine the integrity of the physician-patient relationship as such.[178] Deontological reasons for giving medical confidentiality precedence over the interests in the administration of justice have not been considered by English courts. To the contrary, the courts take it for granted that a patient's interests in the confidentiality of his/her medical confidences cannot override the interests of justice. This attitude is in line with the limited weight given, until recently, to the right of privacy. While the HRA 1998 has brought about changes in the perception of the importance of privacy, it is not likely to trigger a move towards the introduction of medical privilege. The European Court of Human Rights has stated in *Z v Finland*[179] that the Finnish procedural provisions requiring a physician to give testimony in criminal proceedings about confidential patient information without the patient's consent were covered by the exception to the right to private life under Article 8(2) of the ECHR. It can therefore be concluded that a recognition of medical privilege is not required to comply with Convention rights. However, *Z v Finland* concerned very serious crimes. With regard to the balancing of the interest in prosecuting less serious crimes, on the one hand, and the right to medical confidentiality under Article 8(1), on the other, no European case law exists. It could be argued that in the latter case, the general rejection of medical privilege regardless of the

---

[175] For a discussion of the scope of the obligation of confidence see supra, part 1, 3.

[176] *X v Y and others* [1988] 2 All ER 648 (QBD), at 656 per Rose J; *H (A Healthcare Worker) v Associated Newspapers Limited* and *H (A Healthcare Worker) v N (A Health Authority)* [2002] EMLR 23, 425 (CA), at 435-6 per Lord Phillips MR.

[177] [1978] AC 171, at 245-6.

[178] A similar argument was used by Munby J in *Re X (Disclosure of Information)* [2001] 2 FLR 440, at 449, in the context of disclosure to the victims of the findings on sexual abuse made in care proceedings.

[179] (1998) 25 E.H.R.R. 371; see the discussion in chapter 3, part 2, 1.

seriousness of the offence in question might violate the principle of proportionality and that the courts should at least be given the discretion to exclude confidential medical information if the privacy invasion is serious and the offence to be tried of minor importance. However, it is submitted that it is unlikely that English courts would accept this suggestion. While it has been acknowledged by the courts in post HRA cases that the overall fairness of criminal trials is not necessarily compromised where information is protected from disclosure, for example for the purpose of protecting the rights of another person,[180] a decision of non-disclosure is only regarded as acceptable if it is directed towards a clear and proper public objective and represents no greater qualification than the situation calls for.[181] So far, the protection of confidential medical information has not been regarded as such a public objective.[182]

To summarise the principles so far discussed, English law does not recognise medical privilege in criminal court, but the courts have the discretion to exclude confidential medical evidence which is not relevant and material to the proceedings. A recent case regarding the exercise of discretion to order disclosure is that of *Pinochet*.[183] In the context of extradition proceedings for the purpose of conducting a criminal trial in Spain, the Secretary of State was inclined to decide not to extradite Pinochet based on medical reports which unanimously concluded that he was not fit to stand trial. The interested States and parties were invited to make representations as to the course of action proposed by the Secretary of State. They demanded disclosure of Pinochet's medical records for this purpose, a request which was denied by the Secretary of State based on their confidential nature. The court, however, decided in favour of disclosure, arguing that it would give the requesting States the opportunity to comment on the reports; that justice would be seen to be done; and that minds would be set at rest. In short, the demands of fairness and transparency in the decision-making process were held to require disclosure, particularly in the light of the significance of the Secretary of State's decision, as Pinochet, though accused of terrible crimes, would not be triable for them if extradition were to be refused on health grounds. Simon Brown LJ argued that disclosure was justified under Article 8(2), as the prosecution or extradition of alleged offenders fell under the qualifications of that provision. Disclosure was also held to be proportionate, given the pressing social need for fairness in such proceedings. However, his proportionality analysis seems flawed in that he defined the interests to be balanced as the public interest in operating a procedure which would be perceived and accepted by the great majority to be fair, against Pinochet's private interests. Dyson LJ, on the other hand, rightly balanced the public interest in disclosure against the public interest in maintaining the duty of confidence owed to Pinochet, and equally came to conclusion that disclosure

---

[180] See *Brown v Stott* [2001] 2 All ER 97 (PC), at 107 per Lord Bingham, quoting *Fitt v UK* (2000) 30 E.H.R.R. 480, at para.44.

[181] Ibid., at 115.

[182] See *Stevens v Plymouth City Council* [2002] 1 WLR 2583, at 2596 per Hale LJ.

[183] *R v Secretary of State for Home Department ex parte Belgium; R v Secretary of State for Home Department ex parte Amnesty International* [2000] WL 486 (QBD).

was necessary. The proportionality analysis was partly based on the fact that disclosure would only lead to a limited loss of privacy, as large parts of the reports' findings had already been widely publicised and the States would receive the information in confidence.

One cannot help but feel that this decision was based on political rather than legal considerations. Disclosure in this particular case seems to have aimed at appeasing the requesting parties and also the public, without necessarily serving a legal purpose. The representations the parties were asked to make concerned the conclusions to be drawn from the fact that Pinochet was regarded unfit for trial, not the medical findings themselves. Nevertheless, Simon Brown LJ somewhat unconvincingly argued that the requesting parties needed to see the reports, as they might have something constructive to say about the reports' conclusions. This case shows that while the courts now take the right to private life under Article 8(1) of the ECHR into account, the definition of the interests that might override this right pursuant to Article 8(2) as well as the application of the proportionality test are sometimes rather haphazard. The view that a Convention right can be violated so that justice is seen to be done and minds put at rest can hardly stand up to scrutiny.

A more promising indication of how the courts will use their discretion regarding the disclosure of confidential information in the light of the HRA can be found in *Re B (Disclosure to Other Parties)*.[184] In the context of care proceedings regarding four children who were in the care of a local authority under interim care orders, the father (R) of one of the children (H) applied for an order for contact with H. While R contended that he was entitled to see all the documents filed in the proceedings for the purposes of his participation in them, the mother and the children's guardian at litem argued that he should only be given limited access to the documents. The mother suggested that R's application for contact was unlikely to be successful in the light of past violent behaviour both towards her and her children. The judge gave leave to instruct a consultant psychologist to carry out an assessment of the children, the mother and her current partner (W), inviting the psychologist to address issues such as the current needs of each child, the relationship between the children and their mother, and whether there was a need for H to establish a relationship with her father. The documents filed in the proceedings included records of interviews of two of the children, K and S, with the police; care plans in relation to the children; evidence by health visitors and social workers; and letters of instruction to and reports from a consultant psychiatrist who had undertaken a forensic assessment of the mother and W. It was envisaged that in the course of the proceedings reports of the mother's therapist might be filed with the court.

Munby J addressed the problem of the disclosure of documents as one of a conflict between the father's right to a fair trial under Article 6 of the ECHR, and the right to private life under Article 8 of the ECHR of the mother, her children and W. Given the importance of the right under Article 6, the court argued that non-disclosure can only be justified when a compelling case that it is strictly necessary

---

[184] [2001] 2 FLR 1017.

can be made.[185] Munby J then looked at the importance of the different documents for R's participation in the proceedings and came to the conclusion that R should not be given access to the police interviews of K and S, the letters of instruction to and the forensic report of the consultant psychiatrist who had undertaken a forensic psychiatric assessment of the mother and W, the therapist's notes and reports regarding further therapeutic work to be undertaken with the mother, and those parts of the consultant psychologist's report that relate entirely to her sessions with K and S. This was based on the assessment that non-disclosure of these documents would not deprive him of a fair trial, while disclosure would have been traumatic for the individuals concerned. The judge left open the future possibility of disclosure of some of the documents if the need arose at a later stage of the proceedings, but no such qualification was made regarding the non-disclosure of the notes and reports of the mother's therapist. These were regarded as tangential to the proceedings while affecting very intimate parts of the mother's private life, the disclosure of which to R might adversely affect her therapy and amount to a gross invasion of her innermost private life.[186] However, all other documents should be disclosed to R, including the care plan in relation to the children; the witness statements filed in the proceedings by the mother and W; the social workers' and health visitors' evidence; and the letter of instructions to the consultant psychologist and her report, once prepared, save for the parts exclusively referring to K and S.[187]

While this was not a case concerning questions of medical privilege, it is nevertheless informative in that it demonstrates that when exercising their discretion with regard to the disclosure of confidential medical information in the context of court proceedings, courts are now willing to assess the arising conflicts in Convention rights terms. In this case the privacy interests of the parties involved, particularly in respect of the medical and psychiatric reports, were given considerable weight, even though what was at stake was not the confidentiality of the physician-patient relationship, but the general interests of the individuals concerned in the protection of such information from disclosure. However, fair trial rights were regarded as more important than privacy rights, so that the latter can only exceptionally justify non-disclosure where the information the disclosure of which is sought is, if at all, only minimally relevant to the proceedings. This confirms, again, that where confidential medical information might be material to court proceedings, disclosure will be required, but the courts will try to uphold confidentiality as far as possible and, in the light of the HRA, apply a rigid proportionality test. Examining Munby J's holding, it seems as if the more personal the information, the stricter the scrutiny of whether the information is material and its disclosure necessary.

Even if confidential medical information is relevant to the proceedings, confidentiality will still be protected as far as possible. In *Taylor v Serious Fraud*

---

[185] See also *Re D (Adoption Reports: Confidentiality)* [1995] 2 FLR 687, at 694 per Lord Mustill.

[186] *Re B (Disclosure to Other Parties)* [2001] 2 FLR 1017, at 1045-6.

[187] Ibid., at 1044-5.

Office,[188] it has been argued that it was a matter of fairness and justice that the privacy and confidentiality of those whose confidential information was needed in judicial proceedings, was not invaded more than absolutely necessary for the purposes of justice. Thus, only the relevant part of confidential information will have to be disclosed, and the information can normally not be used outside the judicial proceedings in which it has been revealed.

A possibility to exclude medical evidence exists under s.78 of the Police and Criminal Evidence Act 1984 (PACE) which provides that:

> (1) In any proceedings the court may refuse to allow evidence on which the prosecution wishes to rely to be given if it appears to the court, having regard to all the circumstances, including the circumstances in which evidence was obtained, the admission of the evidence would have such an adverse effect on the fairness of the proceedings that the court should not admit it.

It could be argued that the admission of evidence that came about in the course of the confidential physician-patient relationship would adversely affect the fairness of the proceedings and should therefore not be admitted. In *R v McDonald,*[189] the exclusion of a psychiatrist's report based on s.78 was rejected, but the Court nevertheless held that only on rare occasions or in exceptional circumstances would the prosecution seek to adduce evidence of what a defendant had said to his doctor if the issue before the court was not a medical one.[190]

Where does all this leave the physician who is called upon to testify as a witness in criminal proceedings and who feels that his/her testimony would constitute a breach of the legal as well as of the ethical obligation to maintain the medical confidences of his/her patient? With regard to the legal obligation, the law was clearly stated by Diplock LJ in *Parry-Jones v The Law Society:*[191]

> What we are concerned with here is the contractual duty of confidence, generally implied though sometimes expressed, between a solicitor and client. Such a duty exists not only between solicitor and client, but, for example, between banker and customer, doctor and patient, and accountant and client. Such a duty of confidence is subject to, and overridden by, the duty of any party to that contract to comply with the law of the land. If it is the duty of such a party to a contract, whether at common law or under statute, to disclose in defined circumstances confidential information, then he must do so.

It is thus clear that the physician is only under an obligation to maintain the medical confidence of his/her patient as long as this obligation is not overridden by law. Given that the physician is under a legal obligation to give testimony in judicial proceedings and that this obligation is regarded as more important than the

---

[188] [1998] 3 WLR 1040, (HL (E)), at 1049 per Lord Hoffmann.
[189] [1991] Crim LR 122 (CA).
[190] See also *R v Smith (Stanley)* [1979] 3 All ER 605 (CA).
[191] [1969] 1 Ch 1, at 9.

general obligation to respect medical confidentiality, when a physician is called upon to testify he/she is not faced with conflicting legal duties, but is rather only under the legal duty to give testimony, to which the legal duty to maintain medical confidentiality must yield. Thus, while a patient could obtain an injunction to prevent the physician from disclosing confidential medical information outside judicial proceedings,[192] the same information is no longer protected from disclosure when it becomes relevant in the context of litigation.[193] However, these clear legal principles do not necessarily resolve potential conflicts between the legal obligation to testify and the ethical obligation to maintain confidentiality. In *Hunter v Mann*,[194] Widgery LJ described the physician's situation as follows:

> If a doctor, giving evidence in court, is asked a question which he finds embarrassing because it involves him talking about things which he would normally regard as confidential, he can seek the protection of the judge and ask the judge if it is necessary for him to answer. The judge, by virtue of the overriding discretion to control his court which all English judges have, can, if he thinks fit, tell the doctor that he need not answer the question.[195]

In *A Health Authority v X (Discovery: Medical Conduct)*,[196] a decision regarding a health authority's request that a GP hand over patient records for the purpose of an investigation into the compliance by the practice with the health authority's terms of service, the court went even further in arguing that while a physician has to comply with a court order requiring disclosure:

> prior to that point being reached his duty, like that of any other professional or other person who owes a duty of confidentiality to his patient or client, is to assert that confidentiality in answer to any claim by a third party for disclosure and to put before the court every argument that can properly be put against disclosure.[197]

Thus, it seems as if the physician not only has the option of trying to convince the court not to order disclosure, but is even under an obligation to do so. However, once disclosure has been ordered by the court, the physician has to testify.

In *Garner v Garner*,[198] the judge expressly recognised the conflict the obligation to testify would impose on the physician, but was confident that the physician would appreciate that 'in a Court of Justice there were higher considerations than those which prevailed with regard to the position of medical men'. It has also been argued that the good sense and tact of the judiciary makes the recognition of a

---

[192] See, for example, *Goddard v Nationwide Building Society* [1986] 3 All ER 264.

[193] *W v Egdell* [1990] 1 All ER 835, (CA) at 848 per Bingham LJ; *Cross and Tapper on Evidence*, at 494; Matthews, at 93.

[194] [1974] 2 All ER 414 (QBD).

[195] Ibid., at 420.

[196] [2001] 2 FLR 673.

[197] Ibid, at 677 per Munby J. This has been confirmed on appeal, see [2002] 2 All ER 780 (CA) at 788 per Thorpe LJ.

[198] [1920] 34 The Law Times Report 196, per McCardie J.

medical privilege obsolete,[199] and that the courts recognise the public interest in upholding confidential relationships and will therefore not lightly make a decision that could potentially damage the relationship or the reputation of a profession, particularly if no good purpose would be served thereby.[200] One commentator suggested that the *de facto* protection awarded by the courts goes so far that solicitors will normally not even attempt to obtain a court order compelling the physician to divulge confidential patient information, as such an undertaking is doomed to failure unless there is an overwhelming reason for seeking disclosure.[201] There is thus a tendency to suggest that the interest in medical confidentiality is sufficiently, or even overly, protected by the discretion of the courts. The Criminal Law Revision Committee seems to have adopted the same position when it decided against recommending any extension of professional privilege to include the physician-patient relationship[202] because it was regarded as unlikely that any difficulties would occur in practice. The Committee argued that a broad medical privilege allowing the physician to refuse to testify in criminal court about every confidential aspect of the physician-patient relationship would be undesirable, as the interests of justice will often outweigh the public interest in medical confidentiality, for example where a physician obtained information about a criminal offence committed by his/her patient. Even in the case of the psychiatrist-patient relationship no privilege was recommended, as it was seen as unnecessary. In support of this analysis it has been argued that in most cases the prosecution will not even be aware of the confidential information and therefore not be able to seek its disclosure. If the prosecution knows about this information, it is nevertheless unlikely that it will attempt to compel the physician to give testimony.[203] However, it should not be forgotten that the courts' discretion largely rests on the question of the relevance and usefulness of the evidence, a consideration that is not likely to alter the physician's perception of his/her ethical obligation. Accordingly, a physician, though under a legal obligation to give testimony, may nevertheless feel very strongly that he/she ought to uphold the principle of medical confidentiality,[204] regardless of whether or not the evidence in question is relevant to the outcome of the proceedings, and English law takes very limited account of this moral dilemma.

To summarise, no medical privilege exists in criminal proceedings, and as long as the confidential patient information is relevant to the proceedings, either for the prosecution or the defence, the court does not have the discretion to exclude such evidence on the basis of its confidentiality, unless additional public interest considerations point towards non-disclosure. Confidential medical information will

---

[199] Anonymous, (1974) BMJ, at 391.

[200] *Murphy on Evidence*, at 409; see also McHale (1993), at 15; but see Harvard, at 9, who argues that there is very little evidence that the courts are anxious to protect medical confidentiality.

[201] Samuels, at 237.

[202] Eleventh Report, Cmnd 4991, paras 272-6.

[203] May, at 13-43.

[204] See also *Cross and Tapper on Evidence*, at 496.

be protected from disclosure in court, however, as long as its disclosure is not necessary for the proceedings. The conflict between the interest in the preservation of medical confidentiality and the interests in the administration of justice has therefore been resolved by favouring the latter.

The discussion has shown several features of the English approach to medical privilege. Unlike in other legal systems, the focus does not lie on the conflict between medical confidentiality and the interest in criminal prosecution, but rather on the conflict between medical confidentiality and the interests in the administration of justice, which goes beyond the interest in criminal prosecution and in addition protects the integrity of judicial proceedings as well as defence rights. Given that the rejection of medical privilege applies to all court proceedings, not just to criminal trials, the interest in criminal prosecution is not even a necessary component of the interests to which medical confidentiality has to yield. No statutes exist to govern this area, so that the decision as to the recognition of medical privilege rests in the courts. As it is one of the most important tasks of the courts to serve the interests in the administration of justice, it is hardly surprising that they will favour those interests whenever a conflict arises. This stance is also reconfirmed by the predominantly utilitarian approach to medical confidentiality. It is to be hoped that with the increasing importance that is attached to privacy rights, medical confidentiality will no longer be mainly regarded as serving utilitarian goals. Only then will the balancing of interests required by Article 8 of the ECHR in every case of an interference with a patient's privacy rights give sufficient weight to the interests of the patient. At the moment, as soon as the disclosure of medical information is sought in criminal court, the patient whose consent is normally required for disclosure is in an almost powerless position. It is the physician, not the patient, who will decide whether and how to present a case in favour of non-disclosure, and it is the judge and no longer the patient who will decide whether or not disclosure should be ordered. In criminal proceedings, the interests of a patient are thus not sufficiently taken into account.

1.2 Legal professional privilege

The only privilege recognised in English law is that of the legal profession.[205] It is felt that this privilege is justified as the protection of the confidentiality of the lawyer-client relationship directly benefits the administration of justice. As the argument goes, a client might be inhibited in telling his/her lawyer the full truth unless he/she can be certain that the lawyer will treat the information imparted in him/her with the strictest confidentiality. This privilege therefore does not stand in direct conflict to the interests in the administration of justice, but is rather one aspect of this interest, just as the interest that the truth be established. The House of

---

[205] See, for example, *Attorney-General v Mulholland* [1963] 2 QB 477 (CA), at 489 per Lord Denning.

Lords has even held that legal professional privilege is a fundamental condition on which the administration of justice as a whole relies.[206]

Under certain circumstances confidential medical information may be protected against disclosure in the courtroom by legal professional privilege. If, for example, a medical examination takes place in order for the results to be used in litigation, the report of the physician will be covered by legal professional privilege. The fact that communication between the physician and the solicitor had taken place is, as such, not protected. However, the physician's report to the patient's solicitor is privileged. In a case in which the defendant had been charged on counts of rape, incest and indecent assault, and a scientist had carried out a DNA test at the request of the defence solicitor on a blood sample provided by the defendant for that purpose, the Court of Appeal has held, for example, that the sample constituted privileged material and could therefore not be admitted in evidence without the defendant's consent.[207]

Where confidential medical information is protected by professional legal privilege, it receives absolute protection from disclosure. According to the House of Lords in its controversial decision in *R v Derby Magistrates' Court, ex parte B*,[208] this absolute protection is based on the following considerations:

> The principle ... is that man must be able to consult his lawyer in confidence, since otherwise he might hold back half the truth. The client must be sure that what he tells his lawyer in confidence will never be revealed without his consent. ... It is a fundamental condition on which the administration of justice as a whole rests. ... Once any exception to the general rule is allowed, the client's confidence is necessarily lost. The solicitor, instead of being able to tell his client that anything which the client might say would never in any circumstances be revealed without his consent, would have to qualify his assurance. He would have to tell the client that his confidence might be broken if in some future case the court were to hold that he no longer had 'any recognisable interest' in asserting his privilege. One can see at once that the purpose of the privilege would thereby be undermined. ... But it is not for the sake of the applicant alone that the privilege must be upheld. It is in the wider interests of all those hereafter who might otherwise be deterred from telling the whole truth to their solicitors. For this reason, I am of the opinion that no exception should be allowed to the absolute nature of legal professional privilege, once established.[209]

The House of Lords is thus of the view that only through the absolute protection of legal professional privilege which does not allow for any exception can its purpose be achieved. This is based on the utilitarian thought that the good consequences pursued with the protection of confidentiality can only be achieved if there is an

---

[206] See, for example, *R v Derby Magistrates' Court, ex parte B* [1996] AC 487 (HL), at 507 per Lord Taylor; and at 510 per Lord Nicholls.

[207] *R v R* [1994] 1 WLR 758.

[208] [1996] AC 487.

[209] Ibid., at 507-9, per Lord Taylor; for a critique see, for example, Uglow, at 207-28.

absolute certainty that confidentiality will be upheld under all circumstances.[210] Given that the protection of confidentiality in judicial proceedings is limited to legal professional privilege, the costs of an absolute privilege seem to be outweighed by the benefits flowing from confidentiality in that context. It is submitted that the judiciary's view that only an absolute privilege can achieve its purpose is likely to stand in the way of the recognition of other professional privileges, for example medical privilege.

The approach towards legal professional privilege confirms the conclusions reached above with regard to medical privilege. Legal professional privilege does not reflect a decision that the confidentiality of certain relationships as such is more important than considerations of justice, but rather only demonstrates the conviction that justice can best be served by protecting the confidentiality of this particular professional relationship.[211]

1.3 Police access to confidential medical information

While at trial stage, English law does not make a distinction between documents and the oral testimony of a witness, so that a physician can be compelled to give testimony in court as well as forced to submit confidential medical reports and other evidence, the situation is different at the pre-trial stage. As far as the physician's duty to disclose information to the police is concerned, the principle is laid down in *Rice v Connolly*:[212] there is no legal duty to assist the police, and every individual has the right to refuse to answer questions put to him/her by a police officer.[213] At pre-trial stage, therefore, the physician cannot normally be compelled orally to disclose confidential patient information. However, a few statutory provisions impose an obligation on every citizen to disclose information to the police. In the case of traffic offences, for example, s.172(2)(b) of the Road Traffic Act 1988 provides that everybody must, upon request by the police, provide any evidence he/she has which may lead to the identification of the driver involved. While physicians tried to argue that they should be exempt from this obligation given their duty to maintain the patient's confidences, the court in *Hunter v Mann*[214] rejected this view. The Medical Defence Union interprets this provision as imposing an obligation to supply the name and address of the patient only, but is of the opinion that no medical information has to be disclosed.[215]

---

[210] Contrast the considerations which led the House of Lords in *Re L (A Minor) (Police Investigation: Privilege)* [1996] 2 All ER 78, at 85 per Lord Jauncey to the conclusion that litigation privilege does not apply in care proceedings under Part IV of the Children Act 1989.

[211] McHale (1993), at 16-18.

[212] [1966] 2 All ER 649, at 652 per Lord Parker CJ.

[213] See also *A Health Authority v X (Discovery: Medical Conduct)* [2001] 2 FLR 673, at 694 per Munby J.

[214] [1974] 2 All ER 414; referring to s.168 of the Road Traffic Act 1972.

[215] Medical Defence Union, *Confidentiality*, at 7.

Special provisions apply to state access to confidential medical documents in the course of police investigations. Police powers to search for and seize material in the course of a criminal investigation are mainly governed by the provisions of PACE. The Act contains special provisions regarding state access to certain categories of confidential information.

1.3.1 Definition of excluded material

Under s.11 of PACE, personal records as well as human tissue and tissue fluid taken for the purpose of diagnosis or medical treatment are defined as excluded material. According to s.12, personal records are all documentary and other records concerning an individual who can be identified from them and which relate to, *inter alia*, his/her physical or mental health. This embraces patient records kept by doctors or hospitals. Even hospital records of patients' admissions and discharges are excluded material because they relate to the physical and mental health of persons who could be identified from them. This was explained in *R v Cardiff Crown Court, ex parte Kellam*,[216] a case in which the police, in the course of investigating a murder, sought details from a psychiatric hospital about patients who had been absent from the hospital on the day in question. The hospital had kept records of the patients' movements for the purposes of national insurance payments, so that the information the police was looking for was, in fact, available. Morland J argued as follows:

> Section 11 of the Police and Criminal Evidence Act 1984 ... must be given [its] ordinary and natural meaning. ... The definition, in my judgment, is very widely drawn and embracing. The 'records relating to physical or mental health' are not confined to clinical, nursing or surgical notes or treatment. The definition is expressly directed to the identifiability of the patient from the record. Often records of admission and discharge from a hospital or clinic will reveal the aspect of health for which a person is a patient, e.g. mental or maternity hospital, VD clinic or accident and emergency department. Records relating to admission or discharge of a patient from a hospital or clinic exist solely because he is a patient. That applies equally to the secondary records in this case of authorised discharges or leaves of the patient. ... He is a patient because he is suffering or is suspected to be suffering from physical or mental ill-health. He is discharged either permanently or temporarily because either he has recovered his health or temporary discharge is therapeutic or nothing more can be done to help him. In my judgment the records of discharge sought in this case (and the same would apply to unauthorised absences) concern an identifiable patient, in his capacity of being a patient, and are related to his mental health and are therefore 'excluded material' as defined by s.11.[217]

Given the broad interpretation of 'excluded material' in this decision, virtually every document that might be made in respect of a patient, be it clinical or administrative, is now covered by PACE. This outcome has been welcomed as reflecting Parliament's intention as well as being the most practical solution, given

---

[216] [1994] 16 BMLR 76 (QBD).
[217] Ibid., at 79-80.

that it makes any distinction between different types of records held by physicians obsolete.[218]

As objects removed from the human body, for example bullets, are not human tissue, they are not excluded material under the Act.[219] If a crime victim is examined for forensic reasons and for example swabs and smears or blood samples are taken, this material is not being taken for the purpose of medical diagnosis or treatment and therefore falls outside the scope of excluded material.[220] But if this material is held in confidence by the doctor or hospital, it would be special procedure material under s.14 of the Act.[221] Excluded material thus consists of confidential material which is held by a third party who would normally be in breach of an obligation of confidentiality when voluntarily submitting that material to the police. The seizure of such material is excluded because it would constitute an interference with contractual or ethical confidentiality obligations.[222]

1.3.2 Application for an order giving access to excluded material

The police are not completely prevented from access to excluded material, but they have to comply with a certain procedure when seeking access to it. According to s.9(1) of PACE, a circuit judge may, upon application by the police, issue an access order for the purpose of a criminal investigation if the conditions set out in Schedule 1, para.3 to the Act are met, i.e. there must be reasonable grounds to believe that excluded material can be found on the premises for which, prior to the enactment of s.9(2), the issuance of a search warrant would have been appropriate and available under a statutory provision. The effect of s.9(2) thus is that excluded material in regard to which, before the enactment of PACE, a search warrant would have been available under a statute, is now available only where the specific conditions outlined in Schedule 1, para.3 to the Act regarding an access order are met. As the search warrant powers in existence before the enactment of PACE did not refer to situations normally relevant to the physician-patient relationship, the conditions for issuing an access order with regard to confidential patient information will only be met in very rare cases. *R v Cardiff Crown Court, ex parte Kellam*,[223] for example, concerned an investigation for murder. As prior to the enactment of PACE, there was no statutory power for the police to obtain a search warrant in relation to a murder investigation,[224] the disclosure of the excluded material to which the police sought access could not be compelled.

Once it is established that the seizure concerns 'excluded material' and that the prerequisites of an access order are not met, there is no leeway as to a balancing of interests depending on the seriousness of the criminal offence under investigation. As Morland J explained in *R v Cardiff Crown Court, ex parte Kellam*:

---

[218] Grubb, at 371.

[219] Bevan, Lidstone, at 158.

[220] Feldman, at 641.

[221] Bevan, Lidstone, at 158-9.

[222] See Powell, Magrath, at 32-3.

[223] [1994] 16 BMLR 76 (QBD).

[224] See Feldman, at 648.

Section 11 of the Police and Criminal Evidence Act 1984 ... must be given [its] ordinary and natural meaning. This is so even if the result may seriously impede police investigations into a terrible murder and allow a very dangerous man to remain at large and a real risk to others. Parliament defines 'excluded material', as a matter of public policy, presumably, because it considered that the confidentiality of records of identifiable individuals relating to their health should have paramountcy over the prevention and investigation of crime.[225]

However, s.9(2) of PACE does not apply to statutory powers of search created after the coming into force of PACE, unless the creating statute explicitly refers to it. It would, therefore, be possible to introduce new search powers regarding confidential patient information by enacting a statute authorising the search for such information in a certain context, for example regarding drug abuse or gunshot wounds, without making reference to the special procedure set out in PACE.

An exception to the general rule of inaccessibility of excluded material is contained in Schedule 5, paras 5 and 6 of the Terrorism Act 2000, which allows for an application to a circuit judge for access to excluded material where the judge is satisfied that a terrorist investigation is being carried out; that there are reasonable grounds for believing that the material is likely to be of substantial value to the investigation; and that there are reasonable grounds for believing that it is in the public interest that the material should be produced. It follows that, in the course of terrorist investigations, the police could get access to confidential patient information if all of the above mentioned requirements are fulfilled. But as far as police investigations for other than terrorist offences are concerned, confidential information held by a doctor will not be available to the police, since at least one of the prerequisites of an access order to obtain excluded material, i.e. the existence of pre-PACE powers to issue a warrant, will almost never be met. This stands in stark contrast to the law's decision in favour of disclosure in the context of court proceedings. Thus, outside of court proceedings, medical confidentiality is to a large extent given precedence over the interest in the investigation and prosecution of crime. This confirms the view that the rejection of medical privilege in criminal court serves the interest in the administration of justice, of which the interest in prosecuting criminals is just one aspect which, in itself, is not necessarily important enough to outweigh the interest in medical confidentiality.

1.3.3 Access to excluded material without court order
Under certain circumstances, excluded material can be subject to search and seizure without prior application for an access order. Excluded material can be seized according to s.19 of PACE in the course of the execution of a search warrant or post-arrest powers in any circumstances in which the police officer is lawfully on the premises. This means that where a police officer has obtained a warrant, he/she can seize excluded material, if the other requirements of s.19 are met. But it could be argued that almost no situations are conceivable in which the

---

[225] [1994] 16 BMLR 76 (QBD), at 79-80.

requirements of s.19(2) will be satisfied, as there must be reasonable grounds for believing that it is necessary to seize the material in order to ensure that the material will not be concealed, lost, altered or destroyed. Therefore, s.19 of PACE is only of very limited, if any, relevance in the context of the physician-patient relationship.[226] Under s.50(2) of the Criminal Justice and Police Act 2001, excluded material can lawfully be seized by a police officer who is lawfully on any premises if the excluded material is inextricably linked with material he/she would be entitled to seize.[227] The compatibility of these powers with the provisions of the HRA has yet to be tested.[228]

Under s.32(2)(b) of PACE, a police officer is allowed to search the premises on which the suspect was arrested or where he/she was immediately before the arrest, provided that there are reasonable grounds to believe that evidence of the offence for which he/she was arrested is to be found on the premises. If, therefore, a suspect is arrested when leaving the hospital after having been treated for injuries supposedly sustained while committing a serious arrestable offence, the police can legally seize the patient records of said suspect if they have reasonable grounds to believe that the records will contain evidence that the suspect has committed the offence he/she is being arrested for.[229]

Thus, in the situations governed by ss.19 or 32 of PACE respectively, the special protection awarded to excluded material ceases to be effective. These exceptions give the police the possibility to circumvent the otherwise strict rules in respect of the accessibility of excluded material. They hardly seem to be compatible with the principle that excluded material is not accessible in the course of police investigations save in circumstances especially provided for by PACE and subject to careful considerations by circuit judges. It is particularly worrying that police officers are awarded the power to make a decision on the seizure of confidential and often sensitive material, and that they have to make this decision in situations which barely leave any time for a careful balancing of all interests involved. However, overall the provisions of PACE give far-reaching protection to medical records and other confidential patient information and material.

2 Voluntary disclosure by the physician

So far, this chapter has been concerned with the question of state access to confidential medical information by the means of compulsion, either by forcing the physician to testify in court about patient confidences, or by granting the state the power to gain access to medical records. The next problem to be addressed is that of the extent to which the physician might be justified in voluntarily disclosing confidential patient information to the police or the courts.

---

[226] Grubb, at 371.

[227] For safeguards applying to the seizure of excluded material, see ss.55 and 62 of the Criminal Justice and Police Act 2001.

[228] See Fenwick, at 645.

[229] Bevan, Lidstone, at 164.

Where the disclosure of a physician's medical documents is compelled by a court order or they are seized under the provisions of PACE, the physician does not have a choice but rather must comply with the court order or tolerate the seizure, unless he/she is prepared to accept the consequences of disobeying the law. A different question altogether is whether or not it is lawful for the physician voluntarily to submit confidential patient records or other confidential material to the police and/or the courts. Given that the physician is, in principle, under an obligation to maintain medical confidentiality, a voluntary disclosure would normally constitute a breach of confidence. However, in the context of criminal investigations and proceedings it is at least possible that under certain circumstances such a breach could be justified.

2.1 Submission of medical records to the police

It follows from the almost complete exclusion of confidential patient material in the hands of a physician from seizure that the question of whether the doctor has the right voluntarily to submit excluded material to the police is of particular importance. The only English case directly on this point is *R v Singleton*.[230] In that case, a dentist voluntarily submitted his patient's dental records to the police to assist with the investigation of a serious crime. As these records were excluded material under s.11 of PACE, they could not have been lawfully seized by the police. The question before the Court was whether the special access provisions contained in PACE applied not only to the seizure of material, but also to the voluntary submission of excluded material by the material holder, so that the police could then not lawfully receive and use such material, unless it would equally have had the power to seize it. The Court felt that the answer to this question depended on the purposes behind the relevant PACE provisions. According to the Court, s.11 of PACE aims to protect the holder of the confidential material, not the person the information relates to.[231] This approach has been explained by arguing that the seizure of excluded material is prohibited because it would interfere with the physician's contractual or ethical confidentiality obligations.[232] According to this view, while there is an interest in protecting the physician from search and seizure as long as he/she wants the confidential information to be protected, no such interest is involved where the physician voluntarily submits the material to the police, thereby waiving the interest in the confidentiality of the patient records and the protective effect of the PACE provisions. A voluntary disclosure of excluded material by the physician to the police was therefore held to exempt the police from obtaining a s.9(2) order which would not have been available in *R v Singleton* because the requirements under PACE were not fulfilled.

The Court in *Singleton* relied on other decisions which, in a different context, had confirmed that the relevant PACE provisions are designed to serve the protection not of the patient's, but of the physician's interests in the maintenance of

---

[230] [1995] 1 Crim App R 431 (CA).

[231] Ibid., at 439 per Farquharson LJ.

[232] See Powell, Magrath, at 32-3.

confidentiality, as it is the person in possession of the material (the physician), not the suspect (the patient), who has to be notified of an application for an access order.[233] This interpretation of PACE is also supported by the fact that human tissue or tissue fluid only qualify as excluded material under s.11(1)(b) if they have been collected for the purposes of diagnosis and treatment. The protection then depends on the intention of the person taking the tissue or fluid, i.e. the physician, not on the purposes for which the patient consented to the medical procedure.[234] Interpreted this way, the patient's privacy interests are then not protected by the provisions of PACE.

A case can be made, however, for reading the relevant PACE provisions as protecting the privacy right of the person the information relates to,[235] as it was the purpose of the new procedure to improve the protection of confidential material. This view is supported by an analysis of the interests balanced by the provisions on access to excluded material. In *R v Crown Court at Lewes*,[236] Bingham LJ identified the different interests as follows:

> The Police and Criminal Evidence Act governs a field in which there are two very obvious public interests. There is, first of all, a public interest in the effective investigation and prosecution of crime. Secondly, there is a public interest in protecting the personal and property rights of citizens against infringement and invasion. There is an obvious tension between these two public interests because crime could be most effectively investigated and prosecuted if the personal and property rights of citizens could be freely overridden and total protection of the personal and property rights of citizens would make investigation and prosecution of many crimes impossible or virtually so. The 1984 Act seeks to that effect a carefully judged balance between these interests.[237]

If the PACE provisions are interpreted that way, it could be argued that they are meant to protect the personal interests of the patient, as the information relates to intimate details of the patient's, not of the physician's life.[238] Furthermore, if the physician's rights in being free from state intrusions were the protected interest, the distinction between excluded material, specific procedure material and material that, even if in the possession of a physician, can easily be seized cannot be explained.

However, even though both the decision in *R v Singleton* and the academic discussion of this problem focus on the interpretation of the provisions of PACE when the physician voluntarily hands over excluded material to the police, it is submitted that PACE is not relevant in this case. Regardless of whose interests PACE aims to protect, these interests are only protected with regard to state access

---

[233] *R v Crown Court at Leicester, ex parte Director of Public Prosecutions* [1987] 3 All ER 654; *R v Crown Court at Manchester, ex parte Taylor* [1988] 2 All ER 769; *Barclays Bank plc v Taylor* [1989] 3 All ER 563 (CA).

[234] See the discussion by Feldman, at 642-3.

[235] Zuckerman, at 475.

[236] *R. v. Crown Court at Lewes, ex parte Hill* [1991] 93 Cr App R 60.

[237] Ibid., at 65-6.

[238] Zuckerman, at 475.

through search and seizure. It therefore seems more convincing to limit the applicability of PACE to the situation in which the police gains access to confidential material by the use of compulsion. By contrast, PACE does not envisage the situation of voluntary submission of excluded material by the physician. Where the physician voluntarily submits excluded material to the police, it is the physician, not the police who breaches the confidences of the patient. The question of whether or not such a course of conduct, i.e. a breach of the physician's duty of confidence owed to the patient, is lawful depends on whether or not the breach is exceptionally justified, a question which is governed by common law principles.[239] Where this is not the case, a doctor who by such an action breaches patient confidences may be liable to compensation.[240] Thus, in *R v Singleton*, the question should have been whether or not the dentist was justified in handing over the records to the police, a question which cannot be answered according to the provisions of PACE, as these provisions do not govern the relationship between physician and patient. The provisions of PACE are merely relevant in order to decide whether or not material that has been obtained by the police through a physician's breach of medical confidentiality should be excluded under s.78 of PACE.[241]

2.2 Disclosure for the purpose of criminal prosecution

It has already been discussed that English law does not recognise medical privilege in court proceedings so that the physician is no longer under a legal duty to maintain patient confidences once the court has ruled that the information is relevant and therefore needs to be disclosed. However, the situation is different when neither the prosecution nor the defence are aware of the existence of relevant medical information which might be useful in the course of a criminal trial. No court order will then compel disclosure, and the physician is not in any legal conflict, as he/she is under a legal obligation to maintain patient confidences, while there is no competing legal obligation to disclose confidential medical information to the relevant authorities. Whether or not the physician can lawfully volunteer to disclose confidential patient information, thereby violating the duty owed to the patient, depends on whether or not he/she can to that effect rely on a public interest defence that justifies the breach. If disclosure takes place once court proceedings have been initiated and the information is relevant, it is likely that the courts will regard the ensuing breach of medical confidentiality to be justified. The interest in medical confidentiality then competes with the interests in the administration of justice, a conflict that will normally be resolved in favour of the latter interests.[242] Different interests stand in conflict with each other if the physician discloses to the police information which might assist in criminal investigations and might lead to the prosecution of an offender. In that case, the interests in the administration of

---

[239] This question will be discussed in some detail below, infra 2.2.
[240] See Bevan, Lidstone, at 159.
[241] A question which has been discussed supra part 2, 1.1.
[242] See the discussion in the context of medical privilege, supra part 2, 1.1.

justice are not yet affected. Instead, the interests to be balanced against medical confidentiality are the interests of everyone 'to go about their daily lives without fear of harm to person or property', and the interest that serious crime should be effectively investigated and prosecuted.[243]

The professional guidelines issued by the GMC[244] suggest that disclosure will be justified in the public interest if it is made for the purpose of detecting a serious crime, that is a crime that will put someone at risk of death or serious harm. The BMA guidelines[245] equally state that disclosure is justified where necessary for the detection, investigation or punishment of a serious crime. They provide rather detailed guidance regarding the necessary balancing exercise that needs to be performed by the physician in each case of non-censual disclosure of confidential information and suggest, inter alia, the following principles: the crime must be sufficiently serious for the public interest to prevail; without disclosure the task of detecting the crime would be seriously prejudiced or delayed; and the information is not available from another source which would not necessitate a breach of medical confidentiality. The BMA further takes the stance that a distinction can be made between the prosecution of an offender where there is a risk of repetition, and situations in which no such risk seems to exist. According to the guidelines, while arguably in the latter case the interest in disclosure is weakened, the public interest in ensuring that serious crimes are investigated is nevertheless likely to require disclosure even in cases where there is no fear of repetition.

The prosecution of criminal offences can thus, as far as the professional obligation to maintain confidentiality is concerned, justify the disclosure of confidential patient information to the police by the physician, but only where the disclosure is necessary for the investigation or prosecution of serious criminal offences. However, the disclosure for the purpose of prosecuting less serious offences would not be justified.[246] The provisions of the Health Act 1999[247] provide for an exception from the obligation of medical confidentiality created under the Act for the purposes of the investigation of a serious arrestable offence. According to Schedule 5, Part I to PACE, serious arrestable offences are treason, murder, manslaughter, rape, kidnapping, incest with a girl under the age of 13, and indecent assault which constitutes an act of gross indecency. S.29 of the Data Protection Act 1998 which provides for exceptions from data protection provisions and principles where the data are processed for the purpose of the detection of crime or the apprehension or prosecution of offenders, on the other hand, does not distinguish between serious and less serious offences.

---

[243] *Attorney General's Reference (No 3 of 1999)* [2001] 1 All ER 577, at 584 per Lord Steyn, and at 590 per Lord Hobhouse; see also *R (on the Application of S) v Chief Constable of South Yorkshire* [2003] 1 All ER 148, at 161 per Lord Woolf CJ.

[244] General Medical Council, *Confidentiality: Protecting and Providing Information*, para.37(c).

[245] British Medical Association, *Confidentiality & Disclosure of Health Information*.

[246] See also McHale (1993), at 91; Taylor, at 78.

[247] See, for example, s.24(6)(e).

It should be noted that the distinction between different offences according to their seriousness as promoted by the provisions of the Health Act and by the professional guidelines, stands in contrast to the solution the law provides for disclosure in court, where the physician must testify regardless of the seriousness of the offence, and the solution favoured under PACE, where confidential material is excluded from police access regardless of the seriousness of the offence under investigation.

What, then, is the courts' approach to the conflict between maintaining a patient's confidence and the public interest in a physician's disclosure of confidential information that might lead to the prosecution of a criminal offender? No cases directly deal with the disclosure of confidential medical information by a physician for the purpose of criminal prosecution. However, cases from other contexts might, to some extent, shed some light on how the courts are likely to balance the competing interests. In *R v Singleton*,[248] for example, the Court of Appeal suggested, though in the context of an interpretation of the relevant PACE provisions, that a physician can disclose confidential patient records to the police to assist in a criminal investigation.

Another case concerned the disclosure to the regulatory body of the nursing profession of confidential information obtained by the police during an interview.[249] In that case, the Court held that the police was free to pass on confidential information to that body for the purpose of an investigation into the death of a patient in a nurse's care, in the interests of public health or safety. As the police had concluded the investigation without bringing charges against the nurse, the case concerned a situation in which the behaviour fell below the threshold of a criminal offence. If disclosure is justified in such circumstances, it seems unlikely that the voluntary disclosure by a physician of confidential patient information that is relevant to a criminal prosecution will be found to violate the physician's obligation to maintain medical confidentiality. However, it is also at least possible that the courts would distinguish *Woolgar* on the grounds that the interest in preserving the confidentiality of police interviews differs from the interest in protecting the confidentiality of the physician-patient relationship.

Assistance with the balancing exercise can also, to some extent, be derived from wardship cases. Frequently, medical documents form part of such proceedings, for example where the children concerned were examined for possible child abuse, or the parents for potential medical problems that might affect their ability to look after their children. Particularly in child abuse cases, criminal investigations may follow and the evidence that was available to the wardship court, which often includes medical reports, may be of the greatest relevance to the police. However, public interest immunity applies to evidence obtained in wardship proceedings, and judges who have to decide whether or not to allow disclosure in such a case must conduct a balancing exercise. In wardship proceedings, confidentiality serves the purpose of engendering frankness in those who give evidence to the wardship

---

[248] [1995] 1 Crim App R 431 (CA).

[249] *Woolgar v Chief Constable of the Sussex Police and another* [1999] 3 All ER 604 (CA).

court.[250] The privilege is that of the court, not of the child, and its primary purpose is to protect the court in the exercise of its powers.[251] It is thus based on utilitarian considerations. Where the disclosure of information to which such confidentiality applies is sought for the purposes of a criminal investigation, the interest in the confidentiality of wardship proceedings must be balanced against the public interest in seeing that the ends of justice are properly served by making available relevant and material information for the purposes of a criminal trial. At the stage of police investigations, Swinton Thomas LJ described the interest competing with confidentiality as:

> the public interest in the prosecution of serious crime and the punishment of offenders, including the public interest in convicting those who have been guilty of violent or sexual offences against children. There is a strong public interest in making available material to the police which is relevant to a criminal trial.[252]

With regard to the specific questions at issue, i.e. the disclosure of medical reports and of the father's admission that he had caused injuries to his daughter which had resulted in her death, the court came to the conclusion that:

> The medical report and the medical evidence are of first importance in establishing the time of SC's death, which is crucial, and the manner in which her injuries were inflicted, which is also crucial. In preparing for trial and shaping their case, in particular in preparing their medical evidence, it seems to me to be of first importance that the prosecuting authorities should have available the medical evidence and know with precision the admissions that were made by the father.[253]

In that case it was also argued that the weight of the public interest in disclosure depends, *inter alia*, on the nature and seriousness of the criminal offence at issue.[254]

In cases in which a balancing exercise was performed in the context of wardship proceedings, the balance came usually down in favour of disclosure where the evidence to which public interest immunity applied was relevant and material for criminal investigations.[255] An examination of the wardship cases thus further confirms that the interest in the investigation and prosecution of crime will regularly be given precedence over the interest in confidentiality. If this even applies to the situation of information which is, in principle, privileged in order to facilitate the performance of the wardship courts' duties, it is very likely that the

---

[250] *Re D (Minors) (Wardship: Disclosure)* [1992] 1 FCR 297 (CA), at 301-2 per Stephen Brown P; *Re A (Care Proceedings: Disclosure of Information)* [1996] 1 FCR 533 (CA), at 537 per Butler-Sloss LJ.

[251] *Re X, Y and Z (Wardship: Disclosure of Material)* [1992] 1 FLR 84, at 86 per Waite J.

[252] *Re C (A Minor)* [1997] Fam 76 (CA), at 85.

[253] Ibid., at 86.

[254] Ibid.

[255] See, for example, *Re S (Minors) (Wardship: Police Investigations)* [1987] Fam 199, at 203 per Booth J.

same outcome would be reached in cases in which the interest in medical confidentiality, an interest that is not given the same high priority by English courts, conflicts with the interest in criminal prosecution. Given the utilitarian basis of the confidentiality attached to evidence presented in wardship proceedings, the general attitude in favour of disclosure has been explained as follows:

> so long as any further dissemination of such material is limited to circumstances where the court thinks it proper, and so long as the court authorises such disclosure only where there is cogent reason for doing so, the fact that the confidentiality is not absolute will not have any significant effect either upon the willingness of potential witnesses to co-operate or upon their frankness in giving evidence.[256]

Thus, a shift in approach in favour of the protection of confidentiality is only to be expected if either the absolute protection of medical information were to be regarded as essential to protect public health, or if confidentiality were to be given greater significance for deontological reasons, neither of which seems likely. A physician who wishes to disclose confidential medical information to the police for the purpose of a criminal investigation, thereby breaching his/her obligation of confidence to the patient, is therefore likely to be regarded as justified in the public interest. However, this does not mean that a physician should lightly undertake such a disclosure. The case of *Woolgar* is interesting in this respect, as Kennedy LJ established some guidelines for the police when wishing to disclose confidential information to regulatory bodies for the purpose of investigations. According to him, if the police decides to disclose such information, they should inform the person affected so as to enable him/her to seek the assistance of the court as to the lawfulness of such a disclosure.[257] The decision in *A Health Authority v X (Discovery: Medical Conduct)*[258] gives an indication that similar principles should be applied to the disclosure of confidential medical information. According to Munby J, while medical confidentiality might have to give way to the interest in the investigation and prosecution of crime or professional misconduct, the decision of whether disclosure is justified should not be left to the individual physician, but handed over to a court. This is an onerous requirement, but it is to be welcomed, as it gives the physician the security that disclosure in a particular case will be lawful. More importantly, it protects the interests of the patient, at least if the patient is to be informed of the intended disclosure and given the opportunity to oppose it. In cases in which disclosure is sought for the purposes of criminal investigations and prosecution alone, there will usually be no urgency, so that the required involvement of the courts will not endanger the purpose of the disclosure.

---

[256] *Re X (Disclosure of Information)* [2001] 2 FLR 440 (FD), at 449 per Munby J.

[257] *Woolgar v Chief Constable of the Sussex Police and another* [1999] 3 All ER 604 (CA), at 615.

[258] [2001] 2 FLR 673 (FD), at 677 per Munby J; [2002] 2 All ER 780 (CA).

2.3 Disclosure to assist the defence

Given that no medical privilege is recognised in criminal proceedings, the defendant can easily gain access to confidential material that may be useful for his/her defence, as long as the relevance and materiality of the evidence can be established,[259] and provided the accused is aware of its existence. It remains to be discussed whether or not the physician is allowed to disclose confidential patient information which may be of interest to the defence or to someone who is under suspicion of having committed a criminal offence where that person does not know of its existence and can therefore not demand disclosure. There is no case-law directly to this point. However, as case-law in other areas shows, most courts that had to balance confidentiality interests against defence rights have argued that the defence rights of someone who is accused of an offence in criminal proceedings outweigh the interest in confidentiality.[260] The reason behind this outcome of the balancing of interests is that the interests of the accused in his/her liberty are of a very high rank.[261] For a long time, defence rights even prevailed over the confidentiality interest underlying the legal professional privilege.[262] However, *R v Derby Magistrates' Court, ex parte B*[263] has clarified that even where the defence rights of an innocent person are concerned, the importance of legal professional privilege does not allow for any exceptions to the principle of non-disclosure. This seems to be a victory of utilitarian over deontological considerations. Lord Nicholls discussed the difficulties any balancing exercise would have to overcome:

> The court would be faced with an essentially impossible task. ... How does one equate exposure to a comparatively minor civil claim or criminal charge against prejudicing a defence to a serious criminal charge? How does one balance a client's risk of loss of reputation, or exposure to public opprobrium, against prejudicing another person's possible defence to a murder charge? But the difficulties go much further. Could disclosure also be sought by the prosecution, on the ground that there is a public interest in the guilty being convicted? If not, why not? ... There is no evident stopping place short of the balancing exercise being potentially available in support of all parties in all forms of court proceedings. This highlights the impossibility of the exercise. What is the measure by which the judges are to ascribe an appropriate weight, on each side of the scale, to the

---

[259] For the specific problem of the production of confidential documents upon request of the accused under s. 66 of the Criminal Procedure and Investigations Act 1996 see Corker, at 138-41.

[260] See, for example, *Taylor v Serious Fraud Office* (HL (E)) [1998] 3 WLR 1040, at 1049 per Lord Hoffmann.

[261] See, for example, *R v Governor of Brixton Prison, ex parte Osman* [1991] 1 WLR 281 (DC), at 288 per Mann LJ; *Vincent Raymond Agar* [1990] 90 Cr App R 318 (CA), at 324 per Mustill LJ; *Mark v Beyfus* [1890] 25 Q.B.D. 494, at 498 per Lord Esher MR; see also Barnett, at 493.

[262] See, for example, *R v Barton* [1973] 1 WLR 115, at 118 per Caulfield J; *R v Ataou* [1988] 2 All ER 321 (CA), at 327 per French J.

[263] [1996] AC 487 (HL).

diverse multitude of different claims, civil and criminal, and other interests of the client on the one hand and the person seeking disclosure on the other hand?[264]

This argument is interesting in that it sheds some light on the problems arising when having to balance competing interests the respective values of which are difficult to ascertain and qualify. However, the complexity of the balancing exercise is not a reason for awarding one of the two competing interests absolute protection to the detriment of the other. It is submitted that the real reason for giving legal professional privilege absolute precedence over all potentially competing interests is the utilitarian assessment that nothing short of absolute protection will guarantee the interests in the administration of justice.[265] Where such an absolutist approach is not regarded as necessary, courts are prepared to perform balancing exercises regardless of the inherent difficulties.

Unless either medical confidentiality or defence rights are awarded absolute protection, where a conflict between those two interests arises, courts will have to apply a balancing test. An examination of case law will show how the courts have approached the resolution of this particular conflict of interest. In *Note Re an Adoption Application*[266] an originating summons was brought *ex parte* by a local authority, acting as adoption agency. A few years after a schoolgirl's child had been placed for adoption, she had asserted that her stepfather had sexually abused her and he was charged with rape and other sexual offences. The prosecution case depended entirely on the girl's evidence. The stepfather's defence was that the father of the child and the perpetrator of the offences had been a schoolfriend of hers. The stepfather was convicted and sentenced to a long term of imprisonment. He appealed and was allowed to apply for blood tests to establish whether or not he was the father of the baby. The local authority was required to look at their files in order to find out where the baby was. In doing so, the local authority found out that the account of the girl as to how she became pregnant was compatible with the stepfather's defence. The local authority sought the assistance of the court in deciding whether or not to disclose this information. Under Rule 53(3) of the Adoption Rules 1984, any person who obtains information in the course of, or relating to adoption proceedings shall treat that information as confidential and shall only disclose it if the disclosure is necessary for the proper exercise of his/her duties. The court argued as follows:

The information which is now available may be relevant, in the interests of justice, in the Court of Appeal, Criminal Division. In my judgment, a further disclosure of this information to the Attorney-General is necessary for the proper exercise of the social worker's duties. The Attorney-General will be able to decide to what extent the information should be passed on, either to the court or to any other person. I, accordingly, direct that the local authority should inform the Attorney-General of the circumstances of

---

[264] Ibid., at 511-2.
[265] See the discussion supra part 2, 1.2.
[266] [1990] 1 FLR 412 (FD).

this case and of the information which is available in their files, for him to consider further.[267]

In this case the court did not weigh the different interests, i.e. the interest in the confidentiality of adoption proceedings, on the one hand, and the interests of the wrongly convicted, on the other hand, but rather decided in favour of disclosure by interpreting the exception provided by the Adoption Rules in a liberal way. However, this case provides a good example of the interests that can weigh in favour of a breach of confidentiality. If the only possibility to exonerate the accused, or, in this case, the wrongly convicted, is to disclose confidential information relating to the offender or a third party, many will agree that it lies in the public interest to prevent a miscarriage of justice as well as in the accused's interest in freedom from unjust punishment that a breach of confidentiality for this purpose be justified.

Mann LJ held in *R v Governor of Brixton Prison, Ex parte Osman*,[268] a case in which public interest immunity was claimed to protect communications between the magistrates' court and the Home Office, and between the Home Office and other government departments:

> Where the interests of justice arise in a criminal case touching and concerning liberty or conceivably on occasion life, the weight to be attached to the interests of justice is plainly very great indeed. ... In those cases, which establish a privilege in regard to information leading to the detection of crime, there are observations to the effect that the privilege cannot prevail if the evidence is necessary for the prevention of a miscarriage of justice. No balance is called for. If admission is necessary to prevent miscarriage of justice, balance does not arise.[269]

This shows that where the information is needed in the course of criminal proceedings, the interest conflicting with confidentiality is not the interest of the defence, but rather the interest in the administration of justice, of which the protection of defence rights forms part. In that case, in line with the courts' approach in the context of medical privilege, those interests are given precedence. However, just as in cases of medical privilege, this does not necessarily mean that confidentiality will not receive any protection.

In one case of public interest immunity regarding the disclosure of confidential information relating to an abortion which enjoys special confidentiality under the provisions of the Abortion Act 1967 and the Abortion Regulations 1968, the court decided that in case of a conflict between public interest immunity and defence rights, defence rights did not necessarily prevail. Rather, a balancing exercise would have to be performed which in that case led to a decision in favour of non-disclosure, as the court was of the opinion that the documents' value for the

---

[267] Ibid., at 413 per Ewbank J.

[268] [1991] 1 WLR 281 (DC).

[269] Ibid, at 288 and 290; see also *Re D (Minors) (Wardship: Disclosure)* [1992] 1 FCR 297 (CA), at 301-2 per Stephen Brown P.

defence was only slim.[270] Thus, courts apply a materiality test. In *R v K (DT)* *(Evidence)*,[271] for example, a case in which a father applied for disclosure of a video tape of an interview which had taken place with a large part of the family in a hospital for therapeutic purposes, and in which the hospital raised public interest immunity, the court argued that:

> The exclusion of the evidence without an opportunity of testing its relevance and importance amounted to a material irregularity. ... This court recognises the hospital's legitimate concern that interviews which are conducted on a confidential basis for therapeutic purposes ought not, unless the interests of justice so require, to be disclosed outside the family circle of those who are the subject of the case conference and the service which is conducting it. However, where the liberty of the subject is in issue, and disclosure may be of assistance to a defendant, a claim for disclosure will often be strong. In the present case we decided that it was necessary for us to see the video, so as to be able to consider whether there was material which might have been of assistance to this appellant on his trial. ... We are quite satisfied, having done so, that nothing took place at the therapeutic case conference which was filmed on the video could have afforded assistance to the defence had it been ordered to be disclosed. ... We are therefore satisfied that in this case it would not have been appropriate to order disclosure. After seeing the video there really would have been no meaningful balancing exercise for the judge to do, because there was no advantage for the appellant to balance against the claim of public interest immunity. ... It would not be appropriate for us to order that it be disclosed, even for the purpose of allowing counsel to see it.[272]

Another case in which the Court of Appeal explained how the balancing of interests operated in such cases was that of *R v Keane*.[273] It was again Taylor LJ who observed that:

> If the disputed material may prove the defendant's innocence or avoid a miscarriage of justice, then the balance comes down resoundingly in favour of disclosing it. But how is it to be determined whether and to what extent the material ... may be of assistance to the defence? ... The judge has to perform the balancing exercise by having regard on the one hand to the weight of public interest in non-disclosure. On the other hand, he must consider the importance of the documents to the issues of interest to the defence, present and potential ... . Accordingly, the more full and specific the indication the defendant's lawyers give of the defence or issues they are likely to raise, the more accurately both prosecution and judge will be able to discuss the value to the defence of the material.[274]

In *Peter Clowes and Others*,[275] the judge held that the outcome of the balancing exercise depended on the gravity of the offence, so that disclosure upon request of

---

[270] *Morrow, Geach and Thomas v D.P.P.; Secretary of State for Health and Social Security; British Pregnancy Advisory Service* [1994] Crim. L.R. 58.
[271] [1993] 2 FLR 181 (CA).
[272] Ibid., at 184-5 per Taylor LJ.
[273] [1994] 1 WLR 746.
[274] Ibid., at 751-2.
[275] [1992] 95 Cr App R 440, at 454 per Phillips J.

the defendant would be more likely the more serious the offence with which he/she is charged.

In all of these cases, disclosure was requested by the defendant. However, given the courts' insistence that defence rights prevail over the interest in confidentiality, it is submitted that a physician who voluntarily discloses confidential medical information for the purpose of assisting someone's defence or the rehabilitation of a person who was wrongly accused or convicted, will be justified in the public interest, unless the information is not material. The importance attached to defence rights was one of the main reasons for the Criminal Law Revision Committee to reject the introduction of medical privilege.[276] Surprisingly, the latest guidelines on confidentiality issued by the GMC and by the BMA do not make any specific reference to disclosure for the purpose of protecting defence rights. However, both guidelines allow for disclosure in the public interest, based on a balancing of the interests at stake, and it is highly likely that a physician's disclosure to assist someone with his/her defence would be regarded as outweighing the confidentiality interests of the patient.

It can be seen that the approach to the voluntary disclosure of information for the purpose of protecting defence rights is very similar to that adopted towards medical privilege. This is hardly surprising, given that defence rights are normally only at stake in the context of criminal proceedings, so that confidentiality will then conflict with the interests in the administration of justice. It is interesting that the courts do not seem to take account of the factors which according to Lord Nicholls' statement in *R v Derby Magistrates' Court, ex parte B*[277] make the balancing exercise so difficult. His statement suggests that the balancing test is less straightforward than the other cases make believe. It is not obvious, for example, that relevant information should be disclosed if no more than a loss of reputation or a minor charge is at stake. These are problems that deserve more consideration than they have so far received, given that every violation of medical confidentiality constitutes an interference with the patient's right to private life under Article 8(1) of the ECHR.

2.4 Disclosure for the purpose of crime prevention

The physician is under no obligation, and cannot normally be compelled to disclose confidential medical information for the purpose of crime prevention. Therefore, in the context of crime prevention, voluntary disclosure by the physician is of particular importance. The leading case dealing with the voluntary disclosure by a physician of confidential medical information for the purpose of crime prevention is *W v Egdell*.[278] That case, which has already been discussed in a different context,[279] did not concern the disclosure of confidential patient information to the police. The decision nevertheless provides a detailed discussion of the different

---

[276] Eleventh Report, Cmnd 4991, para.272-6.

[277] [1996] AC 487 (HL).

[278] [1990] 1 All ER 835 (CA).

[279] *Supra.*, part 1, 3.5, where the facts of the case are described in some detail.

interests to be balanced where the physician's obligation of confidentiality conflicts with the public interest in the prevention of criminal offences, and the physician decides to disclose the relevant information. As Bingham LJ put it, the crucial question was how the balance should be struck between the public interest in maintaining professional confidences and the public interest in protecting the public against possible violence. According to Stephen Brown P, the balance came clearly down in favour of disclosure. The main reason for this was the number and nature of the killings W had committed, as they:

> must inevitably give rise to the gravest concern for the safety of the public. ... It is clear that Dr Egdell did have highly relevant information about W's condition which reflected on his dangerousness. In my judgement the position came within the terms of r 81(g) of the General Medical Council's rules. ... The suppression of the material contained in his report would have deprived both the hospital and the Secretary of State of vital information, directly relevant to questions of public safety. ... The judge in fact based his conclusion on what he termed 'broader considerations', that is to say the safety of the public. I agree with him.[280]

Bingham LJ also made some interesting observations:

> Counsel for W contended that ... there was ... no question of W's release, whether absolutely or conditionally, in the then foreseeable future. ... I do not find these points persuasive. When Dr Egdell made his decision to disclose, one tribunal had already recommended W's transfer to a regional secure unit and the hospital authorities had urged that course. The Home Office had resisted transfer in a qualified manner but on a basis of inadequate information. It appeared to be only a matter of time, and probably not a very long time, before W was transferred. The regional secure unit was to act as staging post on W's journey back into the community. While W would no doubt be further tested, such tests would not be focused on the source of Dr Egdell's concern, which he quite rightly considered to have received inadequate attention up to then. Dr Egdell had to act when he did or not at all. There is one consideration which in my judgment ... weighs the balance of public interest decisively in favour of disclosure. It may be shortly put. Where a man has committed multiple killings under the disability of serious mental illness, decisions which may lead directly or indirectly to his release from hospital should not be made unless a responsible authority is properly able to make an informed judgment that the risk of repetition is so small as to be acceptable. A consultant psychiatrist who becomes aware, even in the course of a confidential relationship, of information which leads him, in the exercise of what the court considers a sound professional judgment, to fear that such decisions may be made on the basis of inadequate information and with a real risk of consequent danger to the public is entitled to take such steps as are reasonable in all the circumstances to communicate the grounds of his concern to the responsible authorities. I have no doubt that the judge's decision in favour of Dr Egdell was right on the facts of this case.[281]

Bingham LJ made reference to Article 8 of the ECHR, holding that the situation in *Egdell* fell squarely within the exception envisaged by Article 8(2), as Dr. Egdell's

---

[280] [1990] 1 All ER 835 (CA), at 846.
[281] Ibid., at 852.

conduct was necessary in the interests of public safety and the prevention of crime.[282]

In *Egdell*, the court seems to suggest that disclosure may be made only to those to whom it is necessary to convey the information in order to protect the public interest, and that only a risk involving the danger of physical harm justifies disclosure.[283] The approach adopted by the Court of Appeal was mostly welcomed.[284] However, the criteria developed by the Court are extremely vague. The requirement of a 'real' risk, for example, leaves some scope for interpretation, as it can imply a probability of risk or a mere possibility, the latter seemingly having been sufficient in *Egdell*. While the Court professed the view that W posed an imminent risk to the public, it is submitted that this was not the case. There was no imminent risk of W's release, let alone any imminent risk that he might harm anybody. Furthermore, the disclosed diagnosis was no more than the opinion of one physician,[285] and other reports would have been commissioned before making a final decision on W's release. The mere fact that other doctors may not have focused on the same aspects of W's personality and may therefore possibly have come to a conclusion that differed from that of Dr Egdell seems hardly sufficient to justify a breach of the confidential relationship between patient and physician in this case. Another question is how to define the requirement of a danger to the public. It has been suggested that the risk to an individual should be enough to qualify as a danger to the public, as the public has an interest in the protection of its members from violence which is affected by a real risk of danger to the bodily integrity of one individual.[286]

Some commentators, while conceding that the result in *Egdell* may be right in that the public needs to be protected from potentially dangerous persons, nevertheless expressed some unease as to the casualness with which the Court was prepared to disregard the confidentiality interests of the patient.[287] This concern seems justified, as the abstract danger that someone who committed crimes due to a certain psychological disposition might continue to be dangerous in the future seems to be sufficient for the public interest justification to apply. Cases which have applied *Egdell* reconfirm these worries. Based on its decision in *Egdell*, the Court of Appeal held in *Peter Michael Anthony Crozier*[288] that a psychiatrist who was of the firm belief that a patient suffered from a psychopathic disorder and continued to be a danger to the public acted reasonably and responsibly when disclosing this information, as the strong public interest in the disclosure of his views overrode his duty of confidence to the appellant. In *R v Kennedy*,[289] a case in which the appellant, while serving a custodial sentence, was interviewed by two

---

[282] Ibid., at 853.

[283] Kennedy, Grubb, at 1100-1101.

[284] See, for example, Mason, McCall Smith, at 196-7; Jones, at 16-24.

[285] Kennedy, Grubb, at 1101.

[286] Jones, at 19.

[287] McHale (1989), at 719.

[288] [1990] 12 Cr App R (S) 206.

[289] [1999] 1 Cr App R 54 (CA).

psychiatrists and a probation officer and expressed the intention to kill his stepfather upon his release, Lord Bingham CJ stated without further explanation that it followed from *Egdell* that no confidentiality attached to these statements.[290] However, it is submitted that this is a wrong interpretation of *Egdell*, as that decision does not question the confidentiality of the psychiatrist-patient relationship, but merely holds that under certain circumstances medical confidentiality can be outweighed by the public interest in the prevention of criminal offences. The balancing required in order to satisfy the public interest defence and also the requirements of Article 8 of the ECHR should not be circumvented by excluding certain patient information from the scope of protection of medical confidentiality. The courts' approach demonstrates the insufficiencies of the public interest defence. As no clear criteria limit the defence, it is easy for the courts to justify breaches of confidence in the public interests. However, while the criteria developed in *Egdell* could be made workable when given a more specific content, it was seen that they were not fulfilled in the case of *Egdell*. As long as the courts have the perception that certain interests are more important than others, even strict legal criteria are therefore not likely to change the outcome of a case.

Case-law from other areas might be useful in assisting with the analysis of how the courts have balanced and should balance the competing interests. In *Re S (Minors) (Wardship: Police Investigations)*,[291] a case that arose in the context of wardship proceedings, and in which the police applied for leave of the court to permit disclosure to the police of the medical records and video recordings made by a child abuse clinic, Booth J specifically referred to the balancing of interests in cases of crime prevention when stating that:

> The protection afforded to a child by the exercise of the wardship jurisdiction should not be extended to the point where it gives protection to offenders against the law and, indeed, offenders against the wards themselves. The court must take into consideration, as a matter of public policy, the need to safeguard not only its wards but other children against the harm they may suffer as the result of recurring crimes by undetected criminals. The likely outcome and its effects upon a ward of granting an application such as the police now make must be considered in each and every case. But when balanced against the competing public interest which requires the court to protect society from the perpetration of crime it could only be in exceptional circumstances that the interests of the individual ward should prevail. In this case, although the results may be far-reaching and unpleasant for these young and damaged children, their interests are secondary to that greater public need. I am satisfied that on the facts this application is wholly justified and that the police should have the leave they seek in respect of the medical records and video recordings now in the possession of Great Ormond Street Hospital.[292]

In this case, considerations of crime prevention and of criminal prosecution seem to have been mixed up, as the argument is based on the thought that it is necessary

---

[290] Ibid., at 59-60.
[291] [1987] Fam 199.
[292] Ibid., at 203-4.

to prosecute a person who has committed an offence in order to protect the public from the perpetration of crime. In its generality, this argument is problematic. Not in all cases does a risk of repetition exist, and it can hardly be said that the mere fact that someone has committed past crimes and is still at large poses in itself a real risk to individuals or society.

Re V (Sexual Abuse: Disclosure); Re L (Sexual Abuse: Disclosure)[293] are two cases which shed some light on the question of risk assessment and remoteness of risk. In *Re L*, the local authority wished to disclose to another local authority, in the area of which L now lived, the judge's finding made in family proceedings that L posed a considerable threat to the children of single female adults with whom he might cohabit. L had previously been charged with counts of sexual abuse, and acquitted. In *Re V*, the local authority wished to disclose to the football league the judge's finding, again made in family proceedings, that W, who coached the junior teams at the local football club, had committed an indecent assault, and developed an unusual and unhealthy relationship with a 14-year-old. Butler-Sloss argued that:

> In Mr L's case ... it would be difficult to keep the information truly confidential if it is to be of use and its use might well be oppressive, unless a child was actually at risk. ... [In the case of Mr W] For it to be effective they would presumably have to circulate some information to all clubs with which Mr W might be associated. ... Almost inevitably it would have to be passed on probably to numerous people. ... If the dissemination is to be effective, and possibly even if it is not effective, the information provided is likely to be oppressive and consequently unjust to Mr W. Those considerations illustrate the problem for the court when faced with an application to authorise disclosure of information in a case where the risk cannot be related to a particular child or children - because it is not known whether any, or which, children are actually at risk ... . The balance comes down firmly in favour of non-disclosure in each case.[294]

It can thus be seen that the Court of Appeal was not prepared to hold that a risk the existence of which can mainly be inferred from the past behaviour of the person concerned, and which is not specific as to the potential victims, or any other features on how it might materialise, can be sufficient to justify the disclosure of confidential information. The two cases also show that proportionality considerations have an important role to play in this context. Where, because of the vague and general nature of the risk, the interests of the individual that are affected by disclosure will have to be violated to a considerable extent, such a measure does not seem acceptable. However, it must be noted that this decision was concerned with upholding the confidentiality of family proceedings.

Contrast the decision in *R v Chief Constable of the North Wales Police.*[295] In that case the police informed the owner of a caravan site of the presence on his site of two persons with previous convictions for serious sexual assaults against children. It was argued that if the police:

---

[293] [1999] 1 FLR 267 (CA).
[294] Ibid., at 274.
[295] [1997] 4 All ER 691 (QBD); [1998] 3 All ER 310 (CA).

[C]onsider in the exercise of a careful and bona fide judgment that it is desirable or necessary in the public interest to make disclosure, whether for the purpose of preventing crime or alerting members of the public to an apprehended danger, it is proper for them to make such limited disclosure as is judged necessary to achieve that purpose.[296]

Disclosure was held to be at least justifiable where the potential harm to the individual and the community was great and obvious. On appeal, Lord Woolf CJ agreed, stressing that disclosure should only be made when there is a pressing need for it.[297] However, it is difficult to see that such a pressing need existed in that case and that there was an imminent and real risk of physical harm to any individual. It seems as if the seriousness of the harm if it were to materialise was regarded as of such importance that the courts were prepared to substitute 'potential' for 'real and imminent'.

In another case, the court was asked to review the disclosure by the police and social services of information about previous allegations of sexual abuse of children against a person (LM) to the local education department with which he had a contract regarding the transport of school children. The disclosed allegations had not been sufficient to warrant prosecution, but the disclosure led to the termination of the contract.[298] Based on *R v Chief Constable of the North Wales Police*, the court decided that disclosure was only lawful if the pressing need test was satisfied. In order to determine how to balance the interest in protecting children from criminal offences and the individual's right to private life, the court suggested that account should be taken of the disclosing authority's belief in the truth of the allegations, the need of the third party in obtaining the information, and the degree of risk posed if disclosure was not made. In that case, the court concluded that the pressing need test was not satisfied. This assessment was mainly based on the facts that LM did not have a criminal record, that the allegations against him had not been proved, and that the allegations had been made more than 10 years ago.

These cases show that the 'pressing need' test has been strictly applied in cases in which the interest in disclosure had to be balanced against recognised confidentiality interests, as in *Re V (Sexual Abuse: Disclosure)*; *Re L (Sexual Abuse: Disclosure)*.[299] By contrast, in cases in which the information to be disclosed had not been obtained in confidence, the outcome of the balancing seems to depend to a large extent on the past conduct of the subject of the information. It seems likely that the test in the context of medical confidentiality will be less stringent than that applied in the context of preserving the confidentiality of family proceedings, given that more importance is generally attached to confidentiality in

---

[296] *R v Chief Constable of the North Wales Police and others, ex parte AB and another* [1997] 4 All ER 691 (QBD), at 699 per Lord Bingham CJ.

[297] *R v Chief Constable of the North Wales Police and others, ex parte AB and another* [1998] 3 All ER 310 (CA), at 320.

[298] *R v Local Authority and Police Authority in the Midlands, ex parte LM* [2000] 1 FLR 612 (QB), at 622-3 per Dyson J.

[299] [1999] 1 FLR 267 (CA), per Butler-Sloss, LJ.

the latter context. At the same time, considering that medical information is received in confidence, the lax standard of the pressing need test applied in *R v Chief Constable of the North Wales Police* hardly provides sufficient criteria for a proportionality assessment[300] as required by the HRA, given that every breach of medical confidentiality will constitute a breach of the right to private life under Article 8(1) of the ECHR. The test suggested by Butler Sloss LJ in *Re V (Sexual Abuse: Disclosure); Re L (Sexual Abuse: Disclosure)*[301] provides useful guidance as to how such an exercise could be performed.[302] According to that decision, disclosure can only be justified if the risk to be averted goes beyond the general risk, based on past conduct, that a person might commit an offence. Instead, the potential victim must at least be identifiable. In combination with the requirement of a real and imminent risk of physical harm, this provides some guidelines on how to strike a fair balance between the need of the individual and the public to be protected from criminal offences, and the rights of patients to have their medical confidences protected.

The physician who holds confidential information that might help prevent a criminal offence is in the undesirable position of having to perform a risk assessment, especially as to whether or not the risk posed by the patient is real and whether or not it involves a danger to the public. Professional guidelines to some extent assist the physician in making such an evaluation. The GMC is rather vague in stating that disclosure is in the public interest if it may assist in the prevention of serious crimes which might put someone at risk of death or serious harm.[303] The BMA's guidance[304] is more detailed. It equally states that disclosure is justified if it is necessary for the prevention of a serious offence. To determine which offences qualify as serious, reference is made to the definition of arrestable offences in s.116 of PACE. The offences of murder, manslaughter, rape, treason and kidnapping are specifically listed, and as a more general point, it is stated that crimes which might result in serious harm or loss of life for individuals can be regarded as very substantially more significant than crimes involving theft, fraud or damage to property. Disclosure always rests on a proportionality test and can only exceptionally be justified if the crime is sufficiently serious for the public interest to prevail; if without disclosure its prevention would be seriously prejudiced or delayed; and if the information is not available from another source. The BMA recommends that prior to disclosure, advice from professional, disciplinary and indemnifying bodies should be sought.

---

[300] For a critical discussion of the case, see Scully, at 183-92.

[301] [1999] 1 FLR 267 (CA).

[302] However, for a critique of this decision, see Smith, at 249-52.

[303] GMC, *Confidentiality: Protecting and Providing Information*, at para.37(c).

[304] BMA, *Confidentiality & Disclosure of Health Information*.

3 Summary and conclusion

No medical privilege exists in criminal proceedings so that a physician who is called upon to testify in a criminal court has no right to refuse to give testimony. This rejection of medical privilege is mainly based on the consideration that the interests of justice override any interest in confidentiality, unless this interest is supported by public interest immunity. Thus, the fact that the protection of medical confidentiality lies in the public interest is not a sufficient reason for the recognition of medical privilege. Such a privilege is widely seen as undesirable and superfluous, as many are of the opinion that medical confidentiality already receives adequate protection in criminal court. This is because the courts have a discretion to exclude medical evidence where it is not relevant and material. There also seems to be some distrust in the desirability of creating a statutory privilege, probably because it is felt that privilege necessarily relates to a conflict of interests which should not be resolved in a general and abstract manner. Instead, it should be left to the courts to balance the competing interests in the individual case.[305] However, under current case-law the courts will only exercise discretion to exclude medical evidence when it can be established that the evidence is neither relevant nor material to the case. Therefore, at present, not every case of conflict between the interests of justice and the interest in medical confidentiality calls for a balancing of the conflicting interests. Indeed, it is clear that the interests of justice are automatically given precedence where the evidence is material and necessary for a criminal trial.

Medical records that are not protected by the public interest immunity attached to family proceedings or by legal privilege must be produced in criminal court under the same conditions under which the physician has to give testimony. Thus, they are normally only protected if their content is thought to be irrelevant or immaterial. Where the police seek access to medical records in the course of investigations, the provisions of PACE apply. As medical records qualify as 'excluded material', police access to them is only possible where the conditions of an access order are met, which will only rarely be the case. Thus, in the course of police investigations, confidential medical material receives far-reaching protection even if it is highly material to the investigation, which stands in stark contrast to the almost non-existing protection at trial stage. This might be explained by the different interests that are at stake. In the context of police investigations, a balance needs to be struck between the interest in detecting, investigating and prosecuting crime, on the one hand, and civil liberties of citizens, on the other. However, once a case has come to court, the interests involved slightly change. At stake is not only the interest in prosecuting a criminal, but also the interest in the integrity of the judicial system as such, including the protection of defence rights. If the court does not have all information at its disposal to establish the truth, miscarriages of justice may occur and the trust in the legal system may be impaired. These interests are regarded as more important than confidentiality rights.

---

[305] See, for example, May, at 13-43.

Different principles apply, yet again, where the physician voluntarily discloses confidential medical information to the police or the courts. Such a disclosure constitutes a violation of the physician's obligation to maintain patient confidentiality. It will only be lawful if a legal justification is available, a question that is to be decided by the courts. The justification usually applied, that is the public interest defence, is not carefully delineated and court decisions are mainly based on broad considerations of which interest seems more important in a given case. When balancing the interest in medical confidentiality against the interests in the name of which disclosure is made, the courts demonstrate a bias towards disclosure as long as the information is necessary to prosecute a criminal, serve defence rights or prevent the commission of a criminal offence. Decisions usually come down in favour of disclosure, no matter what the criteria according to which the courts perform the balancing exercise. This reflects the traditional attitude that medical confidentiality is mainly protected for utilitarian reasons and that a patient's confidences are only worthy of legal protection if the costs are not too high. Given that disclosure violates the patient's right to have his/her medical confidences protected, it is submitted that clear criteria for the balancing of the competing interests are necessary.[306] However, this in itself will not be sufficient to award greater protection to the patient's right of medical confidentiality. More important is the perception of the value to be attached to medical confidentiality. As long as a utilitarian perspective on medical confidentiality prevails, confidentiality will routinely lose out to the interests behind crime prevention and criminal prosecution.

It seems at first sight inconsistent that the voluntary disclosure of confidential information by the physician for purposes of crime prevention or criminal prosecution is regularly held to be justified by the courts, even in cases in which police access by the way of compulsion has been excluded by statute. This might be explained, yet again, by the different interests that are at stake in each scenario. Voluntary disclosure by the physician only affects the privacy rights of the patient which are not given high priority by the courts when competing with the interests in crime prevention and criminal prosecution. Forced police access to confidential information, by contrast, not only affects the confidentiality interests of the patient, but also the interests of the physician in being free from state intrusion, and in the integrity of his/her professional relationships. It has been demonstrated that the protection awarded by the provisions of PACE mainly focuses on these interests of the material holder, the physician, and not on the privacy interests of the patient. This state of the law only insufficiently protects the patient's right to private life under Article 8(1) of the ECHR. While it is well possible that the balance will in many cases of conflict come down in favour of disclosure, Article 8(2) of the ECHR should not be read so as to give the interests listed therein automatic precedence over the patient's right to confidentiality, without a careful proportionality examination in each case. Unfortunately, only few of the cases so far take the proportionality test seriously in such situations. Whether the HRA will

---

[306] See the discussion in Chapter 8.

bring an increased awareness of the significance of privacy protection, thereby affecting a greater protection of a patient's medical confidences, remains to be seen.

Chapter 7

American Law

This chapter will explain how American law protects medical confidentiality and resolves conflicts between medical confidentiality and the interests in crime prevention and criminal prosecution.

PART 1 – PROTECTION OF MEDICAL CONFIDENTIALITY

The first difficulty such an overview of American law is faced with is that both federal and State law are relevant in this area of the law. Privacy protection is granted under the Federal Constitution, permeating the law of all American States. However, the protection of medical confidentiality by the means of ordinary statutes is almost exclusively at the discretion of the States, so that many different ways of dealing with the relevant legal problems can be found. Some representative approaches to the protection of medical confidentiality through privilege statutes will be introduced, and it will be demonstrated how differently the courts interpret and apply such statutes. In addition, it will be shown how courts react to these problems in the absence of privilege statutes. The different attitudes of the courts regarding the appropriate private law remedies in case of a breach of medical confidentiality will also be discussed.

1 Constitutional privacy protection

In the U.S., constitutional privacy protection can find its basis either in State Constitutions or in the U.S. Constitution. The U.S. Constitution does not expressly protect the right to privacy or the right to medical confidentiality. With regard to the protection of a general privacy right, the U.S. Supreme Court had to struggle to find a constitutional basis for such a guarantee. As Justice Douglas stated in *Griswold v Connecticut*:[1]

> Specific guarantees in the Bill of Rights have penumbras, formed by emanations from those guarantees that help give them life and substance. ... Various guarantees create zones of privacy. ... The Fourth Amendment explicitly affirms the 'right of the people to be secure in their persons, houses, papers, and effects against unreasonable searches and seizures'. The Fifth Amendment in its Self-Incrimination Clause enables the citizen to

---

[1] 381 U.S. 479 (1965).

create a zone of privacy which government may not force him to surrender to his detriment. The Ninth Amendment provides: 'The enumeration in the Constitution, of certain rights, shall not be construed to deny or disparage others retained by the people'. The Fourth and Fifth Amendments were described ... as protection against all governmental invasions 'of the sanctity of a man's home and the privacies of life'. We recently referred ... to the Fourth Amendment as creating a 'right to privacy, no less important than any other right carefully and particularly reserved to the people'.[2]

Under the U.S. Constitution privacy is thus potentially protected by different Amendments.

1.1 Fifth Amendment (Self-Incrimination Clause)

The relevant part of the Fifth Amendment reads as follows:

Nor shall [any person] be compelled in any criminal case to be a witness against himself.

In *Fisher v U.S.*,[3] the Supreme Court discussed whether the Fifth Amendment protected a person's privacy interests in general and rejected that interpretation of the Amendment on the following grounds:

It is true that the Court has often stated that one of the several purposes served by the constitutional privilege against compelled testimonial self-incrimination is that of protecting personal privacy. ... But the Court has never suggested that every invasion of privacy violates the privilege. ... The Framers addressed the subject of personal privacy directly in the Fourth Amendment. ... They did not seek in still another Amendment - the Fifth - to achieve a general protection of privacy but to deal with the more specific issue of compelled self-incrimination. We cannot cut the Fifth Amendment loose from the moorings of its language and make it serve as a general protector of privacy. ... Insofar as private information not obtained through compelled self-incriminating testimony is legally protected, its protection stems from other sources, the Fourth Amendment's protection ... or evidentiary privileges as the attorney client privilege. We adhere to the view that the Fifth Amendment protects against 'compelled self-incrimination, not [the disclosure of] private information'.[4]

According to the Supreme Court in *Fisher*, the Fifth Amendment does not protect privacy interests as such.[5] Instead, its application is limited to protecting the

---

[2] Ibid., at 484-5.
[3] 425 U.S. 391 (1976).
[4] Ibid., at 399-401 per Justice White.
[5] See also, for example, *State v Doe*, 465 U.S. 605 (1983), at 618 per Justice O'Connor, concurring: 'The Fifth Amendment provides absolutely no protection for the contents of private papers of any kind. The notion that the Fifth Amendment protects the privacy of papers originated in *Boyd* ... but our decision in *Fisher* ... sounded the death knell for *Boyd*'.

individual from being compelled to give evidence against him/herself. This was also discussed in *Doe v U.S.*,[6] where it was held that:

> It is the 'extortion of information from the accused', ... the attempt to force him 'to disclose the contents of his own mind', ... that implicates the Self-Incrimination Clause. ... It is consistent with the history of and the policies underlying the Self-Incrimination Clause to hold that the privilege may be asserted only to resist compelled explicit or implicit disclosures of incriminating information. ... These policies are served when the privilege is asserted to spare the accused from having to reveal, directly or indirectly, his knowledge of facts relating him to the offence or from having to share his thoughts and beliefs with the Government.[7]

In that context the question arises whether court ordered psychiatric examinations at the sentencing stage of criminal proceedings violate the defendant's Fifth Amendment rights. It could be argued that in such a case, the defendant is compelled to reveal potentially incriminating facts about him/herself to a psychiatrist who functions as a state agent. In *Buchanan v Kentucky*,[8] the Supreme Court confirmed that where a psychiatrist, upon invitation by the prosecution, goes beyond reporting on the issue of the defendant's competence and presents a prognosis on his/her future dangerousness, based on communication with him/her, the psychiatrist turns into an agent of the state who recounts statements made without *Miranda*[9] warning in a post-arrest custodial setting. This violates the Fifth Amendment rights of the accused.[10] However, the situation changes where the defendant asserts the insanity defence and introduces supporting psychiatric testimony. The Fifth Amendment privilege does then not apply to the introduction of the psychiatrist's testimony by the prosecution, as otherwise the state would be barred from rebutting the defendant's case.

The Fifth Amendment mainly protects a person from having to give testimonial evidence against him/herself. The protection does not extend to the disclosure of possibly incriminating information as such, for example through sources other than the defendant.[11] With regard to confidential medical records, this means that the patient is only protected against having to produce confidential documents that may incriminate him/her, but the protection does not refer to the confidential content of such records. Private documents that have been voluntarily prepared are not protected under the Fifth Amendment, as the Fifth Amendment only protects against having to create incriminating private documents, but not against state access to private documents that an individual has prepared without any state

---

[6] 487 U.S. 201 (1988).

[7] Ibid., at 211-3 per Justice Blackmun.

[8] 483 US 402 (1987), at 421-2 per Justice Blackmun.

[9] *Miranda v Arizona*, 384 US 436 (1966).

[10] See also *Estelle v Smith*, 451 US 454 (1981), at 467 per Chief Justice Burger.

[11] *Couch v U.S.*, 409 U.S. 322 (1973), at 329 per Justice Powell.

compulsion.[12] Another court, while agreeing in principle, qualified this statement by arguing that in such a case the Fifth Amendment could protect the contents of the papers, but only 'where compelled disclosure would break the heart of our sense of privacy'.[13] Confidential medical information thus does not as such receive any specific protection under the Fifth Amendment. The Supreme Court nevertheless argued that the Fifth Amendment can indirectly protect the confidentiality of privileged relationships, as the privilege would be undermined if the person bound by the privilege could be compelled to produce evidence which would be protected by the Fifth Amendment while in the possession of the persons in whose interest the privilege was awarded.[14] For the physician-patient relationship, this means that the physician cannot be compelled to produce confidential medical records if two requirements are met. First, the records would have been protected from production while in the possession of the patient based on freedom from self-incrimination. Even if this were exceptionally the case, the constitutional protection further depends on the existence of a physician-patient privilege, which is not recognised under federal law.[15]

1.2 Fourth Amendment (Unreasonable search and seizure)

The relevant part of the Fourth Amendment provides:

> The right of the people to be secure in their persons, houses, papers, and effects, against unreasonable searches and seizures, shall not be violated.

The protection of the privacy right available under the Fourth Amendment is limited to certain specific situations. As the Supreme Court stated in the leading case of *Katz v U.S.*:[16]

---

[12] See, for example, *In Re Grand Jury Subpoena Duces Tecum*, 1 F.3d 87 (2nd Cir. 1993), at 92-3 per Lumbard, Circuit J.; *Senate Select Committee on Ethics v Packwood*, 845 F.Supp. 17 (D.D.C. 1994), at 23 per Jackson, District J.; *In re: Grand Jury Subpoenas*, 144 F.3d 653 (10th Cir. 1998), at 663 per Stephen H. Anderson, Circuit J.; *In re: Grand Jury Witnesses*, 92 F.3d 710 (8th Cir. 1996), at 712 per Loken, Circuit J.; *Aviation Supply Corp. v R.S.B.I. Aerospace, Inc.*, 999 F.2d 314 (8th Cir. 1993), at 317 per Loken, Circuit J.; but see, on the other hand, *U.S. v North*, 708 F.Supp. 402 (D.D.C. 1989), at 404 per Gesell, District J.

[13] *U.S. v Feldman*, 83 F.3d 9 (1st Cir. 1996), at 14 per Selya, Circuit J.; see also *In re Grand Jury Subpoena*, 973 F.2d 45 (1st Cir. 1992), at 51 per Curiam.

[14] *Fisher v U.S.*, 425 U.S. 391 (1976), at 403-4 per Justice White.

[15] See for example *Hancock v Dodson*, 958 F.2d 1367 (6th Cir. 1992), at 1373 per Contie, Senior Circuit J.; *U.S. v Bercier*, 848 F.2d 917 (8th Cir. 1988), at 920 per McMillan, Circuit J.; *U.S. v Burzynski Cancer Research Inst.*, 819 F.2d 1301 (5th Cir. 1987), at 1311 per Rubin, Circuit J.; *U.S. v Meagher*, 531 F.2d 752 (5th Cir. 1976), at 753 per Morgan, Circuit J.

[16] 389 U.S. 347 (1967).

The Fourth Amendment cannot be translated into a general constitutional 'right to privacy'. That Amendment protects individual privacy against certain kinds of governmental intrusion. ... But the protection of a person's *general* right to privacy - his right to be let alone by other people - is, like the protection of his property and of his very life, left largely to the law of the individual States.[17]

It is thus important to note that the protection awarded under the Fourth Amendment is restricted in two ways. First, it is only directed towards protection against the state, but does not include protection against a privacy violation by other individuals. In the context of medical confidentiality, this means that medical information may be protected against searches by the state, but not against voluntary disclosure by the physician. Secondly, the individual's privacy is not protected as such. Rather, the protection of privacy from governmental intrusions under the Fourth Amendment works as follows:

My understanding of the rule that has emerged from prior decisions is that there is a twofold requirement, first that a person have exhibited an actual (subjective) expectation of privacy, and, second, that the expectation be one that society is prepared to recognise as 'reasonable'.[18]

Given the widespread agreement among American courts that at least some aspects of medical confidentiality deserve constitutional protection as part of the privacy right of the individual,[19] it is fair to say that a patient has, in principle, an expectation that the medical confidences entrusted in the physician will remain confidential and that this interest must be recognised as reasonable. This was recently confirmed by the U.S. Supreme Court in *Ferguson v City of Charleston*,[20] where the Court held that a patient who undergoes diagnostic tests in a hospital has a reasonable expectation that the results of such tests will not be disclosed to non-medical personnel without the patient's consent.[21] In that case, the Supreme Court had to decide about the compatibility of a drug testing programme with Fourth Amendment principles. The Medical University of South Carolina (MUSC) had adopted a policy aimed at identifying and assisting pregnant patients suspected of drug abuse, based on deliberations of a task force consisting of representatives of

---

[17] Ibid., at 350-351 per Justice Steward.

[18] Ibid., at 361 per Justice Harlan; see also, for example, *Smith v Maryland*, 442 U.S. 735 (1979), at 740 per Justice Blackmun.

[19] See, for example, *Whalen v Roe*, 429 U.S. 589 (1977); *Behringer Est. v Princeton Medical Center*, 592 A.2d 1251 (N.J.Super.L. 1991); *Caesar v Mountanos*, 542 F.2d 1064 (9th Cir. 1976); *Falcon v Alaska Public Offices Commission*, 570 P.2d 469 (Alaska 1977); *Hawaii Psychiatric Soc. Dist. Branch v Ariyoshi*, 481 F.Supp. 1028 (D. Hawaii 1979); *Mann v University of Cincinnati*, 824 F.Supp. 1190 (S.D. Ohio 1993); *Schachter v Whalen*, 581 F.2d 35 (2nd Cir. 1978); *U.S. v Westinghouse Electric Corporation*, 638 F.2d 570 (3rd Cir. 1980); *Woods v White*, 689 F.Supp 874 (W.D. Wis. 1988); but see also, for example, *Felber v Foote*, 321 F.Supp. 85 (D. Conn. 1970), where constitutional protection of medical confidentiality was rejected.

[20] 532 U.S. 67 (2001).

[21] Ibid., at 78 per Justice Stevens.

MUSC, the police, the County Substance Abuse Commission and the Department of Social Services. Women who met certain criteria were to be tested through a urine drug screen and a chain of custody was to be followed regarding the urine samples, presumably to make sure that the results could be used in subsequent criminal proceedings. Patients who tested positive were given a choice between consenting to substance abuse treatment or notification of the police which would have entailed their arrest. According to the Supreme Court, the takings of the urine samples were searches to which the protection of the Fourth Amendment applied, as they were performed in a state hospital.[22] The Court distinguished this case from cases in which physicians or psychologists share information with law enforcement officials which they came across in the course of medical procedures. As stated by Justice Stevens:

> While state hospital employees, like other citizens, may have a duty to provide the police with evidence of criminal conduct that they inadvertently acquire in the course of routine treatment, when they undertake to obtain such evidence from their patients for the specific purpose of incriminating those patients, they have a special obligation to make sure that the patients are fully informed about their constitutional rights, as standards of knowing waiver require.[23]

As the medical personnel had performed the tests to collect evidence for law enforcement purposes and law enforcement officers were extensively involved in the design and implementation of the programme, the Fourth Amendment's general prohibition against nonconsensual, warrantless and suspicionless searches applied. However, had the hospital decided to inform the police of a patient's drug addiction which had accidentally come to the knowledge of its personnel, this would presumably not have constituted a violation of the Fourth Amendment.

The Fourth Amendment thus to some extent protects the patient from unreasonable state intrusions in the confidentiality of the physician-patient relationship. There is not much case law in this area, so that it is difficult to delineate the exact scope of this protection. In *State v Summers*,[24] a case in which a police trooper, after learning that the defendant had obtained drug prescriptions from different physicians, had called several physicians and asked whether they knew the defendant and for which medical problem the drug had been prescribed, the court came to the conclusion that the Fourth Amendment had not been violated, for:

> Trooper Wiggin's actions did not constitute a search for purposes of the State Constitution. ... The physician-patient privilege does not apply to the information obtained here. ... The legislature revoked the privilege in precisely the circumstances alleged here by providing that 'information communicated to a practitioner in an effort unlawfully to

---

[22] Ibid., at 76.
[23] Ibid., at 84-5.
[24] 702 A.2d 819 (N.H. 1997).

procure a controlled drug, or unlawfully to procure the administration of any such drug, shall not be deemed a privileged communication' RSA 318-B:21 (1995).[25]

The court thus came to the conclusion that the protection under the Fourth Amendment was excluded because of restrictions laid down in the State's privilege statute. This reasoning is probably based on the consideration that the limitations contained in the privilege statute destroyed any otherwise existing expectation in the confidentiality of this information. If this is the case, the protection of medical confidentiality under the Fourth Amendment is subject to ordinary State legislation determining the patient's reasonable expectation of privacy. However, in *Ferguson v City of Charleston*,[26] the Supreme Court confirmed a patient's reasonable expectation of privacy in medical information even though South Carolina does not recognise a physician-patient privilege.[27]

1.3 Fourteenth Amendment (Substantive due process)

In contrast to the rather limited constitutional protection of certain aspects of medical confidentiality under the Fourth and Fifth Amendments, broader protection is available under the Fourteenth Amendment, the relevant part of which provides:

> Nor shall any State deprive any person of life, liberty, or property, without due process of law.

In *Griswold v Connecticut*,[28] the Supreme Court decided that the right to privacy was a constitutional right and that a statute prohibiting the use of contraceptive methods by and the prescription of contraceptives to married couples violated that right. This view was later confirmed in the abortion case of *Roe v Wade*[29] where Justice Blackmun held that:

> This right of privacy, whether it be founded in the 14th Amendment's concept of personal liberty and restrictions upon state action, as we feel it is, ... is broad enough to encompass a woman's decision whether or not to terminate her pregnancy.[30]

Justice Stewart in the same case outlined the constitutional protection of privacy in broader terms, when stating that:

> The 'liberty' protected by the Due Process Clause of the 14th Amendment covers more than those freedoms explicitly named in the Bill of Rights. ... Several decisions of this

---

[25] Ibid, at 821-2 per Johnson, Justice.
[26] 532 US 67 (2001).
[27] The problem of a patient's reasonable expectation of privacy will be further discussed below, in the context of privacy protection under the Fourteenth Amendment.
[28] 381 U.S. 479 (1965), at 486 per Justice Douglas.
[29] 410 U.S. 113 (1973).
[30] Ibid., at 153.

Court make it clear that freedom of personal choice in matters of marriage and family life is one of the liberties protected by the Due Process Clause.[31]

And Justice Douglas held:

> Many [of the rights acknowledged by the Ninth Amendment] in my view come within the meaning of the term 'liberty' as used in the 14th Amendment:
> ... Second is freedom of choice in the basic decisions of one's life respecting marriage, divorce, procreation, contraception and the education and upbringing of children. ... Third is the freedom to care for one's health and person, freedom from bodily restraint or compulsion.[32]

The constitutional right to privacy thus protects autonomy in personal matters. For this concept to apply in the area of medical confidentiality, it must be demonstrated that medical information is recognised as a personal matter deserving constitutional protection. The patient's privacy interest in his/her medical secrets has been recognised by many American courts.[33] In *US v Westinghouse Electric Corporation*,[34] for example, a case concerning the powers of the National Institute for Occupational Safety and Health (NIOSH) to conduct health hazard investigations, and to be given access to a company's medical records of employees potentially affected by the substances under investigation, the Court stated:

> There can be no question that an employee's medical records, which may contain intimate facts of a personal nature, are well within the ambit of materials entitled to privacy protection. Information about one's body and state of health is a matter which the individual is ordinarily entitled to retain within the 'private enclave where he may lead a private life'. It has been recognised in various contexts that medical records and information stand on a different plane than other relevant material. ... This difference in treatment reflects a recognition that information concerning one's body has a special character.[35]

---

[31] Ibid., at 168-9.

[32] Ibid., at 210-211.

[33] See, for example, *Whalen v Roe*, 429 U.S. 589 (1977); *Behringer Est. v Princeton Medical Center*, 592 A.2d 1251 (N.J.Super.L. 1991); *Caesar v Mountanos*, 542 F.2d 1064 (9th Cir. 1976); *Falcon v Alaska Public Offices Commission*, 570 P.2d 469 (Alaska 1977); *Hawaii Psychiatric Soc. Dist. Branch v Ariyoshi*, 481 F.Supp. 1028 (D. Hawaii 1979); *Mann v University of Cincinnati*, 824 F.Supp. 1190 (S.D. Ohio 1993); *Schachter v Whalen*, 581 F.2d 35 (2nd Circuit 1978); *U.S. v Westinghouse Electric Corporation*, 638 F.2d 570 (3rd Cir. 1980); *Woods v White*, 689 F.Supp 874 (W.D. Wis. 1988); *Doe v Broderick*, 225 F.3d 440 (4th Cir. 2000), at 451 per Traxler, Circuit J.; *U.S. v Sutherland*, 143 F.Supp.2d 609 (W.D. Va. 2001), at 611 per Jones, District J.; *In re Grand Jury Subpoena John Doe No. A01-209*, 197 F.Supp.2d 512 (E.D. Va. 2002), at 514 per Ellis, District J.

[34] 638 F.2d 570 (3rd Cir. 1980).

[35] Ibid., at 577 per Sloviter, Circuit J.

Thus, medical records as well as medical information in general can qualify as personal matters receiving constitutional privacy protection.

In *Whalen v Roe*,[36] the Supreme Court identified two different interests to be protected by the Fourteenth Amendment in the context of medical confidentiality: the interest in avoiding disclosure of personal matters, and the interest in making certain kinds of important decisions independently. It seems as if the secrecy strand of the privacy right, that is the interest in keeping medical information secret, is very closely linked to the question of whether or not a matter is private enough so as to deserve constitutional protection. If this is answered in the affirmative, then the individual has a constitutionally protected interest in keeping this information secret and in controlling the disclosure of such information. However, the constitutional protection is not absolute, but can rather be outweighed by a legitimate state interest in disclosure.[37]

The interests behind the protection of medical confidentiality were further explained in *Hawaii Psychiatric Soc. Dist. Branch v Ariyoshi*,[38] a case which was concerned with the relationship between psychiatrists and patients:

> The Supreme Court has recognised an individual's right to make decisions free from unjustified governmental interference on matters relating to marriage. ... An individual's decision whether or not to seek the aid of a psychiatrist and whether or not to communicate certain personal information to that psychiatrist, fall squarely within the bounds of this 'cluster of constitutionally protected choices'. ... The Supreme Court has consistently been concerned with protecting individuals against governmental intrusion into matters affecting the most fundamental personal decisions and relationships. ... No area could be more deserving of protection than communication between a psychiatrist and his patient. Such communications often involve problems in precisely the areas previously recognised by the Court as within the zone of protected privacy, including family, marriage, parenthood, human sexuality, and physical problems. Constitutionally protected privacy must, at a minimum, include the freedom of an individual to choose the circumstances under which, and to whom certain of his thoughts and feelings will be disclosed. ... This right to choose confidentiality is particularly crucial in the context of communications between patient and psychotherapist. ... The court holds that the constitutionally protected right of privacy extends to an individual's liberty to make decisions regarding psychiatric care without unjustified governmental interference.[39]

This decision highlights both the interest in informational and the interest in decisional privacy. The main aspect behind protecting a patient's decisional privacy through a guarantee of medical confidentiality seems to be that the patient can only seek meaningful medical, and, in particular, psychological advice and treatment when openly disclosing personal information that is subject to privacy protection. If privacy protection were reduced to protecting the patient's interest in

---

[36] 429 U.S. 589 (1977), at 599-600 per Justice Stevens.

[37] *US v Westinghouse Electric Corporation*, 638 F.2d 570 (3rd Cir. 1980), at 577-8 per Sloviter, Circuit J.; *A.A. v New Jersey*, 176 F.Supp.2d 274 (D.N.J. 2001), at 298 per Irenas, District J.

[38] 481 F.Supp. 1028 (D. Hawaii 1979).

[39] Ibid., at 1038-9 per Byrne, District J.

not having to disclose this information, it would not go far enough. The patient would then only have the choice between keeping confidential information to him/herself by not seeking medical advice and treatment, or, alternatively, seeking medical treatment and advice, and, as a consequence, giving up any privacy protection. As was explained in *Mann v University of Cincinnati*:[40]

> If patients have a genuine concern that their private medical information will become publicly known and may adversely affect their reputations or embarrass them, they will be reluctant to seek medical assistance. Thus, patients' interest in making decisions vital to their health care may be impaired by unwarranted disclosures. ... These same reasons support a doctor-patient privilege. Medical care providers ... who create and maintain such information have a concomitant duty to avoid unwarranted disclosures. We believe that duty has its roots in the Constitution.[41]

Thus, autonomy in making personal choices means that the individual must be given the opportunity to decide whether or not to seek help for medical conditions without a fear that his/her secrets may be disclosed to parties outside the physician-patient relationship. Both decisions seem to suggest that the autonomy strand of the right to privacy is, in the context of medical confidentiality, very closely linked to the right to make health care decisions and to the patient's interest in bodily integrity. If the patient cannot be sure that medical information revealed to the physician will be kept secret, he/she may be inhibited to disclose frankly such information to the physician, which may adversely affect the medical treatment available to the patient. A patient who can seek medical advice and treatment only on the basis that the state may be given access to this information can no longer make health care decisions free from state interference, as this possibility may affect and influence the decision the patient is going to take.

Not only informational, but also decisional privacy is thus protected, and the argumentation behind such protection is deontological, rather than utilitarian, as it concentrates on the value of privacy and autonomy as such, rather than on the possible consequences of disclosure. It has been held in various decisions that a stricter standard of judicial scrutiny is required where a person's decisional privacy conflicts with a state interest in the disclosure of medical information.[42] This seems to suggest that while the constitutional guarantee of medical confidentiality is granted both on the grounds of informational and on the grounds of decisional privacy protection, when it comes to a balancing of interests, a higher standard of protection is given to a person whose decisional privacy is at stake.

In *US v Westinghouse Electric Corporation*.[43] the court very briefly touched upon another aspect which may explain why medical confidentiality is given constitutional protection, when arguing that:

---

[40] 824 F.Supp. 1190 (S.D. Ohio 1993).

[41] Ibid., at 1199 per Steinberg, U.S. Magistrates J.

[42] See, for example, *Fraternal Order of Police, Lodge No.5 v City of Philadelphia*, 812 F.2d 105 (3rd Cir. 1987), at 114 per Sloviter, Circuit J.; *A.A. v New Jersey*, 176 F.Supp.2d 274 (D.N.J. 2001), at 298 per Irenas, District J.

[43] 638 F.2d 570 (3rd Cir. 1980).

The factors which should be considered in deciding whether an intrusion into an individual's privacy is justified are ... the injury from disclosure to the relationship in which the record was generated ... . Since Westinghouse's testing and NIOSH's examination of the records are both conducted for the purpose of protecting the individual employee from potential health hazards, it is not likely that the disclosures are likely to inhibit the employee from undergoing subsequent periodic examinations required of Westinghouse employees.[44]

The integrity of the physician-patient relationship is thus also regarded as deserving constitutional protection, but the reasons behind this consideration are not further specified.

American courts have developed a case by case approach when deciding whether specific medical information is or is not constitutionally protected. There seems to be widespread agreement that sensitive health information receives constitutional privacy protection. In *Woods v White*,[45] for example, the court held that a patient had a privacy interest in his medical records containing details of his HIV status, based on the particularly sensitive nature of such information. In another case, a similar reasoning can be found regarding a person's transsexualism.[46] And in *Mann v University of Cincinnati*,[47] the Court explained:

> The student health services file ... includes Ms Mann's answers ... to the following inquiries: history of possible diseases; family history of diseases; ... age at time of first intercourse. ... Additional Student Health Services and University Hospital records contain documents relating to Ms Mann's medical treatment which ... occurred prior to the events alleged in this case. ... There can be no question that the aforementioned information is of such a private nature that a constitutional right to privacy exists.[48]

Thus, patient information that is regarded as highly personal and sensitive clearly receives constitutional protection. More controversial is whether everyday health information or information that is not normally regarded as embarrassing merits the protection of the constitutional right to privacy. Some case law suggests that this should not be the case. In *Cooksey v Boyer*,[49] for example, it was held that the mere fact that a chief of police received psychological treatment for stress did not deserve privacy protection, as it could not be characterised as 'egregiously humiliating'. The court emphasised that not all information related to the mental health of an individual automatically warrants constitutional protection. In *Webb v Goldstein*,[50] this time regarding the disclosure of medical records which contained

---

[44] Ibid., at 578-9 per Sloviter, Circuit J.

[45] 689 F.Supp. 874 (W.D. Wis. 1988), at 876 per Crabb, Chief Justice; see also *Doe v Delie*, 257 F.3d 309 (3rd Cir. 2001), at 315 and 317 per Roth, Circuit J.

[46] *Powell v Schriver*, 175 F.3d 107 (2nd Cir. 1999), at 111 per Jacobs, Circuit J.

[47] 824 F.Supp. 1190 (S.D. Ohio 1993).

[48] Ibid., at 1198-9 per Steinberg, U.S. Magistrates J.

[49] 289 F.3d 513 (8th Cir. 2002), at 516-7 per Melloy, Circuit J.

[50] 117 F.Supp.2d 289 (E.D.N.Y. 2000), at 298 per Raggi, District J.

mental health information and the fact that the patient had been tested for HIV, the court went even further down that road when suggesting that the level of constitutional protection depended upon whether or not the patient could claim that his mental condition had ever been diagnosed as less than normal or that he had ever tested positive for HIV. The court relied on the decision in *Khalfani v Secretary, Dept. of Veterans Affairs*,[51] where it was held that the fact that the information at issue was rather mundane, and not deeply personal, influenced the perception of whether or not it was constitutionally protected. Equally, in *Falcon v Alaska Public Offices Commission*,[52] the court stated that:

> The decisions both of this court and the United States Supreme Court clearly establish that certain types of information communicated in the context of the physician-patient relationship fall within a constitutionally protected zone of privacy. The nature and weight of a privacy interest in an individual's identity as a patient or client, however, presents a more difficult issue. ... Where an individual visits a physician who specialises in contraceptive matters or whose primary practice is known to be giving abortions and the fact of a visit or rendering of services becomes public information, private and sensitive information has, in our view, been revealed. Even visits to a general practitioner may cause particular embarrassment or opprobrium where the patient is a married person who seeks treatment without the spouse's knowledge ... . Similar situations would be presented where, because of a specialised practice, the disclosure of the patient's identity also reveals the nature of the treatment ... . Some examples would include the patients of a psychiatrist, psychologist or of a physician who specialised in treating sexual problems or venereal disease. ... In emphasising these examples, we reiterate that situations involving specialised practice of psychiatry or venereal disease present the exception rather than the general rule and that, ordinarily, identification as a patient of a general practitioner who also engages in some of these functions does not infringe a significant privacy interest.[53]

What becomes clear from all of these cases is that the constitutional privacy protection depends on the degree of sensitivity of the information with particular emphasis on the protection of information the disclosure of which might cause embarrassment to the patient. The situation was recently summarised as follows:

> In determining whether information is entitled to privacy protection, the threshold question is 'whether it is within an individual's reasonable expectations of confidentiality'. ... Generally, 'the more intimate and personal the information, the more justified is the expectation that it will not be subject to public scrutiny'.[54]

What remains unclear, however, is whether so called mundane health information does not benefit from the constitutional privacy protection at all, or whether the degree of sensitivity merely influences the balancing exercise that needs to be performed when the constitutional privacy interest stands in conflict with other interests. While some of the above mentioned cases propose that in such cases all

---

[51] 1999 WL 138247 (E.D.N.Y. 1999), at 6 per Gleeson, District J.

[52] 570 P.2d 469 (Alaska 1977).

[53] Ibid., at 478-80 per Boochever, Chief Justice.

[54] *A.A. v New Jersey*, 176 F.Supp.2d 274 (D.N.J. 2001), at 298 per Irenas, District J.

privacy protection is excluded, the highly influential decision in *US v Westinghouse Electric Corporation*[55] suggests otherwise. There, the Court performed a balancing exercise to decide whether or not the violation of privacy was justified in the particular case. The Court's considerations in that respect are important, as they give some indication as to the different degrees of privacy protection. According to the Court:

> The factors which should be considered in deciding whether an intrusion into an individual's privacy is justified are the type of record requested, the information it does or might contain, the potential for harm in any subsequent non-consensual disclosure ... the adequacy of safeguards to prevent unauthorised disclosure. ... Westinghouse has not produced any evidence to show that the information which the medical records contain is of such a high degree of sensitivity that the intrusion could be considered severe or that the employees are likely to suffer any adverse effects from disclosure to NIOSH personnel. Most, if not all, of the information in the files will be results of routine testing, such as X-rays, blood tests, pulmonary function tests, hearing and visual tests. This material, although private, is not generally regarded as sensitive.[56]

According to the Court in *Westinghouse*, all medical information is, in principle, constitutionally protected. However, the level of protection depends, *inter alia*, on the degree of sensitivity of the medical information concerned. The court proposes an objective test to determine the degree of sensitivity when arguing that certain routine examinations are not generally regarded as sensitive. The reasoning also suggests that the constitutional protection of privacy and therefore medical confidentiality primarily aims at protecting the patient from the adverse consequences of disclosure rather than at guaranteeing the patient's privacy interests as such.

It is submitted that the distinction between sensitive and mundane health related information with its far-reaching consequences is problematic in the light of the objectives of the constitutional privacy protection. Both the patient's informational and decisional privacy can only be effectively guaranteed if it is left to the patient to decide which information he/she regards as sensitive and therefore wants to shield from disclosure. While a societal consensus seems to exist, to the effect that stigmatising information such as that related to an HIV infection, to transsexualism, to sexually related or to mental illnesses, should receive constitutional protection, such a consensus cannot dictate which information the particular patient does or does not regard as private. Of course it could be argued that the constitutional protection is subject to a 'reasonable expectation of privacy', and that reasonableness implies an objective standard. However, every attempt to make privacy protection subject to an objective evaluation of which information deserves to be regarded as private in itself violates the privacy of the individual, as it imposes upon him/her a majority standard instead of respecting the views of the individual concerned. Once it is accepted that information related to a person's physical or mental health is personal enough to be protected by the right to privacy,

---

[55] 638 F.2d 570 (3rd Cir. 1980).
[56] Ibid., at 578-9 per Sloviter, Circuit J.

it should be left to the individual patient to determine which information he/she feels deserves protection. The focus on the potentially embarrassing consequences of a disclosure distracts from the reasons behind privacy protection, which are not primarily the protection of a person from the humiliation and distress of a public revelation of private information. Instead, the more important aspect is that of giving the person control over the dissemination of private information, no matter how positive this information might be perceived by the public. The absurd effects of the 'objective' approach manifest themselves in the case of *Webb v Goldstein*,[57] where the protection of the patient's record depended on his/her health condition, so that communications with a physician would be protected where there is some indication that the patient is, in fact, suffering from the embarrassing illness, while a healthy patient is left unprotected. This, of course, means that from the fact that certain records receive constitutional protection conclusions as to the diagnosis can be drawn. Moreover, in the light of the general perception that HIV infection and mental illness are particularly sensitive conditions, it is submitted that even under the 'objective' approach the mere fact that someone underwent HIV testing or was examined for a potential mental illness might deserve protection, regardless of the outcome of the examination.

Another consideration influencing the outcome of the balancing exercise is whether what is at stake is the disclosure of information to the public, or whether the information will only have to be revealed to a limited number of health care officials. This was, for example, one of the problems raised by the Supreme Court in *Whalen v Roe*.[58] In that case, the Court had to decide on the constitutionality of a statute that, responding to the concern that drugs were being diverted into unlawful channels, classified potentially harmful drugs and provided that prescriptions for the most dangerous legitimate drugs be prepared on an official form. One copy of the form which required identification of the prescribing physician, dispensing pharmacy, drug and dosage, and patient's name, address and age had to be filed with the State Health Department and retained for five years. As to the possible violation of a constitutional right to medical confidentiality as a result of this procedure, the Court first established that the risk of a public disclosure of the medical information was too remote to invalidate the statute, given that adequate safeguards against such a disclosure were in place. The Court went on:

> Even without public disclosure, it is, of course, true that private information must be disclosed to the authorised employees of the New York Department of Health. Such disclosures are not ... meaningfully distinguishable from a host of other unpleasant invasions of privacy that are associated with many facets of health care.[59]

This is problematic, as it does not take account of the fact that even a limited disclosure violates the patient's privacy and should therefore be taken seriously.

---

[57] 117 F.Supp.2d 289 (E.D.N.Y. 2000), at 298 per Raggi, District J.
[58] 429 U.S. 589 (1977).
[59] Ibid., at 602 per Justice Stevens.

1.4 Privacy protection under State constitutions

So far, only the protection of privacy rights under the Federal Constitution has been analysed, but it should be noted that some State constitutions equally recognise such a right. The California Constitution is one example of a constitution that explicitly protects the right to privacy. The leading Californian case in this area is *In Re Lifschutz*.[60] Dr Lifschutz was imprisoned after refusing to obey an order directing him to answer questions and produce records relating to communications with a former patient. The Court first discussed whether or not the forced disclosure of medical information violated a privacy right of members of the medical profession, in this case a psychiatrist, and rejected this view. With regard to the patient's privacy interest the Court then held:

> A patient's interest in keeping such confidential revelations from public purview, in retaining this substantial privacy, has deeper roots than the Californian statute and draws sustenance from our constitutional heritage. ... The confidentiality of the psychotherapeutic session falls within the constitutionally guaranteed zones of privacy. ... Even though a patient's interest in the confidentiality of the psychotherapist-patient relationship rests, in part, on constitutional underpinnings, all state interference with such confidentiality is not prohibited.[61]

This holding does not seem to add any protection not already existent under federal constitutional principles. A similar conclusion could be drawn from *Division of Medical Quality v Gherardini*,[62] where it has been argued:

> While the amendment [to the California Constitution] does not prohibit all incursions into individual privacy, any such intervention must be justified by a compelling interest ... and any statute authorising invasion of such area of privacy must be subject to strict scrutiny.[63]

However, in *Pagano v Oroville Hospital*,[64] the Court held:

> California ... has adopted an explicit constitutional right to privacy, and recognised application of this right to patient medical records. ... The California Supreme Court has interpreted this state constitutional right to be inalienable ... and broader than the federal privacy right. ... The right protects against invasions of privacy by private citizens as well as by the state..[65]

This decision is interesting as it specifies that under California law, the constitutional right to privacy not only creates a right against state interference, but also correlates in a duty of non-disclosure imposed on the physician. This

---

[60] 85 Cal.Rptr. 829 (Sup. 1970).
[61] Ibid., at 839-40 per Tobriner, Justice.
[62] 156 Cal.Rptr. 55 (1979).
[63] Ibid., at 61 per Staniforth, Acting Presiding J.
[64] 145 F.R.D. 683 (E.D.Cal 1993).
[65] Ibid., at 696-7 per Hollows, U.S. Magistrate J.

surpasses the protection awarded under the U.S. Constitution. However, the court at the same time rejected the compelling interest test as too rigid and suggested a less stringent test for the justification of intrusions on the privacy right, which takes away some of the additional protection. It can be concluded that while the privacy right recognised by the U.S. Constitution sets the minimum standard for all American States, some State constitutions provide additional constitutional protection in certain areas of privacy protection.

2 Statutory obligations

In some States, the disclosure of particularly sensitive information, for example the HIV status of a patient, amounts to a criminal offence.[66] At the federal level, the Health Insurance Portability and Accountability Act 1996 (HIPAA), regulating the electronic exchange of health care information, and the Privacy Rule[67] recognise the importance of privacy protection in the health care setting. In many U.S. States, privilege statutes and to some extent licensing statutes create a statutory obligation to maintain patient confidentiality.

2.1 Privilege statutes

In the U.S., privilege statutes are an important means to introduce a statutory obligation of medical confidentiality. No statutory medical privilege exists at the federal level. However, most States in the U.S. now have some form of statutory physician-patient privilege,[68] and in all States privilege statutes protecting the communication between psychiatrists and patients are in force. The scope of the physician-patient privilege varies from State to State. A few State statutes granting medical privilege will now be introduced to give some idea of the nature and scope of such statutes.

In some States, the privilege statutes are formulated so as to give the patient the right to prevent the disclosure of confidential medical information. The Nebraska Revised Statutes, Rules of Evidence, for example, state in § 27-504:

(2)(a) A patient has a privilege to refuse to disclose and to prevent any other person from disclosing confidential communications made for the purposes of diagnosis or treatment of his or her physical, mental, or emotional condition among himself or herself, his or her

---

[66] See, for example, Cal Health & Safety § 120980; Ms St §13-1-21.
[67] Standards for Privacy Protection of Individually Identifiable Health Information (65 FR 82462).
[68] For example Alaska, Arizona, Arkansas, California, Colorado, Connecticut, Georgia, Hawaii, Idaho, Illinois, Louisiana, Michigan, Mississippi, Missouri, Montana, Nebraska, Nevada, New Jersey, New York, Oregon, Pennsylvania, Rhode Island, South Dakota, Texas, Vermont, Virginia, Wisconsin and Wyoming provide for some form of physician-patient privilege. However, for example Alabama, Florida, Kentucky, Maryland, South Carolina and Tennessee do not have a statutory physician-patient privilege.

physician, or persons who are participating in the diagnosis or treatment under the direction of the physician, including members of the patient's family.

And Art.510 of the Louisiana Code of Evidence provides as follows:

> C.(1) General rule of privilege in criminal proceedings. In a criminal proceeding, a patient has a privilege to refuse to disclose and to prevent another person from disclosing a confidential communication made for the purpose of advice, diagnosis or treatment of his health condition between or among himself, his representative, and his physician or psychotherapist, and their representatives.

In other States, the privilege statute is formulated so as to impose an obligation on the physician not to disclose confidential patient information. Illinois Statutes Chapter 735 § 8-802, for example, states:

> No physician, surgeon, psychologist, nurse, mental health worker, therapist, or other healing art practitioner ... shall be permitted to disclose any information he or she may have acquired in attending any patient in a professional character, necessary to enable him or her professionally to serve the patient.

Privilege statutes thus give the patient control over the disclosure of confidential medical information by either awarding him/her the right to prevent the physician from disclosing such information, or by formulating a prohibition, addressed to the physician, not to disclose such information without the patient's consent. However, the protection awarded by such privilege statutes is not as comprehensive as it may seem. First, it must be noted that privilege statutes apply only in the context of judicial proceedings. Moreover, the scope of protection depends on what is meant by 'confidential communication' or 'information' that is protected under the different statutes, as these terms can be given an extensive or a narrow interpretation. The courts' approach when interpreting privilege statutes will largely depend on their perception of the objectives of these statutes and of the importance to be attached to medical confidentiality.

Many different arguments have been advanced in favour of protecting medical confidentiality. There is widespread agreement that medical confidentiality aims to encourage the patient to feel free to disclose openly to the physician all facts which may have a bearing upon diagnosis and treatment.[69] It is felt that the patient may be inhibited to do so unless it is guaranteed that his/her medical secrets are safe with the physician and will not be disclosed to third parties. Therefore, it seems necessary to respect the trust existing in the physician-patient relationship.[70] Only if such confidence is inspired in the patient, will the physician be able to provide effective medical treatment.[71] In the words of Hamilton, J. in *State v Boehme*:[72]

---

[69] *Berry v Moench*, 331 P.2d 814 (Sup. Ct. of Utah 1958), at 817 per Crockett, Justice; *People v Harrison*, 626 N.Y.S.2d 747 (Ct.App. 1995), at 746 per Bellacosa, J.; *Steinberg v Jensen*, 534 N.W.2d 361 (Wis. 1995), at 368 per Steinmetz, Justice.

[70] *U.S. v Bein*, 728 F.2d 107 (2nd Cir. 1984), at 113 per Winter, Circuit J.

[71] *State v Beatty*, 770 S.W.2d 387 (Mo.App. 1989), at 392 per Greene, J.

The judicially proclaimed purpose of statutes such as ours, establishing the privilege, is to surround communications between patient and physician with the cloak of confidence, and thus allow complete freedom in the exchange of information between them to the end that the patient's ailments may be properly treated.

In *Division of Medical Quality v Gherardini,*[73] the court equally emphasised that:

A person's medical profile is an area of privacy infinitely more intimate, more personal in quality and nature than many areas already judicially recognised and protected. ... The patient-physician privilege ... creates a zone of privacy whose purposes are (1) to preclude the humiliation of the patient that might follow disclosure of his ailments ... and (2) to encourage the patient's full disclosure to the physician of all information necessary for effective diagnosis and treatment of the patient. ... The matters disclosed to the physician arise in most sensitive areas often difficult to reveal even to the doctor. Their unauthorised disclosure can provoke more than just simple humiliation in a fragile personality. The reasonable expectation that such personal matters will remain with the physician are no less in a patient and physician relationship than between the patient and psychotherapist. The individual's right to privacy encompasses not only the state of his mind, but also his viscera, detailed complaints of physical ills, and their emotional overtones.

It can thus be said that privilege statutes, just like the constitutional privacy right, have the purpose of protecting the patient's informational and decisional privacy. In addition, they serve the utilitarian goal of protecting public health by creating a confidential environment to encourage patients to seek medical advice and treatment.[74]

Privilege statutes mostly refer to the communication between physician and patient or psychotherapist and patient. Some statutes expressly define the term. Art.510 of the Louisiana Code of Evidence, for example, provides the following definition:

A. (8)(b) 'Confidential communication' includes any information, substance, or tangible object, obtained incidental to the communication process and any opinion formed as a result of the consultation, examination, or interview and also includes medical and hospital records made by health care providers and their representatives.

With regard to the Louisiana statute, Lottinger, Chief J., concluded in *Sarphie v Rowe*[75] that when an individual walks into a doctor's office and opens his mouth, everything spilling out of it, whether it be his identity or his false teeth (a tangible object) is presumptively privileged and beyond the reach of discovery. In *Matter of*

---

[72] 430 P.2d 527 (Wash. 1967), at 533.

[73] 156 Cal. Rptr. 55 (1979), at 60-61 per Staniforth, Acting Presiding J.

[74] For an outline of the deontological value of privacy protection in the context of health care see Secretary of Health and Human Services, *Standards for Privacy of Individually Identifiable Health Information*, 65 Fed.Reg. 82862 (2000), at 82467-82468.

[75] 618 So.2d 905 (La.App. 1 Cir. 1993), at 908.

Commitment of W.C.,[76] however, this statement was somewhat mitigated. There, the court argued that although the definition of confidential communication under LSA-CE art.510 was broad, inherent in the definition was the concept of something being expressed by one person to another and an intent that this information not be disclosed to others. Consequently, the court argued that the definition of 'confidential communication' was not broad enough to include an observation of the patient's behaviour by health care personnel in a situation where the patient was making no attempt to communicate with anyone. Thus, if a patient is seen to strike other patients or if the patient's failure to provide for his/her basic physical needs is observed, these observations are not regarded as privileged communication. This holding was based on the court's interpretation of the purpose behind the provisions of the privilege statute. The court argued that the privilege statute aims to protect the confidences a patient communicates to his/her health care provider and to give heed to the fact that disclosure of the patient's confidences could be detrimental to the health care provider-patient relationship. It is submitted that if this is the purpose of the privilege statute, observations of an in-patient's behaviour should be privileged, as they can only be made because the patient is seeking medical or psychiatric care. Otherwise patients cannot control the dissemination of information and cannot freely decide to seek hospital care without risking such disclosures. Furthermore, the wording of the privilege statute which includes observations made and even opinions formed during the consultation and examination suggests that protection should be awarded to everything the health care provider observes in the course of the physician-patient relationship.

People v Maltbia[77] was decided on the basis of §8-802 of the Illinois Code of Civil Procedure.[78] In that case, a driver was arrested for speeding and lost consciousness before he was put in the squad car. The officers called an ambulance and the physician, Dr Lovell, wanted to analyse the urine of the defendant for the presence of drugs and to check the kidneys for an indication of internal injuries. When the defendant's underwear was removed in order to insert the catheter, Dr Lovell found a bag containing illicit drugs. At that time, no police officers were present. The court argued that the discovery of the drugs on the defendant's person resulted from a medical procedure necessary to diagnose and treat the defendant, and therefore occurred while Dr. Lovell was rendering necessary medical treatment to the defendant. Accordingly, the court concluded that the bag and the drugs contained therein constituted privileged information within the meaning of the privilege statute.

It can be seen that even where the privilege statute provides a definition of the communication which is thereby protected, the exact scope of the physician's obligation must be determined by the courts. Where the relevant statute does not contain such a definition, the courts have even more leeway when deciding what is

---

[76] 685 So.2d 634 (La.App. 1 Cir. 1996), at 638 per Whipple, J.

[77] 653 N.E.2d 402 (Ill.App. 3 Dist. 1995), at 405-7 per McCuskey, Justice.

[78] 'No physician or surgeon shall be permitted to disclose any information he or she may have acquired in attending the patient in a professional character, necessary to enable him or her professionally to save the patient.'

or is not protected communication under the respective statutes. Courts in different States have adopted different approaches in so doing. Most courts decided that 'communication' was not limited to the oral statements of the patient, but also included medical records.[79] Absent a statutory extension of the privilege to observations made by the physicians, the question of whether and to what extent observations should be privileged equally rests with the courts. Most courts have adopted a broad approach. *State v Schroeder*,[80] for example, is a case in which this issue had to be decided. In that case, a patient was brought to the hospital by the police for treatment of a head injury. In the course of the examination of the patient for this purpose, the treating physician made the observation that his patient seemed to have been under the influence of alcohol and the question arose whether or not this observation was protected communication under North Dakota's privilege statute. The court argued as follows:

The privilege authorised by N.D.R.Evid.503 is not limited to verbal statements, but applies to communications. Although N.D.R.Evid.503 does not define communications, it defines when a 'communication is confidential' to include 'the consultation, examination or interview', and 'the diagnosis and treatment'. That definition suggests that the term has a broader meaning than verbal statement. Additionally, Webster's New World Dictionary ... defines 'communication' as 'the act of transmitting' and 'a giving or exchanging of information, signals, or messages by talk, gestures, writing, etc.' That plain, ordinary, and commonly understood meaning of communications is not restricted to verbal statements and also supports a broader meaning for the term. We follow the ordinary meaning of 'communications' and hold that the physician-patient privilege authorised by N.D.R.Evid.503 applies to information and observations made by a physician for purposes of diagnosis or treatment of the patient's medical condition.[81]

This approach was also adopted in *Sims v Charlotte Liberty Mutual Insurance Co*,[82] where the court argued that communication, in addition to the patient's oral statements, also included any information which the physician or surgeon acquired in attending the patient in a professional character, and which is necessary to enable him to prescribe for or treat the patient.[83] The court based its analysis on the purpose behind the privilege statute which it thought could only be achieved by a broad interpretation of 'communication'.

In *Re The June 1979 Allegheny County Investigating Grand Jury*,[84] however, the court took a very narrow approach. Eagen, Chief Justice, explained:

Concerning the statutory physician-patient privilege, our case law has drawn a distinction between information learned by a physician through communication to him by a patient

---

[79] See, for example, *Behringer Estate v Princeton Medical Center*, 592 A.2d 1251 (N.J.Super.L. 1991), at 1268 per Carchman, J.S.C.; *In Re Search Warrant*, 810 F.2d 65 (3rd Cir. 1987), at 71 per Becker, Circuit J.

[80] 524 N.W.2d 837(N.D. 1994).

[81] Ibid., at 840-842 per Vande Walle, Chief Justice.

[82] 125 S.E.2d 326 (N.C. 1962).

[83] Ibid., at 329-30 per Moore, Justice.

[84] 415 A.2d 73 (Sup. Ct. Pa 1980).

and information acquired through examination and observation. ... The distinction is rooted in the purpose of the privilege, merely to create a confidential atmosphere in which the patient will be encouraged to disclose all possible information bearing on his or her illness so that the physician may render effective treatment. Much information acquired by the physician acting in a professional capacity may relate back in some way to an initial communication by a patient, for example, a report of sickness or pain in a particular area of the body. However, the privilege is limited to information which would offend the rationale of the privilege, i.e. information directly related to the patient's communication and thus tending to expose it.[85]

The court concluded that information gained from an analysis of tissue samples was not 'communication' and therefore not protected by the privilege statute. It can be seen that the interpretation of the privilege statute largely depends on the court's view of the purpose behind such a statute. If the purpose of the statute is to encourage frank communication, it seems at first sight sufficient to protect oral communication. However, as the other cases cited above have demonstrated, this approach is rather controversial, as it could be argued that from the patient's point of view, it does not make any difference whether or not the physician obtains confidential information the patient wants to keep secret through direct communication or through an examination of the patient's body or tissue samples. A patient who is concerned about secrecy of medical information may not allow the physician to examine him/her if only direct communication is confidential, but other information the physician acquires in the course of the physician-patient relationship is not protected.

Another question is whether the privilege should only attach to potentially embarrassing information.[86] In *Re The June 1979 Allegheny County Investigating Grand Jury*,[87] the question was answered in the affirmative when the court argued that:

> To fall within the terms of the statute, communications must tend to blacken the character of the patient. Here, the subpoenaed tissue reports contain no statutorily privileged communications. While identifying data such as patient's name and address would tend to reveal communications by the patient, such communications would in no way tend to blacken the character of a patient.[88]

Comparable reasoning can be found in other decisions. In *Falcon v Alaska Public Offices Commission*,[89] for example, a decision already discussed above in the context of constitutional privacy protection, the court argued that in situations involving specialised practice of psychiatry or venereal disease, the identification as a patient of such a specialist could in itself constitute protected information, while the same did not apply to patients of a general practitioner. Thus, the mere

---

[85] Ibid., at 76-7.
[86] For a discussion see, for example, Kendrick, Tsakonas, Smith, at 7-24.
[87] 415 A.2d 73 (Sup. Ct. Pa 1980).
[88] Ibid., at 77 per Eagen, Chief Justice.
[89] 570 P.2d 469 (Alaska 1977), at 479-80 per Boochever, Chief Justice.

facts that the patient received medical treatment and when and where treatment has been administered are normally not protected by medical privilege.[90] In *Weisbeck v Hess*,[91] the court decided differently in stating that the privilege should cover any form of communication made as a part of the therapeutic relationship and therefore protects the name of the patient. However, this statement was made in the context of a psychiatrist-patient relationship, and it is not clear whether the court would extend its holding to the physician-patient relationship. It is submitted that the distinction between embarrassing and non-embarrassing treatment cannot be made objectively. Instead, it should be left to the patient to decide whether or not he/she feels that the fact that he/she receives medical treatment should be kept confidential or made public. Furthermore, it seems artificial to separate the fact that a person receives certain treatment from the protected content of the physician-patient relationship, so that the name of the patient and the fact that he/she has formed a privileged relationship with a physician should be just as protected as physician-patient communications.

With regard to the psychotherapist-patient relationship, it has been held that that privilege does not apply to threats the patient makes in the course of a therapy session.[92] How problematic such an exception is can be seen from the decision in *U.S. v Williams*.[93] In that case, the privilege was excluded on that basis even in a situation in which the patient had not made a direct threat, but had expressed that he felt insulted and demeaned by the judge who had convicted him, and by the investigating FBI agent, and described in great detail what he had done to someone else in the past when he had felt similarly. The Court concluded that the recounting of that episode could reasonably be interpreted as a threat to the judge and the FBI agent. However, it is submitted that if such expressions are not protected by the psychotherapist-patient privilege, its purpose of encouraging the patient frankly to share all feelings and thoughts with the therapist can hardly be achieved, as the expression of anger and aggression will then not be privileged, unless very cautiously phrased.

It seems widely accepted that the privilege does not include information that is unrelated to medical treatment.[94] If, for example, an accident victim seeks medical treatment, those details of the accident that have nothing to do with the injuries sustained would then not be protected.[95] Observations made during home visits to a patient that do not regard the patient's medical condition would presumably also be excluded from protection. However, the exclusion of non-medical observations

---

[90] See also, for example, *Benton v Superior Court Navajo County*, 897 P.2d 1352 (Ariz.App.Div.1 1994), at 1355   per Kleinschmidt, J.; *Elliott v Chicago Housing Authority*, 2000 WL 1774066 (N.D.Ill. 2000), per Manning, Magistrate J.; *Stevenson v Stanley Bostitch Inc.*, 201 F.R.D. 551 (N.D.Ga 2001), where Scofield, U.S. Magistrate J., stated at 558 that privilege does not extend to information such as the dates of therapy.

[91] 524 N.W.2d 363 (S.D. 1994), at 366 per Henderson, Retired J.

[92] *U.S. v Snelenberger*, 24 F.3d 799 (6th Cir. 1994), at 802 per Timbers, Senior Circuit J.

[93] 202 F.3d 271 (table – unpublished opinion) (6th Cir. 2000).

[94] Kendrick, Tsakonas, Smith, at 7-20 to 7-21.

[95] Vilensky, at 39.

from the scope of the privilege is not at all obvious, as they came to the knowledge of the physician in the course of the professional relationship and therefore fall under the wording of many of the privilege statutes. To adopt a narrow approach, excluding non-medical information from the scope of statutory protection does not sufficiently protect the privacy interests of the patient, as the patient would then have to choose between foregoing treatment or risking the disclosure of non-medical but nevertheless private information the physician observes when treating the patient.

The results of medical examinations that did not take place for treatment or diagnostic purposes are not privileged.[96] This refers, for example, to cases where the patient seeks a medical examination for insurance purposes,[97] or where the examination is ordered by a court[98] or is performed at the request of police officers or employers. For blood samples determining the blood alcohol level of a patient, this means that if the test was performed at the direction of the treating physician rather than at the request of law enforcement officials, the privilege will generally be found to apply.[99] By contrast, the results of blood tests exclusively taken to determine the blood alcohol level of a person, and not for diagnostic or treatment purposes are not protected by medical privilege.[100] Even where a treating physician undertakes a course of action for purposes other than treatment, e.g. the drawing of a blood sample to be used in a police investigation, on his/her own account, without any request by a law enforcement official, the privilege may be held to be inapplicable.[101] To reduce the privilege to situations in which a blood sample was taken either for diagnostic or therapeutic purposes seems justified, as the patient does not have a reasonable expectation of privacy if a blood sample is taken upon the request of a police officer. However, the situation is different where blood samples are taken, or existing samples tested, by the treating physician, without the patient's consent, for law enforcement purposes.[102] In that case, the privilege should apply, as the physician's act violates his/her obligation to maintain the patient's confidences, and the patient's reasonable expectation of privacy was not reduced.

With regard to psychiatric treatment, it has been held in *Hinzman v State*[103] that if a psychiatrist had explained to the patient before the session that he would report

---

[96] See, for example, *In re Exxon Valdez*, 270 F.3d 1215 (9th Cir. 2001), at 1249-50 per Kleinfeld, Circuit J.
[97] *Bouligny v Metropolitan Life Ins Co*, 133 S.W.2d 1094 (Mo. Ct. App. 1939).
[98] Snyder at 172-3.
[99] *State v Elwell*, 132 NH 599 (1989), at 605 per Brock, Chief Justice; *State v McElroy*, 553 So.2d 456 (La 1989), at 458 per Calogero, Justice.
[100] *Collins v Howard*, 156 F.Supp 322 (D.C. Ga. 1957), at 334 per Scarlett, District J.; *State v Erickson*, 241 N.W.2d 854 (N.D. 1976), at 865 per Sand, J. Some privilege statutes contain explicit exemptions to this effect; see, for example, Art.510 C (2)(d) of the Louisiana Code of Evidence.
[101] *State v Waring*, 779 S.W.2d 736 (Mo. Ct. App. 1989), at 740-741 per John C. Holstein, Special J.
[102] *Ferguson v City of Charleston*, 532 U.S. 67 (2001).
[103] 922 S.W.2d 725 (Ark.App. 1996), at 731 per Rogers, J.

his findings to the prosecuting attorney's office and the Department of Human Services, the communications taking place during those sessions were not privileged. Furthermore, the psychotherapist-patient relationship between a police officer who was ordered by his employer to attend counselling sessions and his psychotherapists who were expected to provide reports and recommendations to the employer was not covered by privilege.[104] However, such communication is privileged, even if it is ordered by the police officer's employer, if it is understood that the psychiatrist will report back to the employer without disclosing confidential information, for example simply by revealing whether or not the officer is fit to resume his/her duty. In such a case, the police officer's expectation of confidentiality has only been waived with regard to the psychiatrist's final recommendation, but not in respect of the content of the psychiatrist-patient communication.[105] This is convincing, as the purpose of the privilege statute can only be achieved if potential waivers are given a narrow interpretation.

For the privilege statute to apply, the protected communication must be confidential, a term which again leaves scope for interpretation. Under some privilege statutes,[106] a communication is 'confidential' if it is not intended to be disclosed to third persons, except persons present to further the interests of the patient, or persons who are participating in the diagnosis or treatment under the direction of the physician or psychotherapist, including members of the patient's family. Even a clearly professional consultation can lose its privileged status in many States if it takes place in the presence of third parties.[107] It is argued that when third parties are casually present, their very presence neutralises the confidential character and the privilege should not attach.[108] In *State v George*,[109] a case in which a patient, while in police custody, demanded to be seen by his treating physician for a head injury, and then, in the presence of two police officers and his treating physician, performed dexterity tests for the purpose of establishing whether or not he was under the influence of alcohol, the court distinguished as follows: The presence of police officers did not affect the confidentiality of the examination for the head injury and the observations made as a result of it which they could not observe.[110] By contrast, the information acquired from observing the test performances was not confidential, as it could not only be observed by the physician, but also by the police officers. This distinction is highly problematic,

---

[104] *Siegfried v City of Easton*, 146 F.R.D. 98 (E.D. Pa.), at 101 per Huyett, Senior District J.; *Barrett v Vojtas*, 182 F.R.D. 177 (W.D. Pa. 1998), at 181 per Cindrich, District J.

[105] *Williams v District of Columbia*, 1997 WL 22491 (D.D.C. 1997), at 2 per Oberdorfer, District J.; *Caver v City of Trenton*, 192 F.D.R. 154 (D.N.J. 2000), at 162 per Hughes, U.S. Magistrates J.

[106] See, for example, Nebraska Revised Statutes, Rules of Evidence, § 27-504 (1)(e); Art.510 A (8)(a) of the Louisiana Code of Evidence.

[107] *State v Burchett*, 302 S.W.2d 9 (Mo. 1957), at 17 per Storckman, J.; but see also *People v Decina*, 2 N.Y.2d 133 (1956), at 138 per Froessel, J.

[108] *State v Thomas*, 78 Ariz. 52 (1954), at 63 per Udall, Justice.

[109] 575 P.2d 511 (Kan. 1978).

[110] Ibid., at 516 per Miller, Justice.

and it is submitted that the court in *State v Deases*[111] adopted a better approach. In that case, the court emphasised that the presence of a third person during an otherwise confidential communication does not destroy the privilege if the third person is present to assist the physician in some way or the third person's presence is necessary for the defendant to obtain treatment. Thus, if a person under suspicion of having committed a serious crime needs medical treatment and police officers are, for example, present to protect the treating physician, their presence does not negate the privilege. Privilege statutes normally apply to all observations made in the context of the physician-patient relationship, and there is no reason to give less protection to observations that can be made by police officers who are present during a medical examination, where the patient has not consented to their presence but, without it, would not be given medical treatment.

In *Farrow v Allen*,[112] the court held that even where information was intended to remain confidential at the time of the communication, once a patient puts it into the hands of a third party who is unconnected to the treatment and not subject to any privilege, the information is no longer confidential and any privilege applying to the information must be deemed to have been waived.[113] It is submitted that this policy is too restrictive. It seems to imply that whenever the patient shares his/her medical confidences not just with a physician but also, for example, with a close friend, the information loses its confidential character and therefore no longer deserves the protection of the law. However, it can hardly be said that information that the patient imparts to a limited number of people outside the privileged physician-patient relationship is so widely known that it can no longer be regarded as a confidence. Even though it might then be possible for the state to gain access to this information by compelling the party in whose person no privilege exists to disclose the information, this does not justify that the physician should equally be allowed or even obliged to disclose this information.

The law is unclear as to whether information received from family members of the patient or other persons is privileged. In *Grosslight v Superior Court*[114] it was held that the privilege established in s.1014 Evidence Code Cal. includes all relevant communications to psychotherapists by intimate family members of the patient. And the court in *Edington v Mutual Life Ins Co*[115] held that protected communications include knowledge acquired from the statements of others who surround the patient at the time. The rule thus seems to be that the privilege extends to information from any source as long as it is given for purposes of treatment.[116] With regard to the protection of information related to third parties, *Tesser v Board of Education*[117] suggests that while accounts to the psychotherapist

---

[111] 518 N.W.2d 784 (Iowa 1994), at 788 per Ternus, Justice.

[112] 608 N.Y.S.2d 1 (N.Y.A.D. 1 Dept 1993), at 44 per Ellerin, J.

[113] See also *Carrion v City of New York*, (S.D.N.Y. 2002), per Freeman, Magistrate J.

[114] *Grosslight v Superior Court*, 72 Cal.App.3d 502 (1977), at 507 per Kingsley, Acting Presiding J.

[115] *Edington v Mut Life Ins Co*, 67 N.Y. 185 (1876), at 194 per Miller, J.

[116] Kendrick, Tsakonas, Smith, at 7-18.

[117] 154 F.Supp.2d 388 (E.D.N.Y. 2001), at 393-4 per Go, U.S. Magistrates J.

of the patient's feelings concerning a third party are privileged and need not be disclosed, statements made about a person in order to receive advice regarding that person's problems are not privileged, as they were not made in the course of treatment. It is submitted that this is an unworkable and unduly restrictive interpretation of the scope of the privilege statute. If a patient asks for such advice, this expresses the patient's concern about another person which should be privileged. Particularly where a close relationship between the patient and the third person exists, as in the case of husband and wife in *Tesser*, it might be difficult clearly to distinguish between the problems of the patient and those of the other person. Moreover, it is highly likely that such statements are only made because the patient expects them to be as confidential as all other communication with his/her psychotherapist.

2.2 Licensing statutes

In some U.S. States, the licensing statutes for physicians impose upon the physician an obligation to maintain the patient's confidences. The Oregon licensing statute, for example, provides for the disqualification of or other disciplinary sanctions against a physician for 'wilfully or negligently divulging a professional secret'.[118]

3 Private law actions for breach of medical confidentiality

3.1 Obligation of medical confidentiality

Private law actions for a breach of medical confidentiality, be it in contract, in tort, or for breach of a fiduciary duty, all have in common that the patient must be able to show the existence of an obligation imposed on the physician to maintain patient confidences. Some courts have used privilege and/or licensing statutes as a starting point for the development of a general duty to keep the patient's medical secrets. They infer from these statutes a general state policy favouring medical confidentiality that goes beyond the situations envisaged in the respective statutes. In *Saur v Probes*,[119] for example, the court discussed the conclusions to be drawn from the Michigan privilege statutes for out-of court disclosure of patient information by the physician. According to the court, while the privilege statutes cannot be applied directly, as they only address evidentiary disclosures and do not create civil liability for extrajudicial revelations, they can nevertheless be interpreted as exhibiting a public policy of protecting physician-patient confidences absent a superseding public or private interest. The court was thus of the opinion that even though not directly imposing a general obligation on the

---

[118] See *Humphers v First Interstate Bank*, 696 P.2d 527 (Sup. Ct. Or. 1985), at 534-5 per Linde, Justice.

[119] 476 N.W.2d 496 (Mich.App. 1991), at 498 per Kelly, J.; see also *Schaffer v Spicer*, 215 N.W.2d 134 (Sup. Ct. S.D. 1974), at 136 per Biegelmeier, Chief Justice.

physician to maintain medical confidentiality outside of legal proceedings, privilege statutes give a strong indication that the State is dedicated to the protection of medical confidences. In support of this conclusion, the court, in addition, relied on the State licensing statute which also prohibits the disclosure of confidential information by the physician.

It is also interesting to examine the approach adopted in States that do not recognise a general medical privilege. In *Horne v Patton*,[120] the Alabama Supreme Court argued that the absence of a privilege statute does not indicate that medical confidentiality is not protected, as privilege statutes only deal with the limited question of disclosure of medical confidentiality in the judicial setting. Given the existence of State licensing statutes protecting medical confidentiality, the court concluded that a medical doctor is under a general duty not to make extra-judicial disclosures of information acquired in the course of the physician-patient relationship. In *Alberts v Devine*,[121] the court similarly held that the absence of privilege statutes does not indicate that no public policy favouring a patient's right to confidentiality exists.

It can thus be seen that privilege statutes have an impact surpassing their direct applicability. While the existence of a testimonial privilege can be used in support of the view that the relevant State favours the protection of medical confidentiality, so that the protection is then not limited to the judicial setting, the absence of a privilege statute by no means implies that the State does not protect medical confidentiality outside the judicial setting. It rather only expresses the State legislature's attitude that medical confidentiality is outweighed by the state interest in an unhindered administration of criminal justice. Privilege statutes and licensing statutes taken together, or licensing statutes alone in the absence of privilege statutes, have thus been used as a basis for creating a general obligation to maintain medical confidentiality.

3.2 Obligation under contract law

In American law the physician-patient relationship is often based on a contract. In *MacDonald v Clinger*,[122] for example, the court held that the physician-patient relationship is contractual in nature. It is thus in principle possible that the physician is under a contractual obligation to maintain the patient's medical secrets. However, such an obligation will usually not be an express term of the contract. This leaves the courts with the difficulty of deciding whether, absent such an express term, the physician can nevertheless be under a contractual obligation not to reveal the patient's confidences. Some courts have decided in favour of such an obligation. In *Hammonds v Aetna Casualty & Surety Company*,[123] for example,

---

[120] 287 So.2d 824 (Sup. Ct. Alabama 1973), at 827-9 and 832 per Bloodworth, Justice.

[121] 479 N.E.2d 113 (Mass. 1985), at 119-20 per O'Connor, Justice; see also *South Carolina Board of Medical Examiners v Hedgepath*, 480 S.E.2d 724 (S.C. 1997), at 726 per Finney, Chief Justice.

[122] 446 N.Y.S.2d 801 (Sup. Ct 1982), at 802-4 per Denman, Justice.

[123] 243 F.Supp. 793 (N.D. Ohio 1965), at 797-802 per Connell, Chief J.

it was argued that the physician, as an implied condition of the medical contract, guarantees that any confidential information gained in the course of the physician-patient relationship would not be released. A breach of the duty to maintain medical confidentiality is then a violation of the physician's obligation under the medical contract. The court inferred this implied condition on the ground that the public has a right to rely on the code of ethics adopted by the medical profession which imposes on the physician an obligation to keep medical confidences, on the privilege statute, and on the State Medical Licensing Statute which seals the doctor's lips in private conversation. The same conclusion, based on similar considerations was reached in *MacDonald v Clinger*[124] and in *Doe v Roe*.[125] There, it was specified that the physician impliedly covenants to keep in confidence all disclosures made by the patient concerning the patient's physical or mental condition as well as all matters discovered by the physician in the course of an examination or treatment. In the case of breach, the patient has the possibility to ask for an injunction or for compensation.

The problem with an action under contract law is that the plaintiff's recovery is limited to economic loss flowing directly from the breach, and that recovery for mental distress, loss of employment etc. would be precluded.

3.3 Action under tort law

Given the inadequacies of an action in contract, the Court concluded in *MacDonald v Clinger*[126] that the physician-patient relationship contemplates an additional duty springing from but extraneous to the contract and that the breach of such duty is actionable as a tort. According to the Court, the relationship of the parties was one of trust and confidence out of which arose a duty not to disclose. In *Hammonds v Aetna Casualty & Surety Company*[127] the Court came to a similar conclusion in stating that:

> If a doctor should reveal any of these confidences, he surely affects an invasion of the privacy of his patient. We are of the opinion that the preservation of the patient's privacy is no mere ethical duty upon the part of the doctor; there is a legal duty as well. The unauthorised revelation of medical secrets or any confidential communication given in the course of treatment, is tortious conduct which may be the basis for an action in damages.[128]

In *Fairfax Hosp. v Curtis*,[129] the court held that a health care provider owes a duty of reasonable care to the patient which includes an obligation to preserve the confidentiality of patient information which was communicated to the health care provider or discovered during the course of treatment. In the absence of a statutory

---

[124] 446 N.Y.S.2d 801 (Sup. Ct 1982), at 802-4 per Denman, Justice.
[125] 400 N.Y.S.2d 668 (Sup. Ct. 1977), at 674-5 per Stecher, Justice.
[126] 446 N.Y.S.2d 801 (Sup. Ct 1982), at 802-4 per Denman, Justice.
[127] 243 F.Supp. 793 (N.D. Ohio 1965).
[128] Ibid., at 801-2 per Connell, Chief J.
[129] 492 S.E.2d 642 (Va. 1997), at 644-7 per Hassell, Justice.

command to the contrary, or absent the patient's authorisation, a violation of this duty gives rise to an action in tort. The Court then decided that the recovery of damages for humiliation, embarrassment, and similar harm to feelings, although unaccompanied by actual physical injury, was possible under tort law where a cause of action existed independently of such harm. A similar reasoning can be observed in *McCormick v England*,[130] where the court argued that although South Carolina does not recognise a physician-patient privilege, the confidentiality of the physician-patient relationship is an interest worth protecting and that a violation of the physician's obligation can give rise to an action in tort. An action for damages in tort can also sometimes be based on a breach of the general obligation of medical confidentiality inferred from privilege statutes and licensing statutes as outlined above. In *Schaffer v Spicer*,[131] for example, the court decided that the breach of this general duty by an unauthorised disclosure of confidential information may give rise to liability to the patient for resulting damages. In *Horne v Patton*,[132] the Alabama Supreme Court also argued that a medical doctor is under a general duty not to make extra-judicial disclosures of information acquired in the course of the doctor-patient relationship and that a breach of that duty will give rise to a cause of action.

Some courts have based the patient's action on the breach of a fiduciary duty. In *Petrillo v Syntex Laboratories, Inc.*,[133] for example, the court held that there exists, between a patient and his treating physician, a fiduciary relationship founded on trust and confidence. According to the Court:

> The existence of this fiduciary relationship indicates that there is more between a patient and his physician than a mere contract under which the physician promises to heal and the patient promises to pay. There is an implied promise, arising when the physician begins treating the patient, that the physician will refrain from engaging in conduct that is inconsistent with the good faith required of a fiduciary.

In *Brandt v Medical Defence Associates*,[134] the court inferred from the fact that privilege statutes provide for specific exceptions to the physician's fiduciary duty of confidentiality that:

> In the absence of such an exemption, there would be a breach of this duty, which in turn, constitutes a recognition by the legislature of the existence of the physician's fiduciary duty of confidentiality. We believe that a physician has a fiduciary duty of confidentiality not to disclose any medical information received in connection with his treatment of the patient. This duty arises out of a fiduciary relationship that exists between the physician and the patient. If such information is disclosed under circumstances where this duty of confidentiality has not been waived, the patient has a cause of action for damages in tort against the physician.

---

[130] 494 S.E.2d 431 (S.C.App. 1997), at 432-8 per Anderson, J.
[131] 215 N.W.2d 134 (Sup. Ct. S.D. 1974), at 136 per Biegelmeier, Chief Justice.
[132] 287 So.2d 824 (Sup. Ct. Alabama 1973), at 827-9 and 832 per Bloodworth, Justice.
[133] 499 N.E.2d 952 (Ill.App.1 Dist. 1986), at 961 per Linn, Presiding Justice.
[134] 856 S.W.2d 667 (Mo.banc 1993), at 470 per Thomas, J.

In *Inghram v Mutual of Omaha Ins. Co*,[135] this duty was even said to include an obligation not to comply with a subpoena requiring the production of privileged information where a possibility to challenge the subpoena on the grounds of privilege exists. The failure to pursue this option then constitutes a breach of fiduciary duty.

4 Professional obligation

The ethical duty owed by physicians is generally set forth in the Hippocratic Oath, the American Medical Association's Principles of Medical Ethics, and the Current Opinions of the Judicial Council of the American Medical Association. This ethical duty generally prohibits a patient's treating physician from disclosing confidential information without the patient's consent. §5.05 American Medical Association Principles of Medical Ethics states to that effect:

> Information disclosed to a physician during the course of the relationship between physician and patient is confidential to the greatest possible degree. ... The physician should not reveal confidential communications or information without the express consent of the patient, unless required by law to do so.

In some cases, this ethical duty to maintain patient confidences may be broader than the legal obligations imposed on the physician.[136]

5 Summary

While it is uncontested in the U.S. that a physician is under an obligation to keep patient confidences, the legal basis of such an obligation is more controversial. To some extent, confidential medical information is protected by the U.S. Constitution. Constitutional protection is available under the Fourth Amendment which protects an individual's right of privacy against unreasonable search and seizure, if the patient justifiably relied on an expectation of privacy,[137] which will be the case at least where the relevant information is protected by medical privilege. More general protection of medical confidentiality is awarded under the Fourteenth Amendment and its interpretation as protecting substantive due process. According to the Supreme Court, the individual's interest in privacy embraces an interest in controlling the dissemination of private information about him/herself, including the constitutional protection of communications made by patients to

---

[135] 170 F.Supp.2d 907 (W.D.Mo. 2001), at 909-2 per Smith, District J.

[136] *Steinberg v Jensen*, 534 N.W.2d 361 (Wis. 1995), at 370-371 per Steinmetz, Justice; *Falcon v Alaska Public Offices Commission*, 570 P.2d 469 (Alaska 1977), at 478 per Boochever, Chief Justice.

[137] 'Developments in privileged communications', (1985) 98 Harvard Law Review, at 1545-6.

physicians. Courts have also recognised the individual's interest in being free from government intrusion when making important personal decisions concerning matters such as physical or mental health. The right of privacy is thus a fundamental personal right and it encompasses the right to withhold intimate information and communications about oneself, particularly when one's physical condition is at issue, and to have the confidentiality of the physician-patient relationship protected. It has been demonstrated that the scope of the constitutional protection of medical confidentiality is far from uncontroversial. While there is widespread agreement that sensitive and embarrassing information receives constitutional protection, some courts argue that mundane and everyday information is not protected. Others argue that such information is protected in principle, but can be more easily outweighed by competing state interests in disclosure. The courts thus apply an objective standard when assessing the degree of protection awarded to a patient's confidences, which in itself, it is submitted, violates the patient's right to privacy.

The majority of States have enacted privilege statutes, guaranteeing, to varying degrees, the confidentiality of physician-patient communications in court proceedings. The determination of the scope of protection is to a large extent left to the courts which have adopted different approaches, depending on their views of the purpose of the statutory privilege. Some courts limit the protection to verbal communication, while others include all observations the physician made in the course of the exercise of his/her profession. Most privilege statutes and courts exclude protection if third parties could make the same observations as the physician; if third parties were present during the examination when their presence was not necessary for medical purposes; when the examination or treatment takes place for other than medical purposes, for example for insurance or employment purposes, at least as long as there is an understanding that the findings of the physician will be disclosed to a third party; and if the patient discloses the privileged information to a party outside the privileged relationship. It is submitted that courts when interpreting the privilege statutes, and also partly the legislatures when drafting them, do not always give sufficient weight to the patient's privacy interests. While it is unproblematic that a privilege does not apply to medical examinations that take place with an understanding that the results will be disclosed, as the patient then does not have a reasonable expectation of privacy and/or can be said to have waived the privilege, such waivers or exclusions of privilege should be given a narrow interpretation. The purposes of privilege statutes, that is the protection of a patient's privacy in the health care setting and the utilitarian goal of protecting public health, can only be achieved if the patient is given control over the disclosure of confidential information. Therefore, unless a waiver applies, all observations made by the physician in the course of the professional relationship should be protected, be they medical or non-medical and made with or without third parties being present.

In some States, licensing statutes for the medical profession also impose a statutory obligation on the physician to maintain medical confidentiality. Some courts have developed a general legal obligation of a physician to respect patient confidences, mainly based on licensing statutes, and, where existing, also based on privilege statutes. While most courts agree that compensation should be available where the physician has breached his/her obligation of medical confidentiality, different legal bases for such a claim are advanced. The situation can be summarised as follows: while American courts agree that the physician owes a duty to the patient to keep the patient's medical confidences, that a violation of such a duty gives rise to a claim for compensation and that, depending on the circumstances, injunctive relief may also be available, differences can be observed as to the legal basis for such an action. While some courts mainly consider an action for breach of an implied contractual duty, others concentrate on an action in tort law, either as the only cause of action, or as an additional action to the claim under contract law. Still other courts argue that the breach of medical confidentiality by the physician constitutes the breach of a fiduciary duty, and while some courts seem to suggest that this in itself gives rise to an action, others support the view that the breach of such a fiduciary duty results in a claim under tort law.

PART 2 – DISCLOSURE IN THE CONTEXT OF CRIME PREVENTION AND CRIMINAL PROSECUTION

It has been demonstrated that medical confidentiality is, in principle, legally protected. The question then arises of whether or not the physician's obligation to maintain the patient's confidences applies in the context of criminal proceedings and of crime prevention. As there is no uniform American law in this area of the law, federal law and the law of different States have to be examined independently to answer this question.

1 Federal law

The confidentiality of the physician-patient relationship receives protection under different principles of the U.S. Constitution. This does not, however, mean that medical privilege equally receives constitutional protection. Courts have rather always emphasised that the recognition of a medical privilege is not based on the Constitution, but is instead merely a creature of statutory or common law. In *Branzburg v Hayes*,[138] for example, the Supreme Court held that the only testimonial privilege rooted in the Federal Constitution was that of the Fifth Amendment. This means that the state is not under a constitutional obligation to recognise a medical privilege, but that it is at the discretion of the legislature

---

[138] 408 U.S. 665 (1972), at 689-90 per Justice White; see also, for example, *Felber v Foote*, 321 F.Supp. 85 (D. Conn. 1970), at 87 per Blumenfeld, District J.; *Pagano v Oroville Hosp.*, 145 F.R.D. 683 (E.D.Cal. 1993), at 689 per Hollows, U.S. Magistrate J.; *State v Beatty*, 770 S.W.2d 387 (Mo.App. 1989), at 391 per Greene, J.; *State v Boehme*, 430 P.2d 527 (Wash. 1967), at 335 per Hamilton, J.

whether or not to introduce it. Rule 501 of the Federal Rules of Evidence (FRE) which is applicable in proceedings before federal courts provides that:

> Privileges are to be governed by principles of the common law as they may be interpreted ... in the light of reason and experience, except that in civil actions, as to claims or defences grounded in state law, the federal courts are to decide questions of privilege in accordance with applicable state law.

As, traditionally, common law did not recognise a medical privilege,[139] this provision has been interpreted as recognising a medical privilege before a federal court only where the court has to apply state law, and where the law of the relevant State provides for a medical privilege. In contrast, where a federal court has to apply federal law, no physician-patient privilege is recognised.[140] Although FRE 501 allows the courts to protect information from disclosure if they consider it advisable in the light of reason and experience, federal courts have been reluctant to introduce any form of physician-patient privilege in cases in which federal law is determinative. The only authorities supporting the existence of a physician-patient privilege in federal proceedings are *Rosenberg v Carroll*,[141] stating in dictum that such a privilege is applicable before a federal grand jury, and *Mann v University of Cincinnati*,[142] in which the court stated that: 'The federal courts have also recognised a federal common law privilege in the doctor-patient relationship'.

This does not mean, however, that confidential medical information is unprotected in federal criminal proceedings. Even in the absence of a privilege, the constitutional interest in the privacy of confidential medical information requires that where disclosure of such information is sought, a balancing test be performed to decide whether or not the right to privacy is outweighed by the state interest in

---

[139] *Hancock v Hobbs*, 967 F.2d 462 (11th Cir. 1992), at 466 per Curiam; *Brandt v Medical Defence Associates*, 856 S.W.2d 667 (Mo.banc 1993), at 669, per Thomas, J.; *Pagano v Oroville Hosp.*, 145 F.R.D. 683 (E.D.Cal. 1993), at 689 per Hollows, U.S. Magistrate J.; *Benton v Superior Court, Navajo County*, 897 P.2d 1352 (Ariz.App.Div.1 1994), at 1355 per Kleinschmitt, J.; *State v Hardin*, 569 N.W.2d 517 (Iowa App. 1997), at 580 per Vogel, J.; *Fox v Gates Corp.*, 179 F.R.D. 303 (D. Colo. 1998) at 305 per Coan, U.S. Magistrate J.; *Galarza v U.S.*, 179 F.R.D. 291 (S.D.Cal. 1998), at 294 per Battaglia, U.S. Magistrate J.; *State v Smith*, 496 S.E.2d 357 (N.C. 1998), at 361, per Whichard, Justice.

[140] *U.S. v Burzynski Cancer Research Inst*, 819 F.2d 1301(5th Cir. 1987), at 1311 per Rubin, Circuit J.; *U.S. v Bercier*, 848 F.2d 917 (8th Cir. 1988), at 920 per McMillan, Circuit J.; *Hancock v Dodson*, 958 F.2d 1367 (6th Cir. 1992), at 1373 per Contie, Senior Circuit J.; *U.S. v Pierce*, 5 F.3d 791 (5th Cir. 1993), at 791 per DeMoss, Circuit J.

[141] 99 F.Supp. 629 (S.D.N.Y. 1951), at 629 per Goddard, District J.; see also Klieman, at 10.36.

[142] 824 F.Supp. 1190 (S.D. Ohio 1993), at 1197, per Steinberg, U.S. Magistrates J.

obtaining the information.[143] However, this protection is not very far-reaching. A showing that the information is material and relevant to the proceedings seems sufficient to demonstrate a state interest outweighing medical confidentiality.

The situation is rather different when it comes to the question of a psychotherapist-patient privilege. Even though FRE 501 equally applies, the courts that have had to deal with the problem have been influenced by the fact that the recognition of a federal psychotherapist-patient privilege has been recommended by the Advisory Committee on the Federal Rules of Evidence.[144] Congress' failure to enact the recommended provision guaranteeing a psychotherapist-patient privilege in federal proceedings does not imply a rejection of such a privilege. Instead, in *Trammel v U.S.*,[145] the Supreme Court explained the legal situation as follows:

> In rejecting the proposed Rules and enacting Rule 501, Congress manifested an affirmative intention not to freeze the law of privilege. Its purpose rather was to provide the courts with the flexibility to develop rules of privilege on a case-by-case basis.[146]

Recently, in *Jaffee v Redmond*,[147] the Supreme Court reaffirmed its holding in *Trammel* by stating that:

> Rule 501 of the Federal Rules of Evidence authorises federal courts to define new privileges by interpreting 'common law principles ... in the light of reason and experience'. ... The Rule thus did not freeze the law governing the privilege of witnesses in federal trials at a particular point in our history, but rather directed federal courts to continue the evolutionary development of testimonial privileges.[148] ... In rejecting the proposed draft that had specifically identified each privilege rule and substituting the present more open-ended Rule 501, the Senate Judiciary Committee explicitly stated that its action should not be understood as disapproving any recognition of a psychiatrist-patient privilege contained in the proposed rules.[149]

The Court then considered the significance of a psychotherapist-patient privilege and argued in favour of such a privilege on the following grounds:

> That it is appropriate for the federal courts to recognise a psychotherapist privilege under Rule 501 is confirmed by the fact that all 50 States and the District of Columbia have enacted into law some form of psychotherapist privilege. We have previously observed that the policy decisions of the States bear on the question whether federal courts should

---

[143] See, for example, *Fritsch v City of Chula Vista*, 187 F.R.D. 614 (S.D.Cal 1999), at 633 per Aaron, U.S. Magistrate J.; *U.S. v Sutherland*, 143 F.Supp.2d 609 (W.D.Va. 2001), at 611 per Jones, District J.; but see *U.S. v Burzynski Cancer Research Inst*, 819 F.2d 1301 (5th Cir. 1987), at 1311 per Rubin, Circuit J.

[144] 56 F.R.D. 183, at 242.

[145] 445 U.S. 40 (1979).

[146] Ibid., at 47, per Chief Justice Burger.

[147] 518 U.S. 1 (1996).

[148] Ibid., at 8-9, per Justice Stevens.

[149] Ibid., at 15.

recognise a new privilege or amend the coverage of an existing one. ... Because state legislators are fully aware of the need to protect the integrity of the fact-finding functions of their courts, the existence of a consensus among the States indicates that 'reason and experience' support recognition of the privilege. ... The uniform judgment of the States is reinforced by the fact that a psychotherapist privilege was among the nine specific privileges recommended by the Advisory Committee in its proposed privilege rules. ... Because we agree with the judgment of the state legislatures and the Advisory Committee that a psychotherapist-patient privilege will serve a public good transcending the normally predominant principle of utilising all rational means for ascertaining the truth ... we hold that confidential communications between a licensed psychotherapist and her patients in the course of diagnosis or treatment are protected from compelled disclosure under Rule 501 of the Federal Rules of Evidence.[150]

Until this decision of the Supreme Court, the federal courts had been divided between those that accepted a psychotherapist-patient privilege[151] and those that did not.[152] In *U.S. v Corona*,[153] for example, the court had held that no psychotherapist-patient privilege existed in federal criminal trials as neither common law nor statutory law provided for any type of physician-patient privilege in criminal matters. And the court in *Re Grand Jury Proceedings*[154] expressed the view that it was up to Congress to introduce and define such a privilege, and not the task of a court. Those courts that accepted the existence of a federal psychotherapist-patient privilege did so on the grounds that 'reason and experience' (FRE 501) showed that the interests protected by such privilege outweighed the interest in the administration of justice.[155]

This leaves the question of the scope of the non-statutory federal psychotherapist-patient privilege. Prior to the U.S. Supreme Court's decision in *Jaffee*, courts that came to the conclusion that policy reasons mandated the recognition of such a privilege mostly nevertheless argued that it should be recognised only as long as it did not entail undue frustration of other societal interests.[156] They claimed that the recognition of the privilege must be undertaken

[150] Ibid., at 12-15.
[151] *Covell v CNG Transmission Corp.*, 863 F.Supp. 202 (M.D. Pa. 1994), at 205 per McClure, District J.; *Cunningham v Southlake Ctr for Mental Health, Inc*, 125 F.R.D. 474 (N.D. Ind. 1989), at 477 per Rodovich, U.S. Magistrates J.; *In Re Doe*, 964 F.2d 1325 (2nd Cir. 1992), at 1328 per Winter, Circuit J.; *In re Zuniga*, 714 F.2d 632 (6th Cir. 1983), at 639 per Krupansky, Circuit J.; *U.S. v D.F.*, 857 F.Supp. 1311 (E.D. Wis. 1994), at 1321 per Stadtmueller, District J.
[152] *In re Grand Jury Proceedings*, 867 F.2d 562 (9th Cir. 1989), at 565 per Curiam; *U.S. v Corona*, 849 F.2d 562 (11th Cir. 1988), at 567 per Robert H. Hall, District J.; see also *U.S. v Burtrum*, 17 F.3d 1299 (10th Cir. 1994), at 1302 per Kelly, Circuit J. for cases of child abuse.
[153] 849 F.2d 562 (11th Cir. 1988), at 567 per Robert H. Hall, District J.
[154] 867 F.2d 562 (9th Cir. 1989), at 565 per Curiam.
[155] See, for example, *In re Grand Jury Subpoena*, 710 F.Supp. 999 (D.N.J. 1989), at 1004 per Gerry, Chief J.; *In re Zuniga*, 714 F.2d 632 (6th Cir. 1983), at 639 per Krupansky, Circuit J.
[156] *In re Grand Jury Subpoena*, 710 F.Supp. 999 (D.N.J. 1989), at 1007-8 per Gerry, Chief J.

on a case-by-case basis, as the propriety of the privilege as such as well as its scope must be determined by balancing the interests protected by the privilege with those advanced by disclosure.[157] In *Re Doe*,[158] Winter, Circuit J. even held that the privilege amounts only to a requirement that a court give consideration to a witness' privacy interests as an important factor to be weighed in the balance when assessing the admissibility of psychiatric histories or diagnoses. Important for the outcome of the balancing test was the sensitivity of the personal information disclosed, and hence the intrusion on the right to confidentiality. The more sensitive the information, the higher the burden on the state to justify disclosure.[159] *U.S. v D.F*[160] gives some insight into how the courts performed the balancing test in cases in which the interest behind the privilege was in conflict with the interests of justice in criminal proceedings:

> Consistent with the case-by-case approach mandated by Rule 501, the court must now consider whether, in the instant case, the privilege should apply to D.F.'s statements. ... Several aspects of this case suggest that the utilitarian gains from the privilege would be minimal. First, the interest in effective therapy will only be served to the extent that D.F., a fourteen year-old girl, understood the implications of disclosure. ... Second, ... there is evidence in the regard to suggest that she believed that the staff at the Centre was required to disclose her statements. ... To the extent that that is the case, the privilege would have been irrelevant. Third, to the extent that D.F.'s 'therapy' at the Centre was compelled or coerced ... the existence of the privilege likely provided only marginal utilitarian gains. Application of the privilege in this case would do little to promote privacy interests. The facts of this case suggest that regardless of whether the court finds that D.F.'s statements were privileged, her privacy has already been seriously compromised. The statements have already been widely disseminated amongst both governmental officials and other patients. ... On the other hand, the interests weighing against the privilege in this case are considerable. The Government believes that the two infants involved were murdered. D.F.'s statements are clearly relevant to that charge. In fact, the Government has suggested that that charge cannot be sustained without that evidence. Thus, non-disclosure would significantly impair both law enforcement interests and a general interest in the truth-seeking process.[161]

According to the court, the application of the privilege in this case thus depended on whether and to what extent the privilege would promote the interests behind its recognition. The first consideration seems to suggest that children or other people who may not be aware of the privilege will not be protected, as without such awareness, privilege will do nothing to enhance the willingness to receive therapy and to be frank to one's psychotherapist. Secondly, the psychotherapist's mistaken belief that he/she is under an obligation to disclose confidential information seems to negate the privilege. What is even more worrying is the court's remark that the

---

[157] *Re Zuniga*, 714 F.2d 632 (6th Cir. 1983), at 639-40 per Krupansky, Circuit J.
[158] 964 F.2d 1325 (2nd Cir. 1992), at 1328-9.
[159] *Hawaii Psychiatric Soc. Dist. Branch v Ariyoshi*, 481 F.Supp. 1028 (D. Hawaii 1979), at 1043 per Byrne, District J.
[160] 857 F.Supp. 1311 (E.D. Wis. 1994).
[161] Ibid., at 1320-1322 per Stadtmueller, District J.

fact that the patient's privacy has already been widely infringed can justify further invasions. The case shows that the case-by-case approach adopted in cases of federal psychotherapist-patient privilege prior to *Jaffee* gives the courts considerable leeway to do away with the privilege where they think that in the specific case disclosure will yield a better result than non-disclosure. If a court adopts a utilitarian approach towards medical confidentiality as did the court in *U.S. v D.F*, the balancing test can concentrate on costs and benefits for society, while neglecting the privacy and autonomy interests of the individual patient. However, in *Jaffee v Redmond*,[162] Justice Stevens stressed that:

> We reject the balancing component of the privilege implemented by ... a small number of States ... . Making the promise of confidentiality contingent upon a trial judge's later evaluation of the relative importance of the patient's interest in privacy and the evidentiary need for disclosure would eviscerate the effectiveness of the privilege. ... If the purpose of the privilege is to be served, the participants in the confidential conversation must be able to predict with some degree of certainty whether particular discussions will be protected. An uncertain privilege, or one which purports to be certain but results in widely varying applications by the courts, is little better than no privilege at all.[163]

While this very general statement seems to suggest that post-facto qualifications to the psychotherapist-patient privilege are unacceptable because they create unpredictability, thereby undermining the efficiency of the privilege,[164] it must be borne in mind that the argument was advanced in the narrow context of whether or not it was appropriate to make the protection of the patient's interests in non-disclosure subject to the relevance of the information in judicial proceedings. It remains to be seen whether this case-law will in the future be interpreted as a strict ban on any exceptions to the psychotherapist-patient privilege, or whether it will be restricted to its narrow meaning of stating that the psychotherapist-patient privilege must not yield merely because the information the disclosure of which is sought would be relevant in court.

Given the constitutional protection of medical confidentiality under substantive due process principles, it is rather surprising that courts and legal commentators almost unanimously subscribe to the view that medical privilege is not mandated by the Constitution. As medical privilege is an attempt to resolve the conflict between the interests in medical confidentiality and the interests of justice, this opinion expresses the value judgment that the Constitution does not stand in the way of favouring the interests of justice over the interests in medical confidentiality. However, the Constitution does not prevent the statutory recognition of medical privilege, either. It thus follows that the Constitution is neutral with regard to the conflict between the interest in medical confidentiality and the interests of justice. Even the federal psychotherapist-patient privilege

---

[162] 518 U.S. 1 (1996).
[163] Ibid., at 17-18.
[164] See also *Vanderbilt v Town of Chilmark*, 174 F.R.D. 225 (D.Mass. 1997), at 229 per Tauro, Chief J.

recognised by the Supreme Court in *Jaffee*[165] was developed on the basis of the FRE, not based on constitutional principles.[166]

2 State law

Most States in the U.S. now have some form of statutory physician-patient privilege,[167] and in all States, the communication between psychiatrists and patients is privileged by statute.

2.1 Reasons behind the recognition of privilege

Freeman, Chief Justice, explained the problems created by the recognition of a privilege in *D.C. v S.A.*:[168]

> Privileges which protect certain matters from disclosure are not designed to promote the truth-seeking process, but rather to protect some outside interest other than the ascertainment of truth at trial. ... Thus, privileges are an exception to the general rule that the public has a right to every person's evidence. Privileges are not to be lightly created or expansively construed, for they are in derogation of the search for the truth.

As privileges thus constitute a deviation from the normal principles underlying court proceedings, their recognition can only be justified if some other, more important interest is thereby enhanced. In *US v Nixon*,[169] the Supreme Court held that the generalised interest in confidentiality cannot prevail over the fundamental demands of due process of law in the fair administration of criminal justice. Therefore, in addition to general confidentiality considerations there must be more specific reasons to justify medical privilege.

It has already been discussed for what reasons many American States have adopted privilege statutes. To summarise the main considerations, there is widespread agreement that medical privilege aims to encourage the patient to feel free to disclose openly to the physician all facts which may have a bearing upon diagnosis and treatment.[170] This is important to give adequate protection to the

---

[165] 518 U.S. 1 (1996).

[166] *Henry v Kernan*, 197 F.3d 1021 (9th Cir. 1999), at 1031 per Tashima, Circuit J.

[167] For example Alaska, Arizona, Arkansas, California, Colorado, Connecticut, Georgia, Hawaii, Idaho, Illinois, Louisiana, Michigan, Mississippi, Missouri, Montana, Nebraska, Nevada, New Jersey, New York, Oregon, Pennsylvania, Rhode Island, South Dakota, Texas, Vermont, Virginia, Wisconsin and Wyoming provide for some form of physician-patient privilege. However, for example Alabama, Florida, Kentucky, Maryland, South Carolina and Tennessee do not have a statutory physician-patient privilege.

[168] 687 N.E.2d 1032 (Ill. 1997), at 1038.

[169] 418 U.S. 683 (1974), at 713 per Chief Justice Burger.

[170] *Berry v Moench*, 331 P.2d 814 (Sup. Ct. of Utah 1958), at 817 per Crockett, Justice; *People v Harrison*, 626 N.Y.S.2d 747 (Ct.App. 1995), at 746 per Bellacosa, J.

privacy interests of the patient[171] and the interests of society that persons are encouraged to seek medical advice and treatment in order to promote public health. Another consideration is that the privilege helps physicians to avoid a 'Hobson's choice: ... choosing between honouring their professional obligation with respect to their patients' confidences or their legal duty to testify truthfully'.[172] Some courts refer to the constitutional privacy arguments explained above[173] and argue that the patient's privacy rights not only mandate the protection of medical confidentiality in general, but also the recognition of a medical privilege. In *Mann v University of Cincinnati* [174] for example, it was stressed that the reasons favouring a protection of a privacy interest in the non-disclosure of private information and in making health care decisions unimpaired by fear of unwarranted disclosures support the recognition of a doctor-patient privilege. The court thus recognised that without a physician-patient privilege, the patient's privacy and health interests cannot receive adequate protection. Those States that have adopted privilege statutes applicable in criminal proceedings accept that the interests such a privilege guarantees are more important than the competing interests at stake in the course of criminal proceedings.

While the court in *Division of Medical Quality v Gherardini*[175] held the privacy concerns of the general physician-patient relationship to be of equal value to those of the psychotherapist-patient relationship, this view is far from being predominant, as all States provide for a psychotherapist-patient privilege, while not all of them accept that the communication between physicians and patients should be privileged. Similarly, at the federal level, only a psychotherapist-patient privilege, and not a medical privilege, is recognised. The reasons brought forward for this difference in protection are mainly based on the assumption that the psychotherapist-patient relationship concerns a more intimate area of the patient's life than the physician-patient relationship and therefore deserves stricter confidentiality guarantees. As Justice Stevens argued for the Supreme Court in *Jaffee v Redmond*:[176]

Treatment by a physician for physical ailments can often proceed successfully on the basis of a physical examination, objective information supplied by the patient, and the results of diagnostic tests. Effective psychotherapy, by contrast, depends upon an atmosphere of confidence and trust in which the patient is willing to make a frank and complete disclosure of confidential facts, emotions, memories, and fears. Because of the sensitive nature of the problems for which individuals consult psychotherapists, disclosure of

---

[171] *Mann v University of Cincinnati*, 824 F.Supp. 1190 (S.D. Ohio 1993), at 1199 per Steinberg, U.S. Magistrates J.

[172] *People v Harrison*, 626 N.Y.S.2d 747 (Ct.App. 1995), at 746 per Bellacosa, J.

[173] See supra, part 1, 1.3.

[174] 824 F.Supp. 1190 (S.D. Ohio 1993), at 1199 per Steinberg, U.S. Magistrates J.

[175] 156 Cal. Rptr. 55 (1979), at 60-61 per Staniforth, Acting Presiding J.

[176] 518 U.S. 1 (1996), at 10; see also *In re August, 1993 Regular Grand Jury*, 854 F.Supp. 1392 (S.D.Ind. 1993), at 1397 per Tinder, District J.; *Ceasar v Mountanos*, 542 F.2d 1064 (9th Cir. 1976), at 1167 per Jameson, District J. ('Psychotherapy is perhaps more dependent on absolute confidentiality than other medical disciplines'.)

confidential communications made during counselling sessions may cause embarrassment or disgrace.

According to the majority of the Supreme Court, the psychotherapist-patient privilege is thus rooted in the imperative need for confidence and trust, and even the mere possibility of disclosure may impede the development of a confidential relationship that is necessary for successful treatment. The Court then emphasised that the psychotherapist-patient privilege serves the public interest in the mental health of the citizens by facilitating the provision of appropriate treatment for individuals suffering the effects of a mental or emotional problem. Given that the federal psychotherapist-patient privilege does not have a statutory basis, the decision is interesting in that the Court had to perform a thorough balancing of the interests promoted by the privilege and those that might be adversely affected by its recognition:

> In contrast to the significant public and private interests supporting recognition of the privilege, the likely evidentiary benefit that would result from the denial of the privilege is modest. If the privilege were rejected, confidential conversations between psychotherapists and their patients would surely be chilled, particularly when it is obvious that the circumstances that give rise to the need for treatment will probably result in litigation. Without the privilege, much of the desirable evidence to which litigants ... seek access ... is unlikely to come into being. This unspoken 'evidence' will therefore serve no greater truth-seeking function than if it had been spoken and privileged. In addition, given the importance of the patient's understanding that her communications will not be publicly disclosed, any State's promise of confidentiality would have little value if the patient were aware that the privilege would not be honoured in a federal court.[177]

This is a powerful argument. One common criticism of any evidentiary privilege is that it inhibits the truth-finding function of judicial proceedings in making unavailable information that might be relevant and material. The Supreme Court counters that argument by questioning whether, without privilege, the information would in fact be available. Obviously, if privilege is seen to be necessary in order to encourage the patient frankly to disclose information to the psychotherapist, it can at least be argued that without such privilege, the patient will not disclose this information to the psychotherapist, so that even without a privilege the psychotherapist would not be available to testify in court about the patient's mental condition and intimate thoughts. If this is accepted, the costs of recognising a privilege are relatively low and it is very unlikely that much evidence will be lost. This is a utilitarian argument that focuses on the costs and benefits of privilege and it can only be sustained if there is some proof that without psychotherapist-patient privilege, patients would in fact be deterred from sharing their intimate thoughts with their psychotherapists. The rejection of a physician-patient privilege based on these considerations would equally only be justified if it could be shown that the absence of such privilege would not deter patients from seeking medical treatment,

---

[177] *Jaffee v Redmond*, 518 U.S. 1 (1996), at 11-13 per Justice Stevens.

or that the consequences of a risk of disclosure for the physician-patient relationship are outweighed by potential evidentiary gains.

Other courts have argued that even if some relevant information is lost to the courts, a patient in psychotherapy who in order to receive help must lay bare his/her entire self has a right to expect that such revelations will remain confidential,[178] an argument which rests on deontological thought. Thus, in case of a conflict between the interests in the confidentiality of the psychotherapist-patient relationship and the interests of justice, the individual's right of privacy will be given priority.[179] In *Re Zuniga*,[180] the court summarised different arguments in favour of the recognition of a psychotherapist-patient privilege:

> The inability to obtain effective psychiatric treatment may preclude the enjoyment and exercise of many fundamental freedoms, particularly those protected by the First Amendment. ... The interest of the patient in exercising his rights is also society's interest, for society benefits from its members' active enjoyment of their freedom. Moreover, society has an interest in successful treatment of mental illness because of the possibility that a mentally ill person will pose a danger to the community. The court ... finds that these interests, in general, outweigh the need for evidence in the administration of criminal justice.

And *In re Grand Jury Subpoena*[181] the court similarly stressed that:

> Society has a discernible interest in fostering the therapeutic treatment of those of its members experiencing emotional turbulence. This interest consists not only in our altruistic concern for our neighbour's well-being, but in our more selfish interest in the effective treatment of those who may pose a threat because of mental illness or drug addiction. The absence of a privilege seems to have at least some deterrent effect on those seeking treatment. Equally important are the privacy rights of psychotherapy patients.

The public interest in the protection of the confidentiality of the psychotherapist-patient relationship is thus twofold: society has an interest in encouraging mentally ill or unstable persons to seek and receive effective psychiatric treatment so that they will not pose a danger to society. At the same time, society also has an interest in the protection of individual rights and freedoms, such as the privacy right and the right to health. It has been argued that the absence of a psychotherapist-patient privilege would harm both the constitutionally protected interest in avoiding disclosure of personal matters, and the interest in making certain kinds of important decisions autonomously.[182] With regard to the privacy rights of the psychiatric patient, in *Hawaii Psychiatric Soc. Dist. Branch v Ariyoshi*,[183] Byrne,

---

[178] See *In re Lifschutz*, 85 Cal. Rptr. 829 (Sup. 1970), at 831-2 per Tobriner, Justice; *U.S. v Doyle*, 1 F.Supp.2d 1187 (D.Or. 1998), at 1191 per Coffin, U.S. Magistrates J.

[179] In *Re B*, 394 A.2d 419 (Pa. Sup. Ct. 1978), at 429 per Manderino, Justice.

[180] 714 F.2d 632 (6th Cir. 1983), at 639 per Krupansky, Circuit J.

[181] 710 F.Supp. 999 (D.N.J. 1989), at 1009-10 per Gerry, Chief J.; see also *U.S. v D.F.*, 857 F.Supp. 1311 (E.D. Wis. 1994), at 1320-1322 per Stadtmueller, District J.

[182] *In re Grand Jury Subpoena*, 710 F.Supp. 999 (D.N.J. 1989), at 1010 per Gerry, Chief J.

[183] 481 F.Supp. 1028 (D. Hawaii 1979).

District J., held that it includes, at a minimum, the freedom of an individual to choose the circumstances under which, and to whom certain of his thoughts and feelings will be disclosed,[184] and that it extends to an individual's liberty to make decisions regarding psychiatric care without unjustified governmental interference.[185]

It can be seen that the recognition of a psychotherapist-patient privilege is based on a mixture of deontological and utilitarian considerations. While there are many critics of the physician-patient privilege, all legislators as well as most courts agree on the overriding importance of the psychotherapist-patient privilege. However, there are also critical voices with regard to the recognition of a psychotherapist-patient privilege. Justice Scalia, for example, in a dissent to the Supreme Court's decision in *Jaffee v Redmond*,[186] questioned the likelihood that the absence of a psychotherapist-patient privilege might deter a patient from seeking psychological assistance, and he argued furthermore that even if it were certain that the absence of the psychotherapist privilege would inhibit disclosure of information to the psychotherapist, there was no good reason to protect the interest in confidentiality as it seems 'entirely fair to say that if she wishes the benefits of telling the truth she must also accept the adverse consequences'.

It can be seen that the approach towards the recognition of a medical and/or psychotherapist-patient privilege largely depends on the attitude with regard to the purposes that are thereby served. In principle, the arguments in favour of a psychotherapist-patient privilege are very similar to the arguments brought forward in favour of a physician-patient privilege. In both cases, the privacy and health interests of the patient, as well as society's interest in the health of the citizens are important considerations, and the dividing line between the two approaches is mainly the distinction between physical and mental health, a distinction that is not always easy to make, as the growing significance of psychosomatic illnesses shows. But even in cases in which the distinction can be made, it must be questioned whether a different legal approach towards the two situations is desirable and sound. The main reason for a distinction seems to rest on the assumption that the psychotherapist-patient relationship concerns more intimate matters than the ordinary physician-patient relationship, but it should not be forgotten that if confidentiality is guaranteed to protect the patient's interests in making autonomous health care decisions and in controlling the dissemination of confidential information, it is difficult to decide on behalf of the patient which information deserves the strongest protection. Part of the patient's autonomy interest is surely that it should be the patient who decides which information is regarded as particularly sensitive. The fact that most patients will attach more weight to the confidentiality of information imparted to the psychotherapist should not make any difference, as any objective standard regarding the assessment of what information is sensitive impairs the patient's autonomy. Thus, from a

---

[184] Ibid., at 1038.
[185] Ibid., at 1041.
[186] 518 U.S. 1 (1996), at 22-3.

deontological perspective, the distinction between psychotherapist-patient privilege and physician-patient privilege seems hardly justified. With regard to the Supreme Court's consequentialist argument in *Jaffee* that not much, if any, evidence will be lost by introducing a psychotherapist-patient privilege, proof would be needed to decide whether this is true and whether the same does not apply to the physician-patient relationship, for example in respect of certain sensitive areas such as venereal diseases, HIV infection etc. Only if there is a provable difference between the two situations can this argument be used as a reason for different legal treatment. If the stronger protection of the psychotherapist-patient privilege is based on society's interest in preserving the mental health of the population, this argument also needs some evidence to demonstrate that the absence of a physician-patient privilege would then not equally endanger society's interest in preserving the population's physical health.

2.2 Limitations to medical privilege

2.2.1 General considerations

Physician-patient or psychotherapist-patient privileges demonstrate a decision that in case of a conflict between confidentiality and the competing interests in court proceedings, the interest in confidentiality is given precedence. However, it does not follow from a general decision in favour of medical and/or psychotherapist-patient privilege that the privilege should be absolute, trumping other interests under all circumstances. Most privilege statutes provide for exceptions in areas in which the legislature has found certain social interests sufficiently important to override the State's general interest in protecting confidential patient information from being disclosed to third parties. In many States, for example, physicians must report to the police gunshot and knife wounds which may have resulted from illegal activity,[187] and contagious or infectious diseases must be disclosed to the health department.

The scope of the physician-patient privilege varies from State to State. It is first of all important to examine whether or not a privilege statute protecting a patient's confidences from disclosure in court proceedings is applicable in criminal court.[188] In some States, privilege statutes expressly provide that there is no privilege in criminal proceedings.[189] Other States exclude medical privilege 'in trial for homicide when the disclosure relates directly to the fact or immediate circumstances of the homicide';[190] or in cases of criminal charges for abortion.[191] Some privilege statutes, however, expressly provide for a privilege in criminal proceedings. Art.510 of the Louisiana Code of Evidence, for example, states that:

---

[187] See, for example, Wisconsin St 905.04 for wounds and burn injuries.

[188] With regard to this problem, see Slovenko, at 156.

[189] See, for example, §998 California Evidence Code; Alaska R Rev Rule 504(d)(7); Mo. Ann. Stat. §337.636; Pa. Stat. Ann. §5929.

[190] Ill. Comp. State. Ch. 735 5/8-802; Wisconsin St 905.04(4)(d).

[191] Ill. Comp. State. Ch. 735 5/8-802.

C.(1) General rule of privilege in criminal proceedings.
In a criminal proceeding, a patient has a privilege to refuse to disclose and to prevent another person from disclosing a confidential communication made for the purpose of advice, diagnosis or treatment of his health condition between or among himself, his representative, and his physician or psychotherapist, and their representatives.[192]

Other privilege statutes award a general privilege and remain silent as to the question of the applicability of the statute to criminal proceedings. It is then up to the courts to decide whether they will read non-statutory exceptions into the statute. In *People v Reynolds*,[193] for example, the court held that nothing in the statutory physician-patient privilege suggested that the afforded privilege did not apply in criminal cases. Absent such language, the court declined to infer such a broad and conclusive exception to the statutory privilege. And in *State v Ross*,[194] the court explained that the physician-patient privilege had been extended to criminal cases pursuant to RCW 10.58.010 which applies the civil rules of evidence to criminal prosecutions as far as practicable.

Some specific grounds on which a privilege might be limited will now be examined.

2.2.2 Interests in criminal prosecution and the administration of justice
In the context of a privilege in criminal proceedings, the patient's interest in non-disclosure will regularly conflict with the state interest in the prosecution of those charged with a crime, and with the interest in the administration of justice. To understand the balancing process, it is important to be clear about the content and the significance of the interests with which medical confidentiality competes. The discussion of the interests involved differs with regard to the different stages of criminal prosecution. Confidential medical information protected by medical privilege may be relevant in the course of police investigations, in the course of grand jury proceedings in which the grand jury decides on the indictment of a suspect, and, finally, in a criminal trial. As privilege is mainly discussed in the context of criminal trials, this is where the analysis will start.

(a) criminal trials The interest in unlimited disclosure of information in the course of judicial proceedings was best explained by the Supreme Court in *US v Nixon*.[195] There, the Court had to decide whether or not certain presidential communications were protected from disclosure in court by the presidential privilege. In that case, the Supreme Court delineated the interests in favour of disclosure as follows:

---

[192] See also, for example, Rhode Island St §9-17-24.
[193] 195 Colo. 386 (1978), at 648-9 per Carrigan, Justice. See also *Clark v District Court*, 668 P.2d 3 (Colo. 1983), at 9 per Quinn, Justice; *In the Matter of a Grand Jury Investigation of Onondaga County*, 59 N.Y.2d 130 (1983), at 136 per Meyer, J.; *State v Boehme*, 430 P.2d 527 (Wash. 1967), at 533 per Hamilton, J.
[194] 947 P.2d 1290 (Wash.App.Div.1 1997), at 1292 per Coleman, J.
[195] 418 U.S. 683 (1974).

'The twofold aim of criminal justice is that guilt shall not escape or innocence suffer.' ... We have elected to employ an adversary system of criminal justice in which the parties contest all issues before a court of law. The need to develop all relevant facts in the adversary system is both fundamental and comprehensive. The ends of justice would be defeated if judgments were to be founded on a partial or speculative presentation of the facts. The very integrity of the judicial system and public confidence in it depend on full disclosure of all the facts within the framework of the rules of evidence. To ensure that justice is done, it is imperative to the function of the courts that compulsory process be available for the production of evidence needed either by the prosecution or by the defence.[196]

It can thus be seen that evidentiary privileges are regarded as diametrically opposed to the interests of justice which require unlimited disclosure of all evidence that may be relevant to the case, either from the point of view of the defence, or from the point of view of the prosecution. Sissela Bok suggested that in addition to the interests outlined in *Nixon*, the interests in social justice and restitution also have a role to play in the context of prosecuting past crimes.[197]

At State level, in the course of criminal proceedings, potential conflicts between the interest in medical confidentiality, on the one hand, and the state interest in criminal prosecution, on the other, are regulated by either the existence or the absence of privilege statutes. In States which do not recognise medical privilege, the State legislature has not expressed any view on how a conflict between the interests behind medical confidentiality and the countervailing interests in the context of criminal proceedings should be resolved. However, in the absence of privilege statutes, the courts assume that the legislature did not want to make an exception to the principle of the overriding importance of the state interest in the administration of justice, including the interest in criminal prosecution, so that physicians will have to testify about confidential patient information or submit the patient's medical records where this is relevant to the proceedings. The considerations weighing against a recognition of medical privilege were, for example, explained in *Hague v Williams*,[198] where the court argued that the policy to expose confidential medical information to view when it is relevant to the resolution of litigation is in accord with the general theory that society has a right to every citizen's testimony, and that privileges of exemption from this duty can only exceptionally be granted. It has already been discussed in the context of federal law that even where, absent a statutory privilege, courts are willing to protect confidential patient information in court based on the constitutional right to privacy, medical confidentiality will have to yield where the information is relevant and material, as the state has then advanced an overriding interest in

---

[196] Ibid., at 709 per Chief Justice Burger.
[197] At 131.
[198] 181 A.2d 345 (Sup. Ct. N.J. 1962), at 348 per Haneman, J.

disclosure.[199] In the absence of a privilege statute, constitutional protection of patient confidences thus only achieves that irrelevant or immaterial information need not be disclosed. Given the constitutional underpinning of privacy protection, it is surprising that the precedence of the interests of justice over medical confidentiality absent a privilege statute seems to be widely accepted.

Where a privilege statute exists, the legislature has decided the conflict in favour of non-disclosure. However, *State v Boehme*[200] seems to suggest that even where a statutory privilege is in existence, there is still some room to balance the interests behind the privilege against the interest in criminal prosecution, as:

> The privilege, however, should be fairly limited to its purpose. Absent the most cogent of reasons, it should not, by unrealistic or impractical application, become a means whereby criminal activities of third persons may be shielded from detection, prosecution, and punishment. ... To allow the privilege to thus become a device by which the victim of an attempted crime could, without a civically paramount reason, thwart the course of a criminal proceeding against the perpetrator might well promote greater evils than the privilege was designed to avoid. The maintenance of an orderly society, and the circumvention of criminal activities, are functions of government which should not be subject to casual suppression by the operation of a procedural rule primarily designed for the purpose of aiding the healing of physical ailments.

This decision suggests that some courts do not subscribe to the view that the existence of a privilege statute demonstrates that the general conflict between medical confidentiality and the interests of justice was decided in favour of medical confidentiality, excluding that medical confidentiality can be outweighed by the interests of justice. The court obviously thought that the results of such an interpretation of the privilege statute would be unacceptable. It was also argued that 'where confidentiality and privilege are concerned, the rule is that a potential wrongdoer will not be able to hide his deeds behind a physician-patient privilege: crime investigation trumps privilege and confidentiality'.[201] This construction, however, undermines the legislative intention behind privilege statutes. It is thus submitted that in States where privilege statutes are applicable in criminal proceedings, no balancing of the confidentiality interests with the interests in criminal prosecution should be permissible, unless the statute itself provides for an exception, for example for the prosecution of specific crimes such as homicide.[202]

---

[199] See, for example, *Fritsch v City of Chula Vista*, 187 F.R.D. 614 (S.D.Cal 1999), at 633 per Aaron, U.S. Magistrate J.; *U.S. v Sutherland*, 143 F.Supp.2d 609 (W.D.Va. 2001), at 611 per Jones, District J.; but see *U.S. v Burzynski Cancer Research Inst*, 819 F.2d 1301 (5th Cir. 1987), at 1311 per Rubin, Circuit J.

[200] 430 P.2d 527 (Wash. 1967), at 536 per Hamilton, J.; see also *Bryson v State*, 711 P.2d 932 (Okl. 1985), at 934 per Parks, Presiding J.

[201] Oppenheim, at 696.

[202] See also *In the Matter of a Grand Jury Investigation of Onondaga County*, 59 N.Y.2d 130 (1983), at 135-6 per Meyer, J.

(b) Grand Jury proceedings or Attorney General investigations   Given the special character of grand jury proceedings and of investigations by the attorney general, the question arises whether or not privilege is applicable in such proceedings. In *Branzburg v Hayes*,[203] the Supreme Court explained the function of the grand jury in federal proceedings and the consequences for the application of privileges:

> The grand jury ... has the dual function of determining if there is probable cause to believe that a crime has been committed and of protecting citizens against unfounded criminal prosecutions. Grand jury proceedings are constitutionally mandated for the institution of federal prosecutions for capital and other serious crimes (fifth amendment), and its constitutional prerogatives are rooted in long centuries of Anglo-American history. The adoption of the grand jury in the Constitution as the sole method for preferring charges in serious criminal cases shows the high place it held as an instrument of justice. Because its task is to inquire into the existence of possible criminal conduct and to return only well-founded indictments, its investigative powers are necessarily broad. Although the grand jury's powers are not unlimited and are subject to the supervision of a judge, the long-standing principle that the public has a right to every man's evidence except for those persons protected by a constitutional, common-law or statutory privilege is particularly applicable to grand jury proceedings.[204]

Thus, it seems that the interest in disclosure of all relevant information in grand jury proceedings is comparable to the interest in disclosure of all relevant information during a criminal trial. There are, however, differences between grand jury investigations and criminal trials, an important distinction being that information disclosed to the grand jury retains its confidential status and will not be further disclosed. It cannot, for example, be used in criminal court.

In *Chidester v Needles*,[205] the court held that a subpoena *duces tecum*, with which the attorney general demanded access to patients' records, did not violate medical privilege by forcing the physician 'indirectly' to testify, the reasons being that a subpoena *duces tecum* formed part of the county attorney general's investigatory power for use in lieu of a grand jury proceeding, that information thereby obtained could not be used to perpetuate testimony for trial, and that documents produced in response to a county attorney general's subpoena remained confidential unless and until a criminal charge was filed.[206] The court then performed a balancing exercise and came to the conclusion that:

> In weighing the patients' privacy interest against the State's interest in obtaining a thorough investigation, we are also mindful that the privacy interest is partially protected by Iowa Rule of Criminal Procedure 5(6). The records obtained pursuant to a county attorney's subpoena have a confidential status before any criminal charge is filed and may thereafter be kept confidential by court order. ... We conclude that the privacy interest of

---

[203] 408 U.S. 665 (1972).
[204] Ibid., at 686-8 per Justice White.
[205] 353 N.W.2d 849 (Iowa 1984).
[206] Ibid., at 852 per Wolle, Justice.

the clinic's patients must yield to the State's interest in well-founded criminal charges and the fair administration of criminal justice.[207]

The outcome in the specific case, that is that privilege was outweighed by the interest in disclosure, seems at least partly to rest on the assumption that the disclosure does not lead to the use of the information in court, and that the confidential character of the information would be upheld. As was explained in *U.S. v Bein*,[208]

> The danger in the use of privileged material is not that a tribunal may be misled or a party's litigation position unfairly prejudiced, since the reliability of the evidence is not in question. The fear is rather that valued relationships may be disrupted by an apprehension that confidential communications may be disclosed. Given the fact that grand jury proceedings are normally secret, that an authoritative adjudication as to whether material is privileged may have to await subsequent proceedings and that dismissal of an indictment is a most serious step, courts have declined to dismiss indictments because of the use of privileged matter before the grand jury. Such testimony of course is not permitted at trial.

The courts' attitude that privileged information should be available to the grand jury, given the confidentiality of the proceedings and the special role of the grand jury, is problematic, as the privileged information is then nevertheless disclosed to the investigating authority. Contrast the decision in *Re Grand Jury Subpoena*,[209] where the court held that:

> There is something undoubtedly unseeming about requiring psychotherapists to disclose the most intimate of their patient's thoughts and emotions, when such communications merely meet the broad relevancy requirements applicable to grand jury investigations.[210]

While most courts seem to favour unlimited disclosure of confidential patient information in the course of grand jury investigations, some courts thus seem to promote a different approach when suggesting a more stringent test as to whether or not the confidential information is, in fact, relevant to the proceedings. Some courts have decided that absent a statutory exception to that effect, the privilege applies to grand jury proceedings, so that grand jury subpoenas requiring the production of privileged records for *in camera* inspection violate the privilege statute and will be quashed.[211] Only this approach seems to respect the intention of the legislature expressed in the privilege statute that the privacy interests of the patient be given precedence over the investigation and prosecution of crime.

---

[207] Ibid., at 853-4.

[208] 728 F.2d 107 (2nd Cir. 1984), at 113 per Winter, Circuit J.

[209] 710 F.Supp. 999 (D.N.J. 1989).

[210] Ibid., at 1010-1011 per Gerry, Chief J.

[211] *In the Matter of a Grand Jury Investigation of Onondaga County*, 59 N.Y.2d 130 (1983), at 135-6 per Meyer, J.; *In the Matter of Grand Jury Investigation in New York County*, 731 N.Y.S.2d 17 (2001), at 287-8 per Edward McLaughlin, J.

(c) Search and seizure of medical records   When, in the course of criminal investigations, a suspicion arises that a patient's medical records may contain some relevant evidence, it must be determined to what extent the police, the attorney general or the grand jury may obtain access to these records, and to what extent they are protected by medical privilege. In principle, medical privilege not only excludes the physician as a witness in judicial proceedings, but also prevents the state from gaining access to medical records.[212] Thus, in States with a privilege statute medical records are exempt from state access according to the scope of the privilege statute and its interpretation by the courts. In the absence of privilege statutes, many courts will protect medical records from disclosure unless their materiality and relevance to the investigation or proceedings can be shown, as they are protected by the Fourteenth Amendment right to privacy.[213] What remains to be discussed is whether and to what extent the Fourth and the Fifth Amendment might award additional protection of medical records.

It has been explained above that the Fourth Amendment, rather than protecting the privacy interests of the individual as such, only protects individual privacy against certain kinds of governmental intrusion.[214] In the words of Chief Justice Lucas, in *Hill v National Collegiate Athletic*:[215]

> The Fourth Amendment does not proscribe all searches and seizures, but only those that are unreasonable. ... Under the Fourth Amendment ... the reasonableness of particular searches and seizures is determined by a general balancing test 'weighing the gravity of the governmental interest or public concern served and the degree to which the [challenged government conduct] advances that concern against the intrusiveness of the interference with individual liberty'.

Case-law that has developed mainly in the area of the attorney-client relationship, the confidentiality of which is regarded as even more worthy of protection than that of the physician-patient privilege, suggests that searches of law offices, and therefore probably also searches of surgeries or hospitals, as such are not unreasonable under Fourth Amendment standards.[216] In *U.S. v Burzynski Cancer Research Institute*,[217] an action was brought against a physician and a research

---

[212] See, for example, Art.510 A (8)(b) of the Louisiana Code of Evidence; Rhode Island St §9-17-24; *Behringer Estate v Princeton Medical Center*, 592 A.2d 1251 (N.J.Super. 1991), at 1268 per Carchman, J.S.C.; *Comonwealth v Kobrin*, 479 N.E.2d 674 (Mass. 1986), at 680 per Abrams, J.

[213] See, for example, *Fritsch v City of Chula Vista*, 187 F.R.D. 614 (S.D.Cal 1999), at 633 per Aaron, U.S. Magistrate J.; *U.S. v Sutherland*, 143 F.Supp.2d 609 (W.D.Va. 2001), at 611 per Jones, District J.; but see *U.S. v Burzynski Cancer Research Inst*, 819 F.2d 1301 (5th Cir. 1987), at 1311 per Rubin, Circuit J.

[214] *Katz v U.S.*, 389 U.S. 347 (1967), at 350 per Justice Steward. See also supra, part 1. 1.2.

[215] 865 P.2d 633 (Cal. 1994), at 650.

[216] *Klitzman, Klitzman and Gallagher v Krut*, 744 F.2d 955 (3rd Cir. 1984), at 959 per Aldisert, Chief J.; *In Re Impounded Case (Law Firm)*, 840 F.2d 196 (3rd Cir. 1988), at 202 per Seitz, Circuit J.

[217] 819 F.2d 1301 (5th Cir. 1987), at 1310 per Rubin, Circuit J.

centre seeking to enjoin them from violating Federal Food and Drug Regulations, and a criminal search warrant was executed. Some patients, whose treatment records had been seized, alleged a breach of their Fourth Amendment rights, claiming that the seizure had invaded their right to privacy. The court rejected this argument on the grounds that a seizure of documents that was authorised by a warrant can never amount to an unconstitutional invasion of privacy, since a warrant issued upon prior review by a neutral and detached magistrate was the time-tested means of effectuating Fourth Amendment rights. And in *Re search warrant B-21778*,[218] a case of a law office search, the court held that there are no privileged isles beyond the reaches of a properly predicated search warrant, and that anywhere and everywhere within the limits of a court's jurisdiction may be searched, so that the fact that the warrant was directed at a law office did not make the search unreasonable. However, those courts that have allowed the search of law offices or surgeries have held that while the Fourth Amendment does not prohibit searches of such places, privileged information is exempt from seizure.[219] Other courts have argued that privilege is sufficiently protected by the procedure requiring that the government obtain leave of the court before examining any seized items, which gives the parties the possibility to assert privilege.[220] Some courts and legal writers argue that rather than issuing a search warrant to search law firms or surgeries, a less intrusive means to obtain the material sought would be the issuance of a subpoena *duces tecum*. As the argument goes, even the most particular warrant cannot adequately safeguard client confidentiality. In *O'Connor v Johnson*,[221] the court came to the conclusion that:

> Though this may be seen as limiting the ability of the police to obtain information in the early stage of the investigation, we find this measure necessary to protect the overriding interest of our society in preserving the attorney-client privilege. ... Moreover, our decision rests not only on the fourth amendment, but also on Art. I S.10 of the Minn Constitution. We hold that a warrant authorising the search of an attorney's office is unreasonable and, therefore, invalid when the attorney is not suspected of criminal wrongdoing and there is no threat that the documents sought will be destroyed.

The subpoena is less intrusive than a search warrant and a means to protect privileged information, as it enables the physician to gather and produce requested documents, thereby eliminating the threat that law enforcement officials will examine and possibly seize privileged documents in the course of a search authorised by a warrant.[222] Moreover, before producing the evidence the physician may obtain a judicial ruling on the applicability of any relevant privilege by filing a

---

[218] 513 Pa 429 (1987), at 439-40 per McDermott, Justice.

[219] Ibid., at 440; see also Cissell, at 476.

[220] *In Re Impounded Case (Law Firm)*, 840 F.2d 196 (3rd Cir. 1988), at 202 per Seitz, Circuit J.

[221] 287 N.W.2d 400 (Minn. 1979), at 405 per Wahl, Justice.

[222] Bloom, at 26.

motion to quash.[223] The subpoena preference rule is therefore the best practicable accommodation of the legitimate needs of law enforcement, on the one hand, and the important values of privileged relationships, on the other.[224] It can be seen that the Fourth Amendment as interpreted by most courts does not award much protection against state access to privileged records. Indeed, medical records receive additional protection only where the Fourth Amendment is interpreted as requiring the subpoena preference rule.

It remains to examine whether the Fifth Amendment adds anything to the protection of medical records from search and seizure. The protection of confidential medical information under the Fifth Amendment is rather limited, as the Fifth Amendment protects against self-incrimination by having to produce evidence against oneself, rather than guaranteeing respect for the confidential content of documents.[225] As the Supreme Court made clear in *Andresen v Maryland*,[226] information is not exempt from seizure in the hands of the patient simply because the contents are private and confidential. Therefore, confidential medical documents will only be protected from search and seizure where, in addition to their confidential content, they will incriminate the patient, and even then only if they were not voluntarily created. In the hand of the physician, patient records are only protected insofar as they would have been protected by the Fifth Amendment while in the hand of the patient.[227] Given the very narrow scope of Fifth Amendment protection, it is therefore unlikely that the seizure of medical records will violate the patient's Fifth Amendment rights, and the Fifth Amendment does not seem to add much to the protection of medical records under privilege statutes.

As this analysis shows, the true protection of privileged material in the course of searches of surgeries stems from privilege statutes, not from constitutional principles, so that in States without a privilege statute, medical records are far less protected than in States in which privilege statutes apply. Constitutional protection is thus of rather limited practical effect in these cases.

---

[223] *Matter of Witnesses before Sp. March 1980 Gr. Jury*, 729 F.2d 489 (7th Cir. 1984), at 495 per Cudahy, Circuit J.

[224] Bloom, at 54; Mogill, at 354; but see *Zurcher v Stanford Daily*, 436 U.S. 547 (1978), where the Supreme Court declined to hold that the Fourth Amendment imposed a general constitutional subpoena preference rule.

[225] See *Fisher v U.S.*, 425 U.S. 391 (1976), at 397-9 per Justice White; *U.S. v Doe*, 465 U.S. 605 (1983), at 612 per Justice Powell; *In re: Grand Jury Subpoenas*, 144 F.3d 653 (10th Cir. 1998), at 663 per Stephen H. Anderson, Circuit J. See also supra, part 1, 1.1.

[226] 427 U.S. 463 (1976), at 473-6 per Justice Blackmun; see also *Fisher v U.S.*, 425 U.S. 391 (1976), at 402-4 per Justice White.

[227] *In re: Grand Jury Subpoenas*, 144 F.3d 653 (10th Cir. 1998), at 663 per Stephen H. Anderson, Circuit J.; Camp, Levey, at 4-10 to 4-11.

2.2.3 A special problem: child abuse

All States have some form of exception from medical and/or psychotherapist-patient privilege with regard to child abuse.[228] Some have argued that these exceptions show the willingness of legislatures to sacrifice confidentiality for the administration of justice where the crime is outrageous to society,[229] an opinion which seems to suggest that in the particular situation of child abuse the state interest in the prosecution of the offender outweighs the interest in medical confidentiality. Some courts, however, argued differently. In *State v Sypult*,[230] for example, the court argued that 'the central purpose of the child abuse reporting statutes is the protection of children, not the punishment of those who mistreat them', and concluded that child abuse exceptions to a privilege statute must be narrowly construed so that the purpose of the reporting statute may be achieved, while the benefits resulting when those who maltreat children seek confidential therapy programmes are maintained. According to this view, the protection of children from abuse, rather than the prosecution of the offender seems to be the main consideration behind such an exception to medical privilege. In *Pesce v J. Sterling Morton High Sch. Dist. 201*,[231] a case in which a school psychologist was punished for not reporting suspected child abuse of which he learned in the course of confidential communication with a pupil, the court also focused on the element of child protection when arguing that:

> Even if there is here a federal right to confidentiality that can be infringed only to further a compelling state interest, we conclude that such an interest is present in the present circumstances. Of critical importance here is the fact that the state is acting to protect one of the most pitiable and helpless classes in society - abused children. The Supreme Court has recognised the substantial interest of a state in protecting all children.

According to this case, it is obviously the protection of the child at risk of further abuse that is the main reason behind the exception from the obligation to maintain confidentiality, not the interest in prosecuting the offender. The difference in opinion as to the purpose behind the child abuse exceptions is significant, as it may be decisive when courts have to determine whether or not disclosure will be ordered in a given case. If the purpose behind the exception is the interest in protecting the child, then disclosure will be limited to those persons and institutions that will help to prevent further abuse, but disclosure will then normally not be justified in the course of criminal investigations or proceedings against the offender. However, in some States, the privilege statutes provide for an exemption from the privilege for the purposes of testifying in court about child abuse.[232] It can then not be maintained that the child abuse exception merely serves

---

[228] See, for example, Conn. St §52-1460(a)(4); Id St §9-203(4)(A); Il St Ch §5/8-802(7); Wi St 905.04(4)(e).

[229] Domb, at 236.

[230] 304 Ark. 5 (1990).

[231] 830 F.2d 789 (7th Cir. 1987), at 797-8 per Cudahy, Circuit J.

[232] Id St §9-203(4)(A); Il St Ch §5/8-802(7).

the purpose of child protection without at the same time aiming at the prosecution of the offender.

2.2.4 A special problem: drunk driving

In some States, there is no privilege in drunk-driving cases. This is partly due to statutory exceptions to the privilege, partly a creation of case-law. In *State v Dyal*,[233] for example, the court held that in a matter so deeply imbued with the public interest as a case involving a suspected drunken driver, the investigating police should not be deprived of blood test results merely because they had been made for treatment purposes and were thus privileged. As those results were not only relevant, but highly persuasive in determining whether the driver was drunk, and as the patient's interest in the confidentiality of hospital records can be protected adequately by requiring the investigating police to establish a reasonable basis to believe that the operator was intoxicated, medical confidentiality was said to be outweighed by the public interest. Similarly, in *State v Dress*,[234] the court recognised that the privilege was premised on the calculation that the benefits to the protected relationship outweigh burdens thereby imposed, and that the privilege must yield when the public interest outweighs the policy supporting the privilege. This, according to the court, was the case in the context of a prosecution for the offence of driving while intoxicated. As the physician attending a defendant is frequently the sole or most competent source of very relevant evidence, to allow the privilege in such cases would be against the public interest, given that the offence of driving while intoxicated has a great potential for serious injury or death, so that the public interest in prosecuting such offenders is regarded as compelling. This argument seems anomalous in the light of the fact that in many States, not even the prosecution of serious crimes such as murder gives rise to an exception to the privilege. The exception seems to be justified by the specific difficulties in prosecuting drunk-driving offences without resort to medical evidence, rather than by the seriousness of the offence. However, the same would apply to other offences such as sexual offences. The danger to society as a whole by drunk-driving which is thought to surpass the danger of other, more serious offences that mainly affect certain individuals, seems another important consideration behind this exception. The drunk-driving exception to medical privilege seems to rest mainly on utilitarian considerations, taking account of the particularly high costs of a privilege in this context. However, the far-reaching powers under implied consent provisions[235] to order blood tests where a driver is suspected of being intoxicated should be sufficient to satisfy the need to secure evidence against the suspect. An invasion in the privileged physician-patient relationship seems therefore unnecessary, but also unjustified, as this would circumvent the legislative decisions to be found in the implied consent and privilege statutes.

---

[233] 97 N.J. 229 (1984), at 238-9 per Pollock, J.
[234] 461 N.E.2d 1312 (Ohio App 1982), at 1316-7 per Wiley, J (overruled by *State v. Smorgala*, 553 N.E.2d 672 (Ohio 1990)).
[235] See, for example, Ar St § 5-65-202.

2.2.5 Investigations against the physician

Another group of cases in which confidentiality problems frequently arise is that of criminal investigations against a physician or proceedings in which a physician is accused of having committed criminal offences in the context of his/her work. This often concerns cases of fraud against health insurance companies, for example where a physician is accused of having claimed fees for treatment he/she did not administer, or cases in which the physician is accused of prescribing controlled substances for improper and illegal purposes. Different courts have adopted different approaches to tackle this problem. Several courts have made an exception to the application of medical privilege in such cases. The special dilemma the prosecution is facing in these cases was, for example, explained in *State v McGriff*:[236]

> The defendant doctor should not be permitted to invoke his patient's privilege in order to shield himself from prosecution. ... Since the defendant has been accused of prescribing controlled substances for improper and illegal purposes and of committing fraud against various health insurance companies, if there is evidence of wrongdoing it will be contained in notations to his patients' medical records. Without these records, the state will be unable to prosecute its case.

Given the difficulties in investigating and prosecuting such offences, in *Re Search Warrant*,[237] Becker, Circuit J., held that in the case of the investigation of a physician for fraud, the legitimate interests of the state in securing information contained in patient records outweighed the patient's privacy rights, as only the patient's medical records could reveal whether the physician had performed the specified services at the specified time and whether the services were medically necessary. The court thus seemed driven by consequentialist arguments, as it was felt that without this exception to medical privilege, the physician could safely commit criminal offences under the veil of his/her patient's confidentiality rights, thereby posing a danger to society and potentially to public health.[238] It has further been argued that the patient's privacy interests can widely be respected in the course of such investigations, as the relevant and incriminating information, if any, contained in the patient records would be disclosed only to the extent needed to prosecute the defendant. Redaction of the records through erasure or concealment of patients' names and addresses and other information inapplicable to the prosecution of the charged crimes would ensure that each patient's interest in confidentiality and privacy was protected without frustrating the state's interest in prosecuting illegal drug activity.[239] In *Commonwealth v Kobrin*,[240] the court also

---

[236] 672 N.E.2d 1074 (Ohio App. 3 Dist. 1996), at 1075 per Evans, J.

[237] 810 F.2d 65 (3rd Cir. 1987), at 72-3.

[238] *Patients of Dr. Solomon v Board of Physician Quality Assurance*, 85 F.Supp.2d 545 (D.Md. 1999), at 548 per Joseph H. Young, Senior District J.

[239] *State v McGriff*, 672 N.E.2d 1074 (Ohio App. 3 Dist. 1996), at 1075 per Evans, J.; *Schachter v Whalen*, 581 F.2d 35 (2nd Cir. 1978), at 37 per Oakes, Blumenfeld, and Mehrtens.

argued that patient confidentiality should be upheld as much as possible and distinguished between those portions of a psychiatrist's records that recite 'the patient's most intimate thoughts and emotions, as well as descriptions of conduct that may be embarrassing or illegal', as it was difficult to see how this could be helpful to a determination of whether the psychiatrist had in fact furnished a reimbursable service, while the State could properly request that a psychiatrist submit those portions of his/her records documenting the times and lengths of patient appointments, fees, patient diagnoses, treatment plans and recommendations, and somatic therapies. The court summarised its views as follows:

> Those portions of the records, however, which reflect patient's thoughts, feelings, and impressions, or contain the substance of the psychotherapeutic dialogue are protected and need not be produced. ... In sum, a judge confronting the competing demands of the right to privacy ... and the need to supervise the disbursement of Medicaid payments for psychiatric services shall review the psychiatrist's records. Excerpts of those records which reveal that a patient with a given diagnosis saw the psychiatrist on a certain date for a certain length shall be released. The psychiatrist's observations of objective induce of emotional disturbance may be released. Notations of patient prescriptions, blood tests and their results (e.g. lithium carbonate levels), or the administration of electroconvulsive treatment shall be released. Indications of treatment plans (e.g. a recommendation of continuing psychotherapy or of medication) shall be released. The psychiatrist's records of patient conversations shall be withheld.[241]

This distinction seems problematic, as only the patient's expressed thoughts and feelings are protected, but neither the diagnosis nor any other facts related to the treatment which may be highly confidential and which are protected under most privilege statutes, receive protection. In *Hawaii Psychiatric Soc. Dist. Branch v Ariyoshi*,[242] the court tried a different approach by stating that the mere existence of a valid 'public interest' would not be sufficient to justify an intrusion on the patient's privacy for the purpose of a fraud investigation against the physician. Instead, the court required some showing of an 'individualised, articulable suspicion' before access to a psychiatrist's confidential medical records could be had. And in *State v McGriff*,[243] Thomas F. Bryant, J., criticised the approach of placing the state interest in prosecuting the physician above the interest in patient confidentiality. In his view:

> If a patient does not waive the physician-patient privilege, his or her physician may not disclose any privileged communications made during that relationship, subject of course to any statutory exceptions. ... The state suggests that the purpose of the physician-patient privilege statute can be achieved by redacting the patient's medical records to delete information that might identify the patients. I deem this suggestion unworkable and an

[240] 479 N.E.2d 674 (Mass. 1986).

[241] Ibid., at 681-2 per Abrams, Justice.

[242] 481 F.Supp. 1028 (D. Hawaii 1979), at 1047 and 1050 per Byrne, District J.

[243] 672 N.E.2d 1074 (Ohio App. 3 Dist. 1996), at 1078-81; see also Mogill, at 351 for the case of the attorney-client privilege.

invasion of the privilege as well as a blatant attempt to circumvent the application of the statute. To allow the state to delete any identifying information contained in these patients' medical records would necessarily breach the physician-patient privilege without authority to do so. At least one person ... and more likely three persons ... if not more, would have to examine the contents of each patient's medical record to determine what is to be deleted and what is to be shown as evidence. Further, any information not deleted and subsequently used at trial by the state is still information protected by the privilege. ... It is my view that current Ohio law requires that if the state seeks to use the medical records of a non-party patient in order to prosecute that patient's physician, the state must first obtain a waiver of the privilege by that patient.

This approach seems more in line with the purpose behind privilege statutes. While it is conceded that without access to patient records, it will often be impossible to investigate any fraud allegations against the physician, it must nevertheless be respected that in States with privilege statutes that do not contain any exception for such a situation, the legislature seems to have been of the opinion that the privilege should prevail over the state interest in the prosecution of crime. The patient's interests in the confidentiality of his/her medical records is not diminished by the fact that the physician abused the professional relationship. In case of conflict, therefore, the patient's interests should prevail and access to patient records only be allowed with the patient's consent.

2.2.6 Conflicting defence rights

Another conflict frequently arising is that between medical confidentiality, on the one hand, and defence rights of an accused, on the other. Different scenarios are possible for this conflict to occur. It is possible that the prosecution is based on privileged evidence which it may want to withhold from the defendant on the grounds of privilege. If that is the case, the defence is obviously affected, as the accused then does not know against what evidence he/she has to defend him/herself. It is also possible that the defendant wants to resort to privileged evidence either to cast some doubt on the credibility of a prosecution witness, or to prove his/her innocence.

Certain rights of a criminal defendant are guaranteed by the U.S. Constitution. The main constitutional principles discussed in this context are the Confrontation Clause and the Compulsory Process Clause, both contained in the Sixth Amendment to the U.S. Constitution, and the Due Process Clause of the Fourteenth Amendment. The scope of these constitutional principles will be briefly introduced, and the question of the disclosure of privileged information upon request of a defendant in criminal proceedings will then be discussed in some detail.

(a) Confrontation The Confrontation Clause of the Sixth Amendment guarantees every criminal defendant the right physically to face those who testify against him/her, and the right to conduct cross-examination. A violation of these rights is

often alleged in cases in which privilege is asserted. *Pennsylvania v Ritchie*,[244] though not dealing with the specific problem of medical confidentiality, but with that of privilege in child abuse cases, provides a good example of the conflict that frequently materialises. The respondent in that case was charged with various sexual offences against his minor daughter. During pre-trial discovery, the respondent served the CYS (Children and Youth Services) that had investigated the allegations and had conducted interviews with the victim, with a subpoena, seeking access to the records related to the immediate charges, as well as to certain earlier records compiled when CYS had investigated a separate report that the respondent's children were being abused. CYS refused to comply with the subpoena, claiming that the records were privileged under a Pennsylvania statute providing that all CYS records must be kept confidential, subject to specified exceptions, and the trial court confirmed this view. The respondent claimed that by denying him access to the information which he needed to prepare his defence, the trial court had interfered with his right of cross-examination and thereby violated his rights under the Confrontation Clause. It was thus not alleged that a witness was not available because of a privilege, but rather that pre-trial access to certain information was barred, information which the defence thought might have been useful for cross-examination purposes. The Pennsylvania Supreme Court reversed the trial court's decision based on the U.S. Supreme Court's holding in *Davis v Alaska*.[245] In that case, the Supreme Court had had to decide whether or not the confidentiality of juvenile records had the effect that a defendant could not cross-examine a prosecution witness as to the fact that he had such a record. The Supreme Court had argued that:

> Serious damage to the strength of the State's case would have been a real possibility had petitioner been allowed to pursue this inquiry. In this setting we conclude that the right of confrontation is paramount to the State's policy of protecting a juvenile offender. Whatever temporary embarrassment might result to Green or his family by disclosure of his juvenile record - if the prosecution insisted on using him to make its case - is outweighed by petitioner's right to probe into the influence of possible bias in the testimony of a crucial identification witness. ... The State's policy interest in protecting the confidentiality of a juvenile offender's record cannot require yielding of so vital a constitutional right as the effective cross-examination for bias of an adverse witness.[246]

According to the Pennsylvania Supreme Court, it followed from *Davis* that a statutory privilege cannot be maintained when a defendant asserts a need, prior to trial, for the protected information to be used at trial to impeach or otherwise undermine a witness' testimony. The U.S. Supreme Court decided *Ritchie* on due process grounds, but the lead opinion concerning the application of the Confrontation Clause has proved highly influential and shall therefore be introduced. It rejected the Pennsylvania Supreme Court's interpretation of *Davis* by holding that:

---

[244] 480 U.S. 39 (1987).
[245] 415 U.S. 308 (1974).
[246] Ibid., at 319-20 per Justice Burger.

Ritchie argues that the failure to disclose information that might have made cross-examination more effective undermines the accuracy of the truth-finding process at trial. ... If we were to accept this broad interpretation of *Davis*, the effect would be to transform the Confrontation Clause into a constitutionally compelled rule of pre-trial discovery.[247]

While the Court confirmed that the right to cross-examination includes the opportunity to show that a witness is biased, or that the testimony is exaggerated or unbelievable, the Court nevertheless argued that:

The right to confrontation is a trial right, designed to prevent improper restrictions on the types of questions that defence counsel may ask during cross-examination. ... The ability to question adverse witnesses, however, does not include the power to require the pre-trial disclosure of any and all information that might be useful in contradicting unfavourable testimony.[248]

It followed, therefore, that the Confrontation Clause was not violated by the withholding of the CYS file, and that it would only have been impermissible for the judge to have prevented Ritchie's lawyer from cross-examining the witness.[249]

In *U.S. v Haworth*,[250] a case in which the defendants sought discovery of records of the psychotherapist who had examined the witness, the court, after a motion for pre-trial production of these records was granted and *in camera* review was held, similarly argued that defendants who equate their confrontation rights with a right to discover information that is clearly privileged are mistaken, as their confrontation rights permit them to cross-examine the witness fully regarding his/her treatment by the psychotherapist, but will not guarantee access to the psychotherapist's records.

Even where the defendant contends a violation of the Confrontation Clause because the right to cross-examination is restricted at trial, it is not at all clear that the courts will find a violation of the Sixth Amendment. In *Mills v Singletary*,[251] for example, a case in which a violation of confrontation rights under the Sixth Amendment was contended, as the trial court had allowed Ashley, a witness, to invoke the attorney-client privilege and had accordingly curtailed Ashley's cross-examination, the court rejected this allegation based on the following considerations:

During cross-examination of Ashley, Mills' lawyer induced Ashley to admit that: (1) he changed his story of the events surrounding the murder, thereby implicating Mills, after Florida offered him a deal and deciding that 'there was a chance of me getting out and starting a new life'; and (2) the deal that Florida offered Ashley gave him complete immunity from prosecution in the burglary and murder charges in exchange for his

---

[247] *Pennsylvania v Ritchie*, 480 U.S. 39 (1987), at 52 per Justice Powell.

[248] Ibid., at 52-3.

[249] See also *People v Hammon*, 65 Cal.Rptr.2d 1 (Cal. 1997), at 6-7 per Werdegar, Justice.

[250] 168 F.R.D. 660 (D.N.M. 1996), at 661-2 per Hansen, District J.

[251] 161 F.3d 1273 (11th Cir. 1998).

testimony against Mills. We hold that this cross-examination exposed Ashley's prior inconsistent statements and bargain with Florida to the extent that the jury could judge his credibility and Mills could argue effectively that Ashley's testimony was not credible. Mills' lawyer engaged in sufficient cross-examination, and the trial judge neither abused his discretion nor violated the Confrontation Clause in limiting the cross-examination to that which the attorney-client privilege did not protect.[252]

The court's approach mainly seems to depend on the question of whether or not *effective* cross-examination will be possible without touching upon privileged information. Where, as in *Mills v Singletary*, effective cross-examination is not excluded by the restriction of cross-examination to unprivileged information, the defendant's confrontation rights are not violated. In the context of the physician-patient or psychotherapist-patient privilege, some courts have confirmed the view that the mere fact that access to a witness' medical records is denied does not impair a defendant's ability to cross-examine as long as the defendant is not restricted in cross-examination and is able to put before the jury the psychological and behaviour problems, drug and alcohol abuse, and hospitalisation of the witness.[253]

(b) Compulsory process and due process   Another allegation frequently made by defendants who have been denied access to privileged information is that the Compulsory Process Clause of the Sixth Amendment or the Due Process Clause of the Fourteenth Amendment were violated thereby. Under the Compulsory Process Clause, criminal defendants have the right to the government's assistance in compelling the attendance of favourable witnesses at trial and the right to put before a jury evidence that might influence the determination of guilt. The information here is sought either for the purpose of identifying potential witnesses, or for the purpose of its presentation to the jury as part of the defence. The Due Process Clause guarantees a general right to a fair trial. In *Pennsylvania v Ritchie*,[254] the U.S. Supreme Court left open whether and how the guarantees of the Compulsory Process Clause differ from the Due Process Clause and analysed the problem at issue with reference to due process considerations. The Court held that it was well settled that the government has the obligation to turn over evidence in its possession that is both favourable to the accused and material to guilt or punishment.

(c) Disclosure of information for defence purposes   Access to privileged information that is material to the defence, either because it is exculpatory, or because it is necessary for an effective cross-examination, might be constitutionally required. This raises several questions. Should, as proposed in *Ritchie*, a distinction be made between pre-trial discovery and discovery at trial

---

[252] Ibid., at 1288-9 per Curiam.
[253] *U.S. v Skorniak*, 59 F.3d 750 (8th Cir. 1995), at 756 per Hansen, Circuit J.; see also *State v Hanninen*, 533 N.W. 2d 660 (Minn.App. 1995), at 661-2 per Amundson, J.
[254] 480 U.S. 39 (1987).

stage, and between discovery for confrontation purposes or discovery in order to find exculpatory information? And how can the materiality of privileged information be determined prior to its disclosure? Given that two constitutional rights, the right to privacy in one's medical information, on the one hand, and defence rights, on the other, are in conflict with each other, can they be reconciled in a less intrusive way than by disclosure of the material information to the defendant? As in other contexts, the courts have suggested a variety of different solutions to these problems.

The question of pre-trial discovery of privileged information mainly seems to have come up in the context of the psychotherapist-patient privilege. In most cases, pre-trial access to these records was sought on a combination of confrontation and due process grounds by arguing that the records contained information material both for an effective cross-examination of the witness at trial and for the defendant's exculpation, for example by shedding serious doubts on the patient's version of the events which led to the criminal charges against the defendant. The question then arises whether pre-trial discovery should be ordered to protect the defendant's interests, or whether these interests are outweighed by the patient's right to confidentiality. In cases that concern psychiatric records, the principle developed in *Jaffee*[255] that with regard to the psychotherapist-patient privilege, no balancing should be performed on the grounds that the privileged information is relevant in judicial proceedings, might also have a role to play. In *U.S. v Paredes*,[256] a decision was made in favour of pre-trial discovery of a witness' psychological records. In that case, the decision was rendered when the court had already performed an *in camera* inspection of those records. It was held that even though disclosure might be embarrassing to the witness, the defendant's opportunity to cross examine the witness regarding her psychological condition might prove important for an assessment of her credibility, and that his confrontation rights outweighed the interest in confidentiality. The impact of the Supreme Court's decision in *Jaffee* was not discussed. In *U.S. v Alperin*,[257] a California court decided that where a defendant sought pre-trial access to the victim's psychiatric records in order to support his claim of self-defence, a balancing needs to be performed, and came to the conclusion that the victim's strong interest in keeping communications with her psychiatrist confidential was outweighed by the potential evidentiary benefits and the materiality of those records to the defence. Therefore, an *in camera* review of the records was mandated. Interestingly, the court argued that the holding in *Jaffee* did not stand in the way of this conclusion:

> Since an important reason for the Supreme Court's rejection of the balancing test approach in *Jaffee* was concern that patients would not confide in psychotherapists if they thought the information might be disclosed, that reason does not apply in California where the

---

[255] 518 U.S. 1 (1996), at 17-18 per Justice Stevens.
[256] (S.D.N.Y. 2001), per Leisure J.
[257] 128 F.Supp.2d 1251 (N.D.Cal. 2001).

patient would expect from the outset that certain kinds of communications ... are subject to disclosure under appropriate circumstances.[258]

This interpretation of *Jaffee* is rather surprising. In *Jaffee*, the Supreme Court suggested that strict respect for the confidentiality of the psychotherapist-patient relationship was essential to achieve various important goals, and rejected a balancing exercise on the grounds that it would make the privilege unpredictable and therefore inefficient. Under *U.S. v Alperin*, the patient is in exactly the position he/she would be in if the balancing exercise rejected by the Supreme Court were allowed, as the fact that the privilege is 'subject to disclosure under appropriate circumstances' is no more than saying in a different way that, on balance, it can be outweighed by overriding interests. This does not give the psychiatrist-patient relationship the protection required by *Jaffee*. However, *Jaffee* could be distinguished on the basis that it concerned pre-trial discovery in a civil and civil rights action, so that it did not envisage a conflict between the confidentiality of the psychotherapist-patient privilege and defence rights.

In *Goldsmith v State*,[259] the court extended the holding in *Ritchie*[260] that the Confrontation Clause does not award a constitutional right to pre-trial discovery, to a general principle that there is no right to pre-trial discovery of privileged information, whether on confrontation, compulsory process or due process grounds. This argument is based on the consideration that before trial, the court will usually not have sufficient information to conduct a balancing between the defendant's confrontation and the patient's privacy rights. Indeed, before the trial starts, it will often not be obvious which information might be relevant and material for a potential cross-examination or which information might be exculpatory. Therefore, the interest in pre-trial discovery of information the materiality of which is not ascertainable cannot outweigh the interest in upholding the privilege.[261] If the exclusion of pre-trial discovery of privileged information is thus based on the fact that a balancing cannot adequately be performed prior to trial, rather than on the holding in *Jaffee* that it should be excluded in cases concerning the psychotherapist-patient privilege, it equally applies to the pre-trial disclosure of information which is protected by a physician-patient privilege.

The situation is different when discovery, either for confrontation or due process reasons, is sought at the trial stage. Most courts will then hold that, in principle, defence rights are of overriding importance. Thus, in *People v Adamski*,[262] where the defendant was convicted for sexual intercourse with his daughter and where the defendant's claim for privileged statements the victim had made to her counsellor had been denied, the court held that the complainant's prior inconsistent statements to her counsellor were admissible for impeachment despite the bar of the statutory

---

[258] Ibid., at 1254-5 per Zimmermann, U.S. Magistrate J.
[259] 651 A.2d 866 (Md 1995), at 874-5 per Chasanow, J.
[260] *Pennsylvania v Ritchie*, 480 U.S. 39 (1987).
[261] *People v Hammon*, 65 Cal.Rptr.2d 1 (Cal. 1997), at 6-7 per Werdegar, Justice.
[262] 497 N.W.2d 546 (Mich.App. 1993).

privilege, and that the failure of the trial court to allow the defendant to cross-examine the complainant with regard to her statement that the defendant had not acted inappropriately with her, denied the defendant his Sixth Amendment right of confrontation by limiting cross-examination. With regard to the apparent conflict between the right to privilege and the right of cross-examination, the court held that:

> It appears well settled as a matter of constitutional law that common-law or statutory privileges, even if purportedly absolute, may give way when in conflict with the constitutional right of cross-examination. ... The right of cross-examination is not without limit; neither the Confrontation Clause nor due process confers an unlimited right to admit all relevant evidence or cross-examine on any subject. ... Privileges impede the defendant's ability to present a defence by limiting the evidence available. Both this Court and our Supreme Court have not been hesitant to hold that confidential or privileged information must be disclosed where a defendant's right to effective cross-examination would otherwise be denied. ... In the present case, we recognise the important policy underlying the statutory psychologist-patient privilege ... . Weighing against this policy is defendant's interest in his liberty and receiving a fair trial. On its face, the privilege poses an absolute bar to the use of the complainant's statements for impeachment. ... We believe that the statute must yield to defendant's constitutional right of confrontation.[263]

In *Re Doe*,[264] the court equally held that:

> Although appellant's psychiatric files contain material that squarely implicates his privacy interests, the balance in this case weighs overwhelmingly in favour of allowing an inquiry into his history of mental illness. Appellant is not only the person who initiated the criminal investigation against Diamond, but also a witness whose credibility will be the central issue at trial. ... We agree ... that a preclusion of any inquiry into appellant's psychiatric history would violate the Confrontation Clause and vitiate any resulting conviction of Diamond.[265]

Thus, while the Confrontation Clause does not guarantee unlimited access to privileged information merely because this information may be relevant, the interest in medical confidentiality is outweighed where without this information, effective cross-examination is not possible, the reason being that the defendant's interests at stake, i.e. the interest in liberty and in receiving a fair trial, are regarded as more important than the interest in medical confidentiality. This view was also confirmed in *United States v Lindstrom*,[266] where the court held that the interests behind the protection of medical confidentiality could not outweigh the defendant's right to examine and use the psychiatric information contained in the witness' medical files to attack the credibility of a key government witness. The court argued that the desire to spare a witness embarrassment which disclosure of medical records might entail was insufficient justification for withholding such

---

[263] Ibid., at 549-50 per Wahls, Presiding J.
[264] 964 F.2d 1325 (2nd Cir. 1992).
[265] Ibid., at 1329 per Winter, Circuit J.
[266] 698 F.2d 1154 (11th Cir. 1983), at 1167 per Vance, Circuit J.

records from criminal defendants on trial for their liberty. Thus, the defendant's right to present evidence and to cross-examine witnesses may in some cases outweigh a privilege, but only where the probative value of the privileged evidence was considered and found sufficient,[267] and where without disclosure, important interests of the defendant would be impaired.

Even those courts that reject a pre-trial discovery of privileged information come to a different conclusion if the privileged information is sought at trial. In *People v Hammon*[268] where the court had rejected any balancing in the pre-trial setting, the court stressed that its holding was not intended to address the application of these principles to the trial stage, and that when a defendant proposes to impeach a witness with questions referring to privileged information, the trial court might have to balance the defendant's need for cross-examination against the interests behind the privilege. In *U.S. v Haworth*,[269] the court precluded the discovery of the psychotherapist's records, but emphasised that the defendant's confrontation right permitted him to cross-examine the patient during trial. It thus seems that even in the aftermath of *Jaffee*, a balancing of interests will be performed at trial stage where the right to cross-examination conflicts with confidentiality rights, and that the right to an effective cross-examination under the Confrontation Clause is regarded as paramount.

The same conclusion has been reached with regard to the conflict between confidentiality and due process rights. In *State v Knutson*,[270] for example, the court held that the analysis of a discovery issue should start from the premise that due process affords a criminal defendant a right of access to evidence that is both favourable to the accused and material to guilt and punishment, if there is a reasonable probability that, had the evidence been disclosed to the defence, the result of the proceeding would have been different. And in *State Ex Rel. Romley v Superior Court*,[271] the court held that due process of law was the primary and indispensable foundation of individual freedom, and in the case of conflict between due process rights of the accused and the rights of the victim, due process was the superior right. Therefore, when the court is of the opinion that a victim's medical records are exculpatory and are essential to the presentation of the defendant's theory of the case, or necessary for impeachment of the victim, then the defendant's due process right to a fair trial overcomes the statutory physician-patient privilege. In *Ritchie*,[272] the Supreme Court came to the same conclusion when balancing the competing interests as follows:

---

[267] See, for example, *People v Foggy*, 521 N.E.2d 86 (Ill. 1988), at 92 per Miller, Justice.

[268] 65 Cal. Rptr.2d 1 (Cal. 1997), at 7 per Werdegar, Justice; see also *Goldsmith v State*, 651 A.2d 866 (Md 1995), at 874-7 per Chasanow, J.

[269] 168 F.R.D. 660 (D.N.M. 1996), at 661-2 per Hansen, District J.

[270] 854 P.2d 617 (Wash.1993), at 620-622 per Brachtenbach, Justice.

[271] 836 P.2d 445 (Ariz. App. Div.1 1992), at 452-3 per Grant, Presiding J.

[272] *Pennsylvania v Ritchie*, 480 U.S. 39 (1987).

Although we recognise that the public interest in protecting this type of sensitive information is strong, we do not agree that this interest necessarily prevents disclosure in all circumstances. This is not a case where a state statute grants CYS the absolute authority to shield its files from all eyes. ... Rather, the Pennsylvania law provides that the information shall be disclosed in certain circumstances including when CYS is directed to do so by court order. ... Given that the Pennsylvania Legislature contemplated *some* use of CYS records in judicial proceedings, we cannot conclude that the statute prevents all disclosure in criminal prosecutions. In the absence of any apparent state policy to the contrary, we therefore have no reason to believe that relevant information would not be disclosed when a court of competent jurisdiction determines that the information is 'material' to the defence of the accused. ... Ritchie is entitled to have the CYS file reviewed by the trial court to determine whether it contains information that probably would have changed the outcome of his trial.[273]

It can thus be seen that most courts have decided that defence rights principally outweigh the interests protected by medical privilege, as the defendant's liberty may be at stake. However, it does not necessarily follow that a defendant should therefore be given access to all confidential medical and/or psychological files of the witness. Rather, most courts have held that a balancing test must be performed in each case to decide how the conflicting interests can best be protected. While the sensitivity of the information seems to weigh in the balance, on the part of the defendant it must be shown that the information sought is relevant and material for the defence. This, of course, raises the question of how the defendant can be able to meet this requirement before he/she is given access to the information. The solution favoured by most courts is that of an *in camera* inspection of the confidential records by the trial court in order to determine whether or not the files contain information that meets the materiality and relevancy test. In *Ritchie*, for example, the Supreme Court rejected the defendant's claim that his attorney should be given access to the files to search for exculpatory evidence on the following grounds:

We find that Ritchie's interest (as well as that of the Commonwealth) in ensuring a fair trial can be protected fully by requiring that the CYS files be submitted only to the trial court for *in camera* review. ... To allow full disclosure to defence counsel in this type of case would sacrifice unnecessarily the Commonwealth's compelling interest in protecting its child-abuse information. If the CYS records were made available to defendants, even through counsel, it could have seriously adverse effects on Pennsylvania's efforts to uncover and treat abuse. Child abuse is one of the most difficult crimes to detect and prosecute, in large part because there often are no witnesses except the victim. A child's feelings of vulnerability and guilt and his or her unwillingness to come forward are particularly acute when the abuser is a parent. It therefore is essential that the child have a state-designated person to whom he may turn, and to do so with the assurance of confidentiality. Relatives and neighbours who suspect abuse also will be more willing to come forward if they know that their identities will be protected. Recognising this, the Commonwealth - like all other States - has made a commendable effort to assure victims and witnesses that they may speak to the CYS counsellors without fear of general

---

[273] Ibid., at 57-8 per Justice Powell.

disclosure. The Commonwealth's purpose would be frustrated if this confidential material had to be disclosed upon demand to a defendant charged with criminal child abuse, simply because a trial court may not recognise exculpatory evidence. ... An *in camera* review by the trial court will serve Ritchie's interest without destroying the Commonwealth's need to protect the confidentiality of those involved in child-abuse investigations.[274]

In *Ritchie*, the Supreme Court thus balanced the interests as follows: while due process considerations require that a defendant be given access to information that might be material to the defence even if it is contained in confidential files, the right does not go as far as giving the defendant direct access to such files in order to determine whether they include material information. Instead, it is thought that the due process rights of the defendant and the conflicting confidentiality interests can best be reconciled if the confidential information is inspected by the trial court *in camera*. Only material information will be made available to the defendant; with regard to all other information confidentiality will be observed.

However, does this mean that upon the request of the defendant, a court will rummage through all confidential files of a witness to see whether there is anything of interest to the defence to be found therein? Before conducting an *in camera* inspection of privileged documents, most courts require the defendant to make some preliminary showing that the information contained in those documents is relevant to his/her defence.[275] The exact standard the defendant has to meet in order to effect an *in camera* review is, however, controversial. In *State v Green*,[276] the court distinguished between the standard to be met by the defendant in order to compel an *in camera* review of privileged records, and the burden required of the inspecting court when determining whether to disclose the records. The court argued that the materiality standard adopted in *Ritchie* for the disclosure of information to the defendant was too high for the preliminary showing by the defence that *in camera* review was required, as it was difficult to meet before knowing the content of the information. Therefore, it was sufficient that the defendant show 'a "reasonable likelihood" that the records will be necessary to a determination of guilt or innocence'.[277] In *Com. v Fuller*,[278] the court stressed that it did not intend to establish a standard and protocol that would result in virtually automatic *in camera* inspection for an entire class of extremely private and sensitive privileged material, as to do so would make the privilege no privilege at all, and would constitute an unwarranted judicial abridgement of a clearly stated legislative goal. In the court's opinion, *in camera* review, while less intrusive than public disclosure or disclosure to a defendant's attorney, is nonetheless a substantial invasion of the privacy of the witness concerned. A judge should

[274] Ibid., at 60-61.
[275] *State v Speese*, 528 N.W.2d 63 (Wis.App. 1995), at 69 per Gartzke, Presiding J.
[276] 646 N.W.2d 298 (Wis. 2002).
[277] Ibid., at 309 per William A. Bablitch, J. See also *Goldsmith v State*, 651 A.2d 866 (Md 1995), at 877-8 per Chasanow, J.; *People v Stanaway*, 521 N.W.2d 557 (Mich. 1994), at 573 per Brickley, Justice; *State v Pinder*, 678 So.2d 410 (Fla.App. 4 Dist. 1996), at 417 per Gross, J.
[278] 667 N.E.2d 847 (Mass. 1996), at 853-5 per Greaney, J.

therefore undertake an *in camera* review of privileged records only when a defendant's motion for production of the records has demonstrated a good faith, specific, and reasonable basis for believing that the records will contain exculpatory evidence which is relevant and material to the issue of the defendant's guilt. Thus, a privilege should be abrogated only in cases in which there is a reasonable risk that non-disclosure may result in an erroneous conviction. Consequently, even an *in camera* inspection of privileged records may be denied by the courts without violating the Confrontation Clause if the defendant does not specify what information relevant for defence purposes the privileged records are thought to contain.

Some courts only perform an *in camera* review of confidential files of a witness if the witness has consented to this inspection.[279] In *State v Grant*,[280] the court summarised its position as follows:

> In some instances, a patient's psychiatric privilege must give way to a criminal defendant's constitutional right to reveal to the jury facts about a witness' mental condition that may reasonably affect that witness' credibility. ... We have therefore directed trial courts to engage in a specific procedure designed to accommodate this inherent tension. 'If, for the purposes of cross-examination, a defendant believes that certain privileged records would disclose information especially probative of a witness' ability to comprehend, know, or correctly relate the truth, he may ... make a preliminary showing that "there is reasonable ground to believe" that the failure to produce the records would likely impair his right to impeach the witness.' ... If in the trial court's judgment the defendant successfully makes this showing, the state must then obtain the witness' permission for the court to inspect the records *in camera*.[281]

If such consent is not forthcoming, the witness' testimony must be stricken.[282]

It can thus be seen that the courts adopt different approaches with regard to the question of an *in camera* inspection of privileged records. While some courts will examine such records upon the request of the defence without imposing any further conditions, other courts require some showing of the relevance of the information sought before reviewing such files. Even where the defendant has succeeded in making such a preliminary showing, some courts argue that an *in camera* review will only be granted with the patient's consent. The approach largely seems to depend on the court's attitude towards confidentiality. A court that thinks that confidentiality is not affected by an *in camera* review will be more willing to inspect confidential files than a court that is of the opinion that even an *in camera* review affects the patient's privacy concerns

The question remains of what should be the consequence if upon an *in camera* inspection the trial court finds that the confidential records do in fact contain

---

[279] See, for example, *Re Robert H*, 509 A.2d 475 (Conn. 1986), at 482-5 per Arthur H. Healey, J.

[280] 637 A.2d 1116 (Conn. App. 1994).

[281] Ibid., at 1121-2 per Frederick A. Freedman, J.

[282] See *People v Stanaway*, 521 N.W.2d 557 (Mich. 1994), at 577 per Brickley, Justice; *State v. Whitaker*, 520 A.2d 1018 (Conn. 1987), at 1025 per Dannehy, Justice.

evidence material to the defence. Some courts take the stance that in such a case, the defence must be given access to that information, as defence rights will then prevail over any confidentiality interests.[283] Other courts, however, have argued differently and held that in such a situation, the trial court must seek the witness' consent for a disclosure of the relevant parts of the files to the defence. If he/she refuses to do so, his/her testimony shall be stricken and the trial court is ordered to make a redetermination of the respondents adjudications and dispositions based upon the remaining evidence.[284] The courts are thus of the opinion that the privilege bars them from ordering the release of confidential records without the patient's consent. In such a situation, the only method of protecting the defendant's right to a fair trial is to suppress the witness' testimony.[285] In *State v Speese*,[286] where the disclosure of the witness' psychiatric records for impeachment purposes was denied and where the witness had already testified, the court ordered a new trial without the testimony of that witness, as otherwise the constitutional defence rights would be undermined.

The witness whose confidential records are at stake thus has different possibilities to influence the disclosure of his/her medical records. First, in some States it is up to the patient to decide whether or not the court can inspect the confidential records *in camera*. Secondly, where the patient has given such consent and the court has found relevant passages in those records, the patient's consent is needed for a further disclosure of the confidential material to the defence. It is submitted that the approach allowing for a disclosure of material medical records to the defence only with the patient's consent provides a good balance of the interests involved, as this is the best possibility to protect the patient's confidentiality interests. Even where the defence is thus denied access to relevant confidential records, defence rights will not be seriously affected if the prosecution can then not rely on that evidence. However, it is submitted that some compromise might be called for. Even though privilege statutes do not mainly aim at protecting the patient from the embarrassment of a public disclosure of confidential information, so that every unauthorised *in camera* inspection of confidential material violates the patient's privacy right, such an intrusion is rather limited. As long as the patient can be certain that the records will not be disclosed to anyone other than the person reviewing them *in camera*, this limited loss of privacy might be a fair sacrifice to impose, as without such review, the impact of the privilege on the proceedings and therefore on the rights of the defence cannot be assessed. It is difficult to see how defence rights can be adequately protected without such *in camera* review, as courts are not likely to resort to the drastic consequence of striking witness testimony or ordering a re-trial without some knowledge, instead

---

[283] *State Ex Rel. Romley v Superior Court*, 836 P.2d 445 (Ariz. App. Div.1 1992), at 452-3 per Grant, Presiding J.

[284] *Re Robert H*, 509 A.2d 475 (Conn. 1986), at 482- 5 per Arthur H. Healey, J.; *State v Grant*, 637 A.2d 1116 (Conn. App. 1994), at 1122 per Frederick A. Freedman, J.; *State v Solberg*, 553 N.W.2d 842 (Wis. App. 1996), at 844 per Dykman, J.

[285] *State v Shiffra*, 499 N.W.2d 719 (Wis. App. 1993), at 721 and 724 per Brown, J.

[286] 528 N.W.2d 63 (Wis. App. 1995), at 71 per Gartzke, Presiding J.

of some almost inevitably unsubstantiated defence allegation, that the privileged information would affect the case of the defence.

The situation may be different, though, where the defendant, instead of seeking disclosure of privileged information in order to rebut the case of the prosecution, wants to present privileged evidence to prove his/her innocence or to demonstrate mitigating factors. Such cases cannot be resolved according to the principles discussed above, as for example striking out the witness' testimony, if he/she refuses to consent to the disclosure of confidential information, would not help the defendant, if other adverse evidence exists. Given the widespread agreement that, in principle, defence rights outweigh the interest in confidentiality, it has been argued that a criminal defendant should be permitted access to medical records when he/she needs the information contained therein to mount his/her direct defence.[287] This seems particularly important where the privileged evidence could demonstrate the defendant's innocence. An alternative approach would be in such a case to dismiss the charge if the defendant is inhibited by a privilege from adducing favourable evidence.[288] As the argument goes, even though the legislature and not the prosecution is responsible for the existence of the privilege, they are both representatives of the same state and it is therefore fair to shift the burden of a state created privilege on the prosecution rather than on the defence. However, it was suggested that this remedy should only be available to the defendant who meets a high standard of evidentiary need and can demonstrate a probability that the evidence would be exculpatory.[289] This raises the problem of where to draw the line. In the words of Hill:

> Shall the defendant go free because the person he accuses of being the true criminal has a priest or spouse who is *likely* to know something that may be exculpatory, but who cannot be questioned because of a testimonial privilege?[290]

Another possibility would be to limit this remedy to situations in which the witness can demonstrate a likelihood of serious injury resulting from the disclosure of privileged information. It is submitted that the latter suggestion is not convincing, as privacy protection is not granted in order to avert serious injury resulting from disclosure, but rather serves the purpose of giving the patient control over health related information. Accordingly, the disclosure as such constitutes the injury. *In camera* review might yet again present the best compromise in these situations. If upon some initial materiality showing the relevant records were inspected *in camera*, it could be decided, based on knowledge of the records' content, whether or not the information would help the defendant with the direct defence. Only then should the charges be dropped.

---

[287] Oppenheim, at 705; Thomas-Fishburn, at 201-2, for the comparable situation of the attorney-client privilege.
[288] Weisberg, at 982-4.
[289] See for a detailed discussion Hill, at 1189.
[290] Ibid.

With regard to the question of whether or not the physician should be allowed to disclose confidential patient information if he/she is accused in criminal proceedings and that information could assist his/her defence, it has been argued that any professional who is bound by confidentiality has the right of 'self defence' and that a patient who makes allegations against the physician impliedly waives the privilege thereby.[291] However, it must be borne in mind that in criminal cases it is not the patient, but the state who accuses the physician of an offence, and it can hardly be said that by bringing criminal acts committed by a physician to the attention of law enforcement officials, the patient waives medical privilege.[292]

2.2.7 Crime prevention

The conflict between medical confidentiality and crime prevention has not received much attention by American courts. Those cases that touch upon the issue usually do not directly focus on considerations of crime prevention, but rather on considerations of how to avert risks from third parties. The underlying problem is the same, as in most cases the infliction of harm to third parties will amount to a criminal offence. In American law, this conflict is normally discussed in the context of tort law, and the debate is not so much concerned with the question of whether or not the physician is justified when disclosing confidential patient information to protect a third party from a risk. Instead, the conflict is mostly discussed as a conflict between competing duties, i.e. the duty to maintain medical confidentiality and the duty to warn the potential victim. As this work concentrates on the question of exceptions to the obligation to maintain medical confidentiality, the analysis will not concentrate on the particular problems raised by an obligation to disclose as opposed to an authorisation to disclose, but will instead focus on the reasons why confidentiality is overridden.

In the leading case of *Tarasoff v Regents of the University of California*,[293] a patient had told his psychotherapist that he intended to kill Tatiana Tarasoff. Upon the psychotherapist's request, the campus police briefly detained the patient but released him when he appeared rational, without further action being taken. Two months later, the patient killed Tatiana Tarasoff and her parents brought an action in tort against the psychotherapist. The court decided that when a psychotherapist determines or should determine that a patient poses a serious danger of violence to another, the psychotherapist is under an obligation to use reasonable care to protect the intended victim against such danger, either by warning the intended victim, by informing the police, or by taking other steps that are reasonably necessary to avert the risk. The court recognised the interest in the confidentiality of the psychotherapist-patient relationship that might be affected by such a disclosure, but argued that:

---

[291] Slovenko, at 252.

[292] See also, in a different context, *U.S. v Doyle*, 1 F.Supp.2d 1187 (D.Or. 1998), at 1189-90 per Coffin, U.S. Magistrates J.

[293] 17 C.3d 425 (Cal. Sup. Ct. 1976).

Against this interest, however, we must weigh the public interest in safety from violent assault. ... We realise that the open and confidential character of psychotherapeutic dialogue encourages patients to express threats of violence, few of which are ever executed. Certainly a therapist should not be encouraged routinely to reveal such threats; such disclosures could seriously disrupt the patient's relationship with his therapist and with the persons threatened. To the contrary, the therapist's obligations to his patient require that he not disclose a confidence unless such disclosure is necessary to avert danger to others, and even then that he do so discreetly, and in a fashion that would preserve the privacy of his patient to the fullest extent compatible with the prevention of the threatened danger. ... The revelation of communication under the above circumstances is not a breach of trust ... . We conclude that the public policy favouring protection of the confidential character of patient-psychotherapist communications must yield to the extent to which disclosure is essential to avert danger to others. The protective privilege ends where the public peril begins. ... If the exercise of reasonable care to protect the threatened victim requires the therapist to warn the endangered party or those who can reasonably be expected to notify him, we see no sufficient societal interest that would protect and justify concealment.[294]

First, it is worth noticing that the court regarded threats as in principle protected by the psychotherapist-patient privilege. In that respect, the decision provides a welcome contrast to the holdings in *U.S. v Snelenberger*[295] and *U.S. v Williams*[296] which were already discussed and rejected in a different context.[297] With regard to the question of whether or not the physician is justified when disclosing confidential patient information for the purpose of crime prevention, it follows from *Tarasoff* that the interest in medical confidentiality is outweighed where disclosure is necessary to avert a risk from another. This raises several problems. As the decision introduced a balancing exercise into the psychotherapist-patient privilege and argued that confidentiality might have to give way to other interests, it could at first sight be thought that the decision stands in conflict with the U.S. Supreme Court's decision in *Jaffee*. However, in *Jaffee* itself, it was stressed that there may be situations in which the privilege must give way, for example, if a serious threat of harm to the patient or to others can be averted only by means of a disclosure by the therapist.[298] The holdings in *Tarasoff* and in *Jaffee* raise the problem of the type of risk that justifies or even mandates disclosure. In the *Tarasoff* case, the public interest in safety from violent assault was at stake, but it is unclear whether or not other risks, for example the risk of a minor physical injury, or a risk to property interests would equally justify disclosure. Privilege statutes that regulate this question have adopted different approaches. While one statute requires the intent to commit 'a crime involving physical injury, a threat to the physical safety of another person, sexual abuse or death',[299] in another statute it is sufficient that 'there is risk of personal injury to the person or to other

---

[294] Ibid., at 440-442 per Tobriner, Justice.
[295] 24 F.3d 799 (6th Cir. 1994).
[296] 202 F.3d 271 (6th Cir. 2000).
[297] See supra, part 1, 2.1.
[298] 518 U.S. 1 (1996), at 18 per Justice Stevens.
[299] Or St §40.252(1)(a) and (b).

individuals or risk of injury to the property of other individuals'.[300] A broad reference to physical injuries or injuries to property suggests that property and physical integrity will always trump the patient's privacy, no matter how trivial the potential injury and how serious the invasion of the patient's privacy. However, given the importance of a patient's confidentiality interests with their close link to personal autonomy, it is submitted that a careful balancing of the interests which are in conflict in an individual case needs to take place and that disclosure can only be justified where the interest at risk is of sufficient significance to outweigh the patient's privacy right.

Risk assessment also poses a problem. At what point will the physician's obligation shift from an obligation of confidentiality to an obligation to warn? Billings, Chief Justice, argued in a dissent to *Peck v Counseling Service of Addison County*,[301] that it is impossible to predict future violent behaviour and accordingly rejected a duty to warn. Others argue that while the assessment of dangerousness is difficult, it is not impossible, given that psychiatrists have to do just that when certifying individuals for commitment to a hospital because they pose a danger to themselves or to others.[302] According to Or St §40.252(1)(b), it is sufficient that 'in the professional judgment of the person receiving the communications, the declarant poses a danger of committing the crime'. In the recent case of *US v Glass*,[303] it was held that disclosure would only be required if the threat was serious when it was uttered, and if disclosure was the only means to avert the danger. Equally, Or St §40.252(1)(a) requires 'a clear and serious intent at the time the communications are made to subsequently commit a crime'. However, it is not at all clear when a risk is serious enough to justify disclosure. Another question is whether, in addition to being serious, the risk has to be imminent. This is, for example, required by Ct St §52-146c(b)(3). Given that in *Tarasoff*, the threat was only carried out two months after the counselling session, the court seems to have rejected this condition. However, without such a requirement it is difficult to narrow down the cases in which disclosure is justified or even mandated, as it could then be argued that the mere threat that a patient might one day be violent towards a third party would be sufficient to justify disclosure. If that were the case, how can the danger be averted by disclosure? It is submitted that had Tatiana Tarasoff been told that the patient uttered the threat to kill her, the protective effect of the physician's disclosure would have been rather limited.

---

[300] Ct St §52-146c(b)(3).
[301] 499 A.2d 422 (Vt. 1985), at 427-8.
[302] Bok, at 128; Slovenko, at 300-301.
[303] 133 F.3d 1356 (10th Cir. 1998), at 1359-60 per Porfilio, Circuit J.

However, the holding in *Tarasoff* has since been accepted by many courts,[304] and the main problem discussed in the aftermath of *Tarasoff* has been whether or not the duty to warn should only be triggered if the third party at risk is identifiable. In *Gammill v United States*,[305] the court stressed that for a duty to warn to apply the physician must be aware of a specific risk to specific persons. And in *Thompson v County of Alameda*,[306] the court held that no duty to warn arises where the patient is potentially dangerous to a whole community, but where no identifiable victims exist. It makes sense to exclude disclosure where the potential victim is not identifiable, as in such a case, the risk could only be reduced by disclosure to an unlimited number of people, which would constitute a disproportionate invasion of the patient's privacy.

The reaction of commentators to this case-law was far from unanimous. While it was welcomed by some, at least in cases of a danger to the life of others, as life is regarded as more important than the interests of the patient that might be affected by disclosure,[307] others voiced concern. It was feared, for example, that in the light of such a duty psychotherapists and physicians might be reluctant to explore the possibility of dangers to others if a duty to warn is the consequence. If this were the case, then a duty to warn might increase rather than reduce the danger to society. It has been suggested that the potential harm such a duty would inflict upon the physician-patient or psychotherapist-patient relationship might be averted if the doctor informed the patient at the outset that such a duty to warn third parties exists. As the argument goes, patient autonomy could thus be protected, as the patient will then know that the physician or psychotherapist will disclose this information, and, if he/she still reveals such information, this is interpreted as informed consent to the physician's disclosure.[308] This argument, however, is not very convincing. First of all, patient and therapist may have different perceptions of what constitutes a real risk to a third party and what, on the other hand, is just an expression of aggressive tendencies that will never be translated into action. Also, medical confidentiality is protected to spare the patient the choice between seeking health care at the risk of potential disclosure of confidential information, or preserving his/her secrets by not seeking medical treatment, as both alternatives undermine the patient's autonomy.

This leaves the question of whether the exception to the privilege for the purpose of crime prevention and the protection of third parties only permits disclosure to the potential victim or other persons with a need to know in order to avoid the risk,

---

[304] See, for example, *McIntosh v Milano*, 168 N.J.Super. 466 (1979), at 489-90 per Petrella, J.S.C.; *Peck v Counseling Service of Addison County*, 499 A.2d 422 (Vt. 1985), at 426 per Hill, Justice; *Petersen v State*, 671 P.2d 230 (Wash. 1983), at 237 per Dolliver, Justice; but see, on the other hand, *Hasenai v U.S.*, 541 F.Supp. 999 (D.Md. 1982), at 1009 per Frank A. Kaufman, Chief Justice, where the court rejected the *Tarasoff* doctrine.

[305] 727 F.2d 950 (10th Cir. 1984), at 954 per Barrett, Circuit J.

[306] 614 P.2d 728 (Cal. Sup. Ct. 1980), at 734 per Richardson, Justice.

[307] Watson, at 1133-44.

[308] Hermann, Gagliano, at 75.

or whether the physician can choose or is even obliged to testify in criminal proceedings regarding this information. It is submitted that the objective of the crime prevention exception is to avert a risk from an identifiable third person, not to secure the prosecution and punishment of an offender, which has nothing to do with risk aversion. Therefore, in accordance with its purpose, the exception to the privilege should be strictly limited to disclosure that is necessary to avert the risk. Information related to the commission of a future offence, just like all other confidential patient information, should be privileged in the context of criminal proceedings.[309]

3 Summary and conclusion

Given the abundance of approaches throughout the U.S. to almost all questions raised in this chapter, to present a summary is not an easy task. First, it is important to stress that while medical confidentiality is protected by the U.S. Constitution, this protection is not extended to medical privilege, i.e. the protection of medical confidentiality in judicial proceedings is not mandatory under the tenets of the Constitution. It is rather left to the States whether and to what extent to recognise medical privilege.

At federal level, neither a common law nor a statutory medical privilege exists, and the relevant provision of FRE 501 has been interpreted so as not to grant a medical privilege in federal proceedings. A statutory federal psychotherapist-patient privilege does not exist, either, but some federal courts as well as recently the U.S. Supreme Court have decided that such a privilege should be recognised in federal proceedings, given the particular sensitivity of the psychotherapist-patient relationship. This approach partly rests on utilitarian considerations. It has been argued that the benefits of that privilege for society are great, as without its recognition, the mental health of the population could not be preserved. At the same time, the loss of information was said to be negligible, as without privilege, no sensitive information would be imparted to the psychotherapist and such information would consequently not be available through the psychotherapist's testimony. Medical treatment, on the other hand, is felt not to be unduly prejudiced by the absence of a federal physician-patient privilege. This utilitarian approach to the recognition of the physician-patient and the psychotherapist-patient privileges stands in contrast to the protection of medical confidentiality by the constitutional right to privacy, which is predominantly based on the deontological objective of guaranteeing the patient's autonomy in controlling the disclosure of personal information and in making health care choices free from state interference.

At State level, a distinction between the protection of the physician-patient and the psychotherapist-patient privilege can also be observed, as all States provide for a statutory protection of the psychotherapist-patient privilege, while some States do not have privilege statutes protecting the physician-patient relationship. With

---

[309] See also *U.S. v Hayes*, 227 F.3d 578 (6th Cir. 2000), at 584-6 per Ryan, Circuit J.

regard to the physician-patient privilege, it must be distinguished between States with and States without privilege statutes. In States without privilege statutes, the legislature has left open the question of how to resolve the conflict between medical confidentiality and the interests of justice. However, there seems to be a consensus that absent a statutory privilege, the interests of justice and the interests in criminal prosecution should be given primacy over medical confidentiality, so that in case of a conflict, medical confidentiality must yield. This is surprising, given the constitutional protection of medical confidentiality, but it is widely agreed that the constitutional privacy right can be outweighed where information is relevant to court proceedings, as the state interest in disclosure then takes precedence over confidentiality. In States with privilege statutes, the legislature has decided the conflict in favour of medical confidentiality. However, some statutes are silent as to their applicability in criminal proceedings, and it is then for the courts to decide whether or not the privilege should extend to such proceedings. Some privilege statutes are, in principle, applicable to criminal proceedings, but contain exceptions for certain criminal offences.

Privilege statutes are not regarded as absolute, but are rather subject to statutory and common law exceptions. Unlike the constitutional protection of medical confidentiality as part of the right to privacy, privilege statutes not only intend to protect the informational and decisional privacy of the patient, but also serve the utilitarian objective of preserving public health by encouraging patients to seek medical advice and treatment. The courts' interpretation of the respective privilege statutes widely depends on their view as to the purposes thereby served. Where a utilitarian attitude prevails, courts are more likely to interpret privilege statutes restrictively. Some courts have, for example, limited privilege statutes that do not contain any such exceptions so as to be applicable in criminal proceedings only subject to a balancing exercise, an approach which circumvents the legislature's intention, expressed by the very existence of the privilege statute, that medical confidentiality is more important than the interests of justice in criminal proceedings. Most courts do not apply the privilege in the context of grand jury proceedings, given their particular status and their confidentiality. Others, however, rightly argue that even the disclosure of privileged information under limited circumstances violates the patient's privacy rights. Grand jury investigations serve the same interests as criminal proceedings. Absent a statutory exception, the legislative intent to favour medical confidentiality should therefore be just as accepted in the course of grand jury investigations as in criminal proceedings. Most privilege statutes protect confidential patient records from disclosure. In the absence of a privilege statute, such records nevertheless receive some protection from disclosure based on the constitutional guarantee of the right to privacy. They will then only have to be disclosed if a state interest in their disclosure can be demonstrated, which will, for example, be the case when they are relevant to criminal investigations or proceedings. In addition, some limited protection of medical records is available under the Fourth Amendment to the U.S. Constitution, but courts normally do not find searches that are based on search warrants unreasonable. In States without privilege statutes, therefore, patient records can be seized without a violation of the Constitution, as long as a search warrant is first obtained.

In some specific cases, even in States with privilege statutes the conflict between medical confidentiality, on the one hand, and the interest in criminal prosecution, on the other, has been decided in favour of the latter. For child abuse cases, it should be noted, however, that while all States have exceptions to their privilege statutes for this particular situation, many courts have argued that the exception exists not in the interest of facilitating a criminal prosecution, but rather in the interest of protecting children from further abuse. Another situation in which exceptions often apply is that of prosecuting drunk-driving offences. This exception, which is recognised in some States with privilege statutes, is aimed at the prosecution of offences that are regarded as dangerous for society as a whole and the prosecution of which largely depends on medical evidence. An exception for investigations against and the prosecution of physicians is partly based on similar considerations, as particularly fraud regarding the fees for medical treatment can only rarely be detected without resort to confidential medical records. However, as the investigations are then not directed against the patient, some courts try to optimise the interests at stake by restricting disclosure to those parts of medical records that are relevant for the investigation, or by requiring the patient's consent before the records can be used for that purpose. It is interesting to note that in the case of drunk-driving offences and of investigations against physicians, the exceptions seem to be based mainly on pragmatic reasons, as they are not justified by the overriding importance of the competing interests, but rather by the difficulties in prosecuting certain offences without access to medical evidence.

The conflict that has received most attention in the academic and judicial discussion is that between medical confidentiality and defence rights. Defence rights are guaranteed by the Confrontation and the Compulsory Process Clauses of the Sixth Amendment as well as by the Due Process Clause of the Fourteenth Amendment. There seems to be unanimity in the view that, in principle, defence rights outweigh confidentiality, as the individual's liberty is at stake. However, this does not mean that otherwise privileged information is automatically available for defence purposes. Rather, access to privileged information is limited to situations in which effective cross-examination would otherwise be impossible, or cases in which the information is material to the defence. Where the defence can make a preliminary showing that the privileged records will in all likelihood be relevant to the defence, this will only lead to an *in camera* inspection of the relevant material by the court, and some courts decline even *in camera* review without the patient's consent. If the court, upon *in camera* inspection, finds that the records are in fact material for defence purposes, some courts make the material available to the defence. Other courts, however, will do so only with the patient's consent. If the patient refuses to consent to disclosure, the interests of the defence are safeguarded by striking the evidence altogether or, where this is impossible, by ordering a re-trial. No case-law exists with regard to the question of whether or not the same principles should be applied to the situation that the defendant seeks access to the information in order to demonstrate his/her innocence or to present favourable evidence. Some commentators suggest that in such a case, defence rights outweigh confidentiality interests, while others argue that the charges against the defendant should be dropped if the patient refuses to give consent to the disclosure of confidential medical information.

With regard to crime prevention, some privilege statutes provide for an express exemption from the privilege. In the absence of such an exception, American courts focus on the aversion of a risk to third parties. Some courts have held that a physician is not only authorised to disclose information, but is even under a duty to do so, where the disclosure is necessary to avert a risk from an identifiable third party. This approach raises many problems. It is, for example, difficult to assess which interests are important enough to outweigh the constitutionally protected privacy right, and the opinions differ as to whether a risk to life or a risk of physical injuries should be required, or whether a risk to property rights should be sufficient. Another problem is that of risk assessment, that is how to determine whether the risk is serious or not. It is also controversial whether the risk needs to be imminent and if not, how disclosure can then achieve its purpose of averting the risk. It is submitted that the frequently expressed attitude that confidentiality must always yield for the purpose of crime prevention and the protection of third parties is not satisfactory, as it does not take into account that each case of disclosure will constitute a violation of the patient's privacy rights. It is therefore submitted that the interests involved in each case need to be balanced carefully in order to come to a justifiable solution.

The legal situation in the U.S. shows that even in the light of a constitutional guarantee of privacy interests expressed in the federal Constitution, the state has broad leeway in shaping the scope and limits of the protection of medical confidentiality, and is, in particular, not prevented from giving important state interests precedence over the privacy rights of the individual. The fundamental differences in approach among the different U.S. States demonstrate that the federal Constitution only to a limited extent determines the attitude towards medical confidentiality. Of primary practical importance are ordinary statutes and case law. Many court decisions show the predominance of utilitarian considerations, despite the constitutional protection of medical confidentiality. Even the existence of a Constitution granting privacy rights for deontological reasons thus does not necessarily bring about a shift in legal thinking from a utilitarian to a deontological approach, and the prevailing philosophy, rather than legal documents, seems to determine legal reality.

Chapter 8

Comparative Conclusions

The results presented in the preceding chapters show that the potential conflicts between medical confidentiality, on the one hand, and the interests in criminal prosecution, defence rights and crime prevention, on the other, cause difficult problems shared by all of the legal systems that have been examined. To resolve the conflicts arising in this context, value judgments need to be made. An analysis of such problems from the internal perspective of a legal system is inevitably limited. The constraints and conditions existing in a legal system will narrow down domestic perceptions of how to define the problems and of how to resolve them. Factors such as the existence or non-existence of a Constitution, the existing statutory framework, and, most importantly, a specific way of jurisprudential and legal thinking, will be taken for granted and, often unconsciously, confine the analysis. A comparative study broadens the perspective by demonstrating different ways of approaching and resolving shared problems. By going beyond the realities and standpoints of one legal system and by looking at the solutions found elsewhere it becomes possible to identify which factors influence the approach to the problems at hand and which factors, on the other hand, are negligible. If similar approaches to medical privilege can, for example, be found in systems with adversarial and systems with inquisitorial criminal proceedings, the attitude that medical privilege is incompatible with adversarial proceedings[1] needs to be reconsidered. More importantly, where fundamental substantive differences between the law of different systems can be found, as in the case of medical privilege, a comparison provides an impetus to determine what the law should be, instead of concentrating exclusively on how to maximise consistency within a legal system based on the law as it stands.

This chapter will first compare the attitudes of the different legal systems towards the protection of medical confidentiality to see which factors influence the scope of protection granted. The different approaches to the resolution of various conflicts of interests in the context of crime prevention and criminal prosecution will then be compared and assessed in order to develop more consistent and acceptable criteria for the resolution of these conflicts.

---

[1] See, for example, *U.S. v Nixon*, 418 U.S. 683 (1974), at 709 per Chief Justice Burger.

PART 1 – PROTECTION OF MEDICAL CONFIDENTIALITY

With regard to the protection of medical confidentiality, the detailed examination of four different systems has brought to light many similarities as well as many differences. It is common ground in all legal systems that medical confidentiality is a principle worth protecting. However, every legal system has developed its own ways of guaranteeing such protection.

1 Constitutional protection

A first question to be asked is whether and to what extent a constitutional guarantee of the right to privacy influences and strengthens the protection of medical confidentiality. While constitutional protection of medical confidentiality plays an important role both in Germany and in the U.S., it is of only minor significance in France, and does not exist in the UK. However, as in France and Germany, in the UK medical confidentiality is protected as a fundamental right under the ECHR. Constitutional protection, or protection under the ECHR, postulates the general recognition that medical confidentiality forms part of the individual's right to private life and that it is an interest of fundamental significance. It does not, however, provide the answer to the question of how to resolve potential conflicts between medical confidentiality and the interests behind criminal prosecution, defence rights and crime prevention, as constitutional protection does not automatically afford medical confidentiality overriding status. All Constitutions and legal instruments guaranteeing fundamental rights provide for qualifications of these rights in case of conflict. The ECHR states in Article 8(2) that the right to private life can be restricted 'for the prevention of disorder or crime, for the protection of health or morals, or for the protection of the rights and freedoms of others'. Even then, the right can only be limited if the restriction is necessary in a democratic society, that is if it complies with the principle of proportionality. In Germany, the personality right under Arts 2(1) and 1(1) BL which includes the right to medical confidentiality can be limited by overriding community or third party interests, under strict application of the principle of proportionality.[2] In the U.S., the standard to be applied to possible restrictions of the constitutional privacy right is controversial and opinions seem to vary from a compelling interest test[3] to a reasonableness test or the requirement of a balancing of the competing interests.[4] However, the principle of proportionality as applied in Germany and by the European Court of Human Rights does not seem to play a role in the U.S.

---

[2] BVerfGE 34, 238 (1973), at 246.

[3] However, this test seems to have been abandoned in *Pagano v Oroville Hosp.*, 145 F.R.D. 683 (E.D.Cal. 1993), at 698 per Hollows, U.S. Magistrate J.

[4] Ibid.; see also *Fritsch v City of Chula Vista*, 187 F.R.D. 614 (S.D.Cal 1999), at 633 per Aaron, U.S. Magistrate J.; *U.S. v Sutherland*, 143 F.Supp.2d 609 (W.D.Va. 2001), at 611 per Jones, District J.

Even though the standards according to which the right to private life can be restricted differ, none of the systems have adopted the approach that the guarantee of medical confidentiality as part of a fundamental right requires a decision in favour of medical confidentiality when a conflict occurs. In *Z v Finland*,[5] the European Court of Human Rights decided that despite the protection of the individual's private life under Article 8 of the ECHR, States are free to accord the state interest in criminal prosecution overriding importance over the right to private life. In that case, the decision to override medical confidentiality was regarded as proportionate, as the prosecution of serious offences was at issue. Neither in Germany,[6] nor in the U.S.,[7] is it felt that the Constitution mandates the recognition of medical privilege in criminal court, a point that is demonstrated in the U.S. by the fact that many States do not recognise medical privilege. The protection of medical privilege is rather, both in Germany and in the U.S.,[8] a creature of ordinary statutes. In the U.S., the conflict between medical confidentiality and the interest in crime prevention and third party protection is decided according to statutory or case law, not according to the tenets of the constitutional right to privacy as protected by the U.S. Constitution. The approaches as to how to resolve the various conflicts differ from State to State. Judicial decisions in this context are only based on constitutional principles where medical confidentiality stands in conflict with constitutionally protected defence rights.[9] However, in that case the constitutional principle influencing the decision is not that of the protection of medical privacy, but that of the protection of defence rights. In Germany, medical privilege is equally guaranteed by statute, but the Federal Constitutional Court has recognised the constitutional importance of medical privilege.[10] Conflicts of interests between medical confidentiality and third party rights, including defence rights, are resolved by applying the necessity defence contained in the Criminal Code to the disclosure of confidential information by the physician, which, like the Constitution, requires the proportionality of the disclosure.[11] In France, where privacy protection only recently received constitutional protection, medical confidentiality and medical privilege have traditionally been awarded extensive protection by the means of ordinary law, and medical confidentiality is, in principle, regarded as the predominant concept in the case of most conflicts. However, where a conflict occurs, the courts give the physician some discretion when deciding whether or not to disclose confidential patient information.[12] In the UK, where the right to privacy

---

[5] (1998) 25 E.H.R.R. 371.

[6] See BVerfGE 33, 367, 383 (1972) regarding a social worker privilege.

[7] See, for example, *Felber v Foote*, 321 F.Supp. 85 (D. Conn. 1970), at 87 per Blumenfeld, District J.; *Pagano v Oroville Hosp.*, 145 F.R.D. 683 (E.D.Cal. 1993), at 689 per Hollows, U.S. Magistrate J.; *State v Beatty*, 770 S.W.2d 387 (Mo.App. 1989), at 391 per Greene, J.; *State v Boehme*, 430 P.2d 527 (Wash. 1967), at 335 per Hamilton, J.

[8] With the exception of the federal psychotherapist-patient privilege in the U.S.; see *Jaffee v Redmond*, 518 U.S. 1 (1996).

[9] See supra Chapter 7, part 2, 2.2.6.

[10] BVerfGE 38, 312, 323 (1975).

[11] See supra Chapter 5, part 2, 1.3.

[12] See supra, Chapter 4, part 2, 8.

has only been recognised with the coming into force of the HRA 1998 in October 2000, medical privilege is not at all recognised,[13] and conflicts between medical confidentiality and third party protection are resolved according to the not clearly defined criteria of the public interest defence.[14]

This short summary of the different legal approaches demonstrates that the existence of a constitutional guarantee of medical confidentiality is not decisive for the scope of protection accorded to medical confidentiality, as otherwise the different standards of protection that can be observed among U.S. States, and the high standard of protection in France could not be explained. Furthermore, in Germany the statutory protection of medical confidentiality and medical privilege predates the Constitution. It seems as if in all systems, the scope of protection given to medical confidentiality is shaped by ordinary statutes, not by constitutional principles, and the constitutional protection achieves no more than to set a minimum standard of protection. In Germany, constitutional protection nevertheless plays an important role. Reference to constitutional principles is made both by the legislatures and the courts when guaranteeing or extending the protection of medical confidentiality. As statutes and court decisions have to comply with constitutional principles, both legislatures and courts have to take such principles into account.[15] Where, as in the case of s.97 of the German Code of Criminal Procedure, a statutory provision does not give adequate protection to the patient's privacy rights, courts will try to remedy that situation with reference to constitutional principles when applying the provision.[16] The same cannot be said for the U.S. approach. In the absence of statutes regulating conflicts between medical confidentiality and competing interests, courts regularly uphold administrative and judicial decisions restricting medical confidentiality, as long as the state can show an overriding interest in disclosure. The absence of the proportionality analysis is important in this context. In Germany, for a violation of medical confidentiality to be justified, it is not sufficient that confidentiality competes with an interest of overriding importance. It must be demonstrated in addition that this interest cannot be protected by less intrusive means, and that the measure is in fact suitable to protect the overriding interest.[17] This analysis is lacking in the U.S., which facilitates the justification of breaches of medical confidentiality. It can thus be seen that the scope and effectiveness of a protection of medical confidentiality as a fundamental right depends to some extent on the principles according to which this right can be restricted. If it can be legitimately restricted whenever it conflicts with another state interest, without the requirement of a proportionality showing in each case, the constitutional protection is rather weak and will not have much impact on the resolution of conflicts. In the context

---

[13] See, for example, *Attorney-General v Mulholland* [1963] 2 QB 477 (CA), at 489 per Lord Denning; *Hunter v Mann* [1974] 2 All ER 414, at 417 per Boreham J; *Goddard v Nationwide Building Society* [1986] 3 All ER 264, at 271 per Nourse LJ.

[14] *W v Egdell* [1990] 1 All ER 835 (CA), at 846 per Bingham LJ.

[15] Michalowski, Woods, at 72.

[16] BGH NStZ 1997, 562.

[17] Michalowski, Woods, at 83-5.

of the ECHR, where a proportionality test is applied, disclosure can nevertheless be justified more easily than under the standards of German constitutional law, as the States are given a margin of appreciation when deciding individual cases.[18] This means that the ECHR protects fundamental rights, but gives the States some leeway when resolving potential conflicts of interests. It is submitted that while constitutional principles can deliver valid and important arguments supporting a protection of medical confidentiality and facilitating the introduction of medical privilege, the protection through ordinary law is far more influential in the context of specific conflict resolution, as ordinary legislation contains specific rules regulating conflicts and provides the main point of reference for the courts.

In the U.S., like in Germany, constitutional privacy protection is awarded on deontological grounds. However, unlike in Germany, statutory privilege protection is predominantly explained by utilitarian considerations. This demonstrates the attitude that the patient's privacy rights are regarded as less important than the competing interests in the context of crime prevention and criminal prosecution. Of overriding importance are rather utilitarian public health concerns. As a consequence, in the U.S. the decisions of whether or not to implement a privilege statute, and of how to interpret existing privilege statutes is strongly influenced by the view of the legislatures and the courts on how best to promote the utilitarian goals at stake in cases of such conflicts. The scope of protection given to medical confidentiality accordingly depends not just on legal principles, but also on the underlying philosophical approaches adopted by legislatures and courts when giving effect to this interest. The conclusion to be drawn from an isolated analysis of the German approach, that is that constitutional protection of medical confidentiality is of overriding importance for the contours of the ordinary law regulating the details of confidentiality protection, and that deontological considerations underlying constitutional protection will permeate all levels of legal decisions and reasoning, cannot be sustained in the light of the approaches found in the U.S. and in France. The situation in the U.S. shows that constitutional protection as such, and even constitutional protection based on deontological privacy considerations, only has a very limited effect on conflict resolution. The French experience demonstrates, on the other hand, that a strong protection of medical confidentiality can be based on paternalistic perceptions of the physician-patient relationship, and does not necessarily have to focus primarily on the patient's privacy or on utilitarian public health arguments.

Where, as in Germany and the U.S., medical confidentiality is protected as part of the constitutional right to privacy, this constitutional guarantee implies that privacy protection lies in the public interest, as the state has an interest in protecting the fundamental liberties of the citizens. However, the same objective can be achieved through the protection of medical confidentiality by the means of criminal law, as in France and Germany, where the existence of the criminal offences of breach of professional confidences sends a clear statement that medical confidentiality is protected not merely in the private interest of the patient, but also

---

[18] See, for example, *Peter Smallwood v UK* (1999) EHRLR 221, at 222.

lies in the public interest. More surprisingly, a protection of medical confidentiality in the public interest has also been promoted by English case-law,[19] even though medical confidentiality is only protected by private law provisions and remedies, and even though until recently privacy as such was not protected.

With regard to the potential effect of the Human Rights Act 1998 on the protection of medical confidentiality in the UK, it needs to be stated first of all that the Act for the first time recognises a right to private life as part of the domestic law which has already greatly influenced the judicial attitude towards the protection of the right to privacy.[20] To what extent the recognition of a right to privacy and its enhanced protection in the course of private law actions will influence the courts' approach to conflicts of interests between medical confidentiality and competing interests of criminal prosecution and crime prevention remains to be seen. English courts are now more prepared to justify their decisions in Convention terms, far more so than their German counterparts that will only do so when serious doubts as to the constitutionality of a decision materialise. However, given the predominantly utilitarian attitude of English courts, and the prevailing perception that in case of a conflict between medical confidentiality and the competing interests of crime prevention and criminal prosecution utilitarian goals will best be served by a decision in favour of the interests competing with medical confidentiality,[21] no fundamental changes of the law are to be expected. This is particularly likely given the European Court of Human Rights' decision in *Z v Finland*,[22] which does not require a change in approach. The introduction of a fundamental right protecting medical confidentiality as such is thus only of limited value for a strengthened protection of that interest in cases of conflict.

2 Scope and means of protection

With regard to the scope of protection of medical confidentiality, France, Germany, the UK and some of the U.S. States have adopted widely similar approaches, even though the means of protection differ. Medical confidentiality covers not only what the patient expressly confides in the physician, but also all observations the physician makes in connection with the physician-patient relationship. While in Germany, this result is reached by the express wording of s.203 of the Criminal Code, and some U.S. privilege statutes[23] similarly contain

---

[19] *X v Y and others* [1988] 2 All ER 648 (QBD), at 656 per Rose J; *W v Egdell* [1990] 1 All ER 835 (CA), at 846 per Stephen Brown P.

[20] See, for example, *Douglas vHello!*[2001] QB 967 (CA); *Naomi Campbell v Mirror Group Newspapers* [2002] HRLR 28, 763 (QBD); however, see also the in this respect less hopeful decision of the Court of Appeal in *Naomi Campbell v Mirror Group Newspapers* [2003] QB 633.

[21] See supra Chapter 6, part 2.

[22] (1998) 25 E.H.R.R. 371.

[23] See, for example, Art.510 A. (8)(b) of the Louisiana Code of Evidence.

express provisions to this effect, the same result has been reached in France, the UK and some U.S. States in the absence of an express statutory determination, either by judicial interpretation of statutes (France[24] and the U.S.[25]), or by defining the scope of the common law duty to maintain medical confidentiality accordingly (UK).[26] However, some U.S. courts have given their privilege statutes a very narrow meaning when holding that communication protected by a privilege statute is limited to oral communication.[27]

A controversial point is whether or not the protection, or at least the level of protection, should depend on the particular sensitivity and the potentially embarrassing content of the patient information. While French, German, English and many U.S. courts protect confidential medical information regardless of its sensitivity, some courts in the U.S. have adopted a different approach, in arguing that non-sensitive and non-embarrassing information does neither deserve constitutional nor statutory protection.[28] The similarities of the outcome in Germany, France, the UK and some U.S. States, and the dissimilarities among different U.S. States suggest that differences in legal method and the question of whether medical confidentiality is mainly protected by constitutional law, criminal law, private law or by specific privilege statutes which usually form part of procedural law, do not have a great impact on the scope of protection of medical confidentiality. In the U.S. where privacy is constitutionally protected, courts nevertheless partly adhere to a narrow interpretation of statutes that guarantee medical confidentiality. In France, on the other hand, where constitutional protection does not play any role when determining the scope of protection of medical confidentiality, the protection is just as far-reaching as in Germany, where statutory provisions determining the protection of medical confidentiality need to be interpreted in the light of the constitutional right to privacy.

All four legal systems have in common that medical confidentiality is, in principle, protected by ordinary law, and that private law remedies are available for a breach of medical confidentiality. In none of the systems is private law protection of medical confidentiality expressly guaranteed by statute. Rather, courts in all systems have to apply general legal principles to the specific situation of a breach of medical confidentiality by the physician. In Germany, France, and partly also in the U.S., the physician-patient relationship is based on a contract so that a breach of medical confidentiality would amount to a breach of contract, giving rise to a

---

[24] See, for example, 17 May 1973, Ch. crim., D.1973.583; 23 January 1996, Ch. crim., Bull. n°37.

[25] See, for example, *State v Schroeder*, 524 N.W.2d 837(N.D. 1994), at 840-842 per Vande Walle, Chief Justice; *Sims v Charlotte Liberty Mutual Insurance Co.*, 125 S.E.2d 326 (N.C. 1962), at 329-30 per Moore, Justice.

[26] *Hunter v Mann* [1974] 2 All ER 414, at 417 per Boreham J; *W v Egdell* [1990] 1 All ER 835 (CA), at 849 per Bingham LJ.

[27] See, for example, *Re The June 1979 Allegheny County Investigating Grand Jury*, 415 A.2d 73 (Sup. Ct. Pa 1980), at 76-7 per Eagen, Chief Justice.

[28] For a critical evaluation of this approach and an argument in favour of a protection of confidential information regardless of its objectively perceived sensitivity see supra Chapter 7, part 1, 6.

claim for compensation. Where no such contract exists between patient and physician, or where, as in the U.S., contractual remedies are regarded as insufficient, courts have not hesitated to provide other remedies. Thus, in Germany, a breach of medical confidentiality is actionable as a tort under s.823(1) of the Civil Code, and in France, the same result is reached pursuant to art.1382 of the Civil Code. In the U.S., courts have awarded compensation under tort law[29] or for breach of a fiduciary duty.[30] English courts, absent a general action for a breach of privacy, have developed an equitable duty of confidence.[31] Breach of medical confidentiality by the physician is regarded as a breach of confidence and will give rise to compensation. It can thus be seen that regardless of conceptual differences, in all legal systems the courts have recognised the need to protect medical confidentiality under private law. Both in Germany and in the UK, the private law remedies for breach of confidentiality have been expanded in the light of the right to privacy. In the U.S., on the other hand, these remedies were expanded based on the existence of privilege and licensing statutes, so that, again, it is ordinary law, not the constitutional right to privacy, that influences the protection of medical confidentiality in the U.S.

It does not necessarily affect the scope of protection awarded medical confidentiality whether it is protected under the principles of private law, criminal law or procedural law. The means of protection nevertheless makes a difference, as the different types of protection have different functions and effects. Protection of medical confidentiality through criminal law provisions sends a signal that the preservation of medical confidentiality lies in the public interest, that the state is prepared to take measures to guarantee medical confidentiality, and that breaches are to be taken seriously. It also demonstrates that the confidentiality of particular relationships needs increased protection, while private law remedies will usually be available for breaches of privacy or confidentiality, whether or not a professional relationship requiring special trust exists between the parties. Thus, where a breach of medical confidentiality amounts to a criminal offence, this highlights the protection of the confidences of an individual when disclosed to a necessary confidant, that is a person without whose help certain interests, such as the preservation of one's health, cannot be achieved. Under criminal law, every breach of the obligation of medical confidentiality amounts to a criminal offence, unless the physician can demonstrate that a defence applies in the particular case. Unauthorised disclosure is regarded as harmful as such, regardless of its consequences, that is regardless of whether any identifiable harm has been caused, for example in the form of financial harm or a loss of reputation if the information

---

[29] See, for, example, *McCormick v England*, 494 S.E.2d 431 (S.C.App. 1997), at 432-8 per Anderson, J.

[30] *Petrillo v Syntex Laboratories, Inc.*, 499 N.E.2d 952 (Ill.App.1 Dist. 1986), at 961 per Linn, Presiding Justice; *Brandt v Medical Defence Associates*, 856 S.W.2d 667 (Mo.banc 1993), at 470 per Thomas, J.

[31] See *Coco v A N Clark (Engineers) Ltd* [1969] RPC 41, at 47 per Megarry J; *Attorney General v Guardian Newspapers Ltd and others* (2) [1988] 3 All ER 545, at 639 per Lord Keith.

that has been disclosed was embarrassing. This can, to some extent, also be achieved through private law remedies, as long as it is the disclosure, not any additional harm thereby caused, that gives rise to a claim for compensation. However, in most cases the loss will be immaterial, and the damages awarded will then frequently not be significant.

It is highly likely that physicians will take the obligation to maintain a patient's confidences particularly seriously have they to fear the stigma of criminal sanctions in case of an unlawful disclosure. However, the very limited number of criminal cases in this area, both in France and Germany, indicating that breaches of medical confidentiality are rarely prosecuted, and hardly ever lead to a criminal conviction, suggests that criminal law sanctions are not very effective, as prosecutors and courts are reluctant to take the drastic step of criminal prosecution to punish a breach of medical confidentiality. This leads to the conclusion that while criminal law protection might have a deterring effect on physicians and makes a statement regarding the significance of medical confidentiality, private law remedies with all their shortcomings might in practice be the more efficient way to deal with breaches of medical confidentiality. It is submitted that effects similar to those intended by criminal law protection can be achieved by the professional obligation of medical confidentiality, the violation of which might entail disciplinary sanctions resulting, in case of a serious breach, in being struck off the register. As long as the professional bodies supervising any breaches of professional obligations take medical confidentiality seriously, this will deter physicians from lightly disclosing confidential patient information.

Protection of medical confidentiality through procedural provisions, such as the U.S. type privilege statutes and the privilege provisions in the French and German Codes of Criminal Procedure can also add significantly to the level of protection. Unlike private law and criminal law provisions, procedural provisions give medical confidentiality precedence over certain competing interests in the context of court proceedings. However, the protective effect of these provisions depends, again, on their application and interpretation by the courts. If, as in Germany, they are interpreted as giving the physician a right not to disclose confidential patient information, without imposing a correlative obligation, and if they do not lead to the inadmissibility of confidential patient information in evidence, the protection they award is rather limited. If, on the other hand, they prevent the physician from submitting confidential patient information to the court and exclude this information as evidence, the effect of procedural rules is far-reaching. As they only apply to the limited circumstances of disclosure in the context of court proceedings, they can on their own not sufficiently protect medical confidentiality, at least not in Continental systems in which a strict distinction between procedural and substantive law is being made. However, in the U.S. procedural privilege statutes have an impact that goes beyond their direct applicability, as courts have relied on them when developing private law remedies for breaches of medical confidentiality.[32]

---

[32] *Saur v Probes*, 476 N.W.2d 496 (Mich.App. 1991), at 498 per Kelly, J.; see also *Schaffer v Spicer*, 215 N.W.2d 134 (Sup. Ct. S.D. 1974), at 136 per Biegelmeier, Chief Justice.

It can be seen that all forms of confidentiality protection serve different purposes and have different effects. The best possible protection of medical confidentiality can be achieved if they are combined, so that the breach is a criminal and a disciplinary offence, gives rise to private law remedies and leads to the inadmissibility of confidential patient information in court.

3 Differences between common law and civil law approaches

An interesting question is whether or not it is possible to identify fundamental differences in approach between common law and civil law systems. It was already mentioned that both common law and civil law countries broadly achieve the same results when it comes to the protection of medical confidentiality as such. Therefore, it is submitted that with regard to the protection of medical confidentiality and medical privilege, the differences in style are not insignificant, but should at the same time not be over-emphasised, as the results achieved in the various systems are not necessarily affected thereby. At the same time, fundamental differences in approach among common law countries have been identified, as, for example, many U.S. States have adopted privilege statutes, while other U.S. States, as well as the UK have rejected the recognition of medical privilege.

There are, however, differences between common law and civil law countries. Where a common law system recognises medical privilege, this is achieved by the means of privilege statutes specifically drafted for the situation of the physician's testimony in judicial proceedings, providing detailed regulations regarding the scope and limits of medical privilege. Accordingly, these statutes give the physician, as well as the courts, comprehensive guidance for their decisions. Because of this statutory foundation, courts are rarely willing to allow for exceptions to medical privilege that are not outlined in the statute. The main advantage of these statutes is that they are especially formulated to deal with the specific conflicts surrounding medical privilege, and it is usually unnecessary to refer to other provisions or general legal principles when interpreting the statute. Here, U.S. type privilege statutes differ considerably from the relevant statutory provisions in France and Germany.

In France and Germany, the starting point for a legal discussion of medical privilege is that any breach of medical confidentiality by the physician amounts to a criminal offence. Consequently, in the context of medical privilege the main question must be whether the obligation to maintain medical confidentiality extends to the physician's testimony in criminal court. Both the French and the German Code of Criminal Procedure provide for medical privilege in criminal proceedings. To decide whether or not an exception from the obligation to maintain medical confidentiality either in court or outside of judicial proceedings applies, reference must be made to general legal justifications, such as the necessity defence, which are not specifically drafted to deal with the situation of medical privilege. This means that the situation is governed by an interplay of different provisions to be found in different codes. Courts are then faced with the problem of how to apply these different provisions coherently. Although the starting point is the same in France and Germany, the resolution of conflicts nevertheless differs quite considerably. In Germany, conflicts will always be resolved by a strict application of the relevant criminal defences, which poses difficulties, as the situations in which breaches of medical confidentiality most frequently occur do not fit neatly into the framework of existing legal justifications. As a consequence, the German system considerably limits the availability of defences for a breach of medical confidentiality. Also, even though legal justifications provide criteria for the resolution of a given conflict, their application still requires extensive interpretation and a balancing of interests. French courts seem to overcome the problem of the narrow scope of application of legal justifications by referring to general thoughts and interests, rather than to legal justifications when resolving cases of conflict in the area of medical confidentiality. The French approach is thus far more pragmatic than the German approach, and it can be seen that the similarities in written law are to some extent qualified by different ways of applying the law. Accordingly, the impact of differences in legal style between the two civil law countries should not be underestimated.

PART 2 – DISCLOSURE IN THE CONTEXT OF CRIME PREVENTION AND CRIMINAL PROSECUTION

1 Medical privilege in criminal courts

1.1 Recognition of medical privilege

With regard to the conflict between medical confidentiality, on the one hand, and the interests of justice in the context of criminal prosecution, on the other, all legal systems under examination have found a clear approach, at least in respect of the basic issues involved. In France and Germany, under the provisions of the respective Codes of Criminal Procedure, the physician is exempt from the obligation to give testimony in court. Medical confidentiality is thus valued more highly than the interest in criminal prosecution. In the U.S., the situation depends on whether or not a privilege statute exists in the State in which the case has to be decided. In States where privilege statutes apply to criminal proceedings, the physician does not have to, and is not even allowed to testify, while in States without such a statutory privilege, the decision is left to the courts which, absent a legislative decision to that effect, tend to reject medical privilege,[33] so that the physician has to give testimony. Equally, in England there is no physician-patient privilege in judicial proceedings, so that the physician has to testify, unless the testimony is not relevant and material to the proceedings. In that case, English courts have a discretion to exclude evidence in order to uphold the confidentiality

---

[33] See Peiris, at 326-7.

of the physician-patient relationship.[34] Thus, where medical privilege exists in criminal proceedings, it has been introduced on a statutory basis. As far as the Continental legal systems, France and Germany, are concerned, this is hardly surprising, as a privilege introduced by the judiciary would be alien to the legal culture, at least as long as the general obligation to give testimony is regulated by statute. With regard to common law systems, however, it is more note-worthy that where a statutory privilege is missing, the judiciary does not seem willing to introduce medical privilege by case-law. This suggests that the interest in criminal prosecution is, in principle, seen by the judiciary as more important than the interest in medical confidentiality. This result is reached by courts in the UK as well as in the U.S., even though in the U.S., medical confidentiality is protected as part of the constitutional privacy protection.[35] This confirms the conclusion that the existence of a constitutional right to privacy does not necessarily influence the judiciary's approach to medical privilege.

In common law systems, the reluctance to recognise medical privilege is frequently explained by reference to the adversarial system governing criminal proceedings. It is often argued that an adversarial system is particularly dependent upon all evidence being made available to the court.[36] But is this really a distinctive feature of the adversarial system? It is submitted that an inquisitorial system pursues the same purpose as an adversarial system, that is to establish the truth in the course of judicial proceedings in order to come to a fair and just solution in the case before the court.[37] As can be seen from the example of the U.S., where States with and without medical privilege function side-by-side in the setting of the same adversarial system, medical privilege is not alien to an adversarial system and does not undermine its functioning. This suggests that the difference between an adversarial and an inquisitorial system cannot be seen as the decisive factor influencing the recognition or rejection of medical privilege.

Every privilege is based on the assessment that the interests behind the privilege are to be regarded as more important than the interests of criminal justice. It is submitted that the judiciary, as it is mainly concerned with ensuring the purposes of judicial proceedings, is unlikely to make a decision to the detriment of the interests behind criminal prosecution. To the contrary, the judiciary is more likely to attempt to maximise the interest in an unhindered administration of justice. This view is supported by the courts' attitude towards legal professional privilege, which is, at least in England, not recognised to protect the privacy interests of the client, but rather serves the interests of justice which, according to the courts, would suffer if clients did not feel confident to seek comprehensive legal advice and assistance.[38] This is also in line with the discretionary approach adopted by

---

[34] *Hunter v Mann* [1974] 2 All ER 414 (QBD), at 420 per Widgery, LJ.

[35] See, for example, *U.S. v Westinghouse Electric Corporation*, 638 F.2d 570 (3rd Cir. 1980); *Whalen v Roe*, 429 U.S. 589 (1977).

[36] See, for example, *U.S. v Nixon*, 418 U.S. 683 (1974), at 709 per Chief Justice Burger; Hogan, at 418.

[37] Shuman, at 686.

[38] *Reg. v Derby Magistrates' Court, ex parte B* [1996] AC 487 (HL), at 507 per Lord Taylor.

English courts which are willing to consider the exclusion of confidential medical information from judicial proceedings as long as this information is not relevant and material for a just decision in the cases at hand.[39] It is understandable that courts are reluctant to recognise medical privilege where this would lead to the exclusion of relevant and material evidence. In such a situation, the recognition of a privilege would constitute an interference with the smooth functioning of the very system that the judiciary is there to represent. Absent a legislative decision in favour of medical privilege, confidential information will thus only be protected if its costs for an effective administration of justice are relatively low, and it is very unlikely that a general medical privilege will be introduced by case-law.

However, it is interesting to note that some federal courts in the U.S. have recognised a psychotherapist-patient privilege, even though such a privilege is not based on a privilege statute.[40] It was argued that the loss of information would probably be negligible, given that the absence of a privilege would have a chilling effect on the psychotherapist-patient relationship,[41] so that without a privilege, the psychotherapist would in all likelihood not obtain the privileged information. The psychotherapist–patient privilege was therefore introduced on utilitarian grounds. In some U.S. States in which a privilege statute exists but is ambiguous as to its applicability in criminal proceedings, courts have adopted a broad approach and extended the privilege statute to criminal proceedings.[42] This might suggest that once a legislative statement in favour of a privilege exists, courts are more willing to accept its underlying value. However, there are also examples to the contrary, again from the U.S., where the courts' mistrust of privilege statutes has been such that on occasion they have given them as narrow an interpretation as possible.[43]

To interpret the approach of a given legal system once a privilege statute has been enacted is not too difficult a task, as the decision of the legislature then provides a starting point for the evaluation of the legal rules within a legal system. It is immeasurably more difficult to assess whether or not medical privilege should be introduced, given the differences in approach to be found among different legal systems as well as among different philosophical schools. It was seen in chapter

---

[39] See, for example, *Hunter v Mann* [1974] 2 All ER 414, at 417 per Boreham J.

[40] *Covell v CNG Transmission Corp.*, 863 F.Supp. 202 (M.D. Pa. 1994), at 205 per McClure, District J.; *Cunningham v Southlake Ctr for Mental Health, Inc.*, 125 F.R.D. 474 (N.D. Ind. 1989), at 477 per Rodovich, U.S. Magistrates J.; *In Re Doe*, 964 F.2d 1325 (2nd Cir. 1992), at 1328 per Winter, Circuit J; *In re Grand Jury Subpoena*, 710 F.Supp. 999 (D.N.J. 1989), at 1012-3 per Gerry, Chief J.; *In re Zuniga*, 714 F.2d 632 (6th Cir. 1983), at 639 per Krupansky, Circuit J.; *U.S. v D.F.*, 857 F.Supp. 1311 (E.D. Wis. 1994), at 1321 per Stadtmueller, District J.

[41] *Jaffee v Redmond*, 518 U.S. 1 (1996), at 11-13 per Justice Stevens.

[42] See, for example, *Clark v District Court*, 668 P.2d 3 (Colo. 1983); *In the Matter of a Grand Jury Investigation of Onondaga County*, 59 N.Y.2d 130 (1983); *People v Reynolds*, 195 Colo. 386 (1978); *State v Boehme*, 430 P.2d 527 (Wash. 1967); *State v Ross*, 947 P.2d 1290 (Wash.App.Div.1 1997).

[43] See, for example, *People v Doe*, 107 Misc.2d 605 (Sup Ct 1981); *People v Lowe*, 96 Misc.2d 33 (1978).

two that neither the utilitarian nor the deontological approach to medical privilege provide entirely convincing arguments in favour of or against a recognition of medical privilege. Therefore, the question cannot be answered simply by referring to the solutions offered by philosophers or medical ethicists. Given the practical problems of a utilitarian cost-benefit analysis, particularly in the light of the ambiguity of the notion of utility, the utilitarian approach is unhelpful when it comes to deciding a general conflict of interests. It may only be of use as a corrective once a decision has been made, to assist with an evaluation of the consequences of the promoted value judgment. The main problem of the deontological approach is the difficulty of establishing a ranking of the competing interests. As was seen, most deontologists seem to favour medical confidentiality over the interests of justice.[44] The outcome of the balancing test in favour of medical confidentiality seems so obvious that no need is perceived to justify this result by reference to ethical arguments. However, although the philosophical as well as the legal analyses have demonstrated the close link between medical confidentiality, privacy, autonomy, and health, interests which are all of a very high rank, it should not be forgotten that the public interest in the administration of criminal justice which involves such important issues as the trust in the criminal justice system, the investigation of past crimes and the punishment of criminal offenders, is also of great importance. While both of the competing interests are of high value, neither is regarded as absolute. Rather, they can both be outweighed by interests of overriding importance. Consequently, it is not obvious at first sight which of the two interests outweighs the other.

Does it follow that a generalised approach, deciding the conflict in a general and abstract way, is indefensible, and that the outcome of the balancing test should instead be left to an assessment of the particular circumstances of each individual case? All legal systems that have been examined have opted for the first approach and decided the conflict of interests in a general and abstract way. Where a privilege statute exists, it reflects the legislative decision that medical confidentiality is in general more important than the interests in criminal prosecution and will therefore prevail in every case in which the two interests are in conflict with each other. Where no such statute exists and the question had to be decided by the courts, they have equally decided the conflict in an abstract way by principally rejecting medical privilege, thus expressing the judgment that the interests behind criminal prosecution generally outweigh the interests in medical confidentiality. Room for discretion is left only where the confidential information is not relevant and material to the proceedings, and the interests of justice are therefore not seriously affected. Peiris calls the English approach discretionary and argues that this approach has the benefit of according:

> equal recognition both to the privacy of professional relationships and the public interest in maintaining that privacy, and to the countervailing issue in respect of reception of the fullest evidential material facilitating the administration of justice.[45]

---

[44] Krattenmaker, at 90; Louisell, Crippin, at 414.
[45] Peiris, at 309.

Yet this analysis is not entirely accurate, as the English approach very clearly favours the interests in an effective administration of justice over the interest in medical confidentiality.[46] The discretionary approach as applied by English courts does no more than respect medical confidentiality once it has been established that the loss of information is comparatively small. In contrast, a case-by-case approach would start from the assumption that the interests are, in principle, of equal weight, and would look at the particularities of each case to decide whether factors are present in the light of which the balance should shift to one side or the other.

What, then, are the benefits and disadvantages of a generalised approach, on the one hand, and of a case-by-case approach, on the other? The main advantage of a case-by-case approach could be flexibility. None of the competing interests would have to be given a principal precedence over the other, and an attempt could be made to optimise both interests as far as possible in any given case. For example, it would be possible to develop criteria, such as the relevancy and materiality of the evidence, the unavailability of alternative evidence to establish the same facts, the seriousness of the criminal offence at issue, to operate in favour of the interest in criminal prosecution, and the sensitivity of the information, the degree of trust that was placed in the physician, the harm to ensue from disclosure, to operate in favour of a preservation of medical confidentiality. This approach to some extent resembles the case-by-case approach suggested by some utilitarians.[47]

However, such flexibility would be achieved at the cost of uncertainty and of unpredictability of results. None of the purposes behind the protection of medical confidentiality can properly be accomplished this way. Insofar as medical confidentiality serves the purpose of encouraging the patient to seek medical advice and treatment and to disclose all relevant information to the physician, this purpose can hardly be achieved if the patient cannot be certain whether in his/her individual case the balance will come down in favour of or against disclosure.[48] If medical confidentiality is protected to guarantee the patient's autonomy and privacy, this goal will equally not be achieved. A patient who cannot be sure that the information confided in the physician will be protected in the context of judicial proceedings is hardly in a position to make an autonomous decision when deciding whether or not to seek medical advice and treatment and what information to disclose to the physician. This shows that the interest in medical confidentiality is not only adversely affected by forced disclosure,[49] but that the mere possibility that disclosure may be required is sufficient to undermine the purpose behind medical confidentiality. In addition, a case-by case assessment of the particular significance of medical confidentiality in individual cases would require some knowledge of the content of the information in order to assess its sensitivity, the particular features of the physician-patient relationship etc. To obtain such knowledge, medical confidentiality would have to be impaired to some extent.

---

[46] See supra Chapter 6, part 2, 1.1.

[47] See supra Chapter 2, 3.1.1.

[48] Kendrick, Tsakonas, Smith, at 7-10; Thomas-Fishburn, at 194, regarding the attorney-client privilege; Gurfein, at 733, also regarding the attorney-client privilege.

[49] See also Weisberg, at 979-80.

Thus, routine violations of medical confidentiality would be an inherent feature of the case-by-case approach. On the other hand, the interests of justice are directly related to judicial proceedings, so that their determination by the judiciary would be relatively easy and straightforward. As was already seen when assessing the approach of the judiciary towards medical privilege in the absence of privilege statutes, it is highly likely that the courts' bias towards promoting the interests of justice would strongly influence the outcome of the balancing exercise. Therefore, a case-by-case approach would in all likelihood in practice resemble the English approach of giving precedence to the interests of justice unless the confidential patient information is neither relevant nor material to the judicial proceedings.

There are further considerations which weigh heavily in favour of a generalised approach. If it is accepted that medical confidentiality is worth protecting in the interest of patient autonomy, it needs to be protected regardless of the content of the information and of potential adverse consequences of disclosure, as an unauthorised disclosure as such violates autonomy. Medical confidentiality then possesses a value that is independent of the facts of the individual case, so that a case-by-case analysis taking account of the specific circumstances of disclosure in a given case would be unhelpful. The interests of justice can also to a large extent be determined in a generalised way. When it is argued that a generalised approach is too inflexible to accommodate unforeseen circumstances or nuances of a given case,[50] this disadvantage may be outweighed by the benefits deriving from predictability. On the other hand, to adopt a generalised approach does not necessarily mean that no room is left for discretion. Rather, as the English example shows, a generalised approach rejecting medical privilege leaves some discretion for the protection of medical confidentiality where this only marginally affects the interests of justice. Equally, a generalised approach favouring medical privilege does not exclude exemptions from the general rule in certain cases in which exceptional factors are present that might shift the balance towards disclosure.[51]

Coming back to the question of whether or not the recognition of medical privilege is desirable, much depends on which interests the guarantee of medical confidentiality predominantly aims to protect, and on the relationship between those interests and the conflicting interests of justice. It has already been seen that the interests potentially promoted by medical confidentiality include the patient's privacy and autonomy interests; the integrity of the physician-patient relationship; the interests of the members of the medical profession; and the preservation of public health by encouraging patients to receive medical treatment. It therefore needs to be examined whether any of these considerations weigh heavily enough to justify the recognition of medical privilege to the detriment of the interests of justice.

If the main purpose behind medical confidentiality were the utilitarian goal of preserving public health, two abstract public interests would be in conflict when

---

[50] Peiris, at 328.
[51] 'Developments in privileged communications', (1985) 98 Harvard Law Review, at 1548 and 1553.

confidential patient information is needed in court, and a decision about medical privilege would depend on an analysis of its costs and benefits. It has been argued in Chapter two that a utilitarian analysis of the value of medical confidentiality is inconclusive, as no evidence exists to support the view that the existence of medical privilege does in fact enhance the patient's willingness to receive medical advice and treatment. Equally, it is unclear how much evidence would be lost by recognising medical privilege, as it is uncertain whether, absent a privilege, the physician would be given access to all the information that is disclosed to him/her in the light of a privilege. Therefore, it seems as if equally valid arguments can be brought forward both in favour of and against a recognition of medical privilege on those grounds.

If medical confidentiality were mainly protected in the interests of the integrity of the physician-patient relationship, the assessment of whether this interest should prevail over the interests of justice depends on the reasons for which the integrity of this professional relationship is regarded as deserving protection. If the protection were mainly based on the thought that otherwise patients might not be able to receive comprehensive medical advice and treatment, this is no more than a combination of the utilitarian public health argument discussed above, and the interests of the patient to be discussed below. If, on the other hand, as the French approach suggests, the physician's interests in the integrity of the professional relationship were the subject of protection, an individual right of the physician would stand in conflict with the interests of justice. There are, however, no convincing arguments in support of the view that medical confidentiality should be protected in the interests of the physician. The physician may indirectly benefit from medical confidentiality, in that it facilitates the exercise of his/her profession. However, no fundamental right of the physician is affected if medical confidentiality were to be violated. Therefore, it is difficult to see that this interest could be of sufficient importance to outweigh the interests of justice.

This leaves the question of whether medical privilege should be recognised in order to protect the patient's privacy interests. Even though the legislatures of all four systems accept that medical confidentiality should receive legal protection to give effect to the patient's privacy and autonomy in the health care setting, this does not mean that the patient's interest is absolute. Most legislatures seem to agree that the interest in medical confidentiality can be outweighed by a public interest, for example the interest in preserving public health, as they impose on physicians obligations to disclose information about patients who are infected with certain contagious diseases.[52] Equally, most legislatures concur that the interests of justice can sometimes be outweighed by the rights of individuals. Thus, while the truth-finding function of criminal proceedings is regarded as an important value, certain ways of establishing the truth are nevertheless prohibited, such as the extraction of a confession by means of torture, or forced self-incrimination of the

---

[52] For France, see Le Roy, D.1963.280; Pradel, JCP.1969.I.2234; for Germany, see ss.3-5 Bundes-Seuchengesetz (Federal Epidemic Act); for the UK, see s.2 NHS (Venereal Diseases) Regulations 1974; for the U.S., see, for example, A.R.S. §36-621 (Arizona); *Simonsen v Swenson*, 104 Nebr. 224 (1920), at 228; Ensor, at 682-3.

accused. It could be argued that these examples cannot be compared to the situation of medical privilege. Both prohibitions could be said to promote the interests of justice, rather than undermining them. Evidence resulting from torture bears a very high risk of unreliability, as does evidence which emerges due to a disregard for the privilege against self-incrimination. It could thus be argued that both prohibitions are necessary in order to avoid miscarriages of justice. However, it is submitted that both prohibitions at the same time serve other purposes. Confessions induced by torture or forced self-incrimination would seem unacceptable, regardless of whether or not the reliability of the evidence thus obtained can be established in the individual case. Even if it could be demonstrated with certainty that the confession made under torture was in fact correct, its admissibility would nevertheless be unacceptable, as the use of torture constitutes a blatant disregard for human dignity as well as autonomy and bodily integrity.[53] To force a person to incriminate him/herself in the course of criminal proceedings against him/her similarly violates human dignity as well as personal autonomy.[54] It can therefore be seen that evidence or certain means of collecting evidence are not merely excluded on the grounds that they may harm the interests of justice, but that they are also excluded for extra-judicial goals such as the protection of basic human rights. At the same time, it could be argued that it is not in the interest of justice that truth be established at all costs. Rather, while truth-finding is one important goal, the criminal justice system also strives to guarantee a fair trial and achieve results that are in accordance with fundamental principles of justice. These latter concepts may sometimes conflict with and even outweigh the truth-finding function of judicial proceedings. If, for example, evidence has been obtained by unlawful means, justice may be better served by disregarding such evidence than by using it to establish the truth, at least if one adheres to a substantive concept of justice that includes respect for fundamental rights and principles.

When looking at the nature of the different interests that are at stake when a patient's confidential medical information might be needed as evidence against a defendant in a criminal trial, it is obvious that the interest in medical confidentiality directly affects individual freedom, while the interest in criminal prosecution is a public interest. However, it also affects the interests of individuals, such as the interests of the victims of the crime on trial. As States are under a positive obligation to guarantee certain fundamental rights such as the right to life, it could be argued that this includes an obligation to guarantee the effective protection of such rights by the means of criminal law.[55] In order to fulfil this obligation, States might be said to be under an obligation to have adequate procedures in place to prosecute offenders, resulting in a corresponding right of victims or their relatives

---

[53] Kleinknecht/Meyer-Goßner, 3 to s.136(a); Stefani, Levasseur, Bouloc, at 34; *Rogers v Richmond*, 365 U.S. 534 (1961) for confessions obtained through police trickery.

[54] BVerfGE 38, 105 (1974), at 114; BVerfGE 95, 220 (1997), at 241.

[55] *X and Y v The Netherlands* (1985) 8 E.H.R.R. 235, at paras 23 and 27.

to demand the prosecution of offenders who have violated their rights.[56] However, the States' positive obligation to protect the individual rights of victims cannot go as far as giving the individual a right to a particular procedural rule,[57] for example the exclusion of medical privilege, or the admission of all evidence, regardless of the way in which it was collected, especially if such a rule violates the individual rights of others. Rather, the positive obligation of the state towards the victims of crime should not go beyond the duty effectively to investigate crime within the limits set by the rights of others. The European Court of Human Rights therefore rightly stated that the positive obligation of the police to investigate crime is qualified by 'due process guarantees which legitimately place restraints on the scope of their action to investigate crime and bring offenders to justice, including the guarantees contained in Articles 5 and 8 of the Convention'.[58] As effective criminal investigations and prosecutions are not excluded by medical privilege, the recognition of medical privilege accordingly does not affect the individual rights of victims. Instead, in the context of criminal proceedings the patient's interest in medical confidentiality stands in conflict with a public interest, the interest in the administration of justice.

Where the state infringes the fundamental rights or interests of an individual, or, to put it differently, violates its *prima facie* obligation to respect these interests, such an intrusion or violation requires a thorough justification. A right should only be outweighed if it can be demonstrated that the prevailing interest is of overriding importance, and that the violation of the overridden interest is the best and least intrusive course of action in the light of such a conflict.[59] This means that the state would have the burden of showing that the interests of justice override the fundamental interest in medical confidentiality, privacy and autonomy. This also means that there is a presumption in favour of a protection of individual freedom, absent a showing that these interests are outweighed by interests of overriding importance. Where the right that stands in conflict with an important state interest is as broad as the right to privacy, one needs to be clear about the content and the significance of the privacy right that is at stake. In the context of medical confidentiality, the patient's privacy interests go beyond the general interest in keeping personal information private, in controlling one's personal information, in forming relationships with others, and in making personal decisions free from state intrusion. Medical confidentiality further involves aspects that are lacking in other

---

[56] *Avsar v Turkey*, Application No. 25657/94, Judgment of 10 July 2001, at para.393. See also *Akkoc v Turkey*, Application No. 22948/93, Judgment of 10 October 2002, at para.97; *McKerr v UK*, Application No.28883/95, Judgment of 4 May 2001, at para.111; *Kelly v UK*, Application No. 30054/96, Judgment of 4 May 2001, at para.94.

[57] For the approach adopted under the ECHR see *McCourt v UK*, (1993) 15 E.H.R.R. CD 110 regarding the question of the right of a victim's relative to be involved in the parole process. The European Commission of Human Rights not only rejected such a right, but held in addition that with regard to the availability of damages the relative did not have a right that civil proceedings take a particular form.

[58] *Osman v UK*, Judgment of 28 October 1998, (2000) 29 E.H.R.R. 245, at para.116.

[59] See, for example, Beauchamp, Childress, at 19-20.

contexts, as the relationship with the physician or psychotherapist is a relationship with a necessary confidant, that is with a person in whom the patient entrusts information not primarily as a matter of choice, but in order to be able to pursue vital interests, such as health care. The protection of medical confidentiality accordingly serves the purpose of guaranteeing the patient's privacy in health care matters, and the patient's right to make autonomous health care decisions without state control and without having to fear the disclosure of information shared with a necessary confidant in the context of the physician-patient relationship.[60] Only if medical privilege is recognised can the patient's privacy interests as well as the patient's autonomy in the health care setting be adequately safeguarded in the context of criminal proceedings. On the other hand, no case was made by the opponents of medical privilege to demonstrate that medical privilege results in an interference with a public interest that goes beyond the costs that always arise where fundamental individual rights must be respected.[61] Indeed, the experience of France, Germany, and the U.S. with privilege statutes shows that the administration of criminal justice is not markedly impaired by medical privilege. Medical confidentiality as a fundamental right should then not be allowed to be overridden by the public interest in the administration of justice, as the recognition of individual rights only makes sense if they cannot be routinely outweighed by public interest considerations.[62] Absent a showing that the competing state interest is of exceptional and overriding importance and cannot be effectively protected if medical privilege is recognised in criminal proceedings, the interest in medical confidentiality prevails over the interest in the administration of justice, and medical privilege needs to be respected in the context of criminal prosecutions.

To summarise the conclusions reached this far, the question of whether or not to introduce a medical privilege should be decided in a generalised way, not on a case-by-case basis, and the better arguments point towards a recognition of medical privilege in criminal proceedings. This leaves the question of how best to shape medical privilege, a question that will now be discussed from different perspectives.

1.2 Medical privilege only for minor offences?

Should it make a difference whether the physician's testimony is, for example, sought in a case of murder, rather than in a case of minor assault? In the U.S., much depends on the privilege statute that is in operation in a given State, and also on the courts' interpretation of the relevant provisions. In some States, privilege statutes contain express exceptions for cases of serious crime.[63] Other States do not

---

[60] For a detailed discussion of different concepts of privacy and medical confidentiality see supra Chapter 2, 2.2 and 2.3.

[61] For a discussion of the question that the balance might shift in some situations, see infra part 2, 1.2.

[62] Dworkin, at 194-200.

[63] See, for example, D.C. Code Ann. §14-307; Ill. Comp. State. Ch. 735 5/8-802; Kan. State. Ann. §60-427(b).

make such a distinction, and it is neither made in France nor in Germany. In both France and Germany, it is generally accepted that the introduction of medical privilege contains a decision of the legislature in favour of medical privilege, regardless of the seriousness of the crime. Even if the physician wanted to testify in the course of a murder trial, this would only be lawful if a legal justification applied, but no such justification exists for the purposes of criminal prosecution, not even if the trial concerns the most serious criminal offences.[64] In the UK, on the other hand, medical privilege is not even recognised for the prosecution of minor offences. This raises the question of whether the seriousness and the nature of the criminal offence at trial should be irrelevant, as the French, German and English approaches imply, or whether it might be significant, as suggested by some privilege statutes in the U.S.

A general judgment that some offences are so serious that medical privilege should not hinder their prosecution requires a showing that the interests of justice gain so much importance that the balance shifts from a decision in favour of medical confidentiality to a decision in favour of criminal prosecution. Thus, any assessment of the weight accorded to the conflicting interests in such a case depends on the reasons for which the prosecution of serious crimes is said to differ from that of less serious offences. Exceptions in some U.S. privilege statutes for the prosecution of serious criminal offences demonstrate that the costs of the privilege are deemed higher where it could obstruct the prosecution of a more serious criminal offence, and that a decision in favour of medical confidentiality is regarded as less acceptable if it stands in the way of convicting a person who committed a serious crime such as murder.[65] The exceptions thus seem to be based on utilitarian considerations. One such consideration could be that of the risk of repetition. It might seem less tolerable to take such a risk where the commission of serious future offences is to be feared. However, there is no automatic link between a risk of repetition and the seriousness of an offence, as in many cases in which most serious offences have been committed no such risk exists. Moreover, to prevent future offences by someone who has committed a crime raises the same issues as the prevention of the commission of an offence by someone who has not yet committed any offences. It is, accordingly, not a special feature of criminal prosecution, but rather one of crime prevention and therefore needs to be considered in that context.[66] Another argument in favour of an exception to medical privilege for the prosecution of serious crimes could be that the interest in retribution increases with the seriousness of the offence. However, not only is it doubtful whether this interest intensifies sufficiently to justify a violation of the individual right to medical confidentiality which is in no way modified in this scenario. It also needs to be borne in mind that it is difficult to determine which offences are particularly serious. For example, not all cases of murder are of the same seriousness; and neither are all murderers of similar dangerousness. It is therefore submitted that the seriousness of an offence should not be used as a

---

[64] See Chapter 4, part 2, 2, and Chapter 5, part 2, 1.3, respectively.
[65] See, for example, Kendrick, Tsakonas, Smith, at 7-35.
[66] See infra part 2, 3.

criterion to differentiate between cases in which medical privilege should and should not be respected.

The lack of compelling deontological reasons in favour of a distinction between the prosecution of more or less serious crimes is in all likelihood what prevented the legislatures in both France and Germany, where medical privilege is not granted on utilitarian grounds, from introducing such a differentiation. But even from a utilitarian perspective, this distinction is not uncontroversial, as the different approaches in the different U.S. States demonstrate.

In some countries, two types of criminal offences have received special attention: child abuse and drunk driving offences. All American States make exceptions from their privilege statutes for cases of child abuse, and in France, child abuse has also received special legislative treatment. In France, art.434-3 of the Criminal Code makes it a criminal offence not to inform the relevant authorities of cases of child abuse, but physicians are exempt from this obligation. However, art.226-14 of the Criminal Code contains an exemption from the criminal offence of breach of confidence for disclosure in cases of child abuse. Thus, in France the physician is not under any obligation to inform the authorities if he/she comes across a case of child abuse in the course of his/her profession, but neither is the physician under an obligation to maintain medical confidentiality in such a situation. In the U.S., on the other hand, the situation is mostly regulated by an exception to the privilege statute for cases of child abuse, so that the physician is not given a choice, but he/she rather has to disclose the information. In Germany, no exception exists for cases of child abuse, which demonstrates that in the realm of criminal prosecution, child abuse is not given any special attention. A physician would accordingly commit the offence under s.203 of the Criminal Code when disclosing information on child abuse for the purposes of criminal prosecution.

An evaluation of the different approaches depends to a large extent on the purpose to be served by the child abuse exception. In some U.S. States, it is clear that the child abuse exception serves at least partly the purpose of criminal prosecution. Idaho Statutes § 9-203, for example, clearly states that:

(A) Nothing herein contained shall be deemed to preclude physicians from reporting of and testifying at all cases of physical injury to children, where it appears the injury has been caused as a result of physical abuse or neglect by a parent, guardian or legal custodian of the child.

However, in other U.S. States the emphasis very clearly lies on the prevention of further abuse.[67] In France, the place of art.434-3 of the Criminal Code in the context of provisions on the prevention of crimes and of harm to individuals seems to suggest that the provision primarily aims to protect the child from further abuse, rather than at the prosecution of the offender.

A child abuse exception for the purpose of criminal prosecution is undesirable. Though regarded as a particularly horrific offence, child abuse nevertheless covers

---

[67] See, for example, *State v Sypult*, 304 Ark. 5 (1990).

cases of varying degrees of seriousness. Questions of crime prevention will be discussed below, but it should be stated here that the purpose of protecting children can be achieved by disclosing information about detected child abuse to authorities which can take steps to prevent further abuse. A breach of medical confidentiality in order to ensure the criminal prosecution of the offender is then not necessary to achieve that purpose and, accordingly, disproportionate. The proportionality analysis therefore points against a child abuse exception to medical privilege. From a utilitarian standpoint, it must be taken into account that the treatment of the offender as well as the situation of the victims may be adversely affected if confidential information received by the physician can be used for the purposes of criminal prosecution. The offender might then be reluctant to undergo therapy, and may be equally hesitant to seek medical treatment for the abused child. The child, too, may be reluctant frankly to reveal abuse if it cannot be guaranteed that the information will not be used to prosecute the abuser.[68] On the other hand, it is sometimes argued that the child abuse exception is necessary, as medical evidence is particularly essential for the prosecution of the offender, given that other evidence will often not exist, or not be sufficient for a successful prosecution.[69] Again, therefore, the utilitarian analysis does not lead to a conclusive result.

With regard to drunk driving cases, it seems as if only some U.S. States provide for an exception,[70] while this is neither recognised in France nor in Germany. Looking at the reasons given for the drunk-driving exception in some U.S. States, it mainly seems to be based on practical considerations. Thus, it is argued that the prosecution of drunk-driving offences without medical evidence will frequently not be possible and that this should be reason enough to justify an exception to medical privilege. Another argument relates to the particular dangerousness of such offences to the public.[71] However, it is submitted that these arguments are unconvincing. If a blood test was carried out by a physician for the purpose of determining the blood alcohol level of a driver, an obligation to maintain medical confidentiality does not arise, as there is then no confidential relationship between the patient and the physician. The drunk-driving exception would thus only apply to cases in which a blood test was made for treatment or diagnostic purposes, for example after a road accident, and an increased blood alcohol level was detected.[72] It is difficult to see why in a case in which the evidence clearly derives from a confidential physician-patient relationship, practical difficulties encountered when prosecuting drunk-driving offences can outweigh the patient's privacy interests.

---

[68] *Pennsylvania v Ritchie*, 480 U.S. 39 (1987), at 60 per Justice Powell.

[69] *U.S. v Burtrum*, 17 F.3d 1299 (10th Cir. 1994), at 1302 per Kelly, Circuit J.

[70] See, for example, California, Montana, Oregan, Utah.

[71] *State v Dyal*, 97 N.J. 229 (1984), at 238-9 per Pollock, J.; *State v Dress* 461 N.E.2d 1312, (Ohio App 1982), at 1316-7 per Wiley, J. (overruled by *State v. Smorgala*, 553 N.E.2d 672 (Ohio 1990)).

[72] *Collins v Howard*, 156 F.Supp 322 (1957), at 334 per Scarlett, District J.; *State v Erickson*, 241 N.W.2d 854 (N.D. 1976), at 865 per Sand, J.

Furthermore, the powers under implied consent provisions[73] to order blood tests where a driver is suspected of being intoxicated present a better way to satisfy the need to secure evidence against the suspect. In those cases, blood is taken without any reasonable expectation of privacy on the part of the patient.

To summarise, an exception to medical privilege for the prosecution of serious offences or specific types of offences such as child abuse or drink-driving offences should not be recognised.

1.3 Psychotherapist-patient privilege

Should it make a difference if a psychotherapist, rather than a physician, were to be called as a witness in criminal proceedings? In France, Germany and England, the legal situation would be the same as in the case of a physician's testimony in criminal court. In France and Germany, the provisions governing medical confidentiality and medical privilege include both physicians and psychotherapists,[74] so that both professional groups have similar rights and obligations. As medical privilege is comprehensively recognised, there is no need to award any additional protection to the psychotherapist-patient relationship. In England, while some commentators argue that there is a much stronger case for an introduction of a psychotherapist-patient privilege than for the recognition of a general physician-patient privilege,[75] a psychotherapist-patient privilege is no more recognised than medical privilege in general. This demonstrates that the interests of justice even override the confidentiality of the psychotherapist-patient relationship. While the three European systems for different reasons thus treat the psychotherapist-patient relationship similar to the physician-patient relationship, this is not the approach adopted by all American States. In the U.S., all States recognise a psychotherapist-patient privilege, while some States do not provide for a physician-patient privilege. And at federal level, no physician-patient privilege exists, but a psychotherapist-patient privilege has nevertheless been recognised.[76]

What, then are the reasons behind the preferential treatment of the psychotherapist-patient relationship in parts of the U.S.? From a utilitarian standpoint, the main argument would be that psychotherapy depends even more on patient frankness than the ordinary physician-patient relationship, and that a psychotherapist-patient privilege is consequently even more important than a physician-patient privilege to guarantee that professional advice is sought and

---

[73] See, for example, Ar St § 5-65-202.

[74] In Germany, s.53 of the Code of Criminal Procedure only applies to psychological psychotherapists, that is psychologists with a specific degree in psychotherapy.

[75] See, for example, McHale (1993), at 133.

[76] *Jaffee v Redmond*, 518 U.S. 1 (1996); *Covell v CNG Transmission Corp.*, 863 F.Supp. 202 (M.D. Pa. 1994); *Cunningham v Southlake Ctr for Mental Health, Inc.*, 125 F.R.D. 474 (N.D. Ind. 1989); *In Re Doe*, 964 F.2d 1325 (2nd Cir. 1992); *In re Grand Jury Subpoena*, 710 F.Supp. 999 (D.N.J. 1989); *In re Zuniga*, 714 F.2d 632 (6th Cir. 1983); *U.S. v D.F.*, 857 F.Supp. 1311 (E.D. Wis. 1994).

effective treatment given.[77] In addition, it is sometimes argued that patients in need of psychotherapy have less incentive to seek treatment, so that an active encouragement by the way of guaranteeing absolute confidentiality is particularly important in this area of medical practice.[78] Deontological arguments mainly focus on the particularly private, intimate and sensitive nature of psychological information which is said to increase the patient's privacy interest.[79]

It is submitted that any distinction between the physician-patient and the psychotherapist-patient relationship is problematic.[80] First, from a practical perspective, the distinction will often be very difficult to make. Psycho-somatic illnesses, which demonstrate the close link between the body and the psyche, are on the increase. For the distinction to be workable it would have to be determined whether the psychotherapist-patient privilege should be tied to the qualification of the professional as a psychotherapist, or whether it should attach to the content of the information revealed. If a patient seeks medical treatment for a psycho-somatic illness, would all psychological information the patient may reveal to the physician be protected under a psychotherapist-patient privilege? Equally, if a patient in the course of psychotherapy revealed physical problems, would the psychotherapist-patient privilege apply?

In addition to such practical problems, the distinction seems unconvincing for other reasons. The utilitarian gains of a psychotherapist-patient privilege cannot be specified, and therefore cannot be compared to the similarly uncertain gains of a physician-patient privilege, as it is unclear how much evidence would be lost by a recognition of privilege and how many patients would be deterred from seeking treatment in its absence. From a deontological view which values confidentiality because of its close link to privacy and autonomy, it seems inconsistent to make an objective assessment as to the degree of privacy attached to certain information. Rather, a patient's privacy and autonomy can only be safeguarded if this judgment is left to the patient, and is not made on the patient's behalf. For all these reasons, it seems undesirable to treat the physician-patient and the psychotherapist-patient relationships differently. McHale's suggestion for the UK to introduce a psychotherapist-patient privilege, but to leave questions of medical privilege to the discretion of the courts[81] is thus not convincing.

1.4 Medical privilege at the discretion of the physician?

What is the status of privilege should the physician wish to give testimony in a criminal court, for example because he/she feels that his/her duties as a citizen demand that he/she assist the court with the proceedings? In Germany, s.53 of the Code of Criminal Procedure is interpreted by the courts as well as by most legal scholars so as to give the physician the right to refuse to testify, without imposing

---

[77] Kendrick, Tsakonas, Smith, at 7-9 to 7-10.

[78] Ibid., at 7-10; Kottow (1994), at 478.

[79] Kendrick, Tsakonas, Smith, at 7-9 to 7-10; Slovenko, at 49.

[80] See, for example, Saltzburg, at 621.

[81] McHale (1993), at 133.

upon him/her an obligation to that effect.[82] However, when choosing to give testimony, the physician will commit the criminal offence of a breach of professional confidentiality under s.203 of the Criminal Code, and no legal justification will apply in cases in which the testimony merely serves the purposes of criminal prosecution.[83] The German approach not only undermines the patient's autonomy and the utilitarian goal of preserving public health, but it does not even promote the interests of the physicians who are far better off if faced with a prohibition not to testify than if being allowed to make a choice the exercise of which will lead to the commission of a criminal offence for which no justification exists. In France, art.226-13 of the Criminal Code imposes upon the physician the obligation to maintain medical confidentiality, and art. 109 of the Code of Criminal Procedure exempts the physician from the obligation to give testimony in criminal court. It therefore seems as if the legislature has made a clear decision in favour of medical confidentiality.[84] However, it has been suggested by parts of the French legal literature that the physician should nevertheless be given the choice between the two conflicting obligations.[85]

If, as suggested above,[86] medical privilege aims mainly at protecting the patient's interests, it is difficult to conceive of convincing reasons to give a physician the right to disregard medical confidentiality without the patient's consent, as the interests of the patient can only fully be protected if the physician is not allowed to testify in court about confidential medical information. Even if medical privilege were mainly based on utilitarian public health considerations, the physician should not be given a choice between giving testimony or refusing to testify, as the utilitarian goal of a privilege can hardly be achieved if the patient could not rely on the physician's silence. Two possible explanations for giving the physician a choice come to mind. If the privilege statute primarily aimed at protecting the physician against a potential ethical dilemma, it might make sense to give him/her the choice between an obligation to maintain medical confidentiality and a civic duty to give testimony in a criminal court, and to accept whichever choice the physician makes in the individual case. Another possibility to justify giving the physician a discretion to choose between testifying and keeping his/her silence would be the thought that the physician is best placed to decide which of the competing interests is most important in the individual case. With regard to the first suggestion, it is submitted that a decision in favour of medical confidentiality to the detriment of the interests of justice cannot be based on the physician's interests which do not touch upon fundamental values, and can therefore not be regarded as interests that outweigh the public interest in criminal prosecution. And

---

[82] See, for example, BGHSt 9, 59, 61 (1956); 15, 200, 202 (1960); 42, 73, 76 (1996); Karlsruher Kommentar-Senge, 7 to s.53 with further references; Kleinknecht/Meyer-Goßner, 6 to s.53.

[83] Baier, at 117; Haffke, GA 1973, at 69; Kramer, NJW 1990, at 1763; Ostendorf, DRiZ 1981, at 11; Schilling, JZ 1976, at 620; Steinberg-Copek, at 60; Sydow, at 115.

[84] Mazen (1988), at 130; Vouin, at 367.

[85] Chomienne, Guéry, ALD.1995.comm.85.

[86] Supra, part 2, 1.1.

the second argument in favour of giving a physician a choice in these matters is just as unconvincing. The protection of medical confidentiality lies in the public interest and aims at guaranteeing a fundamental right of the patient. The interests behind criminal prosecution are public interests the protection of which lies in the exclusive responsibility of the state. If a decision in favour of medical privilege has been made, this expresses a view that this particular conflict should be resolved in favour of medical confidentiality. To let the physician choose between keeping the patient's confidences and testifying in criminal court means that the physician can substitute his/her own decision of how to resolve a conflict between two public interests for that of the legislature and ignore a clear legal obligation in order to orientate his/her behaviour instead at a conflicting ethical obligation.

In the U.S., the situation is straightforward. The privilege is that of the patient,[87] so that without the patient's consent, the physician is not allowed to give testimony in court, at least not for the purposes of criminal prosecution. If the physician testifies in court despite the existence of a privilege statute, he/she will thereby breach the obligation to medical confidentiality and be subjected to private law and disciplinary sanctions. Only this approach takes account of the interests to be protected by medical privilege.

The differences between the three approaches rest, at least partly, on the different ways of implementing medical privilege. In the U.S., privilege statutes are specifically drafted for the situation of the physician's testimony in judicial proceedings, and they clearly state the physician's obligation not to testify in criminal court without the patient's consent. France and Germany, on the other hand, guarantee medical confidentiality by criminal law provisions. Accordingly, the main function of medical privilege provisions in the respective Codes of Criminal Procedure is to clarify that the obligation of medical confidentiality equally applies to criminal proceedings. It then seems sufficient to formulate medical privilege as an exemption from the obligation to give testimony, rather than as an additional obligation of the physician. It was already discussed in great detail[88] that, properly interpreted, the interplay of all relevant provisions of the French and German codes, respectively, should lead to the same unequivocal result as the application of a U.S. privilege statute. However, it could also be seen that this analysis is not shared by the predominant opinions in France and Germany. The Continental solutions thus leave considerable scope for confusion and inconsistencies. While a U.S. style privilege statute would, in principle, not fit into the French and German systems, the French and German approaches are not satisfactory, and a look to the U.S. may help to avoid the existing problems of interpretation. An interesting solution that may be feasible for all legal systems is that to be found in the Arizona privilege statute, providing in A.R.S. section 13-4062(4) that:

---

[87] Gellman, at 272.
[88] See Chapter 4, part 2, and Chapter 5, part 2, respectively.

A person shall not be examined as a witness in the following cases: ...

4. A physician or surgeon without consent of his patient, as to any information acquired in attending the patient which was necessary to enable him to prescribe or act for the patient.

Here, the privilege statute is addressed to the court, prohibiting the examination of the physician with regard to confidential patient information. This is a more efficient way to protect the patient's privacy interests in court than imposing an obligation upon the physician not to testify. Under a privilege provision thus formulated, the court has to ensure that the physician does not violate his/her obligation, and the physician's testimony in violation of the privilege statute is then clearly inadmissible, as the examination of the physician would constitute a procedural irregularity.

1.5 Effect of the patient's consent

Should the physician be allowed to maintain medical confidentiality where the patient has consented to the physician's testimony in criminal court? In such a case, both in the U.S. and in Germany, the physician would have to give testimony. In the U.S., this purpose is partly achieved by express provisions in privilege statutes,[89] partly by judicial interpretation. As the privilege belongs to the patient, the patient can waive it and the physician will then be under an obligation to give testimony. Thus, the physician can invoke the privilege only in the interests of the patient, and loses this prerogative once the patient has made it clear that he/she favours disclosure. In Germany, the same result is achieved by s.53(2) of the Code of Criminal Procedure stating that the physician loses the right not to testify if the patient authorises disclosure. The French approach differs dramatically, as the patient's consent does not have the effect of relieving the physician from the obligation to maintain medical confidentiality. The patient's consent to disclosure thus does not force the physician to give testimony. However, French courts have held that where a physician decides to testify with the patient's consent, the disclosure is justified.[90] The physician thus has the choice between remaining silent even where the patient has waived his/her interest in confidentiality, and testifying with the patient's consent. The French approach not only leads to inconsistencies within the French legal system,[91] but is also undesirable. There is no need to protect confidential patient information where the patient has waived such protection. A protection of a patient's confidences against the patient's wishes can neither be in the patient's, nor in the public interest. The patient's privacy is not violated if the patient opted for disclosure. The public interest to protect the trust in the confidentiality of the physician-patient relationship is equally not affected if the physician discloses a patient's confidences with the patient's consent. Thus, as

---

[89] See, for example, D.C. Code Ann. §14-307(a) (1981).

[90] Cour de Cassation, 5 June 1985, Bull n° 218.

[91] Mazen (1988), at 90; Waremberg-Auque, at 246; Légal, JCP.1948.II.4141; Savatier, Auby, Savatier, Péquignot, at 303; Savatier, JCP.II.15126; Fénaux, D.1988.106; Honnorat, Melennec, JCP.1979.I.2936; Pradel, JCP.1969.I.2234; Merle, Vitu, at 183.

long as the patient consented to the physician's disclosure, non-disclosure cannot serve any of the purposes of medical confidentiality.

1.6 Medical records

With regard to the problem of state access to medical records for the purposes of criminal prosecution, should the rules governing the physician's testimony in criminal court apply, or should this specific question be treated differently? In the U.S., medical records and the physician's testimony are, to a large extent, governed by the same rules. Thus, where a privilege statute exists, it usually not only excludes the physician's testimony in criminal court, but also bars state access to medical records.[92] In Germany, the prohibition to seize medical records of the accused is seen as a necessary supplement to the physician's right to refuse to give testimony in criminal court, which could otherwise be circumvented by introducing the patient's medical records where the physician's testimony is not available.[93] However, a distinction is made between medical records of a person who is accused in criminal proceedings which are exempt from search and seizure, and those of all other patients to which the prohibition of s.97(1) of the Code of Criminal Procedure does not apply. It has already been discussed that the German approach is unsatisfactory and inconsistent,[94] and that the courts have developed ways to protect medical records of non-accused patients by reference to constitutional principles.[95] In France, medical privilege in criminal court is given far-reaching protection, but medical records can be seized by the examining magistrate, and medical privilege only requires that certain protective procedures are adhered to, but does not restrict access to confidential medical records as such.[96] In England, access to medical records is possible in the course of criminal proceedings. However, in the course of police investigations, medical records receive far-reaching protection from search and seizure by the provisions of PACE.[97] It is nevertheless almost unanimously accepted that the physician will be justified when voluntarily submitting confidential patient material to the police for the purpose of criminal prosecution. Thus, the situation varies from systems in which medical records and the physician's testimony are treated widely similarly (U.S. States with privilege statutes and partly Germany), and a system where the police or the examining magistrate can have access to medical records, while the

---

[92] See, for example, Art.510 A.(8)(b) of the Louisiana Code of Evidence, *Behringer Estate v Princeton Medical Centre*, 592 A.2d 1251 (N.J.Super.L. 1991), at 1268 per Crachman, J.S.C.; *Comonwealth v Kobrin*, 479 N.E.2d 674 (Mass. 1986), at 680 per Abrams, J. For exceptions to this general principle in the context of prosecutions against the physician and for the protection of defence rights, see infra 1.7 and 2.2, respectively.

[93] BVerfGE 32, 373, 385 (1972); BVerfGE 44, 353, 373 (1977); BGHSt 38, 144, 145 (1991); OLG Frankfurt StV 1982, 64, 65; Karlsruher Kommentar-Nack, 1 to s.97.

[94] Supra, Chapter 5, part 2, 3.1; see also Krekeler, NStZ 1987, at 201; Muschallik, at 138; Schmitt, at 128.

[95] BGH NStZ 1997, 562; LG Hamburg NJW 1990, 780, 781.

[96] 24 April 1969, JCP 1970.II.16306; see also Chappart, D.1969.637.

[97] See supra Chapter 6, part 2, 1.3.

physician cannot be forced to testify in court about the same facts (France), to a system in which access to medical records in the course of police proceedings is almost completely excluded, yet the physician would have to give testimony about the same facts when called as a witness in criminal court and could, at trial stage, also be forced to disclose medical records (England).

How can these differences be explained, and which approach is most appropriate? The French approach seems to be based on the thought that the examining magistrate can only adequately perform his/her tasks of investigating criminal offences and deciding whether or not criminal proceedings should be initiated against a suspect if given full access to all evidence. However, the decision that the physician does not have to give testimony in criminal court is based on a legislative assessment that medical confidentiality is more important than the interests in criminal prosecution. This decision is circumvented if access to medical records is possible in the course of investigations into a criminal offence, or if it can be introduced as evidence in criminal court. If the differential treatment is based on the thought that the interest in medical confidentiality is more seriously affected when the physician is forced to testify in court, as this involves the physician's active participation in the disclosure, whereas in the case of a seizure of medical records, the state obtains access to pre-existing records by the use of compulsion, this argument is not convincing. Medical privilege primarily aims at protecting the patient's private sphere which is no less violated where the physician discloses confidential facts in the course of oral testimony, than where confidential medical records come to the knowledge of persons who stand outside of the physician-patient relationship, with or without the physician's active participation. The French approach accordingly protects the physician rather than the patient, as the physician does not actively have to breach the medical secret, while the patient's medical information is not given comprehensive protection from state access. The decision of the English legal system to protect information more comprehensively in the course of police investigations than in the course of judicial proceedings can be more easily explained. Once a case must be decided by a court, the interests to be balanced against medical confidentiality are not reduced to the interest in criminal prosecution; the interests in the administration of justice as such are equally affected. If those interests are regarded as more important than medical confidentiality, it is consistent to deny medical privilege in court while protecting medical confidentiality outside of judicial proceedings. If, on the other hand, as suggested here, medical confidentiality is regarded as outweighing the interests of justice in the context of criminal proceedings, the best approach would be to exclude state access to confidential medical information altogether, be it in the form of the physician's oral testimony or in the form of medical records, and be it in court or in the course of criminal investigations.

With regard to the question of whether or not the physician can be justified in voluntarily handing over confidential patient records to the police or the court, it is submitted that the principles outlined in the context of the general conflict between medical confidentiality and the interests behind criminal prosecution apply, as medical records and the physician's oral testimony should receive the same legal treatment. Therefore, a medical privilege not only means that the physician is not allowed to testify in court for the purposes of criminal prosecution. Instead, he/she would equally not be justified when voluntarily handing over confidential patient records to the police or the court.

1.7 Prosecution of the physician

A last point to be discussed in the context of criminal prosecution is whether it makes a difference if the investigation or the prosecution is directed against the physician. The problem is mainly discussed in the context of the search of surgeries and the seizure of medical records in the course of investigations against the physician for fraud. In Germany, s.97 of the Code of Criminal Procedure does not apply to records of persons who are not accused in criminal proceedings, so that no privilege provision stands in the way of a seizure of confidential patient records. In the U.S., the opinions among different courts are split. While some courts argue in favour of disclosure in such a case,[98] some try to find a compromise by allowing for disclosure, but accepting that individualised patient data need to be anonymised as far as practicable.[99] In France, the courts have come to the conclusion that confidential patient records could be seized, particularly where a physician, after unnecessarily including identifiable and confidential patient information into his book-keeping records, had argued that they could not be submitted without a breach of medical confidentiality.[100] In England, the specific problem did not find any attention of the courts or of legal writers. Thus, the general rules apply, so that medical records would not be privileged in the course of criminal proceedings against the physician. In the course of police investigations such records could be seized if all of the requirements under PACE were satisfied.

The arguments brought forward in the different legal systems in favour of and against disclosure of confidential patient records in this context are very similar. In favour of disclosure, it is argued that the physician-patient relationship does not deserve protection if the physician abuses it to cover criminal activity.[101] However, the practical difficulties in prosecuting the physician without access to patient records seems to be the decisive argument. It is feared that without the power to seize those documents, physicians could use the patient's privilege as a cover for the commission of criminal offences without having to fear discovery.[102] None of these reasons are convincing. The physician's abuse of the confidential professional relationship can hardly negate the protection owed to the patient's medical confidences, as only the patient, but not the physician has the right to

---

[98] *In Re Search Warrant*, 810 F.2d 65, (3rd Cir. 1987), at 72-3 per Becker, Circuit J.

[99] *State v McGriff*, 672 N.E.2d 1074 (Ohio App. 3 Dist. 1996), at 1075 per Evans, J.; *Schachter v Whalen*, 581 F.2d 35 (2nd Cir. 1978), per Oakes, Blumenfeld, and Mehrtens.

[100] 11 February 1960, JCP.1960.II.11604.

[101] Melennec, Gaz. Pal.1980.doct.145; Schlüchter, at 289.

[102] *In Re Search Warrant*, 810 F.2d 65 (3rd Cir. 1987), at 72-3 per Becker, Circuit J.; *State v McGriff*, 672 N.E.2d 1074 (Ohio App. 3 Dist. 1996), at 1075 per Evans, J.; Weyand, wistra 1990, at 6.

waive medical confidentiality.[103] And practical difficulties alone cannot justify a disregard for the patient's fundamental privacy interests.[104] At least where an anonymisation of patient records is not a feasible option or will, in the individual case, not lead to an adequate protection of medical confidentiality, which would necessarily be the case if it were to be performed by a person standing outside of the physician-patient relationship, the only appropriate solution will be to seek the patient's consent to the seizure of his/her medical records.[105] This will in many cases probably be forthcoming, particularly if a considerate use of these data were guaranteed.

1.8 Conclusion

To summarise the conclusions to be drawn from the preceding analysis, medical privilege should be granted in criminal proceedings, regardless of the seriousness of the offence at issue. No difference should be made between a psychotherapist-patient and a physician-patient privilege. Neither should an exception be made for cases in which the prosecution is directed against the physician. The privilege provision should be formulated so as to prevent the court from allowing the examination of the physician as a witness, as this is the best way to ensure that the physician does not breach the obligation of medical confidentiality, and that evidence achieved by such a breach is inadmissible in court. The patient must be allowed to waive medical privilege, so that the physician has to testify if his/her testimony is sought in criminal proceedings and the patient has consented to disclosure. In the context of criminal prosecution, the existence of medical privilege excludes any justification for disclosure apart from consent, so that the physician cannot testify for the purposes of criminal prosecution based on necessity or public interest defences. All of the principles developed for the physician's oral testimony should equally apply to medical records.

The privilege should be enacted by statute, as courts are reluctant to introduce it absent an expression of the legislature's view that medical confidentiality outweighs the interests of justice in the context of criminal proceedings. Such a statutory privilege could be introduced as part of a Code of Evidence or a Code of Criminal Procedure. The content of a privilege provision suggested here would be suitable for all legal systems, and what needs to vary is only the style of drafting the privilege provision.

---

[103] Lorenz, MDR 1992, at 316; Savatier, JCP.1960.II.11604.

[104] *Hawaii Psychiatric Soc. Dist. Branch v Ariyoshi*, 481 F.Supp. 1028 (D. Hawaii 1979), at 1047 and 1050 per Byrne, District J.

[105] *State v McGriff*, 672 N.E.2d 1074 (Ohio App. 3 Dist. 1996), at 1078-81 per Thomas F. Bryant, J., dissenting.

2 Defence rights

A problem for which most systems have not found a consistent and convincing solution is that of the conflict between the interest in medical confidentiality, on the one hand, and defence rights, on the other. Different problems have to be distinguished. First of all, the situation differs depending on whether the defence rights of the patient, a third party or the physician are concerned. Secondly, it could be differentiated between situations in which defence rights of a guilty defendant are at stake, and the scenario that an innocent person is accused in criminal proceedings and the confidential information could help to prove his/her innocence. Lastly, it might make a difference whether the confidential patient information is needed to rebut prosecution evidence, or whether it is needed as part of the direct defence.

2.1 Defence rights of the patient

It is possible that the patient is accused in criminal proceedings and that the physician's testimony or records may be favourable to the defence. In Germany, the U.S. and the UK, no problem arises, as the physician has to testify once the patient consented to disclosure in court. No conflict between medical confidentiality and defence rights would then ensue. The situation is different in France where the patient's consent does not have the effect of forcing the physician to testify even if the patient wants to rely on this testimony for his/her defence.[106] It has already been discussed that the French approach is not convincing, as it is inconsistent with the goals behind the protection of patient confidences to prevent the patient from waiving medical confidentiality.[107] This general consideration is even more powerful where the patient's defence rights are at stake. To deny the patient to introduce his/her own physician as a witness regarding his/her own medical confidences constitutes a violation of the patient's defence rights which is unjustified, as these rights do not stand in conflict with any of the interests that demand the protection of medical confidentiality.

2.2 Defence rights of third parties

It is possible that the patient the disclosure of whose medical information is sought in a criminal court is not the accused, but the victim or a witness. In such a case, a conflict may arise between the patient's interest in medical confidentiality, on the one hand, and the defence rights of the accused, on the other. Defence rights involve the interest of the accused to present a defence against the case of the prosecution, for example by impeaching prosecution witnesses, or by presenting evidence that is favourable to the defence. This interest is protected regardless of the accused's guilt or innocence, as no one should be convicted in criminal

---

[106] See, for example, Cour de Cassation, 22 December 1966, D.1967.122; 5 June 1985, Bull n° 218.

[107] See supra Chapter 4, part 2, 4.

proceedings unless he/she was given the possibility adequately to present his/her version of the event. More importantly, from a legal perspective the guilt of a person can only be established in the course of criminal proceedings, so that a distinction between the defence rights of a guilty or an innocent person does not make sense in the course of a criminal trial. In all legal systems under examination, defence rights are regarded as public interests of very high rank. The U.S. Constitution protects certain specific defence rights, the right to compulsory process and the right to confront witnesses, by the Sixth Amendment, and defence rights in general are also protected by the Due Process Clause.[108] The German Constitution equally protects certain defence rights, such as the right to be heard in judicial proceedings (Art.103(1) Basic Law), and the fair trial principle which follows from the principle of the rule of law.[109] In France, defence rights are also regarded as fundamental rights.[110] The ECHR which influences the law in France,[111] Germany and the UK guarantees certain aspects of fair trial and defence rights in Article 6. In the UK, even before the coming into force of the HRA 1998, defence rights were considered to be important and received the protection of the law.[112]

To understand the significance of defence rights, it is important to realise that for a person who is accused in criminal proceedings, important individual rights and interests, such as personal freedom, financial interests, but also his/her reputation, are at stake. In a criminal trial, the accused is faced with the superior power of the state. Defence rights therefore serve the purpose of mitigating the inequalities inherent in the situation, and it should not be left to the state to abrogate them easily. Given the fundamental importance of defence rights, the legislatures are, therefore, not free to restrict defence rights, but rather have to pay respect at least to the fundamental guarantees contained in the respective Constitutions, or in international documents such as the ECHR. Defence rights are nevertheless far from absolute. They are guaranteed only within the framework of a given legal system, that is they are subject to certain restrictions, and do not go as far as awarding a right of access to evidence regardless of its content or the methods through which it came about. They are, for example, restricted by exclusionary rules and privileges, such as the privilege against self-incrimination, and testimonial privileges. The principal guarantees of defence rights or of a fair trial thus do not give the accused the right to demand that all evidence must be produced in criminal court.

Does it follow from the widespread agreement that defence rights can be restricted by privileges, that the recognition of medical privilege is justified even if it conflicts with defence rights? Different answers to this question seem possible. It

---

[108] *Pennsylvania v Ritchie*, 480 U.S. 39 (1987).
[109] Karlsruher Kommentar-Pfeiffer, 27 to Introduction.
[110] Champeil-Desplats, D.1995.chron.323.
[111] For a discussion of the influence of the ECHR on the French approach toward defence rights see Stefani, Levasseur, Bouloc, at 86-7.
[112] See, for example, *Taylor v Serious Fraud Office* [1998] 3 WLR 1040 (HL (E)), at 1049 per Lord Hoffmann.

could be argued that, as long as confidential evidence is neither available to the prosecution nor the defence, the defence rights of the accused are not unduly prejudiced. There is no inequality of arms, as the prosecution does not deny the defence access to evidence in its possession. However, the validity of this argument is no longer obvious where the defence seeks access to privileged evidence in order either to impeach a prosecution witness, or to present a favourable defence. If, for example, the prosecution presents a key witness, and confidential medical information may cast some doubt on the reliability of the witness, it can no longer be said that the defence is not prejudiced merely because this information is equally unavailable to the prosecution.

In France, Germany and the U.S., it is clear that in the light of medical privilege, the physician cannot be forced to testify in court about confidential patient information. Even if the defence rights of an accused person appear to be adversely affected by medical privilege in an individual case, the court does not have the discretion to order the physician's testimony, which is barred by privilege. Thus, at least as far as the physician's oral testimony in court is concerned, defence rights are restricted by medical privilege, as it is the effect of a privilege provision that physicians are excluded as witnesses with regard to confidential information, and this applies no matter who would want to call the physician to the witness stand. Differences between the approaches can nevertheless be observed when it comes to the question of the availability of medical records to the defence. In theory, this question does not arise in German law, as s.97 of the Code of Criminal Procedure does not protect the medical or psychological records of witnesses from seizure and from use in criminal court.[113] However, the German Federal Supreme Court recently refused to order disclosure of a witness' psychological records for impeachment purposes, even in the light of s.97 of the Code of Criminal Procedure, as this measure was regarded as an unconstitutional intrusion upon the witness' private sphere, at least absent a sufficient showing of materiality.[114] The Court thus protected medical confidentiality to the detriment of defence rights even beyond the scope of the privilege statute. In France, where no provision comparable to s.97 of the German Code of Criminal Procedure exists, the question of the use of medical records in criminal proceedings at the request of the defence has not been discussed. However, it can be inferred from case law in the context of proceedings against the physician that medical records are not absolutely protected from use in criminal proceedings, but that French courts in some instances are prepared to force their production, or, as a less intrusive invasion, instruct an expert witness to inspect the records and prepare a report regarding the relevant part of these records.[115] Absent case law and academic debate in this area, it is difficult to predict whether French courts would extend this approach to cases in which medical records are important for defence purposes. The lack of cases and debate of this question might suggest that it is taken for granted that medical privilege outweighs defence rights even with regard to medical records.

---

[113] S.97 only protects the medical records of those who are accused in criminal proceedings.

[114] BGH NStZ 1997, 562.

[115] Supra Chapter 4, part 2, 7.

In the U.S., the question of defence access to medical records has, even in the light of privilege statutes which usually apply to oral testimony as well as medical records, given rise to an extensive academic discussion and to ample case law. The rights of the accused under the Confrontation Clause of the Sixth Amendment to the U.S. Constitution are not violated by medical privilege as long as the accused or his/her defence lawyer are given the opportunity to cross-examine the witness effectively. If the credibility of a key witness is at stake and the defence wants access to the files of the witness' psychotherapist in order to use them for impeachment purposes, this is not mandated by the accused's confrontation rights, as long as the witness can be cross-examined about the psychotherapeutic treatment, and the witness' psychological problems may thus be introduced and put before the jury.[116] However, if effective cross-examination is not possible without access to confidential and privileged information, such access is, in principle, required by the Confrontation Clause.[117] Compulsory or due process rights are violated if a defendant is denied access to favourable information in the possession of the prosecution, even where the information is privileged, as long as the materiality of the information can be demonstrated.[118] Thus, in the U.S., constitutional principles are infringed if access to confidential medical information which is material either for impeachment purposes or for its assistance with the direct defence is denied, and without it, an effective cross-examination, or the effective presentation of a direct defence is not possible.

However, it does not necessarily follow that the physician or psychotherapist is required to hand over material but privileged information to the defence. Many U.S. courts instead resort to *in camera* review of confidential files. This is based on the assumption that while the defence should not be denied access to potentially favourable information because of medical privilege, medical privilege should not be completely abrogated by the evidentiary needs of the defence. As a compromise, once an initial materiality showing has been made, the court will review the confidential files *in camera*.[119] If the court's *in camera* review establishes that the files would, in fact, be favourable to the defence, some courts have decided that defence rights will then override medical confidentiality,[120] while others argued that even under such circumstances, the files can only be passed on to the defence with the patient's consent.[121] The consequence of a refusal to give such consent would be that the testimony of the witness concerned must either be

---

[116] See, for example, *U.S. v Haworth*, 168 F.R.D. 660 (D.N.M. 1996), at 661-2 per Hansen, District J.; *U.S. v Skorniak*, 59 F.3d 750 (8th Cir. 1995), at 756 per Hansen, Circuit J.

[117] *People v Adamski*, 497 N.W.2d 546 (Mich.App. 1993); *In Re Doe*, 964 F.2d 1325 (2nd Cir. 1992).

[118] *Pennsylvania v Ritchie*, 480 U.S. 39 (1987), at 57-8 per Justice Powell.

[119] *State v Speese*, 528 N.W.2d 63 (Wis.App. 1995), at 69 per Gartzke, Presiding J.; *State v Shiffra*, 499 N.W.2d 719 (Wis.App. 1993), at 724 per Brown, J.

[120] *State Ex Rel. Romley v Superior Court*, 836 P.2d 445 (Ariz. App. Div.1 1992), at 452-3 per Grant, Presiding J.

[121] *Re Robert H*, 509 A.2d 475 (Conn. 1986), at 482-5 per Arthur H. Healey, J; *State v Grant*, 637 A.2d 1116 (Conn. App. 1994) at 1121-2 per Frederick A. Freedman, J.; *State v Solberg*, 553 N.W.2d 842 (Wis. App. 1996), at 844 per Dykman, J.

stricken, or a new trial directed.[122] Some courts resort to *in camera* review only where the consent of the patient to this procedure was first obtained and disregard the patient's testimony where such consent is not forthcoming.[123]

Looking at the situation in the different jurisdictions which have recognised a medical privilege, it is striking that in all three countries, confidential medical records of a witness cannot routinely be used in criminal court at the request of the defence, not even in Germany, where the witness' records are not protected by ordinary statutes. In the U.S., all of the different approaches used by the courts nevertheless point towards a precedence of defence rights whenever it can be established that the confidential information the disclosure of which was sought might be relevant and material. In that case, courts either come to the conclusion that, after *in camera* review, the information should be disclosed to the defence, despite the existence of medical privilege, or they uphold confidentiality, but seek to protect defence rights by ordering that the testimony of the witness, who cannot be impeached because of medical privilege, be disregarded. While in the U.S., the inadmissibility of such records has thus far-reaching consequences and can even result in striking the witness' testimony or ordering a re-trial, no such consequences are envisaged in France or Germany. How can this difference in approach be explained, given that in France and Germany, defence rights are also protected as fundamental rights? First, the protection of defence rights as fundamental individual rights in France and Germany is less specific and less comprehensive than the protection afforded by the U.S. Constitution. Moreover, the differences in criminal procedure may have a significant impact on the solution favoured in each legal system. *In camera* review is alien to the French and German legal systems. One reason for this may be the fact that the decision about the guilt or innocence of the accused is made by the court. If, in such a system, the court could scrutinise confidential material and then deny the defence access to it, either on the grounds that the information was not favourable to the defence, or on the grounds that the patient did not consent to the disclosure, the court would have obtained knowledge of evidence which might influence its later decision, but which is unknown to the defence and to which the defence can therefore not respond. While, from the point of view of the defence, *in camera* review is always problematic, as it allows someone who is not part of the defence team to assess which information is and is not material for defence purposes, it is far more dangerous to the defence where the reviewer is the final decision-maker over guilt and innocence. In France and Germany, unlike in the U.S., the only consequence of an impairment of defence rights by medical privilege is that the court, when making its decision on the guilt or innocence of the accused, will have to consider the fact that access to potentially favourable evidence was barred by medical

---

[122] *State v Shiffra*, 499 N.W.2d 719 (Wis. App. 1993), at 721 and 724 per Brown, J.; *State v Speese*, 528 N.W.2d 63 (Wis. App. 1995), at 71 per Gartzke, Presiding J.

[123] See, for example, *Re Robert H*, 509 A.2d 475 (Conn. 1986), at 482-5 per Arthur H. Healey, J.; *State v Grant*, 637 A.2d 1116 (Conn. App. 1994), at 1121-2 per Frederick A. Freedman, J.

privilege. This may be explained by the thought that courts are in a better position to take account of the fact that evidence was not available for impeachment purposes than is a jury.

While this analysis shows that it would be difficult to transfer solutions from Continental to common law systems, and *vice versa*, it nevertheless seems appropriate to assess whether it is, in principle, more justifiable to resolve the conflict between medical confidentiality and defence rights by deciding in favour of disclosure,[124] by refusing disclosure and making allowances for the impairment of the defence when reaching the final decision, or by respecting medical confidentiality and striking the evidence affected by medical privilege. That defence rights are of fundamental importance is uncontroversial. They serve the interests of the defendant in having a fair trial and in only being found guilty in compliance with procedural rules as well as the interests that are at stake in case of a conviction, such as liberty, property and reputation. Therefore, where medical privilege works to the detriment of a defendant, instead of to the detriment of the state interest in criminal prosecution, the conflict of interests changes. In conflict are no longer individual rights of the patient and the public interest in criminal prosecution, but instead individual rights of the patient and individual rights of the defendant. To resolve that conflict by giving medical privilege, in general, precedence over defence rights could only be justified if the defendant's interests that are at stake are less important than the patient's privacy right, a suggestion that in its generality would be difficult to sustain. On the other hand, given that medical confidentiality equally serves the protection of fundamental individual rights and interests, disclosure against the patient's wishes would only present an adequate solution to the problem if the overriding importance of defence rights could be established.

As two individual rights conflict with each other, one possibility of resolving the conflict would be to apply a case-by-case approach and decide each individual conflict on the basis of the interests that are at stake in a particular case. This would require a careful assessment of the respective values of medical confidentiality and the various interests of the defendant which is difficult to undertake. It would also lead to uncertainty for the physician, the patient and the defendant. Another possible approach would be to decide that one of these fundamental rights is generally less important than the other, so that it would always have to yield in case of a conflict. As a consequence, a fundamental right would routinely be invaded where a conflict occurs. However, fundamental rights should only have to give way if no less intrusive means are available for a satisfactory resolution of the conflict. The U.S. approach of *in camera* review could be regarded as such a less intrusive way of protecting both of the conflicting interests. It is not to be overlooked that this procedure raises several problems. From the perspective of the defence, it can be argued that the court may not be in the best position to assess the materiality of information for the defence, so that

---

[124] See Allan, at 668-9 for cases of legal-professional privilege.

defence rights are not adequately protected by *in camera* review. Furthermore, it has been seen that *in camera* proceedings are regarded as problematic in the context of Continental criminal procedure. However, a feasible solution for Continental systems could be to introduce *in camera* proceedings, but have a judge who is not involved in the criminal trial in which the evidence is sought, inspect the records. This way, the disadvantages for the defendant arising from the particularities of Continental criminal proceedings could be mitigated.

Attaching drastic consequences, such as the striking of a witness' testimony, to the witness' refusal to consent to the *in camera* inspection of his/her medical records would best protect the interests of patient and defendant. It is rather unlikely, however, that the courts would be inclined to adhere to such a petition of the defendant without any possibility to control that the non-disclosure of the privileged records did in fact adversely affect the case of the defence. A more realistic approach therefore is to allow for an *in camera* inspection of medical records even absent the patient's consent, a solution which only leads to a limited loss of medical confidentiality. However, given that an unauthorised *in camera* inspection of medical records nevertheless constitutes an invasion of privacy,[125] particular attention must be given to the determination of the circumstances under which this can be acceptable. It is submitted that as in the U.S., the defence should have the burden of demonstrating a 'reasonable likelihood' that access to the privileged material will be necessary to a determination of guilt or innocence.[126] This requires some showing that there is at least a probability that the evidence the disclosure of which was sought contains favourable information, and that the defence has some idea of the content of the information sought. It would not be sufficient to base a request for a witness' psychotherapeutic records on the knowledge or the assumption that the witness received psychotherapy and that there is the remote possibility that these records contain evidence that might be useful for defence purposes. In such a case, it can hardly be said that the defence is disadvantaged by medical privilege, as this is not different from other cases of 'fishing expeditions' in which access to evidence will also be denied. To conclude, while *in camera* proceedings impose some restrictions on both defence rights and the patient's right to privacy, it gives more weight to both interests than an all-or-nothing approach and seems to present the best possible compromise.

This leaves the question of the consequences to be attached to a patient's refusal to consent to the disclosure of information to the defence once its materiality has been established in *in camera* proceedings. The solution suggested by some U.S. courts was that in such a case, the confidential information should not be disclosed to the defence, but that the testimony of the patient should instead be

---

[125] See *State v McGriff*, 672 N.E.2d 1074 (Ohio App. 3 Dist. 1996), at 1078-81 per Thomas F. Bryant, J.

[126] *State v Green*, 646 N.W.2d 298 (Wis. 2002), at 309 per William A. Bablitch, J. See also *Goldsmith v State*, 651 A.2d 866 (Md 1995), at 877-8 per Chasanow, J.; *People v Stanaway*, 521 N.W.2d 557 (Mich. 1994), at 573 per Brickley, Justice; *State v Pinder*, 678 So.2d 410 (Fla.App. 4 Dist. 1996), at 417 per Gross, J.

disregarded.[127] Indeed, where the patient refuses to consent to the disclosure of information sought for impeachment purposes, to strike the testimony of the witness concerned would provide a less drastic and equally effective means to protect the interests of the defendant than disclosure. At the same time, this would protect the interests of the patient. If testimony can only be disregarded once its materiality was established *in camera*, it need not be feared that this would open the door for defendants to hide behind the medical privilege of third parties and have the testimony of every person disregarded who was a patient once in his/her life. This solution thus does not require a case-by-case analysis of the conflicting interests of patient and defendant. Instead, all that needs to be decided on a case-by-case basis is whether or not the confidential information is material to the defence, which, in all cases, would trigger the same consequences. Such a widely generalised approach is desirable, as it provides predictability for all parties involved and, more importantly, best protects the interests of both the patient and the defendant.

To strike evidence only constitutes a useful remedy for an interference with defence rights where the defence was denied access to information the disclosure of which was sought in order to refute the case of the prosecution. In that situation, the loss of this evidence by the prosecution would provide effective protection of the accused. However, the same would not be true where the evidence was required as part of the direct defence of the accused. In that case, the only effective remedy apart from disclosure would be either to infer that the evidence, if admissible, would have been favourable to the defence,[128] or to drop the charges altogether.[129] It is submitted that in such a case, disclosure of confidential medical information would not be justifiable, given that less intrusive means are available to protect the rights of the defendant. A favourable inference seems more acceptable than to drop the charges, as it is the less drastic measure, and would protect the interests of the accused as effectively as a dismissal of the case. However, it is submitted that, just as in the cases discussed above, this remedy should only be made available upon *in camera* inspection of the records and a finding of their materiality.

2.3 Defence rights of the physician

Where the criminal proceedings or investigations are directed against the physician, and the physician could exonerate him/herself by revealing confidential medical information, the conflict is, in principle, similar to the general conflict between medical confidentiality and defence rights. However, courts and legal writers mostly promote the idea that in such a case, the physician's violation of

---

[127] *Re Robert H*, 509 A.2d 475 (Conn. 1986), at 482-5 per Arthur H. Healey, J.; *State v Grant*, 637 A.2d 1116 (Conn. App. 1994), at 1122 per Frederick A. Freedman, J.; *State v Solberg*, 553 N.W.2d 842 (Wis. App. 1996), at 844 per Dykman, J.

[128] Ibid., at 1184-5.

[129] Weisberg, at 982-4.

medical confidentiality should be justified.[130] This may be based on the view that the physician is in a different position than other persons who are accused in criminal proceedings, as he/she has the potentially exonerating patient information in his/her possession. Accordingly, medical privilege would not prevent access to privileged material that is not already in the possession of the defence, but would rather bar the admissibility of evidence the physician could easily produce. However, the production of confidential medical information for defence purposes would violate the patient's privacy rights. To deny the physician the possibility to introduce such evidence is not different from generally denying the admissibility of certain evidence that is in the possession of the defendant, but the use of which would violate procedural provisions, such as the introduction of conversations that were recorded without the consent of the person concerned.[131] Of course, as the physician is to be treated like every other defendant, he/she can demand an *in camera* inspection of the patient records which, in case of a successful materiality showing, would lead to the consequences suggested above, that is the striking of unfavourable testimony or even the dismissal of the charges. In that case, the physician is better placed than most other defendants, as it will usually be easy for him/her to make a preliminary showing of materiality to trigger *in camera* review.

Differential treatment of the physician could seem mandated in cases in which the patient accuses the physician of criminal conduct in the course of the physician-patient relationship, as in such a case, a meaningful defence might prove particularly difficult without recourse to the patient's records. In this situation, a patient's consent to disclosure will frequently be forthcoming, as the patient then obviously has an interest in the prosecution of the physician. It has been argued that where the patient refuses to consent to disclosure, disclosure could nevertheless be justified as the patient waives medical privilege by making a public accusation against the physician.[132] However, in criminal cases it is not the patient, but the state who accuses the physician of an offence, and it can hardly be said that by bringing criminal acts committed by a physician to the attention of law enforcement officials, the patient waives medical privilege. There is therefore no reason to treat these cases differently and absent consent, the suggested principles of *in camera* review and its consequences apply.

2.4 Protection of the innocent

Would disclosure be justified if the physician were in possession of information that clearly establishes the innocence of the accused? It could be thought that the

---

[130] See, for example, Cour de Cassation, 20 December 1967, D.1969.309; Damien, at 36; Décheix, D.1983.chron.133; Mazen (1988), at 147; Pradel, JCP.1969.I.2234; Rassat, D.1989.chron.107; Reboul, JCP.1979.I.825; Thouvenin, at 99-100; BGHSt 1, 366, 368 (1951); KG JR 1985, 161, 162; Fischer, 31 to s.203; Schönke/Schröder-Lenckner, 33 to s.203.

[131] For the inadmissibility of such evidence in Germany see Kleinknecht/Meyer-Goßner, 43 to s.163.

[132] Slovenko, at 252.

conflict of interests emerging in such a situation differs from the general conflict analysed thus far, in that account has to be taken of the interests of a citizen not to be wrongly convicted or not to be wrongly detained. However, defence rights not only aim at the protection of the rights of the guilty to be convicted only after a fair trial that was conducted in accordance with procedural safeguards, but they also aim at protecting the interests of the innocent not to be convicted at all. Given the presumption of innocence, any distinction between the interests of the guilty and of the innocent seems artificial and unacceptable, as prior to the verdict, every accused person must be regarded as innocent. The rights of the defendant to demand access to confidential material are thus the same, be he/she guilty or innocent, and the innocent defendant can no more force the physician to give favourable testimony or submit exonerating medical records to the defence than the guilty defendant. What needs to be decided in this context, however, is whether or not the physician can be justified when disclosing confidential patient information in order to exonerate an innocent person.

In France, art.434-11 of the Criminal Code makes it a criminal offence not to disclose information establishing the innocence of a person who has either been wrongly convicted of a criminal offence, or is wrongly under arrest for investigation. Physicians are exempt from this obligation and can therefore only lawfully disclose such information where a legal justification applies.[133] However, the predominant opinion among French legal scholars suggests that the physician should nevertheless be justified when disclosing confidential information for this purpose, although the legal basis of such a defence is not explained.[134] While no provision comparable to art.434-11 of the French Criminal Code exists in the U.S., the problem has nevertheless been discussed, and it has been suggested that where the innocence of a person who is wrongly charged with a criminal offence can be established, the physician's disclosure will be justified.[135] In the UK, defence rights are usually given precedence over other interests.[136] However, a different decision has been taken in respect of the conflict between defence rights and legal professional privilege, the only professional privilege recognised in the UK.[137] In Germany, these cases are resolved by an application of the necessity defence which raises several problems. First, it must be decided at what point in time a present danger to the interests of the wrongly accused person materialises. Such an assessment is difficult to make, particularly for a physician who may not be familiar with the details of criminal procedure law and may therefore not be in the best position to evaluate at what moment disclosure would be adequate. Another problem is that of a balancing of interests, as it is controversial whether medical

---

[133] Rassat (1999), at 381.
[134] See, for example, Pradel, D.1978.354; Mazen (1988), at 131; Savatier, Auby, Savatier, Péquignot, at 306.
[135] See Thomas-Fishburn, at 201-2, for the comparable situation of the attorney-client privilege.
[136] See, for example, *Taylor v Serious Fraud Office* [1998] 3 WLR 1040 (HL (E)), at 1049 per Lord Hoffmann.
[137] *R v Derby Magistrates' Court, ex parte B* [1996] AC 487 (HL).

confidentiality is outweighed by the interest in personal freedom, by financial interests, and/or by interests in a good reputation.[138] It can be seen that the criteria advanced in Germany in the context of the necessity defence do not provide a workable solution.

In France, an alternative way has been suggested. Where the physician holds evidence regarding the innocence of a person who is being accused in criminal proceedings, has been convicted or is under detention, he/she should forward this evidence without exposing the identity of the real perpetrator.[139] While this way, the competing interests could widely be reconciled, the decision on guilt or innocence would then exclusively rely on the physician's averment which may frequently not be amenable to any proof, unless corroborative evidence exists in the individual case. However, it is submitted that this would be a less intrusive way to resolve the problem than a full disclosure by the physician. In the context of a criminal trial, the criteria suggested for a solution of the general conflict between medical confidentiality and defence rights can be borrowed. Where the physician has declared to be in the possession of evidence that may exculpate the accused, he/she should therefore merely be allowed to reveal this fact, without at the same time disclosing any confidential patient information. If this is not sufficient to convince the court, an *in camera* inspection of the physician's records or an *in camera* examination of the physician should be performed. Depending on the outcome of this *in camera* examination, it could then be inferred that the physician's testimony, if not barred by privilege, would have been favourable to the accused. However, the information thus revealed should not be used for the prosecution of the real perpetrator. In that regard, the conflict is that between medical confidentiality and the interest in criminal prosecution, and medical privilege bars access to confidential patient information for that purpose.

Should it make a difference whether the real offender is the patient or a third party? A distinction between the two situations has been promoted, as it is felt that a stronger case for medical confidentiality exists where the physician would have to inform on the patient, rather than a party not protected by the physician-patient relationship.[140] However, this distinction is not convincing. First, the patient's privacy interests are not diminished by the fact that the confidential medical information the physician is going to disclose does not incriminate him/her, but rather a third party. Furthermore, the patient may be as interested in protecting a close friend or relative from criminal prosecution as in his/her own protection, so that the harm ensuing from disclosure may be the same regardless of whether the disclosure refers to the patient or a to a third party.

---

[138] See supra Chapter 5, part 2, 1.4.

[139] Anzalec, Gaz. Pal. 1971.113.

[140] Pradel, JCP.1969.I.2234.

2.5 Conclusion

The preceding discussion has demonstrated that defence rights will not necessarily be adversely affected by a recognition of medical privilege, as the two competing interests can widely be reconciled in the case of a conflict. Consequently, the conclusion of the British Criminal Law Revision Committee[141] that medical privilege should not be introduced in the light of the importance of the rights of the defence is not compelling. While allowances need to be made for differences in criminal procedure, the substantive solution can be the same in all legal systems. To that effect, it could be provided as part of the privilege provision that where the defendant can make some initial showing of the materiality of privileged information, an *in camera* inspection of the relevant records will be performed. Where the information is found adversely to affect defence rights and the patient's consent cannot be secured, the records cannot be used in the criminal proceedings. In that case, the relevant adverse testimony needs to be stricken, or the relevant adverse evidence disregarded. Where the privilege impairs the presentation of the direct defence, the consequence should be to infer that the privileged evidence would have been favourable to the defence. No exceptions should be made for the case that the physician is the defendant.

The physician should be justified when disclosing confidential information that can prove the innocence of a person wrongly accused, convicted or detained, but such disclosure must be strictly limited to the information that needs to be revealed in order to achieve this objective. In the context of a criminal trial, an *in camera* review of the relevant evidence could be ordered following the criteria established for *in camera* review of confidential material upon request of the defence. The information thus disclosed should retain its privileged status for all other purposes, including the prosecution of the real offender.

In this context it becomes obvious that a comprehensive solution of the various conflicts that might occur is much easier within the framework of an American style privilege statute which is not limited to strictly evidentiary provisions, but also deals with exceptions to the privilege. This approach makes it possible to perceive all potential problems that might arise in the context of medical privilege as interlinked. It is then more likely that the matter will be resolved with some consistency. In both France and Germany, the question of defence access to privileged material would be one of procedural law, to be regulated by the respective Codes of Criminal Procedure. The question of whether the physician can voluntarily disclose information for the exoneration of an innocent person would be one of substantive criminal law, as it refers to a potential defence for the criminal offence of breach of medical confidentiality, and would therefore have to be governed by the respective Criminal Codes. Whether or not the material, once disclosed, would be privileged or admissible in criminal court would, however, be a question of procedural law. This approach makes it more difficult to give

---

[141] Eleventh Report, Cmnd 4991, para.272-6.

appropriate consideration to the context in which these problems arise. In addition, the drafting of specific defences along the lines suggested here are alien to the Criminal Codes of both Germany and France which deal with matters of criminal defences in a very general matter.

3 Crime prevention

A breach of medical confidentiality for the purposes of crime prevention raises particularly difficult problems. While all legal systems as well as the different philosophical approaches seem to agree that in some circumstances, medical confidentiality may be outweighed by the interest in crime prevention, it is not at all clear how to delineate these cases and which criteria to apply when balancing the conflicting interests in an individual case. This is a problem shared by all legal systems. Even the English system which does not recognise medical privilege has to find a solution to the problem, as medical confidentiality is protected outside the courtroom, and the physician who breaches medical confidentiality to prevent a criminal offence may be held liable for compensation, unless the disclosure is justified. None of the legal systems have succeeded in presenting a coherent approach to this problem, and the same must be said about the philosophical discussions of the problem. A thorough analysis of the different approaches and the results thereby achieved is thus necessary to see whether a convincing approach can, in fact, be developed.

3.1 Obligation to disclose

In France, art.434-1 of the Criminal Code imposes an obligation on every individual to inform the relevant authorities of criminal offences the commission of which can be prevented, or the effects of which can be limited, regardless of the seriousness of the offence. However, physicians are exempt from this obligation. This means that a physician who learns, in the course of his/her profession, that a criminal offence will be committed, is not faced with conflicting legal obligations. He/she is under an obligation to maintain medical confidentiality, from which he/she is not exempt even if disclosure would help to prevent a criminal offence, while there is no obligation on the physician to disclose confidential information for the purpose of crime prevention. In Germany, s.138 of the Criminal Code imposes an obligation on every individual to disclose information about the criminal offences listed in that provision if their commission or consequences can still be averted. S.139(3) of the Criminal Code somewhat mitigates this obligation for physicians. Physicians are only under the obligation to report those offences that are listed in s.139(3) of the Criminal Code, and are, with regard to the offences listed in s.138 of the Criminal Code, exempt from the obligation to disclose if they made a serious effort either to prevent the commission of the offence or to avert its consequences.

Both France and Germany have thus introduced an obligation to disclose criminal offences if their commission or their consequences can be averted, the violation of which amounts to a criminal offence, and both legal systems provide for exceptions to this obligation where physicians would otherwise have to disclose confidential patient information. However, there are also some important differences between the two approaches. In France, the general obligation to disclose refers to all criminal offences, regardless of their seriousness, while the German legislature has opted for an obligation that is limited to certain offences that are regarded as particularly dangerous. In France, the physician is completely exempt from the general obligation to disclose and is therefore not even under an obligation to report the most serious criminal offences in order to prevent their commission. The French system thus makes a general statement that medical confidentiality is regarded as more important than the prevention of criminal offences. The German legislature, on the other hand, adopted a more differentiated view in distinguishing between different criminal offences. The exception for physicians only applies where the physician has tried to avert the danger, but is not at all applicable to the offences listed in s.139(3) of the Criminal Code. This shows that the exception is based on the view that medical confidentiality has to yield where the prevention of the most serious criminal offences could be achieved by a breach of confidence. At the same time, the legislature protects medical confidentiality by allowing the physician to resort to less intrusive means of trying to prevent less serious offences without breaking his/her obligation to medical confidentiality. Here, to achieve the protection of medical confidentiality, the legislature is even willing to take the risk that these less intrusive measures might fail, as it requires no more than that the physician seriously tries to avert the risk, but does not impose an obligation to disclose where such an attempt remained unsuccessful.

In the U.S., the *Tarasoff* decision[142] introduced an obligation of disclosure, but not for the general purpose of preventing the commission of a criminal offence, but rather for the more specific purpose of warning the potential victim, if the victim can reasonably expect to be warned by the physician or psychotherapist. A failure to warn will then amount to a tort. While some U.S. States have since introduced a statutory duty to warn,[143] in other States an obligation to disclose has been rejected.[144]

3.2 Justification of disclosure

So far, it has only been examined whether and under what circumstances physicians may be under an obligation to disclose confidential patient information in order to prevent a criminal offence, and it is clear that in all cases in which such an obligation exists, the physician is justified when disclosing confidential patient information in compliance with the legal obligation imposed upon him/her. However, this does neither necessarily mean that disclosure in such cases would be

---

[142] *Tarasoff v Regents of the University of California*, 17 C.3d 425 (Cal. Sup. Ct. 1976), at 440-442 per Tobriner, Justice.

[143] La. Rev. Stat. Ann. 9:2800.2(A).

[144] See, for example, *Hasenai v U.S.*, 541 F.Supp. 999 (D. Md. 1982).

morally justified, nor that justified disclosure should be limited to cases in which an obligation to disclose exists. It is interesting to note that in both Germany and France, this problem has not occupied the courts and has received only little attention from legal writers. In France, the discussion mainly focuses on the question of whether or not the legislative provisions in this area leave the physician a choice between maintaining confidentiality and disclosure for the purposes of crime prevention, and the majority of legal writers promote the view that disclosure is at the discretion of the physician.[145] For a Continental legal system, the French discussion is surprisingly unsystematic. Given that the physician is under an obligation to maintain medical confidentiality, but under no obligation to disclose information for the purpose of crime prevention, it is inconsistent to argue that the physician can be justified when committing a criminal offence merely on the grounds that he/she has chosen to do so. This certainly contravenes the principles of criminal law, as a criminal offence can only be exceptionally justified where the state has decided that the obligation to follow the criminal law is outweighed by overriding considerations. In that respect, it seems more consistent to follow the German example which allows for a justification of the offence of breach of confidence only where the physician is either under an obligation to disclose the information, or where a legal justification applies. However, the German approach, while formally in line with legal principles, also encounters many problems. As the question of whether or not the physician can be justified when disclosing confidential patient information in order to prevent the commission of a criminal offence is governed by the principles of the necessity defence pursuant to s.34 of the Criminal Code, it must be established whether there is a present and imminent danger to another which cannot be averted without disclosure, and whether the impaired interest is significantly outweighed by the interest protected through disclosure. If these requirements are fulfilled, the justification will depend on the showing that disclosure was an appropriate means to avert the danger.

In the U.S., the problem has first been addressed in the context of whether or not the physician is under an obligation to disclose information where this is necessary for the purpose of crime prevention. Since the influential *Tarasoff*[146] decision, many States have adopted the approach that a physician is under a duty to disclose confidential patient information where this would help avert the risk of harm to another.[147] With regard to the specification of criteria which might help to decide whether or not a disclosure may be justified for the purpose of crime prevention, the holding in *Tarasoff* is rather vague, as it requires no more than a danger of violent assault. In Louisiana, where the *Tarasoff* duty has been enacted by

---

[145] See Colcombet, JOAN 26 September 1991, at 2244; Alt-Maes, at 306; Lepage, JCP.1999.4. See also the discussion supra Chapter 4, part 2, 5.1.

[146] *Tarasoff v Regents of the University of California*, 31 Cal. Rptr. 14 (Cal. Sup. Ct. 1976).

[147] See, for example, *McIntosh v Milano*, 168 N.J.Super. 466 (1979), at 489-90 per Petrella, J.S.C.; *Peck v Counseling Service of Addison County*, 499 A.2d 422 (Vt. 1985), at 426 per Hill, Justice; *Petersen v State*, 671 P.2d 230 (Wash. 1983), at 237 per Dolliver, Justice.

statute,[148] an imminent danger of violence to a specified person is required. Other States provide for justifications to disclose for the purpose of crime prevention, for example in order to avert 'a crime involving physical injury, a threat to the physical safety of another person, sexual abuse or death';[149] or a 'risk of personal injury to the person or to other individuals or risk of injury to the property of other individuals'.[150] In England, disclosure for the purpose of crime prevention can be justified on the basis of the public interest defence. The Court of Appeal's decision in *W v Egdell*[151] suggests that disclosure for the purpose of crime prevention is justified where there is a real risk of danger to the public, and no more specific criteria have yet been developed in order to delineate the scope of the public interest defence in this context.

In France, criteria for a justification of a disclosure of confidential medical information for the purpose of crime prevention are not at all discussed, and the criteria suggested in Germany, the U.S. and England are rather ill-defined and need further specification. Given that the disclosure of confidential medical information by the physician violates the patient's privacy rights, and constitutes a breach of the professional obligation to medical confidentiality as well as, depending on the legal system concerned, a criminal offence, a tort, a breach of contract or a breach of a fiduciary duty, it seems fair to limit instances of justified disclosure to situations in which a compelling case for disclosure can be made. Before criteria for a delineation of a defence will be suggested, some general considerations of the purposes of a defence seem necessary. Defences releasing a person from legal obligations, be it under criminal or tort law, have the function of providing an exemption from legal liability in situations in which, exceptionally, the individual needs to act unlawfully in order to safeguard an interest which cannot otherwise be protected. Normally, however, the protection of the citizens is the task of the state, and only if there is no possibility to resort to state assistance in averting the danger can the individual be justified in disregarding the law in order to guarantee the protection of an interest that is at risk. Otherwise, the individual would be allowed to break the law in situations in which the state can perform its task of protecting the citizens, or be permitted to circumvent the decisions of the law that in a given case a danger must be tolerated.

3.3 Balancing of interests

A first problem when specifying the interests that are at stake when confidential medical information is disclosed in order to prevent a criminal offence consists in defining the dividing line between crime prevention and criminal prosecution. Both problems are often discussed together, apparently because it is felt that the prosecution of a criminal or a crime will at the same time prevent future crimes. However, it is submitted that such a view is not entirely convincing. It is, of

---

[148] La. Rev. Stat. Ann. 9:2800.2(A).
[149] Or St §40.252(1)(a) and (b).
[150] Ct St §52-146c(b)(3).
[151] [1990] 1 All ER 835.

course, possible that a person who has committed a crime in the past may continue to do so in the future. In that case, investigations aimed at prosecuting the perpetrator may at the same time serve the purpose of preventing future crimes. But this is not necessarily the case. Frequently, criminals will not commit more than one offence, and their prosecution can then not be said to be motivated by purposes of crime prevention, apart from the general idea that the prosecution of crime will deter the public from committing criminal offences, an interest that is one feature of the interest in criminal prosecution.

Crime prevention in contrast pursues the primary purpose of preventing harm to potential victims of potential criminal offences. Many uncertainties are involved, as frequently neither the potential victim nor the potential criminal offence can in any way be specified. This complicates the assessment of the weight to be given to the interests in crime prevention in the course of a balancing exercise, as it involves many indeterminable factors.

3.3.1 Weight of the conflicting interests

Given the importance of medical confidentiality as promoting privacy and autonomy, disclosure can be justified only in order to avert a danger to an interest that is of even higher value than medical confidentiality. This, of course, raises the problem of how to rank the competing interests. The German discussion suggests an orientation at the list of offences contained in ss.138, 139 of the Criminal Code, which are all offences that are either directed against weighty public interests, or offences involving some serious form of violence against third parties.[152] In England, reference to the arrestable offences listed in s.116 of PACE has been made, so that the prevention of crimes of murder, manslaughter, rape, treason and kidnapping would justify disclosure. As a more general point, it has been stated that crimes which might result in serious harm or loss of life for individuals can be regarded as substantially more significant than crimes involving theft, fraud or damage to property.[153] In the U.S., it is sometimes required that the danger must involve a threat of physical violence against another.[154] On the other hand, some privilege statutes provide for an exception from the privilege if 'there is risk of personal injury to the person or to other individuals or risk of injury to the property of other individuals'.[155] While English and American courts did not expressly specify this requirement, all case-law existing in this area involves either a threat to the life of third parties, or at least a threat of physical violence or abuse. It seems fair to conclude that there is wide-spread agreement that in cases of a danger to the life or physical integrity of a third party, medical confidentiality may be outweighed by the competing interests of the potential victim.

Is this agreement based on morally justifiable considerations? Most utilitarians seem to agree that the preservation of medical confidentiality in cases of a danger of violence would be more costly than disclosure. However, others disagree and

---

[152] Schönke/Schröder-Lenckner, 31 to s.203; Maurach/Schroeder/Maiwald, at 293.

[153] BMA, *Confidentiality & Disclosure of Health Information.*

[154] See La. Rev. Stat. Ann. 9:2800.2(A).

[155] Ct St §52-146c(b)(3).

argue that it is difficult to assess how many lives might be saved in the long run by maintaining medical confidentiality.[156] Again, therefore, the utilitarian analysis is not helpful for the development of consistent criteria. From a deontological perspective, there seems almost universal agreement that the interest in privacy and personal autonomy has to yield to the interest in life and physical integrity.[157] It should, however, be borne in mind that there may be many cases in which the risk is slim, or in which the injury to be feared might be so minor that it cannot be said to outweigh disclosure. Moreover, it does not seem right to reduce the balancing exercise to a weighing of the potential victim's interests in physical integrity against the patient's interests in autonomy and privacy, as on the patient's side, decisional autonomy serves the patient's health interests and therefore the patient's interests in bodily integrity.

Given the variety of factors influencing the balancing process in the context of crime prevention, it is unsatisfactory to base a decision entirely on the weight of the two interests that stand in conflict with each other. The approaches adopted by the different legal systems reflect this difficulty. Unlike the conflicts occurring in the context of criminal prosecution, none of the legal systems under examination opts for a generalised way of resolving the conflict between medical confidentiality and crime prevention. Rather, all systems adopt a case-by-case approach and make the resolution of the conflict dependent upon the facts of the individual case. The difference between the generalised approaches adopted in the context of criminal prosecution and the case-by-case approach suggested in the context of crime prevention can be explained by the fact that most cases of crime prevention involve a danger to a third party, while cases of criminal prosecution involve a danger to a public interest. Furthermore, unlike the interests behind criminal prosecution which are of a general and abstract nature, the interests behind crime prevention vary from case to case, as crime prevention relates to many completely different potential offences which can have manifold consequences. This means that in every individual case, the outcome of the balancing test will vary, depending on the specific features of the case. Given the imponderabilities of cases of crime prevention, it is thus not appropriate to resolve the conflict between the interest in medical confidentiality and the interest in crime prevention in a generalised way. Instead, it is more adequate to regulate the conflict on a case-by-case basis, as the prevention of harm to third parties requires that the particular risks existing in a given case be assessed and balanced against medical confidentiality. This means that criteria at which the balancing of interests in the individual case can be orientated need to be developed.

3.3.2 Danger, imminence of the risk and general risks of life

Should it make a difference whether or not the danger is present or imminent, and whether there is a danger to the public at large, as opposed to a danger to a specific person? If information can be disclosed whenever there is a risk of danger to another, regardless of whether there is any probability that the risk might

---

[156] Moore, at 193.
[157] Ibid., at 194-5; Beauchamp, Childress, at 426.

materialise in the foreseeable future and whether or not the potential victim is identifiable, this arguably leads to the possibility of disclosure in a large number of cases. Whenever a person shows aggressive or violent tendencies, this could then lead to disclosure, as with such persons there is always at least a slight possibility that the tendencies may one day turn into actual violence. Especially in the context of psychotherapy, where a need for confidentiality is normally perceived as particularly important, this would allow for disclosure in a large number of cases. Given the lack of thoroughly defined legal criteria, the situation is not at all clear. In Germany, the predominant opinion interprets the 'present danger' requirement of the necessity defence to require no more than that the danger might materialise at any time, even though it is not at all clear whether it will occur instantly or at some remote point in time. As long as there is a possibility that the danger could come about immediately, instant action is required and justified in order to avert the danger.[158] The application of this criterion is problematic, as a prediction of the time at which the patient might commit a criminal offence is difficult, if not impossible. The German discussion, for example, raises the problem of whether there is a present danger merely because the permanent dangerousness of a person could at any time lead to the commission of a criminal offence.[159] This puts the emphasis on the difficult problem of risk assessment. In the American case of *Peck v Counseling Service of Addison County*,[160] Billings, Chief Justice, for example, argued in his dissent that it is impossible to predict future violent behaviour, and to determine whether a potentially dangerous person is likely enough to commit an offence so as to pose a danger. Others argue that while the assessment of dangerousness is difficult, it is not impossible, given that it is the normal job of psychiatrists who certify individuals for commitment to a hospital if it is felt that they cause a danger to themselves or to others.[161] Therefore, for a defence justifying disclosure it should be sufficient that the physician or psychotherapist has, in good faith, formed the professional opinion that there is a likelihood that the patient is going to commit the offence. In that moment, the patient will start to constitute a danger, and if it cannot be excluded that the act will be committed immediately, the danger is imminent. Similar considerations can be found in Or St §40.252(1)(b), where it is held to be sufficient that 'in the professional judgment of the person receiving the communications, the declarant poses a danger of committing the crime'.

This raises the question of whether it should be sufficient to base this judgment on the past behaviour of the individual concerned. In *R v Chief Constable of the North Wales Police*,[162] for example, a case in which the police warned the owner of a caravan site of the presence on his site of two persons with previous convictions for serious sexual assaults against children, the English Court of Appeal justified disclosure based on the public interest defence. Contrast the holding in *Re V*

---

[158] Fischer, 4 to s.34.
[159] Schönke/Schröder-Lenckner, 17 to s.34.
[160] 499 A.2d 422 (Vt. 1985), at 427-8.
[161] Bok, at 128; Slovenko, at 300-301; Emson, at 90.
[162] [1998] 3 All ER 310 (CA), at 320 per Lord Woolf MR.

(Sexual Abuse: Disclosure); Re L (Sexual Abuse: Disclosure).[163] In these cases, a local authority wanted to warn single female adults that L posed a considerable threat to the children of women with whom he might cohabit, an assessment that was based on a previous charge with counts of sexual abuse, even though he had been acquitted; and it wanted to disclose to the football league the judge's finding made in family proceedings, that W, who coached the junior teams at the local football club, had committed an indecent assault, and developed an unusual and unhealthy relationship with a 14-year-old. Butler-Sloss LJ held that a risk based on their past behaviour was not sufficient to justify disclosure. This must surely be right. Past actions, however serious and dangerous, cannot in themselves pose a present and imminent danger. Where a person has been released after a criminal conviction, and even more so in the case of an acquittal of a criminal charge, he/she can only pose a present danger if there is a likelihood that he/she will reoffend, which must be based on the individual case, not on a generalised view that sexual offenders cannot be rehabilitated. If one were to accept that such offenders, and even alleged offenders, by their very existence pose an imminent danger to the community, this is a decision that needs to be made by the criminal justice system, not by individual physicians or psychotherapists. Therefore, to apply these considerations to the disclosure of confidential patient information by a physician or psychotherapist, disclosure can only exceptionally be justified where the present condition of the patient gives rise to the fear that an imminent danger for the interests of others might emanate from him/her.

It is submitted that the requirement of a present danger as an isolated criterion is not very helpful. It can achieve no more than exclude disclosure in cases in which no immediate action is, in fact, required and would therefore be disproportionate. This would, for example, apply to the British case of *W v Egdell*,[164] where the Court of Appeal came to the conclusion that the dangerous disposition of a patient as such can be sufficient to justify disclosure under the public interest defence. The result in *Egdell* was reached even though the patient's release from a secure unit was far from imminent. While the Court of Appeal argued that the disclosure was necessary as otherwise the patient's release may have progressed without adequate information being available to the relevant authorities, this seems to be a clear case in which there was no present danger, and in which disclosure should already have been excluded on those grounds.

Is it more meaningful to combine the criterion of the imminence of a danger with the requirement of a specific threat exceeding the general risks of life? In Germany, it is promoted that absent a probability that the risk will materialise, or absent a risk that goes beyond the general risks of life, no danger as required by s.34 of the Criminal Code exists which could be averted by the commission of a criminal act.[165] Considerations resembling the German requirement of a danger exceeding the general risks of life were voiced in the American decision of

---

[163] [1999] 1 FLR 267 (CA), at 274 per Butler-Sloss, LJ.
[164] [1990] 1 All ER 835.
[165] Jakobs, at 415; Schönke/Schröder-Lenckner, 15 to s.34.

Thompson v County of Alameda,[166] and the British decisions in *Re V (Sexual Abuse: Disclosure)*; *Re L (Sexual Abuse: Disclosure)*.[167] In the American case, the court held that no duty to warn arises where the patient is potentially dangerous to a whole community, but where no identifiable victims exist. The focus lies thus less on the probability of the risk, and more on the identifiability of the potential victim. In the British case, the Court of Appeal was not prepared to hold that a risk was sufficient to justify the disclosure where the potential victims were not specified. In *R v Chief Constable of the North Wales Police*,[168] on the other hand, it was held that disclosure for the purpose of preventing crime or alerting members of the public to an apprehended danger can be justified in the public interest.

Is the identifiability of the victim a sustainable criterion for the disclosure of confidential medical information? It may be argued that in cases in which any member of the public, or any member of a large class of people is at risk of becoming the victim of a potentially dangerous person, the general risks of life are not exceeded, while this changes where the potential victim is a clearly identified or at least an identifiable person. However, the significance of the interests to be protected by disclosure is exactly the same in all of these cases. Even if one were prepared to agree that in the first scenario the victim was only exposed to a general risk of life, this in itself can hardly serve as a moral justification for not allowing a disclosure if the risk could be prevented. Therefore, while in most cases only identifiable victims can effectively be protected from criminal acts of others, this cannot be a strict requirement in cases which deviate from the norm.

3.3.3 Avoidability of the risk

The main problem may then be described as a problem of the avoidability of the risk, or the suitability of disclosure as a means to avert the danger, a criterion which can be found in the German necessity defence, and which was similarly promoted in the decision of *US v Glass*[169] and in the English case of *Re V (Sexual Abuse: Disclosure)*; *Re L (Sexual Abuse: Disclosure)*.[170] To avert a risk through disclosure is difficult where the victim is not identified or identifiable, unless disclosure is made to the public at large, or to an unlimited class of potential victims. The question of whether such a wide disclosure can be justifiable was answered in the affirmative by the English Court of Appeal in *R v Chief Constable of the North Wales Police*,[171] when it held that disclosure to alert members of the public to the apprehended danger posed by the mere presence in their area of persons with a past record of sexual abuse of children was justified in the public interest. However, it needs to be borne in mind that disclosure in cases of a risk to a non-identifiable member of a large group or of the public can normally not avert the risk, as it is difficult to see how the potential victim can protect him/herself

---

[166] 614 P.2d 728 (Cal. Sup. Ct. 1980), at 734.

[167] [1999] 1 FLR 267 (CA), at 274 per Butler-Sloss, LJ.

[168] [1998] 3 All ER 310 (CA), at 320 per Lord Woolf MR.

[169] 133 F.3d 1356 (10th Cir. 1998), at 1359-60 per Porfilio, Circuit J.

[170] [1999] 1 FLR 267 (CA), at 274 per Butler-Sloss, LJ.

[171] [1998] 3 All ER 310 (CA), at 320 per Lord Woolf MR.

against the risk, and how any potential protection might go beyond the general precautions of preventing to become the victim of a criminal offence.

This might be different in cases in which the victim is identified or identifiable, which needs to be assessed carefully in each individual case. The possibilities to avert a danger through a disclosure to the police will even then frequently be uncertain. This can be demonstrated at the example of the *Tarasoff* case, where the psychotherapist had informed the campus police, but the police had to release the patient. Disclosure to the police was thus made but proved inefficient to avoid the harm. Given that the time and form of the potential commission of the offence remained unclear, the police could not prevent the offence, even though the victim was clearly identified. This is because the police does not have many preventive measures at its disposal to avert an unspecified risk, as a preventive arrest is rarely lawful and would in most cases be disproportionate.[172] Even disclosure to an identified victim will often not be a suitable means to avoid the danger as can, again, be seen at the example of *Tarasoff*. The victim was killed two months after the threat had been uttered in a therapeutic session. It is very doubtful whether disclosure to the victim would have averted the danger. However, if on the facts of the case there is a possibility that the victim could avoid the risk, disclosure should be justified, if the other criteria identified for a lawful disclosure are equally met.

3.3.4 Proportionality of disclosure

This leaves the question of the proportionality of disclosure. Proportionality requires that the disclosure is a suitable means to avert the risk, and that it is necessary, that is that no less intrusive means are available to avert the danger. The criteria so far developed, that is those of the imminence of the risk and of the avoidability of harm form part of the proportionality analysis. If the danger is not imminent, a less intrusive means would be to wait with disclosure until the risk becomes imminent. Where disclosure cannot avoid the risk, it is pointless and therefore not a suitable means to avert the danger. It has been seen that cases in which disclosure for the purposes of harm prevention might be regarded as desirable are mostly not clear cut, in that it will frequently not be possible to determine with certainty whether or not the risk is imminent and/or could be averted by disclosure. It would therefore not be satisfactory to look at these criteria in isolation, unless the risk is clearly not imminent and/or can clearly not be avoided, so that a justification of disclosure must already fail on those grounds. In all other cases, the uncertainty of the imminence and/or avoidability of the risk should not in itself exclude that disclosure be justified. Instead, it is submitted that the uncertainty of the factors which influence the analysis of whether or not disclosure can be justified needs to be taken into account when making an overall assessment of the proportionality of disclosure.[173] Thus, the decision on whether or not disclosure is proportionate in a given case requires a balancing of the interests

---

[172] Kottow (1994), at 477; see also the discussion in *Osman v UK*, Judgment of 28 October 1998, (2000) 29 E.H.R.R. 245, at para.116.

[173] This conforms with the German approach to the necessity defence, see Fischer, 11 to s.34.

that are in conflict in the individual case, based on an assessment of the
imminence, the avoidability and the seriousness of the risk, on the one hand, and of
the interests to be harmed by disclosure, on the other. The decisions in *Re V
(Sexual Abuse: Disclosure); Re L (Sexual Abuse: Disclosure)* were to some extent
based on such an analysis.[174] In both cases, the risk consisted of the fear that the
potential paedophiliac tendencies of a person could put children with whom the
person might get in contact at risk. In both cases disclosure was regarded as
unjustified, as the risk was so vague that disclosure would only have had a chance
of preventing a potential danger if it had been made to a large number of people, a
drastic measure to which the degree of risk did not give rise, and which, when
contrasted with the certain violation of the interests of the respective applicants,
was regarded as disproportionate. Had such a proportionality analysis been
performed in *R v Chief Constable of the North Wales Police*,[175] it is submitted that
disclosure would equally have been rejected in that case. The probability that an
imminent danger existed was extremely low, as was the avoidability of harm if, in
fact, they did pose a risk. The rights of the couple were severely infringed in order
to avoid a very slight and uncertain risk, and disclosure was therefore clearly
disproportionate. As the example of the persecution in Britain of paedophiles who
have been released from prison shows, a disclosure of these potential risks to the
public at large might not only violate the person's privacy interests, but also raise
concerns for their safety and, therefore, their physical integrity and right to life,
which strengthens the case against disclosure to the public at large.[176] The analysis
as performed by the Court of Appeal in *R v Chief Constable of the North Wales
Police* which was entirely focused on the seriousness of the risk if it were to
materialise, without taking into account the remoteness of the risk and the rights at
stake in case of disclosure, is thus too narrow to provide an adequate assessment of
the specific features of each individual case.

  Based on these considerations, disclosure to the potential victim or the police
cannot be a proportionate means of crime prevention, unless the risk is specific
enough to give preventive measures at least a chance of success, which would
exclude all cases in which the threat merely emanates from potentially dangerous
characteristics of an individual. It is submitted that cases of potentially dangerous
patients who do not pose a danger to another that is specific enough to be averted
by disclosure either to the potential victim or the police need to be dealt with by the
law regulating the commitment to psychiatric hospitals and other supervisory
measures. If in the individual case, the risk potentially emanating from the patient
is not specific enough to justify measures restricting his/her liberty, the law has
made a decision that any remaining risk in these situation needs to be tolerated by
society, just like in the cases of persons with aggressive tendencies whose
preventive arrest in order to make sure that they will never commit violent acts
would be unacceptable. Disclosure, though a less intrusive means, can nevertheless

---

[174] [1999] 1 FLR 267 (CA), per Butler-Sloss, LJ.
[175] [1998] 3 All ER 310 (CA), at 320 per Lord Woolf MR.
[176] *Venables v News Group Newspapers Ltd* [2001] Fam 430 (CA), at 462 per Butler-Sloss, LJ.

only be justifiable if it is proportionate which, as was shown, in almost all of these situations is not the case.

3.4 Conclusion

It has been demonstrated that in cases of a disclosure of confidential medical information for the purposes of crime prevention, a generalised approach that could be easily implemented by a statutory provision, such as a general exception to medical privilege, is not appropriate, as the conflict needs to be decided on a case-by-case basis, taking account of the particular circumstances of each case. The analysis in each case must be based on the following considerations:

- the likelihood, predicted on the basis of the patient's present condition, that the patient poses an imminent risk;
- the likelihood that disclosure might avert the risk;
- the weight to be attached to the interests that would be at risk;
- the extent to which the patient's interest in medical confidentiality would be violated by disclosure.

Based on these factors, a general proportionality analysis needs to be performed in each case, the outcome of which does not depend on an abstract evaluation of the interests at stake, but instead on a detailed analysis of the value of the competing interests, the degree of danger, and the suitability of the disclosure for the prevention of harm.

How these considerations can be implemented in the different legal systems varies. In the U.S., this can best be achieved by including in the respective privilege statutes a provision specifically regulating exceptions to medical privilege for the purpose of crime prevention, which is already the case in some U.S. States. These provisions can make the justification of disclosure subject to the likelihood that the patient poses an imminent risk that can be averted by disclosure, and, most importantly, impose a proportionality analysis. In Germany, where a specific defence for this situation would run counter to the generalised way in which the Criminal Code deals with defences, the necessity defence needs to be the starting point. It already contains the requirement of the imminence and avoidability of the risk and of the proportionality of the disclosure. The main problem in the context of the German analysis is how to specify the criteria of the necessity defence so as to fit the case of disclosure of confidential patient information which could best be achieved by judicial interpretation of the necessity defence. In England, the same could be achieve if the judiciary were to interpret the public interest defence in the context of disclosures for crime prevention according to the criteria suggested above. These considerations to some extent also apply to France. However, in the context of French law, a first step would have to be to apply the necessity defence existing in the French Criminal Code, instead of leaving it to the physician to decide whether and according to which criteria to violate patient confidentiality for the purposes of crime prevention.

PART 3 – CONCLUDING REMARKS

The comparative analysis has illustrated that there are no easy answers to the problems raised. While a surprising unanimity regarding the significance of medical confidentiality among all legal systems as well as the different philosophical schools can be observed, this consensus evaporates as soon as medical confidentiality conflicts with the interests in criminal prosecution, crime prevention or with defence rights. In this area of law, all comes down to value judgments, and the ethical analysis indicates that there are no universally accepted principles at which such judgments could be orientated. This result was confirmed by the comparative legal study which demonstrates that, notwithstanding some similarities, different legal systems not only differ in style and legal method, but also in the value judgments promoted and in the results achieved.

With regard to the reasons for which medical confidentiality receives protection, the value judgments made by the different legal systems reflect the two main ethical approaches to medical confidentiality, that is utilitarian and deontological approaches. Thus, medical confidentiality is regarded in all legal systems as important to promote the patient's privacy and autonomy. All legal systems also accept the consequentialist argument that medical confidentiality is important in order to enhance patient frankness in the context of the physician-patient relationship, which is considered to be important for the preservation of individual and public health. Courts and legislatures in all systems intuitively seem to combine different justifications for medical confidentiality, but mostly, one approach will be given precedence over the other. Thus, the German debate, while occasionally referring to utilitarian ideas, is primarily influenced by deontological thought, while the debate in the UK is predominantly based on utilitarian theory, and deontological justifications are only of secondary importance. The comparative study leads to the conclusion that where medical confidentiality is primarily based on consequentialist thought, it will, in case of conflict, often have to yield to other interests. Particularly with regard to the conflicts examined in this book, the consequences of decisions to the detriment of the interests in criminal prosecution, defence rights and crime prevention will frequently be more obvious and graphic than the consequences of decisions to the detriment of the interests behind medical confidentiality. Where medical confidentiality is protected as promoting privacy and autonomy, the protection will be far more comprehensive, as there is then an increased willingness to accept that such protection may sometimes result in harm to other important interests. As soon as conflicts between medical confidentiality and other interests have to be decided, the weight attached to the right to privacy thus gains importance.

The comparative analysis confirms that values are relative, and that alternative ways of approaching a problem are not only possible, but also practised. It can be seen that different systems function quite well even though they take diametrically opposed approaches to the same problem. This helps to put domestic attitudes into perspective. Thus, the English debate which fears the recognition of medical privilege because of its possibly adverse consequences for an effective administration of justice can draw from a comparative study that other legal systems have made a fundamentally different value decision, and that the administration of justice has nevertheless not ceased to be effective. While the comparison shows that difficulties in balancing competing interests, another reason why medical privilege is rejected in the UK, do, in fact, arise, it nevertheless demonstrates that it is possible to overcome this problem. Consequently, the rejection of medical privilege no longer appears to be the only logical response to this dilemma. On the other hand, the German debate which is imbued with the overriding importance of privacy protection, can infer from the comparative analysis that without medical privilege, patients will not necessarily feel that their privacy and autonomy is fundamentally impaired, as neither the British example nor the example of American States without privilege protection give any indication for such an assumption.

This book has highlighted many of the internal inadequacies and inconsistencies of each of the four legal systems and demonstrated how they could be overcome, both from a domestic perspective, focusing on the internal logic of each system, and from a broader comparative perspective, by illustrating possible ways to change the law so as to enhance the patient's right to medical confidentiality while giving due regard to potentially competing individual rights. Some important issues necessarily remain unmentioned, as they lie beyond the scope of this book. It may, for example, be interesting to examine whether it is compatible with the rationale behind medical confidentiality and medical privilege that the patient can be examined about confidential medical facts, where the physician's testimony about the same information is barred by privilege. Indeed, Shuman's observation made in 1985, that with regard to medical privilege, much work remains to be done,[177] is still valid.

---

[177] Shuman, at 687.

Bibliography

Adams, Jean; 'Confidentiality and Huntingdon's chorea' (1990) JME 196-9

Adshead, Gwen; 'The psychiatrist's view - Preventing violent crime is not a medical role' (1995) 311 BMJ 1619-20

Advisory Committee's Notes on the Proposed Federal Rules of Evidence (1972-1973) 56 F.R.D. 183

Agostini, Eric; 'Le grand secret', D.1996, chron.58

Albucher; Commentary on the decision of Ch. civ. 6 February 1954, JCP.1954.II.8107

Allan, T.R.S.; 'Legal privilege and the accused: an unfair balancing act' (1988) NLJ 668-9

Allen, Anita L.; 'Genetic privacy: emerging concepts and values', in: Rothstein, Mark A. (ed.); *Genetic secrets* (Yale University Press: New Haven, London, 1997), 31-59

Alternativkommentar zur Strafprozeßordnung, Band 1, Rudolf Wassermann (ed.); (Luchterhand: Neuwied, 1988)

Alternativkommentar zum Strafgesetzbuch, Band 2, Teilband 1, Rudolf Wassermann (ed.); (Luchterhand: Neuwied, 1992)

Amelung, Klaus; 'Grenzen der Beschlagnahme notarieller Unterlagen', DNotZ 1984, 195-225

Anonymous; 'Doctors, Drivers and Confidentiality' (1974) BMJ 399-400

Anonymous; 'Developments in privileged communications' (1985) 98 Harvard Law Review 1450-1666

Anzalec, Victor; 'Les seules exceptions au principe du secret médical', Gaz. Pal. 1971.113

Ashworth, Andrew; *Principles of Criminal Law* (Oxford University Press: Oxford, 3rd ed. 1999)

Baier, Helmut; *Strafprozessuale Zeugnisverweigerungsrechte außerhalb der Strafprozeßordnung als Ergänzung der §§ 52 ff StPO* (Peter Lang Europäischer Verlag der Wissenschaften: Frankfurt a.M., 1996)

Bailey, S.H.; Harris, D.J.; Jones, B.L.; *Civil Liberties, Cases and Materials* (Butterworths: London, 5th ed. 2001)

Bainbridge, David; *EC Data Protection Directive* (Butterworths: London, Dublin, Edinburgh, 1996)

Bandisch, Günter; 'Mandant und Patient, schutzlos bei Durchsuchung von Kanzlei und Praxis?' NJW 1987, 2200-2206

Barnett, Kevin; 'Adoption and Confidential Information' (1997) Fam Law 489-93

Baumann, Jürgen; Weber, Ulrich; Mitsch, Wolfgang; *Strafrecht Allgemeiner Teil* (Verlag Ernst und Werner Gieseking: Bielefeld, 10th ed. 1995)

Beauchamp, Tom L.; Childress, James F.; *Principles of Biomedical Ethics* (Oxford University Press: New York, Oxford, 5th ed. 2001)

Bentham, Jeremy; *An Introduction to the Principles of Morals and Legislation*, Burns, J.H.; Hart, H.L.A. (eds.); (Clarendon Press: Oxford, 1996)

Bevan, Vaughan; Lidstone, Kenneth; *The Investigation of Crime* (Buttherworths: London, 2d ed. 1996)

Beyleveld, Deryck; Histed, Elise; 'Betrayal of confidence in the Court of Appeal' (2000) Med Law Int 277-311

Black, Douglas; 'Absolute Confidentiality?' in: Gillon, Raanan (ed.); *Principles of Health Care Ethics* (John Wiley and Sons Ltd: Chichester, 1994), 479-88

Bloom, Lackland H.; 'The law office search: An emerging problem and some suggested solutions' (1980) 69 Georgetown Law Journal 1-100

Bok, Sissela; *Secrets* (Pantheon Books: New York, 1982)

Boyd, Kenneth; 'HIV infection and AIDS: the ethics of medical confidentiality' (1992) 18 JME 173-9

British Medical Association, *Confidentiality & Disclosure of Health Information,* (1999)

Camp, Charles H.; Levey, Stuart; 'The Privilege against Self-Incrimination', in: Stone, Scott N.; Taylor, Robert K. (eds.); *Testimonial Privileges*, vol.2 (Shepard's/McGraw-Hill, Inc.: Colorado Springs, 2d ed. 1994)

Chafee, Zechariah; 'Privileged communications: is justice served or obstruction by closing the doctor's mouth on the witness stand?' (1943) 52 Yale Law Journal 607-17

Champeil-Desplats, Véronique; 'La notion de droit "fondamental" et le droit constitutionnel français', D.1995.chron.323

Chappart, F.; Report on the decision of 24 April 1969, D.1969.637

Chomienne, Christian; Guéry, Christian; 'Secret, révélation, abstention, ou les limites de la liberté de conscience du professionnel dans le nouveau code pénal', ALD.1995.comm.85

Cissell, James C.; *Federal Criminal Trials* (Michie Law Publishers: Charlottesville, Virginia, 4th ed., 1996)

Coad, Jonathan; 'Privacy – Article 8. Who needs it'. (2001) 12 Ent.L.R. 226-33

Combaldieu, Raoul; Report on the decision of Ch. crim. 22 December 1966, D.1967.122

Corker, David; 'Involuntary disclosure of private medical records to the defence in criminal proceedings' (1998) 38 Med. Sci. Law 138-41

Criminal Law Revision Committee Eleventh Report, Cmnd 4991 (1972)

Damien, André (1989); *Le Secret Nécessaire,* (Desclée de Brouwer: Paris, 1989)

Damien, André; 'Le secret professionnel', Gaz.Pal.1982.doct.136

Davies, Michael; *Textbook on Medical Law* (Blackstone Press: London, 2nd ed. 1998)

Décheix, Pierre; 'Un droit de l'homme mis à mal: le secret professionnel', D.1983.chron.133

Desportes, Frederic; Le Gunehec, Francis; *Le Nouveau Droit Pénal, Tome 1 – Droit Pénal Géneral* (Economica: Paris, 7th ed. 2000)

Domb, Brian; 'I shot the sheriff, but only my analyst knows: shrinking the psychotherapist-patient privilege' (1990-1991) 5 Journal of Law and Health 209-36

Dworkin, Ronald; *Taking Rights Seriously* (Duckworth: London, 1977)

Emson, H.E.; 'Confidentiality: a modified value' (1988) JME 87-90

Engelhardt Jr., H. Tristram; *The Foundations of Bioethics* (Oxford University Press: New York, Oxford, 2nd ed. 1996)

Ensor, Judith C.; 'Doctor-patient confidentiality versus duty to warn in the context of Aids patients and their partners' (1988) 47 Maryland Law Review 675-700

Favoreu, Louis; Philip, Loic; *Les Grandes Décisions du Conseil Constitutionnel* (Dalloz: Paris, 11th ed. 2001)

Feldman, David; *Civil Liberties and Human Rights in England and Wales* (Oxford University Press: Oxford, 2nd ed. 2002)

Fénaux, Henri; Commentary on the decision of 5 June 1985, D.1988.106

Fenwick, Helen; *Civil Liberties* (Cavendish: London, 3rd ed. 2002)

Fezer, Gerhard; *Strafprozeßrecht* (C.H. Beck Verlag: München, 2nd ed. 1995)

Fischer, Thomas; *Strafgesetzbuch* (C.H. Beck Verlag: München, 50th ed. 2001)

Flécheux, Georges; Commentary on the decision of Ch. crim. 17 June 1980, JCP.1982.II.19721

Flor, Georg; 'Beruf und Schweigepflicht - Eine Gegenüberstellung', JR 1953, 368-72

Francis, Huw W.S.; 'Of gossips, eavesdroppers and peeping toms' (1982) 8 JME 134-43

Freund, Georg; 'Verurteilung und Freispruch bei Verletzung der Schweigepflicht eines Zeugen', GA 1993, 49-66

Fried, Charles; 'Privacy (A moral analysis)', in: Schoeman, F.D.; *Philosophical Dimensions of Privacy: An Anthology* (Cambridge University Press: Cambridge, 1984), 203-22

Gavison, Ruth; 'Privacy and the limits of the law' (1980) 89 Yale Law Journal 421-71

Gearty, Conor; 'The United Kingdom', in: Gearty, Conor (ed.); *European Civil Liberties and the European Convention on Human Rights, A Comparative Study* (Kluwer International: The Hague; 1997), 53-103

Gellman, Robert M.; 'Prescribing privacy: the uncertain role of the physician in the protection of patient privacy' (1984) 62 North Carolina Law Review 255-94

General Medical Council, *Confidentiality: Protecting and Providing Information,* (2000)

Gillon, Raanan; 'Confidentiality' (1985) 291 BMJ 1634-6

Göppinger, Hans; 'Die Entbindung von der Schweigepflicht und die Herausgabe oder Beschlagnahme von Krankenblättern', NJW 1958, 241-5

Gostin, Lawrence O.; 'Health information privacy' (1995) 80 Cornell Law Review 451-528

Gramberg-Danielsen, Berndt; Kern, Bernd-Rüdiger; 'Die Schweigepflicht des Arztes gegenüber privaten Verrechnungsstellen', NJW 1998, 2708-10

Griffin, James; *Well-Being: its Measurement and Moral Importance* (Clarendon Press: Oxford, 1986)

Grubb, Andrew; Commentary on *R v Cardiff Crown Court, ex parte Kellam*, [1994] 16 BMLR 7, in: (1994) Med. L. Rev. 371

Grubb, Andrew; Pearl, David; 'Medicine, health, family and the law' (1986) Fam Law 227-40

Gulphe, Pierre; Commentary on the decision of Ch. crim. 8 May 1947, D.1947.109

Gurfein, Pamela; 'The assault on the citadel of privilege proceeds apace: the unreasonableness of law office searches' (1981) 49 Fordham Law Review 708-44

Gurry, Francis; *Breach of Confidence* (Clarendon Press: Oxford, 1984)

Haffke, Bernhard; 'Schweigepflicht, Verfahrensrevision und Beweisverbot', GA 1973, 65-9

Harvard, John; 'Medical confidence' (1985) 11 JME 8-11

Henkin, Louis; 'Privacy and Autonomy' (1974) 74 Columbia Law Review 1410-33

Herman, Barbara; 'Mutual aid and respect for persons' (1984) 94 Ethics 577-602

Hermann, Donald H.J.; Gagliano, Rosalind D.; 'Aids, therapeutic confidentiality, and warning third parties' (1989) 48 Maryland Law Review 55-76

Hill, Alfred; 'Testimonial privilege and fair trial' (1980) 80 Columbia Law Review 1173-96

Hogan, Maureen B.; 'The constitutionality of an absolute privilege for rape crisis counselling: a criminal defendant's sixth amendment rights versus a rape victim's right to confidential therapeutic counselling' (1989) 30 Boston College Law Review 411-76

Hondius, Frits; 'Protecting medical and genetic data' (1997) 4 EJHL 361-88

Honnorat, J.; Melennec, Louis; 'Vers une rélativisation du secret médical', JCP.1979.I.2936

Jakobs, Günther; *Strafrecht Allgemeiner Teil* (de Gruyter Verlag: Berlin, New York, 2nd ed. 1991)

Jarass, Hans D.; Pieroth, Bodo; *Grundgesetz für die Bundesrepublik Deutschland* (C.H. Beck Verlag: München, 6th ed. 2002)

Jay, Rosemary; Hamilton, Angus; *Data Protection Law and Practice*, (Sweet & Maxwell: London, 1999)

Jones, Michael A.; 'Medical confidentiality and the public interest' (1990) 6 PN 16-24

Kant, Immanuel; *Foundations of the Metaphysics of Morals*, Wolff, Robert Paul (ed.); (The Bobbs-Merril Company, Inc.: Indianapolis, New York, 1969)

Karlsruher Kommentar zur Strafprozeßordnung und zum Gerichtsverfassungsgesetz, Pfeiffer, Gerd (ed.); (C.H. Beck Verlag: München, 4th ed. 1999)

Kendrick, Martha M.; Tsakonas, Elizabeth E.; Smith, Paul M.; 'The physician-patient, psychotherapist-patient, and related privileges', in: Stone, Scott N.; Taylor, Robert K. (eds.); *Testimonial Privileges*, vol.2 (Shepard's/McGraw-Hill, Inc.: Colorado Springs, 2nd ed. 1994)

Kennedy, Ian; Grubb, Andrew; *Medical Law: Text with Materials* (Butterworths: London, 3rd ed. 2000)

Kielwein, Gerhard; 'Unterlassung und Teilnahme', GA 1955, 225-32

Kleinknecht, Theodor; Meyer-Goßner, Lutz; *Strafprozeßordnung* (C.H. Beck Verlag: München, 45th ed. 2001)

Klieman, Rikki J.; *Representation of Witnesses Before Federal Grand Juries* (Rochester: Deerfield, NY, 4th ed. 1999)

Klöhn, Wolfgang; *Der Schutz der Intimsphäre im Strafprozeß* (Dissertation: Göttingen, 1984)

Klug, Francesca; 'The Human Rights Act 1998, *Pepper v Hart* and all that' (1999) Public Law 246-73

Kohlhaas, Max; 'Strafrechtliche Schweigepflicht und prozessuales Schweigerecht', GA 1958, 65-76

Kottow, Michael H. (1986); 'Medical confidentiality: an intransigent and absolute obligation' (1986) JME 117-22

Kottow, Michael H. (1994).; 'Stringent and predictable medical confidentiality', in : Gillon, Raanan (ed.); *Principles of Health Care Ethics* (John Wiley and Sons Ltd: Chichester, 1994), 471-8

Kramer, Bernhard; 'Heimliche Tonbandaufnahmen im Strafprozeß', NJW 1990, 1760-4

Krattenmaker, Thomas G.; 'Testimonial privileges in federal courts: an alternative to the proposed Federal Rules of Evidence' (1973) 62 Georgetown Law Journal 61-123

Krekeler, Wilhelm; 'Zufallsfunde bei Berufsgeheimnisträgern und ihre Verwertbarkeit', NStZ 1987, 199-203

Kreuzer; 'Aids und Strafrecht', ZStW 100 (1988), 786-816

Lapointe, Eric; Commentary on the decision of 20 December 1967, D.1969.309

Laufs, Adolf; 'Krankenpapiere und Persönlichkeitsschutz', NJW 1975, 1433-7

Laufs, Adolf; Uhlenbruck, Wilhelm; *Handbuch des Arztrechts* (C.H. Beck Verlag: München, 3rd ed. 2002)

Law Commission; *Breach of Confidence*, Cmnd.8388 (1981)

Laws, John; 'The limitations of human rights' (1998) Public Law, 254-65

Le Roy, Max; Commentary on the decision of 2 February 1962, CA Paris, D.1963.280

Légal, A., Commentary on the decision of 8 May 1947, JCP.1948.II.4141

Leipziger Kommentar zum Strafgesetzbuch, Jähnke, Burkhard; Laufhütte, Heinrich-Wilhelm; Odersky, Walter (eds.); (de Gruyter Verlag: Berlin, New York, 11ᵗʰ ed. 2001)

Lenckner, Theodor; 'Ärztliches Berufsgeheimnis', in: Göppinger, Hans (ed.); *Arzt und Recht* (C.H. Beck Verlag: München, 1966)

Lenckner, Theodor; 'Aussagepflicht, Schweigepflicht und Zeugnisverweigerungsrecht', NJW 1965, 321-7

Loiret, Patrick; *La Théorie du Secret Médical* (Masson: Paris, 1988)

Lorenz, Franz Lucien; 'Beschlagnahme von Krankenunterlagen - Prozessuale Anmerkungen zur Memmingen-Entscheidung des BGH', MDR 1992, 313-8

Louisell, David W.; Crippin, Byron M.; 'Evidentiary privileges' (1956) 40 Minnesota Law Review 413-36

Löwe/Rosenberg; *Die Strafprozeßordnung und das Gerichtsverfassungsgesetz*, Rieß, Peter (ed.); 1. Band (de Gruyter Verlag: Berlin, New York, 25ᵗʰ ed. 1999)

Markesinis, Basil; Unberath, Hannes; *The German Law of Torts: A Comparative Treatise* (Hart Publishing: Oxford, 4ᵗʰ ed. 2002)

Marsden, Andrew K.; 'Helping the police with their enquiries' (1992) 85 Journal of the Royal Society of Medicine, 187-8

Mason, J. Kenneth; McCall Smith, Alexander; *Law and Medical Ethics* (Butterworths: London, Edinburgh, Dublin, 5ᵗʰ ed. 1999)

Matthews, Paul; 'Breach of confidence and legal privilege' (1981) 1 Legal Studies 77-93

Maurach, Reinhart; Schroeder, Friedrich-Christian; Maiwald, Manfred; *Strafrecht Besonderer Teil 1* (C.F. Müller Verlag: Heidelberg, 8ᵗʰ ed. 1995)

May, Richard; *Criminal Evidence* (Sweet and Maxwell: London, 4ᵗʰ ed. 1999)

Mazeau, Henri; Mazeau, Léon; Mazeau, Jean; Chabas, François; *Leçons de Droit Civil - Les Personnes*, Tome 1 vol. 2 (Florence Laroche-Gisserot, Montchrestien: Paris, 8ᵗʰ ed. 1997)

Mazen, Noël Jean; Commentary on the decision of 17 January 1980, CA Lyon, Gaz.Pal. 1981.2.491

Mazen, Noël Jean; *Le Secret Professionnel des Praticiens de la Santé* (Vigot: Paris, 1988)

McHale, Jean V. (1989); 'Confidentiality, an absolute obligation?' (1989) 52 MLR 715-21

McHale, Jean V. (1993); *Medical Confidentiality and Medical Privilege* (Routledge: London and New York, 1993)

Medical Defence Union; *Confidentiality* (1993)

Melennec, Louis; 'Perquisitions, saisies et secret professionnel médical', Gaz.Pal. 1980.doct.145

Mémeteau, Gérard; 'L'honneur d'un président', Gaz.Pal. 1996, 754-9

Merle, Roger; Vitu, André; *Traité de Droit Criminel*, Tome II, *Procédure Pénale* (Editions Cujas: Paris, 4ᵗʰ ed. 1989)

Michalowski, Sabine; Woods, Lorna; *German Constitutional Law* (Ashgate Dartmouth: Aldershot, Brookfield USA, Singapore, Sydney, 1999)

Mill, John Stuart; *Utilitarianism*, Crisp, Roger (ed.); (Oxford University Press: Oxford, 1998)

Mogill, Michael A.; 'Avoiding "the big chill": protecting the attorney-client relationship from the effects of *Zurcher*' (1988-1989) 21 Connecticut Law Review 293-363

Montgomery, Jonathan; 'Confidentiality and the Immature Minor' (1987) Fam Law 101-4

Monzein, Paul; 'Réflexions sur le "Secret médical"', D.1984.chron.107

Moore, Nancy J.; 'Limits to attorney-client confidentiality: a "philosophically informed" and comparative approach to legal and medical ethics' (1985-86) 36 Case Western Reserve Law Review 177-247

Müller, Klaus; 'Die Schweigepflicht im ärztlichen Standesrecht', MDR 1971, 965-71

Müller-Dietz, Heinz; 'Juristische Grundlagen und Dimensionen der Schweigepflicht des Arztes', in: Jung, Heike; Meiser, Richard Johannes; Müller, Egon; *Aktuelle Probleme und Perspektiven des Arztrechts* (Enke Verlag: Stuttgart, 1989), 39-57

Murphy, Peter; *Murphy on Evidence* (Blackstone Press: London, 7th ed. 2000)

Muschallik, Thomas; *Die Befreiung von der ärztlichen Schweigepflicht und vom Zeugnisverweigerungsrecht im Strafprozeß* (Dissertation: Köln, 1984)

Neill, Sir Brian; 'Privacy: A challenge for the next century', in: Markesinis, Basil S. (ed.); *Protecting Privacy* (Oxford University Press: Oxford, 1999), 1-28

Newdick, Christopher; 'Common law and the GMC's standards of ethical conduct' (1996) 3 EJHL 373-81

Nomos Kommentar zum Strafgesetzbuch (Nomos Verlag: Baden Baden, 1995)

O'Neill, Onora; 'Universal laws and ends-in-themselves' (1989) 72 Monist 341-61

Oppenheim, Elliott B.; *The Medical Record as Evidence* (Lexis Law Publishing: Charlottesville, Virginia, 1998)

Orentlicher, David; 'Genetic privacy in the patient-physician relationship, in: Rothstein, Mark A. (ed.); *Genetic Secrets* (Yale University Press: New Haven, London, 1997), 77-91

Ostendorf; 'Der strafrechtliche Schutz von Drittgeheimnissen', JR 1981, 444-8

Ostendorf; 'Die Informationsrechte der Strafverfolgungsbehörden gegenüber anderen staatlichen Behörden im Widerstreit mit deren strafrechtlichen Geheimhaltungspflichten', DRiZ 1981, 4-11

Palandt, Otto; *Bürgerliches Gesetzbuch* (C.H. Beck Verlag; München, 61th ed. 2002)

Parent, W.A.; 'A new definition of privacy for the law' (1983) 2 Law and Philosophy 305-38

Peiris, G.L.; 'Medical professional privilege in Commonwealth law' (1984) 33 ICLQ 301-330

Petry, Horst; *Beweisverbote im Strafprozeßrecht* (Dr. N. Stoytscheff Verlag: Darmstadt, 1971)

Peytel, Adrien; 'Les médecins et le délit de commission par ommission,' Gaz.Pal. 1952.2.doct.13

Picard, Etienne; 'The right to privacy in French law', in: Markesinis, Basil S. (ed.); *Protecting Privacy* (Oxford University Press: Oxford, 1999), 49-103

Powell, Greg; Magrath, Chris; *Police and Criminal Evidence Act 1984, a Practical Guide* (Longman: Guildford, 1985)

Pradel, Jean; 'L'incidence du secret médical sur le cours de la justice pénale', JCP.1969.I.2234

Pradel, Jean; Commentary on the decision of 14 February 1978, D.1978.354

Pradel, Jean; Danti-Juan, Michel; *Droit Pénal Spécial*, Tome III (Editions Cujas: Paris, 1995)

Rassat, Michèle-Laure; 'La révélation médicale', D.1989.chron.107

Rassat (1999), Michèle-Laure; *Droit Pénal Spécial* (Dalloz: Paris, 2nd ed. 1999)

Reboul, Marcel; 'Des cas-limite du secret professionnel médical', JCP.1950.I.825

Rengier, Rudolf; *Die Zeugnisverweigerungsrechte im geltenden und im künftigen Strafverfahrensrecht* (Ferdinand Schöningh Verlag: Paderborn, München, Wien, Zürich, 1979)

Rivero, Jean; *Les Libertés Publiques*, Tome 1, *Les Droits de l'Homme* (Presses Universitaires de France: Paris, 8th ed. 1997); Tome 2, *Le Régime des Principales Libertés* (Presses Universitaires de France: Paris, 6th ed. 1997)

Ross, W.D.; *The Right and the Good* (Clarendon Press: Oxford, 1930)

Roujou de Boubée, Gabriel; Bouloc, Bernard; Fancillon, Jacques; Mayaud, Yves; *Code Pénal Commenté* (Dalloz: Paris, 1996)

Roxin, Claus; *Strafverfahrensrecht* (C.H. Beck Verlag: München, 25th ed. 1998)

Rudolphi, Hans-Joachim; Anmerkung zu BGH NStZ 1998, 471, in: NStZ 1998, 472-4

Ryckmans, Xavier; Meert-Van de Put, Régine; *Les Droits et les Obligations des Médecins*, Tome 1 (Larcier: Bruxelles, 2nd ed. 1971)

Saltzburg, Stephen A.; 'Privileges and professionals: lawyers and psychiatrists' (1980) 66 Virginia Law Review 597-651

Samson, Erich; 'Im Irrgarten von Zeugnisverweigerungsrecht und Beschlagnahmefreiheit', StV 2000, 55-6

Samuels, Alec; 'A question of privilege: reflections by a lawyer' (1986) 26 Med. Sci. Law 235-7

Savatier, René; Auby, Jean-Marie; Savatier, Jean; Péquignot, Henri; *Traité de Droit Médical* (Librairie Technique: Paris, 1956)

Savatier, René; Commentary on the decision of 11 February 1960, JCP.1960.II.11604

Savatier, René; Commentary on the decision of 22 December 1966, JCP.1967.II.15126

Savatier, René; Commentary on the decision of 24 April 1969, JCP.1970.II.16306

Savatier, René; Commentary on the decision of Ch. civ. 22 January 1957, D.1957.445

Schilling, Georg; 'Strafprozessuales Zeugnisverweigerungsrecht für Sozialarbeiter, Sozialpädagogen und Psychologen?' JZ 1976, 617-22

Schlüchter, Ellen; *Das Strafverfahren* (Carl Heymann Verlag: Köln, Berlin, Bonn, München, 2nd ed. 1983)

Schmidt, Eberhard; 'Ärztliche Schweigepflicht und Zeugnisverweigerungsrecht im Bereich der Sozialgerichtsbarkeit', NJW 1962, 1745-50

Schmitt, Petra; *Die Berücksichtigung der Zeugnisverweigerungsrechte nach §§52, 53 StPO bei den auf Beweisgewinnung gerichteten Zwangsmaßnahmen* (Duncker & Humblot: Berlin, 1993)

Schmitz, Roland; 'Verletzung von (Privat)geheimnissen – Der Tatbestand des § 203 StGB', JA 1996, 772-7

Schmitz, Roland; 'Verletzung von (Privat)geheimnissen – Qualifikationen und ausgewählte Probleme der Rechtfertigung', JA 1996, 949-55

Schöne-Seifert, Bettina; 'Medizinethik', in: Nida-Rümelin, Julian (ed.); *Angewandte Ethik* (Kröner: Stuttgart, 1996), 552-648

Schönke, Adolf; Schröder, Horst; *Strafgesetzbuch Kommentar* (C.H. Beck Verlag: München, 26th ed. 2000)

Schünemann, Bernd; 'Der strafrechtliche Schutz von Privatgeheimnissen', ZStW 90 (1978), 11-63

Schutte, Peter; 'Medical confidentiality and a police murder inquiry' (1989) Journal of the Medical Defence Union 21

Scully, Anne; 'Is a sense of proportion needed in the judicial review of emotive cases?' [1999] CFLQ 183-92.

Secretary of Health and Human Services, *Standards for Privacy of Individually Identifiable Health Information*, 65 Fed.Reg. 82862 (2000)

Shuman, Daniel W.; 'The origins of the physician-patient privilege and professional secret' (1985) 39 Southwestern Law Journal 661-87

Shuman, Daniel W.; Weiner, Myron S.; 'The privilege study: an empirical examination of the psychotherapist-patient privilege' (1982) 60 North Carolina Law Review 893-942

Siegler, Mark; 'Confidentiality in medicine - a decrepit concept' (1982) New England Journal of Medicine 1518-21

Slovenko, Ralph; *Psychotherapy and Confidentiality* (Charles C. Thomas Publisher Ltd.: Springfield, Ill., 1998)

Smith, Victor; 'Passing on child abuse findings – *Re V* and *Re L*' (1999) Fam Law 249-52.

Snyder, David V.; 'Disclosure of medical information under Louisiana and federal law' (1990) 65 Tulane Law Review 169-202

Spickhoff, Andreas; 'Erfolgszurechnung "Pflicht zum Bruch der Schweigepflicht"', NJW 2000, 848-9

Stefani, Gaston; Levasseur, Georges; Bouloc, Bernard; *Droit Pénal Général* (Dalloz: Paris, 17th ed. 2000)

Stefani, Gaston; Levasseur, Georges; Bouloc, Bernard; *Procédure Pénale,* (Dalloz: Paris, 17th ed. 2000)

Steinberg-Copek, Jutta; *Berufsgeheimnis und Aufzeichnungen des Arztes im Strafverfahren* (Dissertation: Berlin, 1968)

Steiner, Eva; 'France', in: Gearty, Conor (ed.); *European Civil Liberties and the European Convention on Human Rights, A Comparative Study* (Kluwer International: The Hague, 1997)

Stern, Kristina; 'Confidentiality and Medical Records', in: Kennedy, Ian; Grubb, Andrew (eds); *Principles of Medical Law* (Oxford University Press: Oxford, 1998), 495-545

Sydow, Fritz; *Kritik der Lehre von den "Beweisverboten"*, (Holzner Verlag: Würzburg, 1976)

Systematischer Kommentar zum Strafgesetzbuch, Band 2, Rudolphi, Hans Joachim; Horn, Eckhard; Samson, Erich; Günther, Hans-Ludwig; Hoyer, Andreas (eds.); (Luchterhand: Neuwied, 6th ed. 1999)

Tapper, Colin; *Cross and Tapper on Evidence* (Butterworths: London, 9th ed. 1999)

Taylor, J. Leahy; *Medical Malpractice* (John Wright and Sons: Bristol, 1980)

Terré, François; Simler, Philippe; Lequette, Yves; *Droit Civil, Les Obligations* (Dalloz: Paris, 7th ed. 1999)

Thomas-Fishburn, Julia; 'Attorney-client confidences: punishing the innocent' (1990) 61 University of Colorado Law Review 185-211

Thouvenin, Dominique (1987); *Juris-Classeur Pénal* - ancien code pénal, Art.378 (1987)

Thouvenin, Dominique (1982); *Le Secret Médical et l'Information du Malade* (Presses Universitaires de Lyon: Lyon, 1982)

Timm, Manfred; *Grenzen der ärztlichen Schweigepflicht* (Deutscher Ärzte-Verlag: Köln, 1988)

Turkington, Richard C.; 'Confidentiality policy for HIV-related information; an analytical framework for sorting out hard and easy cases' (1989) 34 Villanova Law Review 871-908

Turpin, Dominique; *Droit Constitutionnel* (Presses Universitaires de France: Paris, 4th ed., 1999)

Uglow, Steve; *Evidence, Text and Materials* (Sweet & Maxwell: London, 1997)

Ulsenheimer, Klaus; *Arztstrafrecht in der Praxis* (C.F. Müller Verlag: Heidelberg, 2nd ed. 1998)

Véron, Michel; *Droit Pénal Spécial* (Armand Colin: Paris, 8th ed. 2001)

Vickery, Alan B.; 'Breach of confidence: an emerging tort' (1982) 82 Columbia Law Review 1426-68

Vilensky, Robert; 'New York Law on confidentiality of medical records – Part 1' (1994) 66 New York State Bar Journal 38-42

Vouin; *Droit Pénal Spécial*; (Dalloz: Paris, 6th ed. par Michèle Laure Rassat, 1988)

Wagner De Cew, Judith; 'The scope of privacy in law and ethics' (1986) 5 Law and Philosophy 145-73

Waremberg-Auque, Françoise; 'Réflexions sur le secret professionnel', Revue de science criminelle et de droit pénal comparé 1978, 237-56

Warren, Samuel D.; Brandeis, Louis D.; 'The right to privacy' (1890) 4 Harvard Law Review 193-220

Warwick, S J; 'A vote for no confidence' (1989) JME 183-5

Watson, Shelly Stucky; 'Keeping secrets that harm others: Medical standards illuminate lawyer's dilemma' (1992) 71 Nebraska Law Review 1123-44

Weinmann, Günther; 'Die Beschlagnahme von Geschäftsunterlagen des Beschuldigten bei Zeugnisverweigerungsberechtigten'; in: Hanack, Ernst-Walter; Rieß, Peter; Wendisch, Günter (eds.); *Festschrift für Hans Dünnebier* (de Gruyter Verlag: Berlin, New York, 1982), 199-213

Weisberg, Robert; '*Defendant v Witness*: Measuring confrontation and compulsory process rights against statutory communications privileges' (1978) 30 Stanford Law Review 935-91

Welp, Jürgen; Anmerkung zu BGH JR 1997, 32, in: JR 1997, 35-8

Welp, Jürgen; Anmerkung zu BGH JZ 1974, 421, in: JZ 1974, 423-6

Welp, Jürgen (1973); 'Die Geheimsphäre des Verteidigers in ihren strafprozessualen Funktionen', in: Lackner, Karl; Leferenz, Heinz; Schmidt, Eberhard; Welp, Jürgen; Wolff, Ernst Amadeus (eds.); *Festschrift für Wilhelm Gallas zum 70. Geburtstag* (de Gruyter Verlag: Berlin, NewYork, 1973), 391-425

Westin, Alan; *Privacy and Freedom* (The Brodley Head Ltd: London, 1967)

Weyand, Raimund; 'Arzt- und Steuergeheimnis als Hindernis für die Strafverfolgung?' wistra 1990, 4-9

Wigmore, J.; *Wigmore on Evidence*, vol.8, McNaughton rev. ed. (Little, Brown and Company: Boston, Toronto, 1961)

Woesner, Horst; 'Fragen ärztlicher Geheimhaltungspflicht', NJW 1957, 692-4

Wright, Jane, *Tort Law and Human Rights: the Impact of the ECHR on English Law,* (Hart: Oxford, 2001)

Würtenberger, Thomas; 'Der Schutz des Berufsgeheimnisses und das Zeugnisverweigerungsrecht des Sozialarbeiters', in: Conrad, H.; Jahrreiß, H.; Mikat, P.; Mosler, H.; Nipperdey, H.C.; Salzwedel, J. (eds.); *Gedächtnisschrift für Hans Peters* (Springer Verlag: Berlin, Heidelberg, New York, 1967)

Zuckerman, A.A.S.; 'The weakness of the PACE special procedure for protecting confidential material' (1990) Crim LR 472-8

Index